Advance Praise for

UNSETTLED LAND

"This is the book we desperately need on the Texas Revolution. *Unsettled Land* shows Texas as it was, not as it has appeared on the set of *The Alamo*. Sam W. Haynes's Texas was a multiracial society, where free African Americans became prominent merchants, and where white land speculators staged revolts with Indigenous allies. For the likes of Sam Houston and Stephen Austin, the Texas Revolution promised freedom from Mexican rule. But for the Indigenous peoples and African Americans who had forged lives in Mexican-era Texas, independence signaled a loss of freedom. With gripping prose, Haynes captures both the drama and the complexity of the Mexican province that would eventually become the Lone Star State."

—ALICE L. BAUMGARTNER, author of *South to Freedom*

"No chapter in American history calls more for a thorough retelling than the origins of Texas. In the vividly written *Unsettled Land*, Haynes meets that challenge, and his story is vastly more revealing than the tired myths that have held the stage for so long. Once one of the most ethnically and culturally diverse areas on the continent, Texas underwent a steady narrowing of possibilities until by the war with Mexico it was saddled with an iron Anglo rule that shoved to the margins the Native peoples, Hispanos, Blacks, and others who had played so prominently in its early years. It is a fascinating, if dispiriting, story."

—ELLIOTT WEST, University of Arkansas

UNSETTLED
LAND

Published in Cooperation with the William P. Clements
Center for Southwest Studies, Southern Methodist University

UNSETTLED
LAND

FROM REVOLUTION TO REPUBLIC,
THE STRUGGLE FOR TEXAS

SAM W. HAYNES

BASIC BOOKS
New York

Basic Books
Hachette Book Group
1290 Avenue of the Americas, New York, NY 10104
www.basicbooks.com

Printed in the United States of America
First Edition: May 2022

Published by Basic Books, an imprint of Perseus Books, LLC, a subsidiary of Hachette Book Group, Inc. The Basic Books name and logo is a trademark of the Hachette Book Group.

The Hachette Speakers Bureau provides a wide range of authors for speaking events. To find out more, go to www.hachettespeakersbureau.com or call (866) 376-6591.

The publisher is not responsible for websites (or their content) that are not owned by the publisher.

Print book interior design by Linda Mark.

Library of Congress Cataloging-in-Publication Data has been applied for.

ISBNs: 9781541645417 (hardcover), 9781541645400 (ebook)

LSC-C

Printing 1, 2022

For Lisa

CONTENTS

LIST OF MAPS AND ILLUSTRATIONS

MAPS

ILLUSTRATIONS

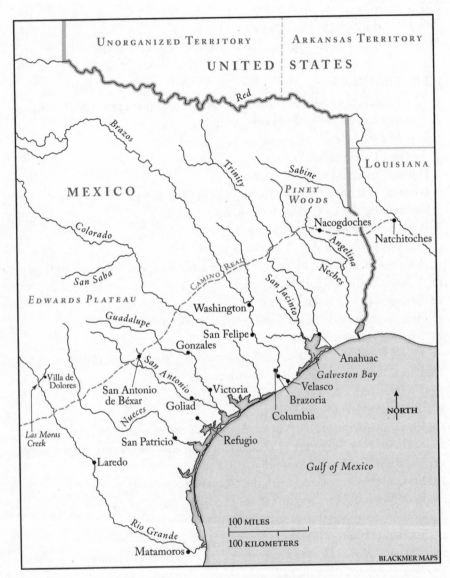

Mexican Texas, 1821–1835

INTRODUCTION

I T WAS CLEAR FROM THE BEGINNING THAT THE BEALES COLO-nists were out of their depth. They were not weather-beaten, hardscrabble frontierspeople. Some had never wielded an axe or plowed a field in their lives. But in the spring of 1834 they found themselves on the banks of Las Moras Creek, a few miles above the Rio Grande, lured to this remote spot by the promise of free land. Numbering about sixty men, women, and children, they had been recruited in New York City by an English land agent, John Charles Beales, authorized by the Mexican government to settle an area on the upper Rio Grande, about three hundred miles from the Gulf Coast. A handful were Americans, but most hailed from the British Isles, France, and Central Europe. They included Eduard Ludecus, a well-educated twenty-six-year-old native of Weimar, Germany, whose résumé included a job as a clerk in a dry goods store. Another settler, John Horn, owned a shop in London before setting out for America with his wife, Sarah, and their two boys. Even Beales, a doctor by training, was himself a stranger to Texas, with no experience in the business of settling a raw and untamed wilderness.[1]

As the immigrants surveyed the land on which they would make their new homes, they were overcome by feelings of despair. Stretched out before them lay an unending vista of thornscrub and mesquite. They may not have been seasoned farmers, but they needed only to look at the hard, sunbaked soil, where rattlesnakes and scorpions seemed to lie under every rock, to know that little could grow there,

1

at least not without costly irrigation. And even if they could bring in a decent crop, there were no markets for their produce. The closest Mexican town was a two days' ride away, and the Rio Grande, they had just learned, was not navigable this far upriver. Ludecus was dumbfounded. Back in New York, he had read glowing reports about the thriving American colony established by another land agent, Stephen F. Austin, apparently unaware that it lay far to the east in the fertile savannas of the Brazos River valley. "There were no tall green trees and no luxuriant vegetation," a miserable Ludecus wrote of the South Texas chaparral in one of his letters home. "Nature seemed to have died there."[2]

Incredibly, no one had told Ludecus about the Comanches, either. From their encampments on the Low Plains far to the north, raiding parties on horseback regularly passed through the area on their way to plunder the ranches below the Rio Grande—an important piece of information Beales neglected to share with the colonists until they arrived. To protect the group, the land agent hired a few dozen armed men from the Mexican towns along the river. Some were longtime veterans of the northern frontier's many years of conflict with the tribe, but others seemed as frightened of the Comanches as the Europeans were. The immigrants could at least be thankful for the presence of a band of Shawnees, who happened to be on a hunting expedition in the area. They, too, were far from home, having drifted onto the prairies of northeast Texas some years earlier, one of many American tribes that migrated into Mexico after the turn of the century. Bitter enemies of the Comanches, the Shawnees had befriended the greenhorns, providing the little colony with a steady supply of wild turkeys from the woods along the creek.[3]

Whatever their misgivings, the immigrants were here now, and they tried to make the best of it. They spent several days clearing away the underbrush for what they hoped would one day be a town plaza, and erected huts with the only materials available to them: mesquite poles daubed with mud for the walls, clumps of prairie grass as thatch for the roofs. In late March they held an elaborate ceremony—or as elaborate as the primitive conditions would allow—

christening Mexico's newest town the Villa de Dolores, after Beales's wife. Laying a cornerstone where they intended to build a church, the members of the little community then swore loyalty oaths to the Mexican republic and held elections for municipal offices. Their business concluded, the settlers ended the day with a "concert and a ball," as Ludecus wryly put it.

That night, under a star-studded, obsidian sky, the residents of Dolores—Europeans, Americans, Mexicans, and Indians—gathered around a large, blazing fire. For such a special occasion the colonists donned their most formal attire, better suited to a New York City promenade than a rugged wilderness, the men in round felt hats, frock coats, and stiff-collared white shirts, the women in their finest embroidered dresses. Some members of the audience lounged on deerskins; others sat on the newly cut trunks of mesquite trees.

The entertainment began with a war dance performed by the Shawnees. Daubed in war paint and wearing a horse mane head-dress, the leader of the band moved deliberately around the fire, brandishing a tomahawk, moving left, then right, as his men beat time with sticks. Suddenly he stopped, his body taut, letting loose with a guttural war cry that startled and delighted the immigrants. It was "as if hell itself is threatening to erupt and release its captive spirits," Ludecus wrote. Next, the Mexicans performed a fandango. Ludecus was not impressed by the dance, and still less by the vocal accompaniment, the songs delivered by one of the men in a trembling falsetto. The European immigrants followed with renditions of traditional songs from their native lands, their voices ringing out in the enveloping darkness. Presumably the Americans offered their own musical contribution, though Ludecus did not find it worthy of mention. It was, nonetheless, an extraordinary transcultural moment in which peoples from vastly different worlds came together in a spirit of fellowship and goodwill. For a few precious hours, the colonists could forget that Beales had brought them to a godforsaken place in the middle of nowhere.[4]

The colony was doomed, of course—thanks to its location and Beales's gross mismanagement. But a storm was brewing on Mexico's northern frontier that would hasten its demise. In the well-established colonies closer to the Gulf Coast, Anglo settlers from the American South had once exhibited a similar readiness to reach across racial and ethnic lines, forging constructive and mutually beneficial alliances with area Hispanos, and sometimes with local Indian tribes, in their effort to build a new community. But as their numbers swelled they chafed under Mexican rule. They became increasingly determined to recreate the world they had known in the United States, a rigid, color-coded world of masters and slaves that bore little resemblance to Mexico's multiracial society. Anglo colonists clashed with Mexican troops in the fall of 1835, plunging the region into chaos.

The impact of the upheaval that would come to be known as the Texas Revolution would soon be felt on Las Moras Creek. Some settlers had already decamped—one South Texas summer was enough for Ludecus and the Germans. The rest scattered, abandoning the Villa de Dolores when they learned that a large Mexican army was crossing the Rio Grande a few miles away to put down the revolt. The Horn family joined a party bound for the Gulf Coast, intending to make their way back to England. They managed to avoid Mexican troops, who torched the town, but not the Comanches. A raiding party slaughtered the group on the banks of the Nueces River, sparing only Sarah, her two sons, and another Englishwoman. Separated from the boys, who became adopted members of the tribe, Sarah lived as a captive until American merchants bought her from the Comanches eighteen months later in New Mexico. Traumatized by the ordeal, she would never see her sons or England again, dying a short time later.

The reverberations of the Texas war for independence would be felt in the Las Moras Creek area for many years afterward. Mexico refused to accept the loss of its northern province, waging an on-again, off-again border war with the newly created Lone Star Republic. Claimed by both countries, the area between the Rio Grande and the Nueces River became a contested space, a bloody no-man's-land where armed gangs of Anglos and Mexicans stole cattle, killed civilians, and skirmished with Comanches. Elsewhere, land-hungry whites turned on Native Americans who occupied some of the republic's most valuable territory. When the Shawnees, whose war dance had so thrilled the colonists on Las Moras Creek, returned to their homes below the Red River, they became embroiled in a turf war with Anglo-American settlers, and in 1839 they were driven beyond the borders of Texas as part of President Mirabeau Lamar's ethnic cleansing policy. In short, the revolution ignited a doom loop of primordial violence that would not begin to subside until Texas became a state in 1845.

ON THE EVE OF THE REBELLION, TEXAS WAS A REGION OF EXtraordinary ethnic diversity, having been a place of convergence for the peoples of North America for more than a century. In the 1700s, its indigenous population saw the influx of the Comanches and Apaches, nomadic tribes following the buffalo herds that came down off the High Plains. At the same time, the Spanish Crown began to make a tentative effort to colonize the region, establishing a string of missions, military outposts, and civil settlements from the Rio Grande to the Sabine River. The flow of migrants increased sharply in the early nineteenth century, with the arrival of Cherokees, Shawnees, and other refugee Indian tribes from the United States. They were followed in turn by white Americans, some of whom brought enslaved men and women of African descent. European immigrants, like those of the Beales colony, were also beginning to make their way to Texas. Together they created a patchwork of overlapping borderlands and ethnic enclaves on Mexico's northern frontier, each group trying to navigate and make sense of the turbulent world in which they found themselves.

The region's unique multiracial character is not, of course, what first comes to mind when one thinks of Texas during this period. The traditional narrative of the revolution is a gripping saga in which outsized figures, all white males, crowd the stage, elbowing aside everyone and everything else. It is a story of men like Sam Houston, David Crockett, William Barret Travis, and James Bowie, who led

a ragtag band of "Texians" in a life-or-death contest against Santa
Anna's armies. Emphasizing the epic drama of the Alamo siege, the
Goliad Massacre, and the Battle of San Jacinto, this hyper-masculine
version of events emerged in the early twentieth century as a symbol
of an American "manifest destiny" to hold sway over the continent.
With its tales of martial heroism and lessons of patriotic sacrifice, the
struggle for independence continues to occupy a prominent place in
the national historical imagination, a creation story Americans have
been happy to call their own.

So powerful is this mythology that scholars in recent years have
largely ceded the field to popular writers, who have been content to
revisit, again and again, the same thrilling acts of valor. Some, in a
quest to find something new to say, have delved into its more arcane
mysteries. Did Davy Crockett surrender at the Alamo? Did William
Barret Travis draw a line in the sand? To be sure, some newer works
have challenged this celebratory narrative, often pointing to the
economic motives of the slaveholders who led the revolution. But
even a critique of the familiar Texas story cannot fundamentally alter
the way we look at these events; we are still hostage to a narrative
dominated by Anglo-American actors. Thus, much has been written
about the settlement of Texas by white colonists in the decade prior
to independence, but little about the migration of large numbers of
Native Americans from the United States during the same period.
Much has been written, too, about the revolution from the viewpoint
of the Texas rebels, but little about how Mexico City saw the crisis on
its northern frontier. While the role of Tejanos has garnered more
scrutiny in recent years, scholars have tended to draw attention to
the few Mexican Texans who supported the Anglo cause, rather than
the many who did not. Even our geographical orientation reflects
this racial bias, with vast swaths of the state viewed as marginal, peripheral spaces not worthy of mention—until they are populated by
large numbers of Anglos. In the end, the basic contours of the narrative we know so well remain more or less intact, with a small group
of white males in tight focus.[5]

Above all, the revolution is still defined as a war to free Texas from Mexican rule, a war that ended with Sam Houston's decisive victory at San Jacinto. But Anglo-Americans were not the only inhabitants of Texas to experience the upheaval of revolution. For a large segment of the population, independence from Mexico meant the *loss* of freedom, a fact that only became evident in the years that followed, as the Lone Star Republic moved aggressively to expel Indians, marginalize Mexicans, and tighten its grip on the enslaved. Thus the revolution was far from over in 1836. The work of creating a new society, radically different from anything Texas had known under Mexico, had only just begun.[6]

When a wider lens is used to see the Texas Revolution, the alpha male heroics and moral clarity of the familiar narrative dissolve, and a new, more chaotic picture emerges. More than a contest between the Mexican army and Anglo rebels, the struggle for independence is also the story of ordinary people in an extraordinary time, of lives upended by the seismic shift from a multiracial society to white rule. If the birth of early modern Texas is a story of triumph, it is also in equal measure one of tragedy, which saw the coming together, then pulling apart, of people in an unsettled land.

ONE

WHAT MUST BE DONE WITH US POOR INDIANS?

As dawn broke over the cloud-capped Blue Ridge Mountains on a cold day in mid-January 1810, the village of Little Hiwassee was a hive of activity. A tiny settlement on the edge of North Carolina's western border with Tennessee, the community consisted of about a dozen families, who lived in cabins clustered near the banks of the Hiwassee River. The villagers had decided to relocate to lands west of the Mississippi, a journey of five hundred miles. If all went according to plan, they would reach their destination just in time for the spring planting season. As the pioneers loaded their belongings onto a flat boat and several canoes, herds of restless oxen, cattle, and horses grazed nearby. A team of drovers would guide the animals along the river bank as the party made its way west. At last, when the bundles of clothing, farm implements, spinning wheels, and cotton looms had all been fastened securely, the villagers clambered into the canoes, pushing off into the mist that hung over the silent waters of the Hiwassee River.

Heading the expedition was a vigorous, athletic man in his fifties. While most of the villagers knew little of their final destination, he had made hunting trips to the region several times before. For many years he had been the undisputed leader of this small community, but he was well-known far beyond it, a familiar figure to the people throughout the North Carolina–Tennessee backcountry.

"His eyes were gray, his hair was of a dirty sandy color," someone who met him many years later recalled, "but he did not speak the English language."[1]

His people knew him as Duwali—Bold Hunter. But in the years ahead, whites would come to know him simply as Chief Bowls. Though half-white himself—his father was a Scottish trader who lived with the tribe for several years—Bowls had spent the better part of his adult life fighting whites living on the western edge of the Blue Ridge Mountains. During the American Revolution, his village joined a militant splinter group, the Chickamaugas, allying with the British against backcountry settlements, in open defiance of tribal elders who wanted to make peace with the Americans. As a lieutenant of the famed war chief Dragging Canoe, Bowls with his men ranged across the American Southeast. The War for Independence ended in 1783; Bowls's war did not. Aided by the British, and later the Spanish, the Chickamauga villages continued to fight against white encroachment well into the 1790s.[2]

By the time peace returned to the Tennessee River Valley around the turn of the century, the Cherokees were a people in transition. Many Cherokee men, at the urging of US Indian agents, took up farming and stock raising, occupations once performed exclusively by women. Cherokee women, with a long tradition of basket weaving, learned to spin clothing from wool and cotton. Little Hiwassee had made some concessions to these changes in recent years; Bowls's wives and daughters, for example, had become accomplished weavers. But the men of the village preferred to cling to traditional folkways. Theirs was a world in which manhood was still defined by warfare and the hunt.[3]

The US government's Indian resettlement policy aggravated these tensions in Cherokee society. Pressuring the tribe to cede its land in the Tennessee River Valley, the War Department created an Indian reserve in the west, offering gunpowder, lead, and farming supplies to all who chose to go. Well-to-do Cherokees wanted no part of the proposal, but Bowls disagreed. Painful as it was to abandon the forested highlands of his birth, he knew that his way of life was already in full retreat, and he saw little reason to stay. The deer and black bear, once so plentiful in the area, were slowly disappearing, decimated by overhunting. Reluctantly, the people of Little Hiwassee decided to abandon their homes and accept the government's offer.

A quarter of a century later, the Indians who stayed in their villages on the Hiwassee River would be forcibly removed by the federal government in the Trail of Tears. Though voluntary, this first wave of the Cherokee exodus from the southeastern United States would also be marred by misfortune and tragedy. But Bowls and his people left Little Hiwassee with feelings of hope, tinged with regret, believing a life of peaceful abundance awaited them in the vast open country just west of the Mississippi River. In 1810, Bowls had never heard of Texas, then a province of New Spain's far northern frontier. On that cold day in January, the Cherokees embarked on a decade-long journey that would lead them there.[4]

THE WESTERN CHEROKEES, AS THEY WOULD NOW BECOME known, would make their home between the St. Francis and Mississippi rivers in the Missouri Territory. Finding game plentiful, they did not regret their decision—at least not at first. But within a year the War Department closed a nearby trading post, requiring the Cherokees to rely on unscrupulous whites, who sold farm implements at exorbitant prices and offered liquor in trade for Indian peltries. At the same time, resentful tribal leaders back East refused to share the subsidies that they received from the federal government, insisting that the Western Cherokees were no longer a part of the tribe.[5]

Then disaster struck. On the night of December 14, 1811, one of the strongest earthquakes ever experienced on the North American continent hit the midsection of the Mississippi River Valley. The ground rolled in waves. Whole forests were uprooted. Rivers flowed backward. Destroying the nearby town of New Madrid, the temblor ripped enormous seams in the earth, sending clouds of sulfur gas,

dust, and water vapor into the air, blocking the sun and turning day
into night. The earthquake would be felt along the Atlantic seaboard,
ringing church bells as far away as Boston. Two more quakes of similar intensity and hundreds of aftershocks followed over the next
twelve weeks. For local whites the seismic events presaged the Day
of Judgment; the Cherokees attributed the disaster to the writhing
of a great serpent beneath the earth. But in the Stygian darkness that
enveloped southeastern Missouri, both came to the same conclusion:
the end times had arrived.[6]

With their homes and farms washed away, the Cherokees had
no choice but to abandon the land allocated to them by the federal
government. So they fled west, across present-day Arkansas into the
foothills of the Ozarks, a region long claimed by the Osage, one
of the dominant peoples of the Low Plains. Regarding the Cherokees as invaders, the Osage fiercely defended their hunting grounds.
Hapless Indian agents struggled to keep the peace, but the two
tribes were soon locked in an unending cycle of violence, of raids
and counterraids. Much of the trouble stemmed from the Cherokee
tradition of blood revenge. While it was customary among Osage
families to accept gifts as compensation for the death of a warrior,
only blood could atone for the killing of a Cherokee man by members of another tribe. As Bowls explained the warrior credo at a
tribal council some years later, "Men shall not fall unrevenged."[7]

Grievances on both sides mounted over the next few years. The
Cherokees claimed to be innocent victims of Osage depredations,
though both sides were equally to blame. Bowls and other Cherokee
headmen, fired by the desire to avenge murdered kinsmen, appealed
repeatedly and unsuccessfully to federal authorities for permission to
inflict a decisive blow against their enemies. Finally, in the summer
of 1817, they decided they had waited long enough. Following the
deaths of two Cherokee men killed at the hands of Osage raiders, the
chiefs held a council to discuss their plans, then penned a letter to
the territorial governor. Uncharacteristically blunt, the communiqué
made it clear that the time for further negotiation had passed, stating
simply, "we are going to do mischief."[8]

It was not an empty threat. In fact, the "mischief" the Cherokees had in mind had probably been in the planning stages for several months. Organized by Bowls and three other head chiefs, the campaign against the Osage would not be fought only by Cherokee warriors in Indian Territory. During the late summer and early fall, squads of Cherokee men from villages back in Tennessee arrived along the Arkansas River to take part in the fighting. Warriors from other tribes with grievances against the Osage also joined the campaign.

In mid-October, a time when most Osage warriors, as well as many women, would be away on their annual buffalo hunt, a flotilla of pirogues and flatboats carried a force of five hundred Cherokees and their allies up the Arkansas to the Verdigris River. They landed near one of the Osage's main villages, nestled at the foot of a limestone hill known as Claremore Mound, a few miles north of present-day Tulsa, Oklahoma.[9]

Camping for the night a short distance away, the Cherokees prepared for battle by performing a series of elaborate rituals. Casting aside the Western influences that had seeped into their way of life, they took off their homespun cotton and woolen clothing and put on leather breechclouts. Removing the distinctive colorful turbans that had been a staple of their daily attire for more than a generation, they cut their hair close to the scalp and donned feather headdresses. Their faces painted with vermillion, Bowls and the other war chiefs led their followers in traditional war songs and dances. That night, the Cherokees returned to the world of their warrior ancestors.[10]

To make sure that they would encounter little resistance, Bowls sent a runner to the Osage village the next morning to request a parley, offering to negotiate a peace with the tribe. The runner soon returned to the camp with an old man, who told them that the tribe's principal leaders were gone. Hearing this, Bowls felled him with a single blow.

The Cherokees and their allies entered the town, finding it occupied by old men, women, and children. They began killing indiscriminately, the inhabitants scattering in all directions. Some of

1. Chief Bowls (Duwali), Western Cherokee leader (ca. 1756–1839). Bowls crossed the Red River into Spanish Texas at the head of a band of Cherokees in 1819. Thousands more Native American refugees from the United States would make their way into the province in the decade that followed. Courtesy of Texas State Library and Archives Commission.

the Osage fled into lodges, which the Cherokees set alight. Others tried to escape by hiding in the wooded mound behind the town. Still others were pursued to the Verdigris River, several drowning as they tried to reach the west bank. By the time the blood-letting frenzy had run its course, the Cherokees had killed more than eighty Osages, taking the scalps of many and emasculating some of the teenage boys. After destroying the Osage vegetable gardens and food stores, they plundered the town, driving out herds of stolen horses laden with furs and skins, tools and cookware. Leaving Claremore in flames, the attackers made off with more than one hundred captives, most of them children, who would later be sold to cover the costs of the campaign.[11]

The primal ferocity of the Claremore Mound Massacre forced the US government to act. In a belated effort to quell the violence and prevent the outbreak of a full-scale Indian war, the War Department hurriedly sent troops to build a post on the Arkansas River, Fort Smith. Siding with the victors, the government ordered the Osage to abandon their claim to land along the Verdigris River, pushing the tribe farther west.

The Western Cherokees would have little time to savor their victory. Within two years the federal government created the Arkansas Territory, opening up land along the Arkansas River to thousands of Anglo-American settlers. At the same time, as Washington became increasingly committed to an Indian resettlement program, it sought new and even larger land cessions from Eastern Cherokee chiefs. A treaty signed in 1817 prompted a new wave of migrations, and by the following year the number of Cherokees living along the Arkansas River doubled to around six thousand.[12]

Western Cherokees like Bowls resented the new migrants, and not just because their presence contributed to overhunting and put a strain on available resources. Ever since Bowls and his followers left the Tennessee River Valley, there had been bad blood between two groups over the distribution of the federal government's annual payments to the tribe. The rift between the Cherokees' two main branches had grown wider in recent years, as the Eastern Cherokees began to adopt the cultural practices of their white neighbors. In Tennessee, Presbyterian and Moravian missionaries enjoyed some success in converting the Indians to Christianity. Some members of the tribe embraced American ideas of private property, and a few had become wealthy farmers and slave owners.

Richard Fields in many ways typified the second wave of Cherokees who made the trek west in 1817. One-eighth Cherokee, he owned a large farm and several slaves on the Chickamauga River. He was fluent in English, though he could read and write it only with great difficulty, and for several years worked as a translator for US Indian agents and Moravian missionaries. The missionaries got to know him well and found to be him a likeable companion as they traveled from one Cherokee village to another, spreading the gospel in the Tennessee River Valley (one noting ruefully there was no sign that Fields himself "has been moved by the word of Jesus' suffering").[13]

Leaving behind three wives and several children, Fields—he does not seem to have been known by an Indian name—was in his early forties when he decided to take advantage of the government's resettlement program. For a time he prospered in US Indian Territory, acquiring six hundred acres on the St. Francis River, where he raised cattle and horses. Dressing according to his station in Cherokee society, he favored buckskin clothing lined with coral beads, and sported an exquisitely crafted long rifle with ornate silver mountings and inlays. As part of a bustling commercial network that connected whites and Indians on the North American frontier, he was an engaging, self-confident man, who lived at the intersection of two worlds and seemed comfortable in both.[14]

The new migrants' attachment to Anglo-American values brought about significant changes in the tribe's relationship with its indigenous neighbors on the Low Plains. Less attached to the old ways, the newcomers disapproved of the warrior ethos that had fueled the Western Cherokees' ongoing conflict with the Osage. For Bowls, matters came to a head when an Osage raid resulted in the death of three men of his village. As he had done so often in the past, the chief called for swift retribution. This time, a tribal council that included several Eastern Cherokee chiefs sided with local authorities and denied his request. Bowls angrily packed up and left, separating from the Western Cherokees entirely. During the winter of 1819–1820 he would lead sixty warriors and their families south across the Red River into Spanish Texas.[15]

SPAIN'S NORTH AMERICAN COLONIAL EMPIRE WAS IN ITS DEATH throes when the Cherokees crossed the Red River. For almost a decade, Mexico had been wracked by a bloody war for independence that was now grinding toward a conclusion. Home to no more than three thousand Hispanos, Texas had never occupied a significant place in Spain's imperial project. Nonetheless, it was not spared the wrenching upheaval of revolution, and in recent years the area had devolved into virtual anarchy. So feeble was Spain's hold over the northern frontier that Texas had begun to attract the attention of American adventurers, who launched a number of filibustering expeditions into the province. At first, such enterprises were undertaken in cooperation with Mexican revolutionists. But as the War of Independence dragged on, American soldiers of fortune began to pursue an agenda all their own, with the goal of establishing an independent Texas that could one day be annexed by the United States.[16]

Despite the political chaos, Texas remained, for all intents and purposes, a Native American world, inhabited by a constellation of peoples as culturally distinct as the region was vast. Bowls's Cherokees were not the first refugee Indians from the United States to find a home in East Texas. For several years, this remote corner of New Spain had become a destination of choice for Native Americans displaced by white encroachment. A few Western Cherokees received permission from Spanish officials to reside in East Texas as early as 1807. About the same time, small groups of Alabama, Coushatta, and Biloxi Indians from the Lower South crossed the Sabine River into Texas, to settle in the bayou country between the Trinity and Neches rivers. Still others, the Shawnees, Delawares, and Kickapoos, Algonquin-speaking peoples from the Ohio River Valley, drifted into East Texas after Tecumseh's efforts to establish a pan-Indian alliance ended in failure during the War of 1812.[17]

The Indian refugees who came to Texas from the United States would find an even more diverse collection of Native peoples already living there. Before the arrival of the Spanish, East Texas was one of the densest population centers in North America, home to a flourishing confederacy that extended into northern Louisiana and Arkansas. Known collectively as Caddos, the woodland tribes had been decimated by European diseases, but one or two thousand still remained, living in small villages between the Sabine and Trinity rivers. Seminomadic Wichitas, driven off the Low Plains by the Osage several decades earlier, occupied the prairies of northeast Texas, while some drifted farther south, into the central part of the province, establishing fortified towns along the Brazos and Navasota rivers. Nomadic tribes, the Comanches and Apaches, vied for control of buffalo grazing lands, having displaced Tonkawa bands that now roamed the post oak savannahs closer to the coast. Along the Gulf Coast, several hundred

Karankawas fished and hunted in area bays and waterways, rarely venturing more than a few miles inland.[18]

For Bowls's Cherokees, the first couple of years would be difficult ones, as they sought to find land not already claimed by Native peoples. After crossing the Red River, they made their way south, to the headwaters of the Trinity near present-day Dallas. There they clashed with the Taovaya Wichitas, who jealously guarded the area's creeks and streams, heavily timbered with the bois d'arc tree, essential for making bows. Within a year one-third of Bowls's warriors had been killed in clashes with the tribe.[19]

On the move again, the Cherokees followed well-worn Caddo trails into the forests of East Texas. An immense wedge of timberland comprising roughly one-third of the province, the area was part of a great pine belt that spanned much of the American South, a humid region of slow-moving rivers, languid creeks, and stagnant bayous. Its gently undulating landscape flattened out as it stretched southward, the pine barrens giving way to the wetlands of the Gulf Coast. The Cherokees settled between the Neches and Angelina rivers, about a day's ride north of the small Spanish town of Nacogdoches. The Caddo Indians resented the newcomers, but unlike the Osage and Wichitas lacked the numbers to expel them. A recent smallpox pandemic had wiped out more than half the indigenous population, leaving the survivors severely scarred from the effects of the disease. Here, under a canopy of loblolly, longleaf, and shortleaf pines, the Cherokees built villages of log cabins where Caddo brush tipis once stood, and returned long-abandoned, weed-choked fields and pastureland to productivity. The forests teemed with black bear, wild turkeys, peccary, and white-tailed deer. No less important, with Natchitoches, Louisiana, one hundred miles to the east, the Cherokees had a ready market for their skins and furs. Having spent the last decade wandering across the Mississippi Valley, Bowls and his people had at last found a home.[20]

Or so they thought.

No sooner had the Cherokees arrived in East Texas than they received news that caused them to question their decision to migrate to Texas. In the summer of 1821, a party of government officials rode into Nacogdoches to escort a twenty-seven-year-old American land agent, Stephen F. Austin, to San Antonio. One year earlier, Austin's father, Moses, had received permission from the provincial governor to establish a colony of three hundred Anglo-American settlers in Texas. When Moses died of pneumonia, his son decided, after some initial hesitation, to move forward with the project, and had come to Texas to scout out a suitable location for the colony. News of Austin's plans created considerable buzz in Louisiana, prompting some families to move across the Sabine River. For the Cherokees, reports of Anglo-American migration were a troubling development, given the failure of federal and state officials to protect them from white encroachment in the United States. Complicating matters still further, they learned a few months later that the Spanish viceroy had ratified the Plan of Iguala, confirming Mexico's independence. What all this meant for the Cherokees remained to be seen. They were no longer under the protection of Spain, and as squatters had no legal claim to the land they were now working so hard to improve.[21]

Richard Fields was especially keen to have some clarity on the Cherokees' status as residents of Mexico. He had recently moved south into Texas, possibly a victim of the economic downturn that gripped the United States in 1819. Joining Bowls in the Piney Woods, he quickly assumed a position of some authority with the tribe, although the two men, separated by a generation that had seen dramatic changes in Cherokee life and culture, had little in common. Unlike Bowls, Fields saw land as a commodity, a perspective that gave him a clearer understanding of the value of legal title.

Early in 1822 Fields wrote to Mexican authorities, introducing himself as "a chief of the Cherokee Nation." The Spanish had given the immigrant Indians land grants to settle in Texas, he explained. Did the new Mexican government intend to honor these commitments? In fact, no such contracts existed; Spanish officials had merely given a few refugee Indian groups informal permission to settle the area. It would not be the only time Fields would exhibit a casual disregard for the truth in his dealings with Mexican authorities. "I wish to humbly fall at your feet and ask you," he inquired plaintively, "what must be done with us poor Indians?"[22]

Several months passed without a response. Tired of waiting, Fields decided to lead a delegation to San Antonio to meet with the provincial governor, José Felix Trespalacios. That fall, after the tribe held their annual Green Corn Dance, a weeklong celebration of the corn harvest, Fields and Bowls set out on their journey with a party of twenty Cherokee men.

Two translators accompanied the Indians, one of them a twenty-three-year-old native of Jalapa, a town in Mexico's central highlands. José Antonio Mexía had spent much of the recent civil war in exile with his family in Natchitoches, a haven for many Mexican expatriates, and he had probably met Fields during one of the Indian leader's cattle drives across the Sabine. Handsome and ambitious, Mexía looked forward to making a new life for himself in post-revolutionary Mexico. He had already given some thought to a military career, and with the government apparently willing to do business with American land agents like Austin, he was equally excited by the prospect of investing in Texas lands.[23]

The party followed the Camino Real (Royal Road) that stretched in a gentle north-south arc across the midsection of Texas. Little more than a footpath marked out by the Spanish, the road took the Cherokees out of the dense pine barrens of East Texas into the rolling hills and post oak savannahs of the Brazos River valley. At that time of year they would have encountered large herds of buffalo and pronghorn antelope following the grasslands down to the Gulf Coast. Beyond the Colorado River some seventy miles farther west, the undulating prairie gave way to a chain of rugged, limestone hills, the southeastern edge of the Edwards Plateau. Here the Camino Real traversed a web of spring-fed streams and creeks, winding its way up hillsides dotted with thickets of mesquite and live oak, and down into ravines where dense cedar brakes crowded upon the trail.[24]

At length the party reached the edge of a broad basin, where it caught the first glimpse of its destination, several miles distant. From afar, the former capital of Spanish Texas appeared to good advantage.

Founded more than a century earlier, San Antonio de Béxar was a town of some two thousand inhabitants (Bexareños), an oasis of whitewashed stone and adobe buildings clustered around two main plazas. The San Fernando church in the city center dominated the landscape; five Franciscan mission complexes built in the eighteenth century to Christianize the area's indigenous peoples sat along a fifteen-mile stretch of the San Antonio River south of town.

A closer inspection, however, revealed a crumbling colonial outpost that had been in a state of decay long before Spain lost control of its New World empire. The Catholic Church had abandoned its efforts to convert the Indians decades earlier. Now the missions lay in ruins, occupied by a handful of Indian families. The few Hispanos that passed for well-to-do raised cattle and sheep, which they sold in the towns along the Rio Grande. Cash poor, some were lucky enough to supplement their income as government functionaries. But most Bexareños eked out a hardscrabble existence, living in *jacales*, crude huts of mud-daubed cedar poles and thatched roofs. The town had been especially hard hit by the ravages of civil war. Royalist troops routed republican forces on the nearby Medina River in 1813, leaving the bodies of hundreds of rebels strewn along the roadway into town. There they lay for nine years, until Governor Trespalacios ordered the bones removed and given a proper burial, a few weeks before Bowls and Fields arrived.[25]

War and imperial neglect were not the only reasons for San Antonio de Béxar's forlorn condition. The town had been a target of the nomadic tribes of central Texas for decades, its ranching economy devastated by Comanche, Apache, and Tonkawa raiding parties. Things had only gotten worse in the final years of Spanish rule. With its colonial empire in a state of collapse, the Crown could not afford the gifts that traditionally kept the tribes at bay, and drastically cut back its military presence in the area. In San Antonio only a skeleton crew of a few dozen soldiers remained, whose weapons were in disrepair, and who lacked even enough horses to go in pursuit of large parties of Indian raiders. Unable to develop the region's rich agricultural potential for fear of attack, Bexareños lived in a

perpetual defensive crouch, reduced to growing corn and other sub-
sistence crops on small plots of land just outside town.[26]

In recent years the Comanches had become nothing less than an
existential threat to the town's survival. Known by the name given
them by the Utes, meaning "people who fight all the time," five major
Comanche bands numbering about ten thousand people held sway
over the Southern Plains. The easternmost band, the Penatekas, or
"Honey Eaters," lived in large rancherías (encampments) along the
headwaters of the Colorado River. Riding down off the Edwards Plateau, Penateka warriors menaced not only San Antonio but the string
of half a dozen towns along the Rio Grande, the villas del norte.
They seized captives (invariably women and children), stole horses
and mules, and killed cattle. With little fear of Spanish troops, they
sometimes sauntered boldly into town to demand trade goods and
supplies. The captives they incorporated into the tribe or sold back to
local officials. The horses and mules they drove north, trading them
to American merchants on the Red River for guns and ammunition.[27]

In his meeting with Fields and Bowls, Governor Trespalacios
quickly saw that the Cherokees were nothing like the Comanches,
or any of the nomadic or seminomadic tribes he was familiar with.
"They work for their living and dress in cotton cloth which they
themselves manufacture. They raise cattle and horses," he wrote in a
glowing report to his superiors in Saltillo and Mexico City, who were
as unfamiliar with the Cherokees as he was. It occurred to him that
the immigrant Indians offered a possible solution to his intractable
Comanche problem. Giving the Cherokees a parcel of land in East
Texas would be a small price to pay, he reasoned, if their warriors
would help to interdict the flow of Comanche contraband across the
US-Mexico border.[28]

The governor lacked the authority to grant Fields's request, but
he was happy to do what he could. Drafting an eight-part agreement with the Cherokee leader, he ruled that the Indians could stay
where they were for the present, giving the tribe full rights and
privileges as "Hispano-Americans." Since a formal land grant could
only be issued by the national government, Trespalacios gave Fields

2. Penateka Comanches in War Dress. By Lino Sánchez y Tapia. Courtesy of the Gilcrease Museum, Tulsa, Oklahoma.

and Bowls permission to proceed to Mexico City, where a constitutional monarchy had been established under Agustin de Iturbide. Advising them to make their case in person to the new regime, he provided the Indian leaders with a small military escort for the eight-hundred-mile journey. The young Mexía, aware that he could pursue his own interests more successfully in Mexico City than anywhere else, readily signed on to serve as translator for the group on its long trek to the capital.[29]

Given the delegation's warm reception in San Antonio, Fields must have had high hopes for the success of his mission. Indeed, Trespalacios had been so encouraging that he may have assumed that Mexico City's approval of his land grant request was merely a formality. But the path toward a permanent Cherokee homeland in Texas would be a long and tortuous one, strewn with obstacles that Fields could not have foreseen. As the little group set out for the nation's capital, the Cherokees' Texas journey had only just begun.

TWO

INNOCENTS ABROAD

EARLY IN 1823 FIELDS AND BOWLS REACHED MEXICO CITY. Built on the ruins of the Aztec metropolis of Tenochtitlan, with a population of 150,000, it was the largest city in the Western Hemisphere. Situated at the southern end of a broad valley anchored by a pair of snow-capped volcanoes, the seat of Spanish power in the Americas had experienced a massive construction boom in the second half of the eighteenth century. Draining shallow marshlands where Aztec floating gardens once stood, colonial architects built a Baroque city that served as a testament to the vast mineral wealth the Crown had extracted from its colonial possessions, a crowded urban space of churches, monasteries, convents, and public buildings, each an ornamented marvel of stucco and stone. The city could boast a major university, an academy of fine arts, and an engineering college. What London was to England and Paris to France, Mexico City was to Mexico—its political, economic, and cultural epicenter.

Visitors to the capital were invariably struck by its extremes of rich and poor. Impressed by the great homes of its upper classes, the German scientist Alexander von Humboldt dubbed it "the city of palaces." But it was also a city in which grinding poverty was the norm for many, with a homeless population, according to some estimates, as high as twenty thousand. While elite families took leisurely promenades along the Alameda and other municipal parks, the city's urban poor, composed largely of non-Hispanicized Indians and known disparagingly as *léperos*, scrounged and begged for food.[1]

Fields and Bowls arrived to find a gaggle of Americans in residence in the capital, who had come for much the same reason: to seek the government's permission to settle the northern frontier. The approval of Moses Austin's land grant in the waning days of Spanish rule had sparked a flurry of interest in the United States, especially among entrepreneurially minded men with the money to invest in Texas lands. For its part, the new government recognized that its underpopulated frontier was a problem that required urgent attention. Comanche raiding parties, having laid waste to many of the ranchos of the lower Rio Grande valley, were beginning to probe ever deeper into Mexico's interior in their search for mules and horses. At the same time, the activities of American filibusters during the War of Independence had not gone unnoticed, alerting the government to the very real possibility that it might lose Texas altogether if it did not act quickly to establish control over the area. A colonization program that allowed private land agents to recruit settlers from the United States, Europe, and Mexico with the promise of cheap land seemed a cost-effective way to populate the northern frontier in the shortest amount of time.[2]

Clutching maps and land grant petitions, the Americans spent their days lobbying for various colonization schemes, roaming the dimly lit corridors of the National Palace, a sprawling building on the central plaza that housed Iturbide's official residence, chambers of congress, and government offices. They whiled away their nights drinking and gambling. The high roller of the group was Haden Edwards, a land agent from Kentucky, who bought a roulette wheel and turned his lodgings into a gaming house.[3]

The American contingent included Stephen F. Austin, who had made the same journey as Fields and Bowls nine months earlier. Austin's colony along the Brazos River had gotten off to a promising start, but since his father's land grant was awarded by Spain, he had come to Mexico City to make sure that the new government would honor the contract. In the nation's capital, Austin displayed the qualities that would make him Texas's most successful empresario (land agent). Unlike the other American entrepreneurs loitering about the city, he understood that his colonization project depended upon his ability to navigate the terrain of a foreign culture. Try as he might, Austin never entirely escaped the burden of his own racial prejudices. He was shocked, for example, by the squalor of the city's poorest classes, confiding to his brother that the *léperos* "want nothing but tails to be more brutes than the apes." Yet he applied himself diligently to a mastery of the Spanish language, which enabled him to forge not only effective working relationships but close friendships with Mexicans both in Texas and the nation's capital.[4]

From the outset, the Cherokees were at a disadvantage, handicapped by a lack of funds. Little expecting when they left East Texas that their trip would turn into a thousand-mile trek deep into the heart of Mexico, they were ill-prepared for the costs of a long journey, much less an extended stay in the nation's capital. Fortunately, they had been able to rely on the kindness of strangers along the way. With a letter of safe conduct from Trespalacios, they received small sums of money from Mexican officials in the towns they passed; hacienda owners along their route provided lodging and food for the party free of charge. Arriving penniless in the capital, the Cherokees also gained the sympathy of Emperor Iturbide, who ordered the treasury to cover their living expenses.[5]

The Indians soon discovered they had another problem—a competitor for the East Texas lands they were seeking to obtain from the Mexican government. The young translator José Antonio Mexía, his mission on behalf of the Cherokees at an end, now appeared at the National Palace to put forward his own land grant petition. Evidently he had been working on the proposal for some time—even before he signed on as Fields's translator, in fact—having already lined up American investors. Mexía proposed to settle several hundred Louisiana farmers on a swath of land between the Angelina and Neches rivers—the very land the Cherokees now occupied.[6]

As it turned out, political events would soon conspire to wreck the plans of both the Indians and their former translator. For several months hostility toward Iturbide had been building among regional leaders, who saw the monarchy as a threat to their own authority.

3. José Antonio Mexía (1800–1839).
One of the first Mexican citizens to
recognize the economic potential
of Texas, Mexía would acquire
title to more than a quarter of a
million acres of land in the province
before he was thirty. Courtesy of
the Bancroft Library, University of
California, Berkeley.

One by one the provinces began to declare their opposition to the
empire, forcing Iturbide to abdicate in March. The provisional
government—a three-man executive body that would rule until a
new constitution could be drafted—promptly voided all legislation
passed by his regime, throwing the entire Texas land grant program
into doubt and confusion. But it allowed Austin's contract to stand—
evidence of the young empresario's skill in cultivating influential
friends. Austin left the capital soon afterward, free to devote his energies to establishing the first Anglo-American colony in Texas.

The new government took a decidedly cooler attitude toward
the Indian delegation, however. A ruling on their petition would
now be made by Lucas Alamán, Minister of Interior and External
Relations. A wealthy arch-conservative, Alamán felt no affection
for Indians of any kind, having watched in horror when lower-class
mobs sacked Guanajuato, slaughtering the town's well-to-do residents, during the War of Independence. While the Cherokees' land
grant petition still enjoyed support in Congress, he was eager to be
rid of them. The government promptly stopped the allowance they

had received from Iturbide, leaving Fields no choice but to turn to the well-heeled Haden Edwards for money. Issuing a quick decision on their petition, the minister ruled that the agreement Fields had signed with Trespalacios could remain "provisionally in force," but no more Indians could be settled in Texas until passage of a new colonization law. Grudgingly, Alamán agreed to cover the chiefs' travel costs for the trip back to Texas, but any future petitions would have to be submitted in writing. The dismissive tone of Alamán's ruling was unmistakable: the Cherokees had overstayed their welcome. For Fields and Bowls there was nothing left to do but pack up and start the long journey home.[7]

Mexía, for his part, took the change of government in stride. After another unsuccessful attempt to obtain a Texas land grant, he secured an appointment in the army and seems to have had little difficulty gaining access to the right social circles. A few months after his arrival in the capital, the dashing young officer married Charlotte Walker, the daughter of a prosperous British merchant. And like Austin, he spent much of his time networking. Among the most prominent political contacts he would make during this period was Lorenzo de Zavala, a Yucatecan delegate to congress who sat on the colonization committee. It would prove to be the most important and enduring friendship of his life.[8]

Short, paunchy, with a crop of curly, thinning black hair, the thirty-five-year-old Zavala was a rising star on the Mexican political scene. A liberal newspaper editor and physician, he had spent three years in prison during the War of Independence, during which time he learned English and immersed himself in the writings of the political thinkers of the Enlightenment and the American Revolution. A great admirer of the American political experiment, he was not so naive as to believe that the new Mexican nation could follow a path identical to its republican neighbor to the north. At the same time, as a firm believer in popular sovereignty and a fierce critic of the wealth and power of the Catholic Church, he saw in the United States an emerging democracy that drew a line between church and state in civic life, a beacon that would light the way for the fledgling republics of Latin America as they sought to free themselves from the vestiges of Spanish colonial rule.[9]

Despite the thirteen-year age difference between Zavala and Mexía, theirs was not strictly a mentor-protégé relationship. Mexía had spent many years in the United States, and Zavala would come to value his opinions on American life. Perhaps even more important, the young Mexía possessed a well-honed business sense that the urbane politician could not have failed to appreciate. An enthusiastic booster of Texas commercial development, Mexía was one of only a handful of Mexicans in the 1820s who saw what American land speculators saw: a region destined to become the new frontier of a rapidly expanding cotton economy. There was a fortune to be made in Texas lands, and together Mexía and Zavala were eager to take advantage of the opportunity.

After the fall of Emperor Iturbide, the fault lines that would define the Mexican political landscape became clearer. Resembling the partisan divide that had emerged in the early days of the American republic, Mexico's ruling class coalesced into two broad factions that would engage in a decades-long struggle to determine the proper balance between national and regional power. Wealthy conservatives favored a strong, centralized form of government. As representatives of the country's privileged interests, such as the Church and large hacendados, they sought to preserve the colonial social order, advocating a constitutional monarchy or some other form of central authority to contain the widespread disruptions that the struggle for independence had unleashed. Middle class liberals, on the other hand, saw the end of Spanish rule as an opportunity to effect sweeping change, championing a federal republic on a Jeffersonian model that would give greater political power to provincial elites.[10]

In the fall of 1824, in a repudiation of the authoritarian rule of Iturbide, liberal federalists dominated the new Constituent Congress, and with Zavala serving as president drafted a constitution that limited the power of the national government. On the Texas lands issue, congress took a position consistent with the shift toward federalism and regional autonomy. Passing a new colonization law, the national government gave the nineteen states the authority to manage and distribute their public lands. Henceforth the state legislatures, not Mexico City, would rule on the petitions of prospective empresarios.[11]

The news was a major setback for Haden Edwards, who had spent more than two years in the capital. But he had come too far to abandon the enterprise at this point. With an American companion the businessman headed to Saltillo, the new state capital of Coahuila y Texas (no doubt taking his roulette wheel with him). The almost five-hundred-mile journey was a dangerous one that twice required them to fight off bandits on the road. Edwards hoped the legislature would act quickly, but again he would be disappointed. Before it could approve any land grant petitions, the state government would first have to draft its own colonization law. Accustomed to waiting, he now waited some more, settling into the dusty town on Mexico's northern frontier, where he was soon joined by a new crowd of American speculators looking to colonize the lands north of the Rio Grande.

By this time, Richard Fields was back in East Texas, believing the Mexican government would rule separately on the Indians' petition. But once the Cherokees left the capital, Alamán did not give their land grant request another thought. As for the national colonization law, it said nothing about a provisional agreement with the tribe. Presumably, if Fields wanted to establish a formal claim to lands in East Texas, he would have to present a petition to the state legislature like everyone else. Mexican officials would later assert that Fields would have received a favorable hearing from sympathetic lawmakers in Saltillo had he done so. But the Cherokee leader had other plans. And the consequences would be felt far beyond his little corner of the Piney Woods.

Fields had been given the brush-off in Mexico City, but that is not what he told the Cherokees when he returned to East Texas. As far as he was concerned—or so he told the tribe—the mission had been an unparalleled success. The Mexican government, he claimed, had given the delegation everything it asked for, and more. It had approved the tribe's land grant petition and entrusted him with the task of uniting the East Texas tribes under his leadership. Not only that, but Fields seemed to have conveniently forgotten Alamán's ban on further Indian immigration from the United States, insisting that he had been given "full powers to distribute the vacant lands of this country" to the tribes above the Red River.[12]

Clearly, something had gotten lost in translation.

It is hard to make sense of Fields's behavior during this crucial period. One explanation is that it was all a colossal misunderstanding. According to this interpretation, the Indians were unfamiliar with the language and political institutions of their new country, and were unaware of the procedures and protocols needed to bring their claim to the attention of Mexican authorities. Since Fields spoke no Spanish, he may not have known that the informal agreement made with Trespalacios in San Antonio could be superseded by leaders in the capital. As one historian charitably—but patronizingly—put it, the Cherokees "did the best they knew how."[13]

Yet Fields was hardly a simple child of the forest. For much of his adult life he had bought and sold land from whites, and he was in contact with a number of American speculators with business interests in Mexico. Possibly his trip to Mexico City convinced him that the Cherokees could not compete with the deep-pocketed and well-connected entrepreneurs seeking the favor of Mexican leaders. So he opted instead to disregard Alamán's ruling and proceed with his own plans to settle the area with refugee Indians from the United States. Such a strategy was fraught with risk, but if he could make national leaders see the advantages of a large Indian population that could defend the northern frontier from the Comanches, it might be a risk worth taking. He could always plead ignorance later, and chance the consequences. Even if Mexico City disapproved of his actions, Fields was well aware that the government's control over the area was tenuous at best. Once the Indians took possession of East Texas, there would be little Alamán could do about it.

Thus while Edwards was cooling his heels in Saltillo, Fields headed north, into US Indian Territory above the Red River, where he issued a call to all "oppressed and dissatisfied" Native Americans to join the Cherokees in Texas. Soon US Indian agents tasked with monitoring the Native peoples west of the Mississippi began to detect signs of unusual activity. One agent informed the War Department that a group of Texas Cherokees, headed by a chief described only as "the most daring and intelligent man in the nation," had been spotted in southeast Arkansas. Another reported that some Shawnee and Delaware bands had abruptly abandoned their villages and were moving below the Red River. But the reports were fragmentary and incomplete; US officials did not know any more about Fields's plans than their counterparts in Mexico did.[14]

To the south, in the Brazos River valley, the first Anglo-American settlement in Texas was well underway. Stephen F. Austin quickly fulfilled the terms of his first contract, bringing almost three hundred colonists and their families to Texas by the summer of 1824. In a country that depended heavily on ranching, Mexico's empresario program was crafted to attract stock-raisers, offering prospective colonists enormous tracts of grazing land. Most of Austin's settlers, however, hailed from the American South and had come to cash in on a worldwide cotton boom that had sent prices for the crop soaring. As a result, a Texas colonist could receive more than a league of land, or about 4,600 acres, for one hundred dollars, to be paid in installments, at a time when public lands in the United States were selling for $1.25 an acre. Single men who married Mexican citizens would receive even more. There were surveying fees—Austin charged twelve and a half cents an acre—but it was still an unbelievable bargain. Equipped with an ox and a plough, settlers could cultivate only a small portion of the land they were allotted, leaving the remainder undeveloped, to increase in value as the colony grew.[15]

Austin selected as the site of his colony a prime chunk of real estate in the central part of the province, bounded by the Camino Real to the north and the San Jacinto and Lavaca rivers to the east and

west. Most of Austin's colonists gravitated to the well-watered savannahs of the Brazos and Colorado river valleys running through the
middle of his land grant, which were ideally suited to cotton farming
and offered relatively easy access to the Gulf Coast and markets in
New Orleans.

In later years, the empresario liked to say that the first Anglo-
American colony in Texas had "redeemed a wilderness." In fact, Austin's early settlers would find a sparsely populated region, but hardly
an uninhabited one. More than two thousand Native Americans lived
within the boundaries of his land grant in the early 1820s. The Texas
coastal region had long been the domain of the Karankawas, the
name given to three main groups of hunter-gatherers that fished and
hunted in inlets and marshes. Farther inland, Austin's colonists would
find roving bands of Tonkawas, buffalo hunters pushed off the Low
Plains by more aggressive tribes decades earlier. Although the two
groups sometimes resisted Spanish intrusion, in recent years they
had come to accept the small numbers of Hispanos in their midst.
Bitter enemies of the Comanches, the Tonkawas saw royal officials
in San Antonio as valuable allies and as an important source of trade
goods. For the Karankawas, the Spanish were a welcome source of
food, allowing the Franciscans to build a couple of missions near the
coast as part of the Crown's ambitious but largely unsuccessful effort
to Hispanicize the native population.[16]

The workable peace forged by Tonkawas, Karankawas, and Hispanos would be shattered—and quickly—when Anglo-Americans
began to settle the area in the 1820s. Austin's first encounter with
Tonkawas and Karankawas had occurred during a fact-finding mission to Texas in the fall of 1821. Visiting the villages of both tribes,
he was greeted warmly by their chiefs. But he hurried on his way,
spending as little time among the Indians as possible. His journal
reveals an all-consuming interest in the quality of the soil, timber,
and water in the area—features essential to its commercial development. But he gave no thought whatsoever to the place Native peoples would occupy in his future colony. The Tonkawas he regarded
with contempt as "great beggars." His view of the Karankawas was

4. Stephen Fuller Austin (1793–1836). Known after his death as the "Father of Texas," Austin was the most successful Anglo-American colonizer on Mexico's northern frontier. Courtesy of the Palestine Public Library.

even less charitable, no doubt prejudiced by the writings of some Franciscans who, embittered by their lack of success in converting the tribe to Christianity, portrayed them as almost subhuman. Despite the Karankawas' cordial welcome, Austin's mind was already made up. He described the coastal Indians in his journal as "universal enemies of man," ominously offering the opinion that he saw no future for the tribe but their ultimate "extermination."[17]

Austin's colonists felt much the same way. "They were the most savage looking human beings I ever saw," one early settler remembered of the Karankawas. "Their ugly faces were rendered hideous by the alligator grease and dirt with which they were besmeared from head to foot as a defense against mosquitoes." In the very first encounter between Karankawas and the new arrivals, at the mouth of the Colorado River in 1823, a shoving match ensued when the Indians demanded a share of the provisions the colonists had brought with them. The Americans proceeded upriver, leaving a couple of men to guard their supplies. When they returned, they found the men dead and the supplies gone. There were clashes with the Tonkawas, too, and always over the theft of livestock and food. Both tribes were accustomed to supplementing their meager diet by

poaching from isolated ranchos and the nearby missions, a practice
Hispano residents grudgingly tolerated. The Indians soon found
that the Anglo newcomers held very different ideas about private
property, invariably responding to thefts with swift and often brutal
reprisals. Aware that his fledgling colony could not fight both tribes
at once, Austin sought to curry favor with the Tonkawas with gifts
of farm implements and seed corn. Free to adopt more aggressive
measures toward the Karankawas, the empresario would eventually
call for a shoot-on-sight policy toward the tribe. Bands of settlers
pursued the Indians into bottomlands and canebrakes, wiping out an
entire village in the Dressing Point Massacre in 1826. Soon afterward, fragments of the tribe relocated below the Lavaca River, out
of harm's way.[18]

Local authorities generally gave Austin a wide berth in his dealings with Native peoples, sharing his desire to populate the region
with loyal and productive citizens. Given the absence of any official
administrative or judicial presence in the area, the Mexican government expected an empresario to be more than a real estate agent, but
a benevolent *patrón* to the colonists under his care. It was a role that
Austin, who inherited from his Connecticut-born father a decidedly
Whiggish disposition, was born to play.

Establishing his headquarters on the west bank of the Brazos
River about eighty miles from the Gulf Coast, from which would
emerge the crude beginnings of a town, San Felipe de Austin, the
empresario supervised every facet of the life of his colony. A man of
prodigious work habits, he authored a civil and criminal code for the
settlement, and for the first five years served as its only civil authority. Screening potential immigrants carefully, he wrote to a business
associate, "Let *us have no black sheep in our flock*." Austin hoped to
attract individuals who were "enlightened by education and matured
by experience," not "hot headed youths" or "ignorant" frontiersmen.
This was, of course, wishful thinking, since well-established planters in the American South had little reason to relocate. Austin's colonists were upwardly mobile but unlettered farmers looking for a
fresh start, who sometimes chafed at his paternalistic manner, not

to mention the twelve-and-a-half-cent surveying surcharge. He had spent much of his life west of the Appalachians, yet he had little in common with the roughhewn men and women who gravitated to his colony. Ill-suited to the dictates of a democratic age, he remained, at heart, a snob.[19]

To THE NORTHEAST, IN THE PINE FORESTS NEAR THE TEXAS-Louisiana border, Fields was quietly building a power base of his own. The Cherokees were not the largest or the most powerful Indian group in East Texas. But under Fields's leadership the tribe now emerged as the head of an ad hoc confederation, which outsiders would come to know as the Cherokees and their "associated bands." After recruiting Indians above the Red River for more than a year, he decided the time had come to let Mexican authorities know what he had been up to.

In two remarkable letters, one to the *jefe politico* (political chief) in San Antonio, the other to the *alcalde* (chief magistrate) of Nacogdoches, Fields took the opportunity to lay out his plans for the future. In a tone that suggested he was not telling them anything they did not already know, he explained that he had received a land grant from the national government, as well as a commission to unite the Indians of East Texas. Almost nonchalantly, he informed them that he would be holding a grand council of the tribes in Cherokee territory that summer in an effort to bring about peace on the northern frontier. To the local alcalde he added that, if he wished, he was welcome to attend.[20]

The Mexican officials were flabbergasted. If Fields had been awarded a land grant in the forests of East Texas, or been given permission to form a coalition of the immigrant tribes, it was certainly news to them. Unsure how to proceed, they forwarded the letters to Mexico City and awaited instructions. The response from Lucas Alamán did little to shed light on things. Nothing Fields had told them was true, the minister replied. When concerned local officials asked the Cherokee leader to produce the documents he claimed to have received from the government, Fields blithely ignored the request. He was a loyal citizen of the Mexican state, he repeatedly assured them, and he would prove it by unleashing his warriors against the Comanches and any other tribes who raided the settlements on the northern frontier.[21]

While Alamán was trying to figure out how an obscure Indian leader had managed to bring thousands of refugees into East Texas without the government's knowledge, in Saltillo state lawmakers were finally getting around to passing a colonization law. The legislature soon issued to American empresarios the first of some two dozen land grants above the Rio Grande. Haden Edwards's patience was finally rewarded with a contract to settle eight hundred families on a parcel of land that stretched across eleven present-day East Texas counties. His son-in-law, Frost Thorn, got one, too, a contract to settle four hundred families farther north. The exact boundaries of these grants were anything but clear—legislators had only a vague knowledge of the lands they were giving away—but there could be little doubt that Thorn's contract, and perhaps part of Edwards's as well, included the dense timberlands the Cherokees and other immigrant tribes called home.

The news that the state legislature had awarded land grants that effectively annulled Indian territorial claims sparked a flurry of rumors in Texas about what Fields might do next. On the Brazos River, Stephen F. Austin heard disturbing reports that the Cherokee leader was so angry that he intended to raise a force of immigrant Indians to sweep the area of Mexicans and Anglos, and immediately notified the political chief in San Antonio, José Antonio Saucedo. "I do not believe that Fields wants war, but he is discontented," he wrote, and urged Saucedo to appease him by giving the Indians land.[22]

Fields was mulling his options—and a war against the Mexican government may well have been one of them—when a short, stocky white man appeared in his village. To the Cherokee leader, the unexpected arrival of John Dunn Hunter, one of the most famous men on the North American frontier, must have seemed nothing less than providential. Though only in his late twenties (he did not know his exact age), Hunter claimed to have been kidnapped by the Kickapoos as a child and raised by the Kansas and Osage Indians. He had recently authored a widely read memoir, though its authenticity would be questioned by some who resented its harsh critique of Anglo-American treatment of indigenous peoples. He became an international celebrity, sought out as an expert on the western tribes by such figures as Thomas Jefferson and James Madison and feted by British high society. All were captivated by the young American, who spoke with such passionate authority on the plight of the Indians that some likened it to "a storm that agitated his entire soul."[23]

Convinced that the western tribes could be readily assimilated if taught the necessary agricultural skills, Hunter in 1824 embarked upon a personal crusade to extend "the benefits of civil life to the Indians." He made his way to Arkansas, intending to live among the Quapaw, only to find that the tribe had been pushed farther west by the War Department. It was then that he began to hear reports of a Cherokee chief in Texas who was gathering the Native peoples under his leadership.[24]

It was an auspicious meeting for both men. As a boy, Hunter had been stirred by a fiery speech the Shawnee chief Tecumseh delivered to the Osage in 1813, during his campaign to unite the tribes of the Mississippi River Valley. In Richard Fields he saw a similarly charismatic figure, a leader with the vision to forge a new pan-Indian movement. The two men decided that Hunter should go to Mexico City to make a second plea for a land grant, reasoning that a famous American might succeed where two Cherokee leaders had failed. Mindful that the government would no longer pay for Indian visits to meet with the nation's leaders, Fields sold off his cattle to cover Hunter's expenses.[25]

Arriving in Mexico City in the spring of 1826, Hunter, as expected, met with a very different reception than that of Fields and Bowls. Lucas Alamán was no longer serving as Minister of Interior and Exterior Relations, which certainly helped matters. But even more important, Great Britain and the United States, two nations Mexico could ill afford to ignore, had recently opened diplomatic relations with the new government, and both saw that a Cherokee land grant in East Texas would have enormous implications for their ambitions on the North American continent.

The British minister to Mexico, Henry George Ward, was not impressed with Hunter personally. He found his language "coarse, his appearance dull, and his manner totally devoid of energy and grace." But he understood that a large Indian population in East Texas could serve as an effective barrier to the expansion of the United States, a country his government viewed as a serious rival to British power in the Western Hemisphere. As Hunter's enthusiastic patron, Ward drafted a land grant petition on behalf of the Cherokees that pledged to establish a homeland in East Texas for thirty thousand displaced US Indians. Hunter then copied the document in his own hand and presented it to President Guadalupe Victoria. To no one's surprise, the president endorsed the plan. Having borrowed heavily from British banks, his government had no desire to antagonize its principal creditor.[26]

Unfortunately for the Cherokees, Ward's American counterpart in Mexico City, Joel Poinsett, was not without influence of his own. Tapped by President John Quincy Adams to serve as the first US minister to the Mexican Republic, Poinsett had established a reputation as a zealous representative of American interests. A South Carolinian with extensive experience in Latin America, the diplomat spoke fluent Spanish, developing a rapport with the country's prominent liberals. Poinsett even helped to create, with Zavala, Mexía, and other federalists, a new Masonic order in the nation's capital, the York Rite Lodge, to rival the Scottish Rite Lodge dominated by wealthy conservatives. With the *yorkinos* holding lodge meetings at his official residence, Poinsett commanded a solid bloc of support in Congress, much to the dismay of conservatives who accused the diplomat of meddling in the country's internal affairs.[27]

Like many Americans, Poinsett exhibited a lively fear of the British Empire, which seemed poised to thwart US interests at every turn. Ward had already bested his American counterpart on one important policy issue, inking a major trade deal with Mexican leaders. Poinsett had no intention of allowing the British diplomat to get the better of him again. Instructed by the State Department to see if the Mexican government would sell all or a part of Texas, he was genuinely alarmed when he got wind of Hunter's plan, and Ward's role in it. Keeping Washington apprised of the Cherokee emissary's progress in coded dispatches, the US minister turned to his *yorkino* allies in Congress to scuttle the bill. Zavala, sitting on the Senate's colonization committee, made sure the Cherokee land bill never came up for a vote. A frustrated Hunter left the capital empty-handed, and returned to Texas to tell Fields the bad news.[28]

FIELDS HAD BEEN BUSY DURING HUNTER'S ABSENCE, recruiting more Indians from above the Red River as he sought to establish his authority over the East Texas tribes. Anglo settlers watched with mounting concern as Delawares, Shawnees, Kickapoos, and others groups streamed into the area. Their fears were compounded by the fact that the Indians' actions, to whites at least, were shrouded in secrecy. "Their numbers are increasing daily from some unknown cause," one American wrote. When he asked a band of refugees why they had come, he received only a laconic reply: Richard Fields had summoned them.[29]

By the spring of 1826 the Cherokee leader would claim that as many as eight thousand Indians had crossed the Red River, with more on the way. While there is no way of knowing how many refugee Indians entered the province during the mid-1820s, Fields's estimate was almost surely an exaggeration. Still, to the Cherokee leader belongs much of the credit for the sudden and dramatic increase in the population of Texas during this period. No empresario, not even Stephen F. Austin, would bring in so many settlers in so short a time.[30]

To allay the growing concerns among Mexican officials of a pan-Indian alliance, Fields rarely missed an opportunity to assure them that he bore no ill will toward the government. Far from it, he insisted; the immigrant Indians considered themselves to be "sons of the Mexicans" and would gladly offer "the last drop of our blood for the defense of the country." Again and again he reminded them that the East Texas tribes stood ready and willing to beat back the Comanches and block the flow of contraband goods across the US-Mexico border. All he needed was the go-ahead from Mexican leaders.[31]

Their reluctance to give it must have baffled and irritated Fields. Defending the frontier against the hostile, nomadic tribes was, after all, one reason why the government had been so keen to settle the region in the first place. Part of the problem was that Mexican authorities were not yet ready to embrace the Cherokees and their associated bands as full-fledged allies. They knew little about the tribes that were moving into Texas and preferred to keep them at arm's length, at least for the time being. It was a view Anglo-Americans did little to discourage. "Although they declare that they are friendly," warned one settler to the political chief in San Antonio, "they do not cease to be Indians."[32]

And part of the problem was Fields himself. The Cherokee leader's declarations of loyalty did little to satisfy local officials, who detected in his letters a troubling self-importance, a sign that Fields might be driven by another, more personal agenda. Styling himself the "Superior Chief" of the East Texas Indians, he sought to project an image of power he did not possess, referring to them as "my people." Yet Fields ignored, or seemed oblivious to, the fact that the tribes still acted independently of one another, deferring to the Cherokees only when it was in their interests to do so. No doubt Fields hoped to impress upon Mexican officials that he was a figure to be reckoned with. Instead, he only gave them grounds for concern.[33]

Such fears would be confirmed when John Dunn Hunter returned to East Texas. Fields was furious to learn of Hunter's rebuff by the Mexican government. He had been tricked and humiliated, he raged; the immigrant tribes must now rise up and claim by force what had been promised to them. Hunter was not yet ready to support such a drastic course of action. Rather than risk a destructive war, he argued, the tribes should simply move across the Red River, into US Indian Territory. But for Fields there was no turning back; he had staked his reputation and his personal property on behalf of a "poor orphan tribe of red people that look up to me for protection." The Indians could no longer put any faith in Mexican promises, he declared. "I am a red man and a man of honor. We will lift up our tomahawks and fight for land."[34]

THREE

THE RED AND WHITE REPUBLIC OF FREDONIA

RICHARD FIELDS WAS NOT THE ONLY LEADER IN EAST TEXAS whose anger at the Mexican government had reached a breaking point in the summer of 1826. The land speculator Haden Edwards, following in the footsteps of Stephen F. Austin, had been working for more than a year to establish his colony in the Piney Woods. It had not gone exactly as planned.

The land grant Edwards had received from the Saltillo legislature differed from Austin's in one crucial respect: there was a Mexican community already living there. The little village of Nacogdoches sat at the tail end of the Camino Real, a day's ride south of Cherokee country. In the colonial era, the town was far too remote to be integrated into the economy of New Spain, managing to survive only because of a lively smuggling trade with Natchitoches. During Mexico's War of Independence it had been all but abandoned, the Hispano townsfolk fleeing across the Sabine River to escape the violence. Now the town was sputtering back to life, with a population of about five hundred. Located on the seam that joined the frontiers of Mexico and the United States, Nacogdoches was a hybrid community. Its Hispano residents returned from exile with newly acquired American customs and habits, even speaking their native language, according to one disapproving Mexican visitor, with "marked incorrectness." After independence, Nacogdoches attracted a motley assortment of Anglo-Americans, French Creoles, and runaway slaves, while Indian refugees like the Cherokees also became a part of the life of the town, which served as a market for their cattle, skins, and furs.[1]

In Nacogdoches the color line was blurry at best, and no one was more representative of its multiracial character than the local blacksmith, a free person of color named William Goyens. Light-skinned and powerfully built, the forty-year-old Goyens had been born in the foothills of North Carolina, at one time a frontier not unlike East Texas, where racial boundaries were very much in flux. The son of a free person of color and a white woman, probably an indentured servant, he could also claim Cherokee roots, some North Carolina Indians having been enslaved and absorbed into the African American population in the mid-eighteenth century. He spoke the Cherokee language fluently, and as a teenager served in the Cherokee Regiment, fighting at the Battle of Horseshoe Bend in 1814. How Goyens wound up in the remote pine barrens of East Texas many years later is unclear. At any rate, in Nacogdoches the enterprising blacksmith had become one of the town's most well-respected citizens. He had recently started a freight-hauling business, carting Cherokee peltries and other goods across the Sabine River to Natchitoches. In a world where hardship and poverty tended to muddy distinctions of race and class, Nacogdoches offered a welcoming refuge to anyone willing to help it rebuild.[2]

Welcoming, that is, until Haden Edwards showed up. For all his lobbying and glad-handing in Mexico City and Saltillo, Edwards turned out to be a lousy empresario. Displaying a conspicuous lack of tact in the day-to-day business of running a colony, he quarreled bitterly with Nacogdoches town leaders. According to the terms of his contract, Edwards was required to respect all preexisting land claims. Instead, he promptly notified families living within the boundaries of his grant to produce valid titles or face eviction.

When residents objected and threatened to take their complaints to political chief Saucedo in San Antonio, Edwards refused to back down, insisting that he took orders only from the state government in Saltillo. Stephen F. Austin was concerned by Edwards's high-handed conduct, and bluntly told him so: "The imprudent course you have commenced will totally ruin you," he warned, hastening to add that it also threatened to prejudice the government against the entire empresario program.[3]

Rather than seek a compromise, Edwards turned for support to a new settlement that had sprouted farther east, near the US border. Most residents of Ayish Bayou were Anglo-American squatters who had moved across the Sabine River after the War of Independence. The settlement was home to a number of so-called border ruffians, too, gangs of men who engaged in a lively contraband trade in stolen horses, livestock, and enslaved people, who had been run out of western Louisiana when the US Army established a post in Natchitoches to police the area.

The rift between Edwards and Nacogdoches residents soon centered on the election for the office of alcalde. As the Mexican government's sole functionary in northeast Texas, the alcalde served as a kind of bureaucratic jack-of-all-trades. Magistrate and mayor of the district, he was also the custodian of the town's municipal archives, and thus responsible for the safekeeping of all land records. With the Ayish Bayou settlers voting as a bloc, the Edwards faction defeated longtime resident Samuel Norris and installed Edwards's son-in-law in the job. The angry locals took their case to Saucedo, and in the spring of 1826 they received a reply: Norris must be reinstated, and the archives returned.

Edwards did not take the defeat graciously. On the night Saucedo's letter arrived in Nacogdoches, the Mexican residents held a fandango to celebrate their victory. The blacksmith William Goyens, who was known to be fond of the dances held regularly in the town's Hispano community, was almost certainly in attendance. The empresario and some of his Ayish Bayou friends crashed the party, and angry words quickly degenerated into a violent scuffle. Passions ran so high that the melee resumed the following day, with the locals giving Edwards and his son-in-law a sound thrashing in the town square.[4]

5. Haden Edwards (1771–1849).
Land speculator Haden Edwards
devoted several years and much of
his fortune to his Texas colonization
enterprise. When state authorities
rescinded his empresario contract,
he led the first Anglo rebellion
against Mexican rule in 1826.
Courtesy of Ralph W. Steen Library,
Stephen F. Austin State University.

Tensions continued to escalate between the Edwards faction
and Nacogdoches residents with a series of minor disturbances in
the months that followed. One episode involved Goyens and one
of the Ayish Bayou men who had instigated the ruckus at the fandango, a slave dealer with a particularly unsavory reputation named
William English. Since Goyens's freight-hauling business required
him to cross the border into Louisiana, he was an easy target for
English, who had him arrested as a runaway slave. Under normal
circumstances, an unclaimed slave would be sold at public auction,
with the slave catcher receiving the proceeds. But not in this case.
Goyens was a man of some means, and unlike most free persons of
color he could afford to buy his freedom. The seizure amounted to a
poorly disguised extortion attempt, one in which English must have
had the cooperation of the local sheriff, since it was hardly a secret
in Natchitoches that Goyens was a Mexican citizen. The blacksmith
languished in jail until he paid English off, purchasing a female slave,
then signing the deed over to his abductor. It was a stark reminder
that for those of African descent, the Sabine River represented more
than just a border between the United States and Mexico, but a de-
marcation line separating two very different worlds, one enslaved
and one free.[5]

Norris and other local leaders kept up a steady barrage of complaints about the behavior of the Ayish Bayou rowdies to Saucedo in San Antonio, who in turn forwarded them to Governor Victor Blanco in Saltillo, who promised to rule on the matter. By the summer of 1826 they had new grounds for concern: Haden Edwards had signed up seven hundred colonists from Mississippi and Louisiana, who would be arriving early the following year. This was, of course, the whole point of the empresario program—Stephen F. Austin was doing the same thing at his colony on the Brazos River. But the citizens of Nacogdoches needed little imagination to see that the presence of a large group of white Southerners, many of them slaveholders, threatened to completely Americanize the area, shattering the peaceful coexistence of their small multiethnic community.[6]

THE BATTLE LINES BETWEEN THE EDWARDS FACTION AND THE town were clearly drawn when John Dunn Hunter appeared at the Ayish settlement to request a meeting with the empresario. Recently returned from Mexico City, he informed Edwards of his failed mission to secure a land grant for the Cherokees, and of Fields's angry reaction when he learned of its failure. Edwards could certainly relate; he had long been exasperated by the country's cumbersome bureaucracy and seemingly capricious land policies. As the two men commiserated with each other, Hunter broached the possibility of an alliance with the Indians to seize the territory for themselves.[7]

The empresario balked at the suggestion, or so he later claimed, confident that he still had the backing of the state legislature. A few months passed, and in early October Edwards received Governor Blanco's long-awaited ruling on the empresario's feud with the town. His first reaction upon reading the letter was that it had to be a forgery written by his enemies. The governor not only sided with the locals, he upbraided Edwards for behaving in an arbitrary manner, and for acting as if he believed himself to be "absolute Lord and Master of those lands." Blanco annulled the empresario's contract and ordered his expulsion from Texas. If Edwards wished to appeal the ruling, he could do so by mail, but only after he had left the country.[8]

The news was a gut punch for the empresario, one that, perhaps surprisingly, he had not anticipated. He had devoted several years of his life and invested a substantial part of his personal fortune on his land project with nothing to show for it. Hunter's proposal suddenly began to take on a certain appeal.

The plot to wrest East Texas from Mexican control was not as harebrained as it might seem. With no formal military presence in the area, Saucedo would be unable to mount a response to the uprising for several weeks. By that time, Edwards believed, more Americans would join the insurgency. Anglo-Texans were then in a state of alarm over rumors that the state legislature in Saltillo was planning to abolish slavery. In Austin's colony on the Brazos, the province's chief cotton-growing region, newly arrived settlers were known to be especially concerned by the news. In addition, the empresario reasoned that an uprising involving Americans so close to the US border might force Washington to intervene, and in a best-case scenario, persuade the Mexican government to part with its troublesome province for the right price.[9]

The success of the rebellion would depend on the alignment of all these factors, but at this point Edwards believed he had little to lose. On December 16, the empresario, his brother Benjamin, and a handful of conspirators rode into Nacogdoches. They fired their guns, hallooed, and galloped around the town square—there was no one to stop them. Making their headquarters in a building on the square then known as the Stone House, they raised a flag they had made the night before. Half red and half white, to symbolize the union between the Anglo-American rebels and their Indian confederates, the banner bore a legend written in black ink: "Independence, Freedom and Justice."[10]

Fields and Hunter showed up a few days later with a small group of Cherokees. Forming a thirteen-member "General Council of Independence," the rebels gathered at the Stone House and announced their intention to secede from Mexico. Clearly oblivious to the strangeness of the moment, they pinned red and white cockades to their hats and grandly declared their new state the "Republic of Fredonia." Then they got down to the business of primary concern to both groups: the distribution of land. The General Council divided Texas into two, roughly equal parts. The lands just north of Nacogdoches and extending west along a line all the way to El Paso would be reserved for the "Red People." Anglo-Americans claimed the territory below the line. In an effort to win the support of the other empresarios, the council promised to honor all land grants awarded by the Mexican government. Squatters, and there were lots of them in East Texas, would receive secure title to any lands they had cleared and improved.[11]

It is tempting to view the Fredonian Rebellion as a uniquely biracial moment in which whites and Indians overcame seemingly insurmountable cultural barriers to work toward a common goal. But from the outset it was clear that the rebels did not speak for either constituency—at least not yet. Despite their claim to represent the Americans of Texas, the white rebels were all residents of the tiny Ayish Bayou settlement. And while Richard Fields liked to boast that he was the chief of no fewer than twenty-three tribes, the four Indian signatories were all Cherokees. In fact, Edwards and Fields had made a bold gamble. They would declare independence now and worry about finding support for their revolt later. Despite the stunning symbolism of the rebels' red and white banner, the uprising was less an alliance of two peoples than a marriage of expedience, a conspiracy hatched by two men, one a somewhat shady land speculator, the other a one-eighth Cherokee with a messiah complex, linked only by their hostility toward Mexican rule.

IN THE DAYS THAT FOLLOWED, THE CONSPIRATORS BEGAN THE work of raising a rebel army. Fields and Hunter rode back to their village after the signing ceremony, having promised to recruit four hundred warriors for the campaign. They were disappointed to find that most of the tribe's young men had gone on a winter hunt and would not be back for several days. Fields soon left to make a tour of the other Indian villages, leaving Hunter to make the case for the uprising to the Cherokees. In Nacogdoches, the Edwards brothers printed up handbills justifying their actions, dispatching riders to distribute them to the Anglo settlements in Texas and across the river in Louisiana. Drawing upon the rhetoric of the American Revolution, the Fredonians claimed to be fighting against a tyrannical regime. Their cause was identical to that of "those long departed patriots, who, when their rights were invaded, nobly grasped their arms, and planted the standard of liberty and independence in our native land." It was a familiar refrain to white Americans, who had spent much of the past year commemorating the fiftieth anniversary of their country's independence.[12]

The uprising in Nacogdoches did not come as a surprise to political chief Saucedo. For weeks he had been receiving updates from Samuel Norris on the feud between Nacogdoches residents and the Edwards brothers, warning him that a crisis was at hand. Days before the conspirators gathered at the Stone House, he had assembled in San Antonio a force of three hundred men to march on Nacogdoches, though rain-swollen rivers would delay his progress. At San Felipe, Stephen F. Austin was also following the worsening situation in East Texas closely. In full damage control mode, he dashed off frantic letters to members of the Edwards faction to tell them that they could expect no support from his own colony. Their actions "cast a stain on the hitherto high character of Americans," he wrote to a friend known to be sympathetic to the rebels. "I am unwilling to believe that you have all run mad."[13]

Fortunately for Mexico, the province's newly appointed Indian agent appeared on the scene as the rebellion began to unfold. A colorful, freewheeling soldier of fortune, Peter Ellis Bean was forty-three years old in 1826. He had fought under Andrew Jackson at the Battle of New Orleans and alongside the revolutionary leader José María Morelos in the early years of Mexico's War of Independence. Competent, despite a messy private life—he had a wife in Texas and another in central Mexico—Bean learned of the uprising as he was making his way back to his home in the Piney Woods after a yearlong sojourn in the capital. He would act as the government's point man during the crisis in the weeks ahead, coordinating his efforts with Saucedo and Austin. He soon discovered he had another, more personal reason to quell the revolt: his American wife, believing he had died in Mexico, had married one of the Fredonian ringleaders.[14]

Bean initially dismissed the reports of trouble in Nacogdoches; it seemed a minor fracas, of the kind not uncommon in rowdy border towns. He gained a clearer sense of the situation when he arrived at his farm in East Texas. The Edwards brothers and their confederates could be dealt with, he believed, but to Austin he frankly admitted that "if all the Ingins Joine them this will be a serious affair." Bean wrote several conciliatory letters to Fields, urging him to disavow his alliance with the Fredonians and suggesting a meeting with Saucedo to address Cherokee grievances. No word came until the end of December, when an Indian messenger appeared at Bean's farmhouse with a blunt reply. Fields was not interested in a conference with the political chief, or anyone else. The time for negotiation had passed.[15]

Fields would soon regret his decision to spurn Bean's olive branch. Recruiting the army of Indians he had promised Edwards was proving harder than he expected. About the time Bean received the Cherokee leader's message, John Dunn Hunter was riding back to Nacogdoches, having scraped together a party of just thirty warriors. There the situation was hardly one to inspire confidence in the success of their enterprise. In the days since their capture of the town, Edwards's men had busied themselves fortifying the Stone House and taking whatever supplies they needed from the locals. But with no Mexican troops in the area and none expected for some time, they had little to do. Most went home; those who remained entertained themselves with idle, endless talk about a possible attack on San Antonio. They also began drinking and quarreling among themselves. When Hunter arrived, he found the rebels engaged in an inebriated brawl. Half of his men promptly turned around and rode back to their villages in Cherokee country.[16]

With the Fredonians in disarray, alcalde Norris decided he did not need to wait for Saucedo's troops to put an end to the revolt. In early January he rode into town at the head of a column of several dozen armed Anglo and Hispano Nacogdoches residents. Beating a drum and carrying the Mexican flag, the group dismounted and prepared to make an assault on the Stone House. Before they could do so, Edwards's men, who had evidently sobered up by this time, charged out of the building, accompanied by Hunter's Indian followers. Their yells and war whoops unnerved the citizens, who turned and ran. In a skirmish that lasted only a few minutes and left one resident dead, they chased Norris and his men back down the street and out of town.[17]

The battle was a minor victory for the Fredonians, but it failed to generate any momentum for the rebellion. In the nearby Anglo settlements and across the river in Natchitoches, Edwards's call for volunteers was met with disapproval or bewildered indifference. The response in San Felipe, where Austin took energetic measures to stamp out any thought of rebellion, was hardly better. When letters arrived addressed to men the Fredonians believed would be sympathetic to their cause, the empresario confiscated them before they could be delivered. Eager to demonstrate his colony's loyalty to Mexico, Austin issued a proclamation denouncing the rebels as a "small party of infatuated madmen," and called for volunteers to help put down the revolt. The natural affinity that his Anglo-American colonists may have felt for the Fredonians was offset by the sensational news that the Edwards brothers had entered into an "unnatural and bloody alliance" with the immigrant tribes, a fact Austin exploited to discredit the uprising. The Indians, he asserted, intended to lay waste to all the white settlements on Mexico's northern frontier. When Saucedo's troops arrived in San Felipe, a company of one hundred men was waiting to march with them as they pushed on toward Nacogdoches.[18]

If Edwards had badly misjudged the willingness of Anglo-Americans to join him in a revolt against Mexico, Richard Fields had also overreached. He would get no help from Bowls, who had been conspicuously absent when the Fredonians met to sign their declaration of independence in Nacogdoches in December. While it is unlikely that the meeting could have taken place at all if the old chief opposed the idea, there is no evidence that he ever shared Fields's enthusiasm for a war against the Mexican government. The historical record sheds little light on the relationship between the two men, but it is likely that Bowls distrusted Fields, a Westernized Indian who had always been something of an outsider among the more traditional Texas Cherokees. And he distrusted Hunter, a white man with no connection to the tribe, even more. No doubt Fields's claim to the imaginary title of "Superior Chief" of the Indians rankled Bowls and the other head men of the immigrant tribes. And none could forget their long history of conflict with the whites, whom Fields now insisted that they embrace as allies.[19]

Fields's inability to rally the immigrant tribes also revealed a fundamental misunderstanding about the nature of Native American warfare. The Cherokee leader called upon the Indians to "fight for land," which was certainly reason enough for white Americans, who routinely took up arms to achieve political and economic objectives. But Indians went to war to avenge the deaths of kinsmen or to redress some other form of deeply held grievance, and up to this point the Mexican government had left them undisturbed in their villages in the Piney Woods. The decision to fight was not made lightly, and it was one each man would make alone, without regard for a war chief's personal ambitions. "They are free to go or stay," Bowls would state at a war council on another occasion, "it is as the heart of the warrior directs."[20]

For the Indians, matters came to a head on January 25, when Bean met with several immigrant chiefs, probably at Bowls's village forty miles north of Nacogdoches. Fields and Hunter had deceived the tribes with false promises, he told them; any further association with the Edwards brothers would result in disaster for the Cherokees and their associated bands. The Kickapoos needed no convincing; they had been against the uprising from the start. Although he had no authority to do so, Bean assured the Cherokees, Shawnees, and Delawares that the Mexican government would look favorably upon their land claims if they took no part in the uprising. Even without such a promise, it is likely that they, too, wanted nothing more to do with the Fredonians. By this time they knew that Mexican troops were approaching Nacogdoches, and the support from the other American settlements Edwards had promised would not be forthcoming. If they still had any doubts as to what course to pursue, a promise of amnesty from Saucedo for all who abandoned the Fredonians settled the matter.[21]

For the Cherokees, one issue remained to be resolved: what to do with Fields and Hunter. The question was probably decided after the grand council by a meeting of tribal elders. There seems to have been no disagreement as to the fate of Fields. He had committed an unpardonable sin, placing his own ambition above the welfare of the community. Only a verdict of death would reassure Mexican officials of the Indians' loyalty. As for Hunter, Bean appealed for clemency. He was not an Indian but a white man, the agent argued, and should be handed over to local authorities. The head men disagreed, evidently deciding that both men were equally to blame for leading the tribe into an unwanted war.[22]

The pair fled when they learned of the verdict. Fields escaped into the forest, headed for Louisiana, but he did not make it to the US border. A party of Cherokee men tracked him to a camp he had made for the night and stabbed him in the heart. Hunter attempted to rejoin Edwards and the Fredonians in Nacogdoches, accompanied by two Cherokees he believed he could trust. When he stopped at a creek to water his horse, they shot him in the back. Pursued by his assailants as he staggered into the water, Hunter begged them not to fire. It was hard, he was reported to have said in his final moments, to die by the hands of his friends.[23]

By the end of the month the rebellion had collapsed. A party of Alabama-Coushatta Indians joined Mexican loyalists in capturing some of Edwards's men, who had taken refuge at Ayish Bayou. The Fredonians abandoned Nacogdoches three days later. As Saucedo's army closed in on the town, the Edwards brothers and the last of the rebels skedaddled, riding hard down the Camino Real into Louisiana.

The red and white Republic of Fredonia had come to an inglorious end. It was indeed a "silly, wild, Quicksotic scheme," as one American described it, hatched by men who represented neither whites nor Indians. Their adversaries, however, *did* represent an alliance of the region's ethnic groups. The Fredonian movement failed because Hispanos, Anglos, immigrant Indians, and even a few blacks like William Goyens all closed ranks in defense of the Mexican regime.[24]

Relieved that a major crisis had been averted, the Cherokees and the Mexican government both made public gestures of reconciliation in the months that followed. Local officials presented Bowls with a lieutenant colonel's commission and an army uniform for his role in thwarting the rebellion. For his part, the chief announced that his two youngest sons would be educated as Mexicans to help foster better relations between the Indians and their adopted country. And in a sign of the strong community values that Fields had defied, Bowls asked the government to provide for the relief of Fields's wife and children, who had been reduced to poverty since his death. The tribe did not visit the sins of the father upon the sons. It took care of its own.[25]

Richard Fields's dream of a pan-Indian alliance would die with him. The Cherokees still assumed a position of prominence among the East Texas tribes, representing the associated bands in negotiations with the government and Anglo settlers. But Bowls had no interest in empire building; never again would an Indian presume to speak for all the region's Native peoples. Fields's quest to secure for the Indians a permanent homeland was also unsuccessful. Yet his efforts had not been entirely in vain. In the years that followed, Bowls and other headmen would press the Mexican government to formally acknowledge their ownership of the lands they occupied in East Texas. Even without such a guarantee, the Cherokees and their associated bands were in a much stronger position than before.

From the prairies below the Red River to the Piney Woods, Mexico's northern frontier was now dotted with Indian villages, and a distant government lacked the resources to dislodge them. The Indians still faced an uncertain future, but there was, at least, strength in numbers, something Richard Fields had known all along.

FOUR

AN ELYSIUM OF ROGUES

T HE RESIDENTS OF LAREDO HAD NEVER SEEN ANYTHING LIKE the enormous, ornately carved coach with silver inlay that rolled into the sleepy town in February 1828. The denizens of the villas del norte, the chain of half a dozen communities along the lower Rio Grande, had long been left to fend for themselves by the government in Mexico City, and formal visits by high-ranking dignitaries were rare. Part of a convoy of three dozen troops and several wagons of supplies, the coach brought Manuel de Mier y Terán, a thirty-eight-year-old brigadier general, to the northern frontier.[1]

Terán would spend the next year in Texas, leading a Boundary Commission tasked with drawing a line between Mexico and the United States. When Spain signed the Adams-Onís Treaty with Washington establishing a boundary in 1819, its North American empire was on the verge of collapse. Newly independent Mexico promised to abide by the treaty, but the US government, having never ratified the agreement, now insisted it was not legally bound to honor its provisions. Fully aware of Washington's interest in acquiring a part or all of Texas, the Guadalupe Victoria regime wanted Terán's Boundary Commission to conduct a survey to define the border between the two countries, as well as to undertake a comprehensive study of the frontier's natural resources. The expedition had been in the planning stages for some time, but in the wake of the Fredonian Rebellion Terán's mission assumed a more urgent purpose. While the Edwards brothers had certainly not acted with

Washington's knowledge or approval, the influx of large numbers of
Americans, both illegally and as colonists under the empresario program, suddenly became a serious concern for national leaders suspicious of US territorial ambitions. Thus Terán's mission would also
take stock of the immigration question and develop a plan to defend
the frontier should Mexico need to do so.[2]

In a country still reeling from the effects of a decade-long war
for independence, Mexican military leaders all too often played a
destabilizing role in civic life. Terán, however, was a notable exception. An engineer by training, he had acquired a reputation as a dutiful public servant rather than an ambitious military chieftain. He
leaned conservative politically, counting Lucas Alamán as one of his
closest friends, but had taken little part in the increasingly acrimonious debate between the country's federalist and centralist leaders.
His new assignment as head of the Boundary Commission was a
task uniquely suited to his talents. Accompanied by a scientific team
that included a cartographer, a botanist, and a mineralogist, Terán
was himself an enthusiastic student of the natural environment. As
the group made its way into the interior of Texas, he kept careful
notes of the region's plant life and geological features, and at night
spent his time pleasantly stargazing with a telescope he had brought
on the trip.[3]

After a month in San Antonio, the expedition lumbered eastward
along a path that would take it into two of the colonies established by
American empresarios. Following distance markers carved into the
live oaks that dotted the rolling hills of this part of Texas, the party
soon reached the Guadalupe River and the struggling settlement of
Gonzales. Founded by a Missourian, Green Dewitt, the hamlet—it
could hardly be called a town—consisted of half a dozen shacks near
the water's edge. It had been temporarily abandoned when Comanches swept through the area two years earlier, and the few dozen
Americans on the farms nearby still "lived in terror of being killed."
The colony would grow fitfully in the years ahead, though Dewitt
would never come close to settling the four hundred families required by his empresario contract.[4]

Not until Terán and his entourage crossed the Lavaca River, the western boundary of Stephen F. Austin's land grant, did they see the first signs of a permanent American presence. In 1828, the colony was home to more than two thousand people, one-fifth of them enslaved. Most lived on the waterways that fed into the Colorado and Brazos rivers, where they raised cattle and mules and grew corn and cotton. Only about two hundred people lived in San Felipe de Austin, which stretched for half a mile along the roadway and looked like any American backwoods town, with a tavern and a few dozen ramshackle cabins. Two poorly stocked general stores offered a few staples the settlers could not produce themselves: liquor (whiskey and rum), coffee, rice, flour, and cheap cloth. But the colony was clearly prospering, and whatever concerns Terán may have had about the loyalty of the American immigrants seemed to subside during the fortnight he spent at San Felipe. Here the colonists "try to understand and obey the laws of the country," he noted, a fact he attributed to the "enlightenment and integrity" of Austin himself.[5]

The expedition left San Felipe in something of a hurry when a storm came up, making it necessary to ferry quickly over to the east bank before the waters rose. Bad weather followed the little expedition as it headed northeast, toward the Piney Woods. In the forests, they encountered a web of rain-swollen streams, creeks, and sloughs, some too deep to ford. Wagons sank in the bog, and almost every day a wheel broke or an axle snapped and had to be repaired using the timber available. Then the weather turned hot and humid, and in the evenings mosquitos descended upon the camp in great, unforgiving clouds. Terán and his men awoke to find their faces so swollen they were almost unrecognizable. The bites soon became infected, leaving sores that oozed blood and pus. A third of the men came down with fever, including Terán himself, who gave up his carriage to others too sick to ride. It would take the party almost a month to reach the Trinity River, a distance of barely one hundred miles, where they learned that the flatboats to ferry the wagons across had been destroyed in the recent storms. Sending most of the soldiers back to

San Antonio with the wagons, equipment, and his ornate carriage, Terán pressed on with a handful of men to Nacogdoches, where he finally arrived, feverish and exhausted, in early June.[6]

In the Piney Woods, the news of Terán's visit caused no little excitement among the Cherokees and the immigrant tribes. Bowls and the other chiefs insisted on meeting the Mexican dignitary, riding into town at the head of large delegations. They crowded, uninvited, into his lodgings, some lounging on the furniture, others on the general's steamer trunks or on the floor, their pipe smoke filling the room. The courtly Terán found the Indians' lack of decorum irritating, but he listened patiently to their concerns. The Cherokees impressed him, perhaps because they were more Western in appearance than the other tribes. Of the Alabamas and Coushattas, he wrote, "These forest people live in great contentment" and "satisfy their needs abundantly through their labors in a fertile land." Likewise, he developed a favorable view of the Shawnees and Delawares, who came down from the northern prairies to introduce themselves. Expressing a keen desire to be Hispanicized, they asked the government to send teachers so they could learn to read and write Spanish.[7]

But again and again, the Indians turned these awkward encounters to the topic of most concern to them: their desire to obtain clear ownership of the lands they occupied. White squatters were encroaching upon their hunting grounds, they told him, and the game population once so abundant in the forests of East Texas was dwindling. Deforestation was partly to blame. Indians and settlers alike showed little restraint in their exploitation of the Piney Woods' most important natural resource, felling great stands of hardwoods for firewood and lumber. Farther south, area residents cut down bald cypresses just for the Spanish moss that hung from the tree limbs, which they used for bedding, rope, and blankets. But the principal reason for the disappearance of deer, black bear, otter, and beaver was overhunting. In one year alone, area merchants shipped a staggering eighty thousand deerskins along the Camino Real into Louisiana. By necessity rather than choice, the Indians were now less reliant

6. General Manuel de Mier y Terán (1789–1832). After his tour of Texas in 1828, General Mier y Terán urged national leaders to limit Anglo-American immigration, which he believed would lead to the loss of the province to the United States. Courtesy of Special Collections, the University of Texas at Arlington Libraries.

on hunting, spending much of their time improving their farms and pasturelands. For all these reasons, a guarantee from the government that the tribes could not be removed from their lands was more important than ever before.[8]

Eager to dispel any lingering doubt about their allegiance to the Mexican republic following the Fredonian affair, the Indians held a grand council at one of the Cherokee villages during Terán's visit. Attended by more than three hundred tribal representatives, the conference took place in a council house constructed especially for the occasion, a brush tipi eighty feet long and thirty feet wide. The Cherokees, Shawnees, Delawares, Kickapoos, Choctaws, and Caddos solemnly declared their desire to be peaceful neighbors and, in times of war, reliable allies to their Mexican "fathers."[9]

Terán was sympathetic to the Indians' plight. Although he had received no firm instructions from his government on the question of Indian land claims, the idea of a land distribution program for the immigrant tribes seemed to him a sound one, if managed properly. His letters to his superiors in the National Palace left no doubt that he thought some of the tribes—he singled out the Cherokees and the Shawnees—could be located on lands not already awarded to empresarios. Convinced of their loyalty to Mexico, he believed they could one day be fully "incorporated into the Mexican nation."[10]

He could not say the same for Anglo-Americans. If he had been impressed by the progress of Austin's colony on the Brazos River, the situation in East Texas troubled him. In the Piney Woods, the settlers exhibited a defiant Americanism, treating Terán and his companions with suspicion and even disdain. The general was especially annoyed by their readiness to flout the laws of their adopted country, a tendency he found in evidence among Americans of all classes. During the course of his tour he met indigent squatters living in forested bottomlands who had no right to be there, and cotton farmers with little regard for Mexico's restrictions on slavery. The overwhelming majority of settlers had arrived only within the last couple of years, yet all insisted that the province deserved special treatment and should be governed separately from Coahuila. In matters big and small, he found them obnoxiously independent-minded and quarrelsome, a people who "go about with their constitution in their pockets," ever alert to any infringement of their putative rights and liberties as Anglo-Americans.[11]

With Nacogdoches as his base of operations, Terán would spend seven months in East Texas, making a detailed study for his government about this region of "strange and incoherent elements." Though his health slowly returned after the difficult journey, he had always struggled with depression, a battle he continued to fight during his stay. At times he was overwhelmed by a profound melancholy, feelings he described as "the fateful scars left in the heart by the tempests of human life." When he was well enough, he took long walks alone in the woods outside town, where he could indulge his passion for the collection and study of plants and insects. In the "eternal forests of Tejas," he found a tranquil refuge and a measure of peace. In the end, he was sorry to leave.[12]

For the rest of his life, the fate of Mexico's northern province would never be far from Terán's mind. While most national leaders gave little thought to the distant, sparsely populated lands above the Rio Grande, Terán saw a region of enormous value, a potential breadbasket for the country's eight million people. Even more important, his inspection tour convinced him that Texas was vital to the security of the Mexican republic, an Achilles heel that left the country vulnerable to an aggressively expanding United States. To be sure, the US government had made no headway in its efforts to buy Texas, and the threat from the Fredonian revolt never rose above the level of comic farce. The real danger, Terán feared, was more insidious: the "silent means" of Americans moving across the border. Unless Mexico took prompt action, Anglo immigration would soon accomplish what US diplomats and American filibusters could not.[13]

As he rode southward on the journey back across the Rio Grande, Terán despaired that the nation's leaders possessed neither the will nor the means to meet the challenges he saw in Texas. The 1828 presidential election, held four months earlier, had plunged the country into a state of anarchy. Terán lamented "the dismal situation in the center of my nation," sensing that he was about to be drawn into an "abyss of passions that causes my country to groan."[14]

Responsibility for the electoral chaos in Mexico could be laid squarely at the feet of two men with little in common but a driving ambition: the federalist politician Lorenzo de Zavala and a general from the state of Veracruz, Antonio López de Santa Anna. When it became clear that Manuel Gómez Pedraza, a moderate conservative, had won the election, the two men refused to accept the result. Santa Anna battled centralist forces in the countryside, while Zavala's followers seized control of the armory in the nation's capital. President-elect Pedraza fled the city, and later into exile. The crisis unleashed the fury of the working poor, and in early December mobs of léperos stormed the markets in the city square, destroying the Parián, an enormous bazaar in the main plaza that catered to the city's elite. Shaken by the civil unrest, congress annulled the election results and handed the presidency to the federalist candidate, Vicente Guerrero, an African-Indian hero in the War of Independence.[15]

It was the beginning of an intense and stormy relationship between the intellectual and the *caudillo*. The two men could hardly be
called friends, but each saw the value of their alliance and rarely let
an opportunity pass to flatter the vanity of the other. "Never before
has such a brilliant field presented itself for the noble ambition of a
warrior," Zavala gushed in a letter to the general during the revolt.
Santa Anna repaid the compliment in full. "No one but you can steer
the Ship of State in the midst of so many reefs," he wrote soon afterward. A master of political intrigue, Zavala probably believed he
could control Santa Anna, and for a time that proved to be the case.
But he had abandoned his principles for a taste of power. The revolt
effectively sheared away the guardrails of stable governance, ush-
ering in an era of political dysfunction that would last for the next
quarter of a century.[16]

In the short term, at least, Zavala emerged from the turmoil of
the 1828 election as the country's dominant political figure. Holding
the cabinet post of secretary of the treasury, he also served as chief
adviser to President Guerrero, who proved to be a guileless politician, though popular among the country's working poor. No one in
the National Palace doubted that the canny Zavala held the reins of
power in the new regime. And behind Zavala stood another figure of
outsized influence: the US minister to Mexico, Joel Poinsett.

The Mexican liberal had been a stalwart champion of American
interests in the capital since the birth of the republic, as John Dunn
Hunter learned when Zavala blocked the Cherokees' land grant petition three years earlier. In fairness to Zavala, his close relationship
with the US minister was consistent with a sincere belief that the
two North American republics were natural allies. At the same time,
the federalist leader's political ideology and financial interests were
closely intertwined. For some months Zavala had been lobbying for
an empresario contract of his own in East Texas, probably at the urging of his young friend, José Antonio Mexía, who knew the area well.
The treasury secretary pledged to settle five hundred families on a
choice swath of real estate that included a twenty-six-mile stretch
of the Sabine River. The application was not without controversy.

7. Lorenzo de Zavala (1788–1836). With his protégé, José Antonio Mexía, the Yucatán intellectual and statesman speculated in Texas lands and worked tirelessly to promote Anglo-American immigration on Mexico's northern frontier. Courtesy of Dolph Briscoe Center for American History, University of Texas at Austin.

Running along the Texas-Louisiana border, the grant was part of the same territory Poinsett had been badgering the Mexican government, so far unsuccessfully, to sell to the United States. It was widely believed in the National Palace that Zavala had no interest in establishing a colony at all, but saw the contract as an opportunity to make a quick profit in the event that East Texas came under American control. The contract was eventually granted, though the suspicious Minister of the Interior did manage to insert a provision that explicitly barred Anglo-Americans from settling in the colony. Undeterred, Zavala promptly began seeking American investors for the project, who were likewise willing to gamble that any lands acquired on the cheap from Mexico would skyrocket in value should the area be ceded to the United States.[17]

Mexía was engaged in the scramble to acquire Texas lands on his own account. Following a brief but lucrative stint as a customs house officer, a patronage post secured through the influence of powerful friends, he seized on a provision in the state colonization law that offered eleven league grants at nominal prices to Mexican citizens. Although the law limited individual buyers to one grant, Mexía snatched up five of them. Acting on his behalf, friends of

Mexía purchased the land, then transferred the deeds to his children.
By the end of the decade he had acquired title to almost a quarter of
a million acres along the Trinity and Navasota rivers, making him,
at least on paper, one of the largest landowners in Texas.[18]

While men like Zavala and Mexía were intent on downplaying Terán's concerns about American immigration, the government
faced more immediate crises that rendered a quick response to its
Texas problem impossible. Emboldened by Mexico's political turmoil, Spain dispatched an expeditionary force in July to seize the
Atlantic port town of Tampico in a bid to reconquer its former colony. Santa Anna, accompanied by Mexía serving as his aide-de-camp,
rushed to take charge of the siege, where he was soon joined by
Terán. Yellow fever took its toll on the Spanish expeditionary force,
which surrendered six weeks later. Santa Anna got the lion's share of
the glory, catapulting to national prominence as the "Hero of Tampico." Much like Andrew Jackson after the Battle of New Orleans,
the general enjoyed an unrivalled popularity that took on the character of a personality cult. Santa Anna still called himself a federalist, but Zavala would increasingly find him to be an unreliable ally.
With a power base of his own, the *caudillo* stood ready to exploit the
country's political turmoil for his own ends.

AS MEXICO RICOCHETED FROM CRISIS TO CRISIS, AMERICAN
migration into Texas continued unabated. Some settlers came legally,
receiving parcels of land from empresarios, though in East Texas,
where few colonists had been recruited since the expulsion of Haden Edwards, Americans simply carved out clearings in the woods
and called them their own. The army stationed a small garrison in
Nacogdoches after the Fredonian Rebellion, but it was wholly inadequate to police the area, much less defend it. Left to its own de-
vices, the town saw the trickle of Anglo-American settlers swell into
a steady stream, its economy bound ever more tightly to that of the
United States. With a population approaching one thousand by 1830,
Nacogdoches became a boom town, a great woodland emporium for

Mexicans, Indians, and Anglo-Americans who drove horses and cattle and carted wagonloads of skins, furs, and agricultural produce along the Camino Real into Louisiana.[19]

As Terán had feared, East Texas continued to attract an undesirable element. Dubbed an "Elysium of rogues" by one American traveler, the area enjoyed a dubious reputation as a refuge for immigrants with checkered pasts. Once the dust settled over the Fredonian affair, Haden Edwards returned to make his home in East Texas, as did a number of his followers. The slave catcher William English speculated in lands and made a fortune. By the 1830s, the town's prominent civic leaders included Robert Potter, a former North Carolina congressman who had castrated two men he accused of sleeping with his wife, and Richard Robinson, a New York City shop clerk who changed his name to Parmalee after being acquitted of the axe murder of a prostitute, Helen Jewett, in one of the most sensational murder trials of the Jacksonian era.[20]

The unsavory character of some of its Anglo-American residents notwithstanding, a resurgent Nacogdoches managed to retain its distinctly creole charm. The multiethnic coalition that had thwarted the Fredonians remained intact during these years and continued to shape the life of the town. The Catholic Church played an especially important role in promoting racial diversity, with Anglos, Hispanos, and African Americans all receiving the formal sanction of the local priest for mixed-race unions. The blacksmith William Goyens lived openly with Mary Sibley, the widow of a white man, and her eleven-year-old son before exchanging marriage vows in the Catholic Church in 1832. Virginia native David Towns arrived in Nacogdoches in 1826 with seven slaves—his partner Sophie and their six children. He promptly freed them all, marrying Sophie a short time later. Their two teenage daughters were much in demand at the fandangos in the Mexican quarter, with one refusing a marriage proposal from a white suitor on account of his being "not strictly temperate."[21]

The absence of formal racial barriers also helped to fuel Nacogdoches' dynamic frontier economy. Moving easily among the

Hispano, Anglo, and Indian communities, William Goyens soon became one of the town's most prosperous businessmen, and surely its
most diversified. His blacksmithing business allowed him to branch
out into lucrative sidelines as a gunsmith and cartwright. The garrison provided Goyens with a steady income shoeing horses and
repairing weapons and wagons. Meanwhile, as the town grew, his
freight-hauling business along the Nacogdoches-Natchitoches corridor thrived. With the profits from these activities he built a house
in town, which he and Mary operated as a boarding house. In the
early 1830s, he purchased a nearby tract of land, afterward known
to the locals as Goyens Hill, overseeing his far-flung enterprises
from a large, two-story home. Taking advantage of the area's natural
springs, he would eventually operate a sawmill on the property to
serve the area's growing need for lumber, and a gristmill to grind
flour and corn meal.[22]

The multiracial character of the Piney Woods tended to offset the impact of Anglo-American immigration. Though Terán still
fretted that a lawless element—"vicious and wild men of evil ways,"
he called them—would subvert Mexican rule, East Texas was a long
way from becoming an extension of the United States. But in the
Brazos River valley, Stephen F. Austin's colony did not have to contend with a well-established, nonwhite population loyal to Mexico.
There, American settlers were busily creating a world that closely
mirrored the one they left behind, a more rigid, color-coded world
of masters and slaves. Under Austin's steady leadership, the colony
had thus far been peaceful and prosperous. Yet its very success made
José Maria Sanchez, a scientific illustrator who accompanied Terán
on his tour of Texas, wonder if Mexican authorities had not been
"lulled . . . into a sense of security." Sharing Terán's concern that the
province might one day be lost to the Americans, he believed that
the country had more to fear from the industrious cotton farmers of
the Brazos than the indigent squatters of East Texas. "The spark that
will start the conflagration," he confided to his diary, "will start from
this colony."[23]

FIVE

TEXAS MUST BE A SLAVE COUNTRY

J ARED GROCE WAS HARDLY TYPICAL OF THE HARDSCRABBLE cotton farmers drawn to Austin's colony during these early years. Born in Virginia, he had already amassed a fortune investing in timberlands, cotton, and enslaved people during a career spanning two decades on the edges of the American South. Some of that time seems to have been spent skirting the edges of the law as well. In 1817, he helped finance the illegal importation of Cuban slaves into Spanish Florida. Upon learning that the Austins had obtained an empresario contract in Texas, he dissolved his business partnership and hastily made plans to relocate, leaving his associates holding $10,000 in promissory notes which he never repaid.[1]

Ordinarily, allegations of financial impropriety might have concerned Stephen F. Austin, who vetted prospective colonists with fastidious care. But when Groce arrived in 1822 with almost a hundred enslaved people and fifty wagons laden with supplies, he was happy to make an exception. Desperate to attract men of substance to his new colony, the empresario promptly awarded him a grant of forty-five thousand acres of prime cotton-growing land along the Brazos River. Groce's plantation, Bernardo, would quickly become a self-sufficient community, producing its own food, with a kitchen and nursery for field hands, a full-time doctor, even a "Bachelor's Hall" that provided lodging for travelers.[2]

Bernardo flourished under the strict supervision of its owner. A shrewd if somewhat irascible businessman, Groce quarreled with just

about everyone—his neighbors, Mexican officials, land surveyors—
and always about money. For all his wealth, he had little interest in
mimicking the aristocratic pretensions of the Old South's seaboard
gentry. A widower, he lived simply, in a two-story home of square-
hewn cottonwood logs. Like many frontier oligarchs, Groce was
too intent on growing his fortune to aspire to a life of gentlemanly
ease. "To make money was their chief object," one Texas pioneer remarked of such men, "all things else were subsidiary to it." To that
end, productivity, not appearances, guided the day-to-day activities
at Bernardo. Slaves felled trees at the plantation by a process known
as girdling, cutting rings around the trunks, then leaving them to rot
and die. The technique transformed large swaths of timberland into
vistas of bleak desolation. And while a night or two at Bachelor's Hall
offered a welcome respite on a long journey, visitors were surprised
when the tight-fisted Groce presented them with a bill at the end of
their stay.[3]

It might come as something of a surprise, therefore, to find that
Groce's approach to slave management was not entirely transac-
tional. To be sure, the master of Bernardo calculated the annual cost
of clothing and feeding the families on his plantation down to the
penny. Yet even Mier y Terán, who abhorred slavery, was obliged to
concede during a brief stopover at Bernardo that they appeared to
be well-provided for. "On this evening," Terán noted in his diary
during his 1828 inspection tour, "the black men and women gathered at the master's house and held a dance, which I am told is customary every Saturday night." A slave list that has survived suggests
that Groce understood the correlation between strong kinship ties
and productivity. Most of those living in the quarters belonged to
two-parent families, though such unions were no doubt arranged by
Groce himself. Only one single adult male resided on the plantation
in 1831.[4]

Ironically, the unsettled conditions of the frontier may have
helped to mitigate the worst abuses of chattel slavery. The ever-
present danger from the Karankawas demanded some degree of cooperation between master and slave, redefining, at least up to a point,

the power relations of the plantation. Bernardo's male field hands did much more than pick cotton and engage in other forms of manual labor; they assumed a civil defense role as well. When Stephen F. Austin sought to drive the tribe from the Gulf Coast in 1824, Groce armed and mounted a company of thirty enslaved men. They rendered an even more valuable service when it came time to bring his crop to market. During the plantation's early years, Groce sold his cotton to a merchant in Matamoros at the mouth of the Rio Grande. He transported the bales overland by mule train, making the dangerous three-hundred-mile journey with a team of armed men to guard against the Comanche raiding parties that roamed the South Texas chaparral. Groce and his crew returned several weeks later, apparently without incident, the mules laden with bags of silver coins.[5]

While Groce was eminently suited to life in an unsettled country, with its many privations, it was not one he wanted for his daughter, Sarah. The crusty cotton baron doted on the girl, who had spent five years at boarding schools in Tennessee and New York City. In 1827, having finished her education, the seventeen-year-old rejoined her father and two brothers at Bernardo.

Eligible suitors for the young woman were few. According to Austin family lore, the empresario, still unmarried at thirty-four, briefly courted the young Sarah. If true, she seems to have shown little interest in the "small spare little old batchelor," who fretted constantly over his empresarial duties. Having been awarded a second colony from the Saltillo government in 1825, and a third the year Sarah arrived, he seemed unable to talk of anything else.[6]

Fortunately for Sarah, there appeared at Bernardo another visitor that summer. William H. Wharton, a twenty-five-year-old Nashville lawyer, had come to Texas in search of new opportunities, looking to speculate in land. His parents having died when he was a child, William and his younger brother John were raised by an uncle, Jesse Wharton, a former congressman and confidant of Andrew Jackson. Ambitious and well-connected, William moved in the same social circles as Sam Houston, a Jackson protégé who would soon be elected governor of Tennessee. Endowed with a keen intellect and a healthy self-confidence, he could seem haughty to those around him. At the same time, the cultured young lawyer exhibited a refined and worldly manner, a quality in short supply among the coarse, unlettered farmers of the Brazos River valley. As one settler dryly remarked, Wharton was "fond of poetry and such things." Sarah seems to have been instantly attracted to him.[7]

After a short courtship, the couple married at Bernardo in December 1827. The reason for the brief engagement would soon become evident. Sarah would give birth to a son seven months later.

The newlyweds planned to return to Nashville after the wedding, though Groce made every effort to induce them to stay. Offering the couple two leagues of land—almost ten thousand acres—he vowed to turn the property into a plantation that would rival any in the American South. No doubt the proposal tempted Wharton. But since his arrival in Texas he had cooled on the idea of a new life as a citizen of Mexico. Like many prospective immigrants from the South, he had come to realize that the future of slavery in the Latin American republic was anything but clear.[8]

The system of bonded labor that white Southerners were beginning to refer to as the "peculiar institution" had long been in a state of decline in Mexico. Perhaps as many as two hundred thousand Africans were transported to the region during the colonial period, many to work in silver mines and sugar cane fields, but over time most had been absorbed into the general population. When the Mexican republic was established in 1824, the issue was of such little concern that the constitution did not bother to address it. National leaders saw the institution as a uniquely American problem—the white republic's recessive gene. The liberal Lorenzo de Zavala, despite his great admiration for the United States, acknowledged the jarring contradiction of a nation that granted unfettered freedoms to some of its people while enslaving others. During a visit to Baltimore, conservative leader José María Tornel felt a twinge of pride upon finding that the Catholic Church was the only place in the city where whites and people of color could stand alongside each other as equals. "Not even in the theater can whites mix with blacks and mulattos," he observed, "but God, in his Catholic temples, calls to the same table a mother of duchesses and a slave."[9]

The immigration of Southern whites into Texas forced Mexican leaders to confront the slavery issue, drawing them into the same moral debate that was quickly becoming an existential part of American civic discourse. In the absence of any specific prohibitions against the institution, slaveholders like Jared Groce had given little thought to the future of slavery in Texas when they arrived in the early 1820s. By the middle of the decade, however, it became clear that strong antislavery sentiment existed among leaders in the state capital, as they began work on a constitution for Coahuila y Texas. With much of the state's economy devoted to ranching, many delegates were unsympathetic to the slaveholding cotton farmers who migrated to the fertile river valleys of central Texas.[10]

The Constituent Congress in Saltillo took its time drafting the document—two years—and no one followed its deliberations more closely than Stephen F. Austin. Consumed by his land business, the empresario was not a planter, owning only a few people himself, though he sometimes hired out those of his neighbors for various tasks. In 1829, he owned one—"an old decreped woman, not worth much." Occasionally he exhibited pangs of conscience over the morality of slavery, but they never lasted very long. For Austin, plantation agriculture was the key to the success of his colonization enterprise. "Texas," he would later declare, "must be a slave country." He was therefore not a little alarmed by reports that state legislators might abolish slavery, or limit ownership to those settlers who had already arrived. As the debates over the issue dragged on, Austin estimated that half the families in his colony would return to the United States if emancipation became law.[11]

Uncertain as the situation seemed for the future of slavery in Texas, Austin could always count on influential Mexican friends to work on his behalf. Although most prominent Hispano-Texans were ranchers with no stake in plantation agriculture, they generally welcomed the newcomers from the United States. As more immigrants arrived, land values rose, as did the prices for horses, mules, and livestock. Anglos also came armed and ready to defend themselves against the prairie tribes, the Comanches and Wichitas. Austin thus had little difficulty getting well-to-do Mexican Texans to echo the pleas of white Southerners to leave the institution undisturbed. In the summer of 1826, the San Antonio *ayuntamiento* (town council) drafted a memorial to the state legislature insisting that slavery was indispensable to the economic development of the region.[12]

Despite these lobbying efforts, the antislavery delegates in Saltillo stood firm, drafting a constitution that sharply curtailed the American labor system. Ratified in the spring of 1827, the document decreed that no child could be born into slavery, and it barred the importation of any more enslaved people into Texas after a six-month grace period. Austin's worst fears had come to pass. Seeing no future for bonded labor in Texas, he now began to consider recruiting colonists from non-slaveholding states.

Saltillo's vigorous moral objections proved to be short-lived, as the legislators became aware of the economic costs involved. Under continued pressure from Austin and Texas Hispanos, the state government relented a few months later, passing a law that kept American slavery in Texas more or less intact. Slaveholders could simply draw up labor contracts before leaving the United States, reclassifying their bonded laborers as "lifetime" indentured servants. Although intended as a stopgap measure, the policy effectively voided the constitutional restrictions on slavery. Said one Anglo-Texan, "They have indeed abolished the name but not the Thing."[13]

With the issue apparently settled and the future of bonded labor in his colony secure, Austin redoubled his efforts to recruit cotton farmers from the American South. The prospects of Texas had never been brighter, he assured family members and friends, urging them to relocate. Always keen to attract a "better class" of settler to his colony, the empresario imagined the Brazos River valley settled by "southern gentlemen," not the poor squatters who eked out a living in the forests of East Texas.

Men, in other words, like William Wharton. "There is nothing but plain sailing ahead," the normally dour empresario gushed

8. William H. Wharton (1802–1839).
A wealthy planter, Wharton would
become a leader of Anglo-American
resistance to the Mexican government
in the 1830s. Courtesy of Friends
of the Governor's Mansion, Austin,
Texas.

in a letter to the Nashville attorney. Now that all obstacles to the development of plantation agriculture had been removed, Wharton should reconsider his father-in-law's offer and return with his family to Texas. There could no longer be any doubt, the empresario believed, that Texas would soon become "the best, the brightest star in the Mexican constellation." If Wharton had any lingering reservations, the 1828 presidential victory of Andrew Jackson surely put them to rest. Nashville's favorite son was a diehard expansionist and vowed to make the purchase of Texas a top priority of his administration. Finally, Wharton was sold on the idea of a move to the Brazos River valley.[14]

The Whartons would not be the only prominent Nashville residents who looked to the West for a fresh start in 1829. That spring, the town was rocked by scandal when Governor Houston's wife, Eliza Allen, a woman fourteen years his junior, left him without explanation after less than three months of marriage. The abrupt separation became fodder for Houston's political enemies, while his refusal to issue any kind of public statement on the matter only intensified speculation about the cause of the breakup. Amid unsavory but unsubstantiated rumors of adultery and spousal abuse, Houston resigned. Neither he nor Eliza spoke of the matter ever again, lending an aura of mystery to the scandal. Yet the cause of the breakup seems clear enough. It was a time of changing expectations of marriage, a sentimental, romantic age in which young women no longer saw matrimony exclusively in terms of status or economic advantage. Smitten though he may have been by Eliza, Houston's affections were not reciprocated. No doubt her family was thrilled by their daughter's marriage to the governor who, as a protégé of Andrew Jackson, had a bright future in American politics. But Eliza had other suitors, and she was reportedly in love with one of them, a man closer to her own age.[15]

His marriage over and his political career in ruins, a distraught Houston drank himself into a stupor. He raved to anyone who would listen about his future plans, which included a "grand scheme" to separate Texas from Mexico. Having lived with a band of Cherokees in his youth, he decided to move to US Indian Territory in Arkansas, and talked of placing himself at the head of an army of Cherokee warriors and marching into Texas. To Wharton he mused about the possibility of inciting a rebellion among Austin's colonists. The substance of these conversations soon reached President Jackson, who was alarmed enough to write to Houston, insisting that he abandon such an enterprise. The last thing Jackson wanted was another Fredonian debacle on his hands that would upset his diplomacy with Mexico.[16]

Houston's filibuster fantasies may have been little more than idle talk, but they revealed much about the way Anglo-Americans saw the land beyond their borders. The United States had experienced such rapid territorial growth since the turn of the century that its citizens had become accustomed to the shape-shifting impermanence of the nation's boundaries. Texas seemed an especially likely candidate for acquisition, and not just because the American population already eclipsed the number of Hispanos in the province. Many Southerners subscribed to the fanciful belief that Mexico did not have a legal claim to the region anyway, contending that Texas had been part of the 1803 Louisiana Purchase. Even Stephen F. Austin viewed the province's place within Mexico's orbit in purely conditional terms.

Dutiful Mexican citizen though he was, the empresario deplored the country's political turmoil and would not foreclose the possibility that Texas might one day declare its independence or become part of the United States.[17]

In the fall of 1829 the Whartons were finally ready to depart for Texas. With a crew of enslaved house servants they embarked on a steamboat at the Nashville wharf, traveling up the Cumberland River, then down the Mississippi to New Orleans. The Whartons lingered in the Crescent City for several days, purchasing household furniture, a piano, and other furnishings for their new home. For the last leg of their journey, a week-long voyage to the Texas Gulf Coast, they would book passage on one of the schooners that regularly carried supplies to Austin's colony, returning to New Orleans with cotton picked, ginned, and baled by Brazos River slaves.

As it turned out, Austin's promise to Wharton that there was nothing but "plain sailing ahead" proved to be somewhat premature. In September, José María Tornel, governor of Mexico's federal district, devised an ingeniously simple plan to prevent Texas from becoming a beachhead of an expanding plantation economy. It had become a tradition for the government to commemorate the anniversary of the nation's independence with a public act of charity. Having tried unsuccessfully to pass an emancipation bill in congress, Tornel suggested that President Guerrero use his executive authority to issue a decree to that effect. Guerrero, an African-Indian himself, happily agreed, whereupon Tornel drew up a brief document freeing all enslaved people in the Mexican republic forthwith, adding the vague proviso that slave owners would be compensated for the loss of their property "when circumstances may permit."[18]

For the overwhelming majority of Mexicans, who had no stake in slavery, the decree was seen as a magnanimous if largely empty gesture. But in Texas the decision touched off a minor panic, as Tornel must have known it would. The outcry would have been far worse, but quick-thinking officials decided to withhold the edict from publication and await further guidance. "In the name of God what shall we do?" wrote one agitated settler to Austin when he heard the news.

Fearing the decree would plunge the Anglo settlements into chaos, he wailed, "We are ruined forever."[19]

Austin by now had become accustomed to these shocks to the system. Counseling caution, he contacted the new political chief in San Antonio, Ramón Músquiz, a close friend, who did not need the empresario to tell him of the devastating economic impact which the decree would cause. Once again, Mexican officials on the northern frontier served as the witting instrument of American slaveholders. Defusing what could have been a potentially explosive situation, Músquiz drafted a lengthy memorial to the governor, asserting the Anglo-Americans' right to property, and warning of serious civil unrest should the new policy go into effect. The governor seconded Músquiz, endorsing the view that Texas slave owners should be exempted from the ruling. President Guerrero relented, rendering the emancipation decree virtually meaningless.[20]

The furor in Texas over Tornel's antislavery gambit had not yet died down when the schooner carrying the Whartons successfully navigated the sandbar at the mouth of the Brazos River and deposited its passengers and cargo at Velasco. The entry point for many Texas immigrants, Velasco was a desolate strip of beach, uninhabited save for the flocks of herons and egrets, and thick clouds of mosquitos that ranged over the treeless, coastal wetlands of the Brazos River delta. Here and for several miles inland, the river overflowed low sandy banks, carving a labyrinth of streams and creeks on its lazy path into the sea.

The Whartons would make their home on the edge of this coastal plain, a prairie of rustling grasslands, interspersed with groves of black walnut, hackberry, and mulberry trees. Jared Groce had already picked a site for the main house, several acres of land on an oxbow on Oyster Creek—the couple would name it Eagle Island—about ten miles from the Gulf. Work on the site was well underway when they arrived, with Groce supervising a crew of slaves who cleared land for planting and built livestock pens. A kiln was already in operation, making bricks for an outdoor kitchen, slave quarters, and walkways throughout the property.

True to his word, Groce spared no expense to ensure that his daughter would live in a manner comparable in every way to the planter elite in the American South. At a time when even a well-to-do Texas cotton farmer lived in a two-room log dogtrot chinked with mud, with one room for family members and the other for the enslaved, the newlyweds would move into a colonnaded, two-story Greek Revival style home, a replica of a house Groce had seen in Alabama. The lumber for the main house he purchased precut from a sawmill in Mobile, every plank sawed and numbered. The doors, window facings, and stairway were carved from mahogany ordered from Cuba.[21]

Unlike his crusty father-in-law, William Wharton cultivated the image of the planter aristocrat. He would make additional improvements to the property in the years that followed, and visitors to Eagle Island would soon find a main house surrounded by fruit orchards and landscaped grounds, the work of a full-time Scottish gardener. Fond of entertaining, the Whartons frequently opened their home to the planter families along the river. Sarah was an accomplished pianist; her husband, an avid collector, amassed the finest library in Texas, as well as shells, fossils, and other curiosities, which he delighted in showing his guests. Wrote one visitor, "Mr. Wharton lives as gentlemen do in other countries, with the associations of literature & taste."[22]

By the early 1830s, a string of large plantations sprouted along the waterways of the Brazos River valley, though none would rival Eagle Island as a showplace of manorial elegance. From San Felipe down to the Gulf, a rough facsimile of the cotton-producing regions of the Old South began to emerge. Stephen F. Austin's dream of a prosperous colony of "southern gentlemen" was well on its way to being realized.

SIX

THE MOST AVID NATION
IN THE WORLD

A S 1829 DREW TO A CLOSE, GENERAL MIER Y TERÁN'S anxiety about the future of Texas was giving way to a full-blown sense of alarm. Stationed in Matamoros as commandant general of the Eastern Interior Provinces (a post that gave him political and military authority over three northeastern states—Coahuila y Texas, Tamaulipas, and Nuevo León), he had spent much of the year waging a one-man crusade to alert national leaders to the dangers of unrestricted Anglo-American immigration. But the problem was growing progressively worse. As the numbers of illegal immigrants rose, so too did their complete disregard for Mexican laws. Terán could hardly believe the effrontery of the newcomers, who "do as they please, and settle where they please." Even more galling, they talked as if US acquisition of the area was a foregone conclusion. Only a dramatic increase in the number of Mexican troops to close the border and police the area, he believed, could prevent Texas from falling into the hands of the United States, the "most avid nation in the world."[1]

But the winds of political change in Mexico were about to shift again, this time in Terán's favor. After only eight months in office, President Guerrero had become a pitiable figure, viewed largely as an instrument of Zavala and US minister Joel Poinsett. Conservatives and men of property, the so-called *hombres de bien*, chafed at a series of sweeping economic reforms implemented by Zavala in his capacity as secretary of the treasury. But the cabinet member's cozy relationship with the US minister had drawn the ire of Mexican leaders of both factions. Loathed as a kind of Svengali who seemed to exert a strange hold over Zavala, Poinsett had interfered so regularly in domestic politics that even many federalists acknowledged that it was time for him to go.

In a belated show of independence, Guerrero insisted that Washington recall its troublesome diplomat. The president soon parted ways with Zavala, too. Pressured to resign from the cabinet, Zavala accused his former ally, Santa Anna, of conspiring against him. The general denied it, but he had begun to tire of Zavala's pro-American maneuvering. Guerrero's actions failed to quiet the conservatives, and in December 1829, Vice President Anastasio Bustamante staged a palace coup, driving the chief executive from office. In a sign of the new regime's rightward shift, the aristocratic Lucas Alamán became Bustamante's most trusted adviser, the role formerly occupied by Zavala in the Guerrero cabinet.[2]

Alamán lost no time acting on Terán's recommendations. In the spring of 1830, the Mexican Congress passed a sweeping law designed to put a stop to American penetration into Texas once and for all. The most controversial provision of the Law of April 6, 1830, Article XI, not only prohibited further immigration from the United States, but ordered, rather vaguely, that all empresario contracts "not already completed" be immediately suspended. In a move designed to further discourage Anglo-American immigrants, the law barred the introduction of enslaved people into the province. In addition, the law sought to raise revenues by imposing new taxes on cotton exports, funds that would be earmarked for a new resettlement program of Mexican nationals, and to establish a more robust military presence in the area. And since no one knew conditions in Texas better than Terán himself, the government appointed the Mexican general to serve as the region's new commissioner of colonization.[3]

In barring American immigration altogether, the law actually went further than Terán's own recommendations. He knew that

Anglo-Americans drew no distinction between their economic ambitions and their "rights and liberties," and he did not think they would take the news well. He quickly reassured Stephen F. Austin that his was one of two American colonies that had already been established and would be allowed to remain. For his part, the empresario quieted settlers' concerns by downplaying the law's severity; he even went so far as to delete the article prohibiting further immigration from the United States when an English translation of the act was published in a Texas newspaper.[4]

The validity of Zavala's contract was another matter. In the year since the awarding of the grant, Zavala had made no effort to colonize his East Texas lands, failing to recruit a single colonist. This was reason enough to raise Terán's suspicions that Zavala was only holding on to the land until it could be acquired by the United States. Zavala would deny it, but he had already brought into his colonization project as business partners the two men who were working to bring about that very result: his friend Joel Poinsett, and the outgoing minister's successor, Anthony Butler. When Terán wrote to the minister of war, "He who consents to and does not oppose the loss of Texas is an execrable traitor," he did not need to mention Zavala by name.[5]

Zavala seemed entirely oblivious to Terán's opposition to his land scheme. Adopting a broad interpretation of the new law, he somehow convinced himself that it did not apply to his own grant, which had been awarded before the law was passed. In any case, in the spring of 1830 Zavala had bigger problems: surviving the collapse of the Guerrero regime. Refusing to go quietly into exile after Bustamante's coup, Guerrero raised a people's army of Indians and mixed-race Mexicans in the south; he would be captured and executed several months later. Zavala, too, felt the wrath of the new regime. Swept up in a purge of leading federalists, he was arrested on charges of corruption. The charges were eventually dropped, but his abrupt fall from grace left him financially ruined. Strongly advised to leave the country by the few friends in the government he had left, Zavala packed his sole remaining asset, his East Texas empresario contract, safely away in a steamer trunk and sailed into exile. He was bound for the United States, a country he had long admired from afar.

ZAVALA LIKED THE AMERICAN REPUBLIC EVEN BETTER UP CLOSE. Traveling part of the way with José Antonio Mexía (who had not only survived the purge of prominent federalists but received a plum diplomatic assignment in Washington) and part of the way with Poinsett, Zavala wrote a memoir of his journey, which he would later publish, joining the ranks of the many foreign visitors who wrote accounts of the American republic in the first half of the nineteenth century.

Unlike most European travelers, he found little to criticize. Aside from the institution of slavery, which he deplored, Zavala saw in the United States what he wanted to see: a liberal democratic utopia. With letters of introduction from the well-connected Poinsett, he met with several prominent political leaders, including Martin Van Buren, John Quincy Adams, and, on two separate occasions, Andrew Jackson. A great admirer of the president, whom he regarded as a true man of the people, Zavala first encountered Old Hickory during a visit with Mexía to Cincinnati. He marveled at the outpouring of genuine, spontaneous enthusiasm that greeted the republic's head of state, who was received without pomp or circumstance. And he was equally impressed by the delegation of civic leaders that welcomed the president to the city. Composed mostly of artisans and tradesmen, Zavala described it as "the simplest court in the world."[6]

A greater appreciation for one's native land is often a happy consequence of foreign travel. In Zavala's case, the experience only seemed to fill him with shame. At times the memoir is an unabashed love letter to Americans, while his fellow citizens invariably fare poorly by comparison. Indulging in the kind of broad ethnic stereotypes that Americans would soon use to describe the people of his country, he could assert: "The Mexican is easy going, lazy, . . . superstitious, ignorant and an enemy of all restraint." Unlike the

Americans, who are "wise, economical, and fond of accumulating capital for the future," in Mexico "the few who have anything are careless with it and fritter it away."[7]

Zavala found American women beautiful, too. Although not as "voluptuous" as the women of his homeland, they "have very good color, large bright eyes, [and] well-shaped hands and feet," he noted approvingly. Perhaps these were the qualities that drew Zavala to Miranda West, a striking, raven-haired woman twenty years his junior, whom he met during a brief stopover in Albany. Raised in a nearby farming community, Miranda worked as a domestic servant at Crosby's Hotel, a popular watering hole for the Democratic Party. Unwed, and with an infant son, she also seems to have supplemented her income, to use the parlance of the day, as a "girl of the town," an occupation not uncommon to women of her class.[8]

Zavala had courted scandal before. Estranged from his wife for many years, he had been the subject of gossip as a result of his relationships with other women. Now, far from home, he evidently believed there was little likelihood that his private life would set tongues wagging back in Mexico. He seems to have corresponded with Miranda after leaving Albany, although no letters between the couple have survived, and a few months later he would return to the town on his way to New England.[9]

From a financial standpoint, the highlight of the trip was Zavala's visit to New York City, where he sold a controlling interest in his empresario project to a group of investors. The directors of the newly formed Galveston Bay and Texas Land Company, who had already purchased two adjoining East Texas grants, reportedly paid Zavala $100,000 in cash and stock. Not one to forget his friends, Zavala doled out shares in the company to Mexía, who would lobby on its behalf in Mexico, as well as Poinsett and Butler, who would continue to press for the US acquisition of East Texas in Washington and Mexico City.

Suddenly flush with cash, Zavala treated himself to a trip across the Atlantic, embarking upon an extended, leisurely sojourn of the capitals of Europe. While there he received important personal

9. Emily West de Zavala (1809–1882). Born in rural upstate New York, Emily West was a domestic servant in Albany before she married Lorenzo de Zavala in 1831. Courtesy of Dolph Briscoe Center for American History, University of Texas at Austin.

news. He learned that Miranda was pregnant again, and still unmarried. At about the same time, word reached him that his wife had died in the Yucatán. Now free to "live honorably" with the young woman from Albany, he wrote to Miranda with a proposal of marriage. Facing life as a single mother with two illegitimate children and few prospects, all of them unappealing, she replied immediately, accepting the offer.

When Zavala returned to New York City after almost a year abroad, Miranda, seven months pregnant, was waiting for him at the harbor. The next day the couple exchanged marriage vows in a quiet ceremony at a Catholic church in the Five Points. The Mexican leader may have had no qualms about the union, but he clearly recognized that any future he hoped to have in Mexican politics would be seriously jeopardized if Miranda's past became public knowledge. In an apparent attempt to obscure the truth, he changed her name to Emilia on the marriage license.[10]

They were an unlikely couple. He was one of his country's most prominent political figures and leading intellectuals; she had little formal education, and her reading habits did not extend beyond a fondness for romance novels. Nonetheless, Zavala seems to have eased comfortably into his new domestic life. The couple took lodgings in Greenwich Village, where Emily, as she would hereafter be known, gave birth to a son at the start of the new year. Zavala adopted her first child a few months later. A teenage son from his first marriage, Lorenzo Jr., having recently graduated from a school in New England, soon joined the growing family. Zavala spent much of his time over the next several months on various writing projects, completing the second volume of *Ensayo Histórico*, a history of postcolonial Mexico. "I think I will be happy in this marriage," he confided to his journal, then added, cryptically, "as much as a mortal can be in my circumstances."[11]

Did the Mexican leader miss his homeland after two years in exile? Perhaps, but it is much more likely that he missed the one thing he could not live without—politics and the proximity to power. Zavala's time abroad had weakened his attachments to his native land, even as a fierce nationalism was beginning to emerge among his contemporaries. A key ingredient of this sense of nationhood (*Mexicanidad*) was a deep anxiety toward the United States, which was becoming increasingly aggressive in its efforts to expand westward at Mexico's expense. Such anti-American sentiments were completely foreign to Zavala, now a resident of New York City with an American wife and adopted American children, living on the income from his business dealings with American land speculators. He still considered himself a Mexican patriot, and so he was—at least up to a point. But he was too complex a man to indulge in an unconditional love of country. Quick to see its faults and imperfections, which he blamed in large measure on the legacies of Spanish rule, he saw little reason to fret about maintaining the boundaries Mexico had inherited from its colonial parent, especially when his own economic interests were involved.

Zavala's cavalier attitude toward preserving the integrity of the national domain filled Terán with disgust. While the intellectual-in-exile saw Mexico more as an idea than a place, Terán's determination to prevent the United States from acquiring Texas had become nothing short of an obsession. Alarmed by the news that Zavala had sold his empresario contract to the Galveston Bay and Texas Land

Company, he began monitoring the activities of the group closely. At first, Terán seems to have been willing to let the project go forward, so long as it recruited colonists from Europe. Aware of the colonization commissioner's concerns, the company issued land titles to a few dozen settlers, who arrived in Galveston in 1831. They were not Americans, the directors insisted, but recently arrived European immigrants recruited in New York City. Terán was skeptical and ordered the colonists removed. Evidently concluding that the company could not be trusted to comply with the restrictions of the Law of April 6, 1830, he then ruled that it must cease operations altogether on the grounds that the consortium had never been authorized by the Mexican government.

Stunned and angry, Zavala regarded Terán's decision as a personal insult. He quickly wrote to his American business partners to assure them that all was not lost. Since his initial grant had been awarded before April 6, 1830, the government would surely overrule the order, he told them; Mexía, who had returned to Mexico and was lobbying furiously in the nation's capital for an exemption for the company, was confident that it would do just that. If not, there was always hope that a new regime would take a different view of the matter—hardly an unreasonable expectation given Mexico's volatile political climate.[12]

WHATEVER SATISFACTION TERÁN TOOK FROM THWARTING ZAVala and his American investors, he knew he had won a pyrrhic victory. With Mexico wholly lacking the resources to adequately police the border, his campaign to stanch the flow of Americans was proving to be an impossible task. Still, he did the best he could under the circumstances, ordering six new forts to be built above the Rio Grande, and reinforcing the garrisons at San Antonio, Nacogdoches, and Goliad. Stationed at likely points of entry and commonly used river crossings, the garrisons amounted to only a few hundred troops, poorly equipped and irregularly paid. They did little to deter squatters and smugglers who, once they learned of the new troop locations, were usually able to avoid detection without too much difficulty.[13]

A bigger problem for Anglo immigrants was the Wichitas, who had clashed with Austin's colonists since the earliest days of American settlement. The Wacos and the Tawakonis, two subgroups of the tribe, lived in large villages high on the Upper Brazos, about 150 miles north of San Felipe. For young Wichita men, like the Comanches, raiding was an essential ritual of manhood. They ventured deep into wooded river valleys to steal horses and mules, often killing those who tried to stop them. Equal opportunity offenders, the Wichitas did not discriminate, raiding the farms and ranches of Anglos, immigrant Indians, and Mexicans alike.

Even when such encounters did not result in violence, they could spell ruin for the Anglo-American farmer. When horses and mules were stolen, transportation came to a halt. Fields could not be plowed; crops could not be carted to market. Occasionally the colonists mounted expeditions to punish the Wichitas, relying on Tonkawas and Lipan Apaches as scouts, who had their own grievances against the tribe. But for the isolated homesteader who had the misfortune to have his animals stolen by Wichita raiders, the only recourse was to set out after them, usually in the company of a few helpful neighbors. Following the tracks that invariably led north, back to the Indians' villages on the Upper Brazos, they sometimes caught up with the horse thieves. More often than not, they returned home empty-handed.

Although white settlers did not hesitate to use force to defend their property, the Cherokees would have more success in dealing with the Wichita problem, launching major attacks on the tribe in 1829 and again the following year. Horse thefts were also the root cause of their long-standing feud, but the Cherokees' insistence on repaying blood with blood ensured an especially severe and brutal response whenever Bowls's warriors died at the hands of their neighbors to the west. The murder of three members of a hunting party by the Wichitas, who then dragged the scalped, naked corpses back

10. Tahchee (aka William Dutch), Western Cherokee leader (1790–1848). Watercolor by George Catlin in 1846. A war chief of the Western Cherokees in Texas and Oklahoma, Tahchee led the tribe to its greatest victories against the Wichitas in 1829 and 1830. Courtesy of Gilcrease Museum, Tulsa, Oklahoma.

to their village and put them on public display, so enraged the Cherokees that they appealed to tribal leaders above the Red River to help them avenge the insult. Now in his seventies, Bowls did not take part in the expedition. A Cherokee *uku*, or "beloved man," he left military affairs to younger members of the tribe. The duties of war chief had recently passed to a charismatic leader known to the Americans as William Dutch, and to the Cherokees as Tahchee. Described as a man with "black, keen restless eyes" more than thirty years Bowls's junior, Dutch had acquired a legendary reputation as a hunter-warrior in Arkansas before migrating to Texas. In late May 1830, he led more than one hundred Cherokee men on a march in torrential rains into Wichita country. Warriors from other immigrant tribes who held their own grudges against the Wichitas also joined the campaign. Reaching a palisaded Tawakoni village undetected, the Cherokees launched a surprise attack at dawn. During the day-long battle, Dutch's warriors set fire to the Grand Lodge, where many of the Indians had taken refuge. Killing their prisoners, they returned home in triumph with dozens of scalps.[14]

Mexican troops would also play an important part in rooting out the woodland Wichitas. A few months after Dutch's victory, the military commander in San Antonio launched a major campaign against the tribe, destroying their heavily fortified villages on the Brazos River. The Wichitas soon regrouped, erecting makeshift encampments along nearby creeks. The following year the Mexican army fielded an even larger search-and-destroy campaign against the Indians. It took three weeks to find them. Launching a predawn attack on a Tawakoni camp, the army routed the Indians, who scattered, making their way west into the hill country of central Texas. Mexican troops gave chase, leaving the bodies of several warriors hanging from two oak trees near Marble Falls. Unable to withstand these sustained attacks, the Wacos and the Tawakonis retreated to the northern prairies, joining another Wichita group, the Taovayas, just below the US border, near present-day Wichita Falls.[15]

The expulsion of the Wichitas (which proved to be only temporary) brought a measure of peace to the river valleys of central Texas. But peace only brought more American immigrants. As whites continued to extend their hold over the province, Terán unveiled an ambitious scheme to populate the area with Mexican citizens. Appealing to the governors of the northern states to help with the relocation effort, Terán set aside generous parcels of land for fifteen hundred families. The plan also called for convict soldiers to assist with the construction of the forts and other public works projects, who could be integrated into the civilian population when their sentences were completed. The results were nothing short of abysmal. State leaders saw little reason to contribute their own resources for such an undertaking, while impoverished Mexican families lacked the means to move north on their own. The northern governors proved similarly reluctant to send convict labor to Texas, contributing a total of only thirty-five men.[16]

Forced to accept the fact that Mexicans could not be resettled in anything near the numbers needed to counterbalance the growing American population, Terán had only one option left. For the better part of a decade, the Cherokees and their associated bands had petitioned Mexican authorities for legal title to their lands. The time had come, Terán decided, to give it to them. A clear policy on the issue

of Indian land ownership, and the will to implement it, finally began
to emerge. Hoping to encourage the Cherokees to adopt Western
values, Terán favored giving two-hundred-acre parcels to each Indian family. If successful, the plan could be extended to include the
Shawnees, the Delawares, and perhaps some of the other tribes as
well. As commissioner of colonization, Terán coordinated his efforts
with the new governor, José María Letona, ordering him to set aside
land for the Cherokees in East Texas between the Trinity and Angelina rivers.[17]

At long last, the stars seemed to be in alignment for the Cherokees. Richard Fields's dream of a permanent Indian homeland in
Mexico appeared to be within reach.

Inevitably, there would be pushback from Anglo-Americans.
Stephen F. Austin was happy to see the Cherokees make war on the
Wichitas. But he was fiercely opposed to any plan that would reward
them for their military service. To Mexican officials he painted grim
pictures of the misfortunes that would befall the province should the
"savages" be allowed to settle permanently in East Texas. Peter Ellis
Bean, the Indian agent who persuaded Bowls in 1826 to abandon
Richard Fields and the Fredonians, now took the position that the
Cherokees should be relocated to the western prairies. There, he argued, they could better serve as a buffer between the Comanches and
the Anglo settlements. He neglected to mention that their removal
would eliminate a potential stumbling block to his own efforts to
secure a land grant in East Texas.[18]

Local Mexican officials, always ready to protect American interests, also tried to sabotage Terán's plans. Just as he had done on
the slavery issue, political chief Ramón Músquiz dragged his feet,
offering several reasons why the land distribution plan could not
go forward. The Cherokees, he reminded Governor Letona, would
first need to engage an attorney to represent them in the state capital. And then there were the legal fees to process land titles, and
surveying costs to be considered. Who, he wanted to know, would
pay for it all? Letona soon realized that Músquiz was stonewalling
and bypassed the political chief. Writing directly to the garrison

commander at Nacogdoches, Colonel José de las Piedras, he ordered that land titles be issued directly to the Indians.[19]

But once again, there were complications. Terán's plan to turn the tribe into small yeoman farmers was unfamiliar to traditional Western Cherokees like Bowls, who viewed land ownership in communal terms. Piedras, already overburdened with his duties as garrison commander, would now have to assume the role of land commissioner as well. Land would have to be surveyed, and titles issued to each Cherokee family.

All this would take time, and time was something Terán did not have. After a year on the job as commissioner of colonization, he felt weighed down by the burdens of his office. His mood darkened; poor health and overwork had taken a severe toll. Filled with a sense of foreboding, he viewed the loss of Texas as imminent. Illegal immigrants were streaming across the border in open defiance of the government, which for all its good intentions was powerless to stop them. At every turn, he had met with lassitude and indifference from some state and local authorities, outright resistance from others. Worst of all, prominent national figures like Zavala and Mexía were colluding openly with the business interests of a foreign power and using their influence to try to overturn the government's anti-immigration policy for their own financial gain. It was all going horribly wrong, and for Terán the tragedy was compounded by the fact that the fault lay not only with the people of the United States, but with Mexicans themselves.

SEVEN

LONG LIVE SANTA ANNA!

I N 1831 A FEW DOZEN MEXICAN TROOPS SAILED UP THE COAST from Matamoros and waded ashore at Velasco beach. The place was still uninhabited, just as it had been when the Whartons arrived two years earlier. Setting up makeshift shelters, they began collecting driftwood, flotsam from the vessels that had run aground on the sandbar at the mouth of the Brazos River. During the next several months they would build a customs house, and later a circular stockade. Sixty miles up the coast, on a bluff where the alligator-infested waters of the Trinity River flowed into Galveston Bay, the construction of another fort, Anahuac, was already well underway.

By and large, the Anglo-American colonists in the upland regions of the province had welcomed the troops sent by General Terán to police the northern frontier. They were grateful for any help they could get in driving the Wichitas from the area. A very different reception awaited the soldiers sent to the Texas coast, who would not be fighting Indians but collecting customs duties. According to the state's colonization law, American immigrants had been promised tax-exempt status for a period of ten years. The Bustamante government rescinded the exemption, intending to use the revenue to defray the costs of Terán's military buildup.

For American coastal settlers, troops and taxes proved to be a toxic combination. Schooled in the history of their own country's struggle of colonial resistance, they would have probably opposed the new policies under any circumstances. But relations between the colonists and Mexican authorities soured even more quickly than expected, due in large part to a series of unpopular rulings made by the newly appointed Anahuac commander, Colonel Juan Davis Bradburn. A native Kentuckian who had spent several years in the service of Mexico, Bradburn displayed a unique ability to antagonize local residents. Among his more controversial decisions was to require all outgoing vessels to obtain clearance at Anahuac, since a customs collector had not yet been appointed at Velasco. The policy was a major headache for Brazos shippers, obliged to ride overland to Anahuac to complete the necessary paperwork, a delay of about four days. Few bothered to obey the ruling, and instead tried to slip past the small garrison at the mouth of the river. When Mexican troops boarded unauthorized vessels, seizing their cargos, tempers flared.[1]

William Wharton and other cotton planters bristled at the new regulations. Late in 1831, only a few months after the troops had arrived, he and the captain of the *Sabine*, a schooner bound for New Orleans, appeared before the garrison commander. During the course of the meeting, Wharton offered a fifty-dollar bribe to allow the vessel to leave without clearance from the Anahuac customs house. The Mexican officer demanded one hundred. Wharton refused, and after a heated argument, the two Americans returned to the ship. The affair seemed to be over.

A few hours later, a cry went up from the Mexican troops at the mouth of the river. Gliding toward the open water under full sail, cotton bales stacked on its deck for protection, was the *Sabine*. Seeing that the vessel intended to run past the garrison, the crew of another ship moored nearby quickly followed suit. The troops fired frantically on the two vessels as they sailed into the bay, causing only minimal damage. The garrison commander arrested Wharton and the *Sabine*'s captain for the stunt, but soon bowed to the public outcry that followed and released the two men.[2]

The episode set in motion a series of events that would lead to a dramatic escalation of tensions along the Texas coast. Holding a public meeting the following day, Wharton and other Brazoria firebrands were ready to fight, and promptly raised eight hundred dollars to buy powder and lead in New Orleans. They also sent a group of men to Anahuac, where Bradburn had become embroiled in a seemingly endless series of petty disputes with local residents. There they met with William Barret Travis, a twenty-two-year-old Alabama lawyer, who had emerged as the commander's principal tormenter since his arrival in Texas earlier in the year.

Austin tried to tamp down tensions on the Brazos River, without success. When the vessel carrying the powder and lead purchased in New Orleans arrived at Brazoria, he implored the ship's owner to dump the cargo into the river. His request was flatly rejected. Writing to Terán of the affair, Austin condemned the "wild intemperance" of the agitators, but also tried to justify their behavior, noting the hardship of having only one customs house in all of Texas. The Mexican general was not persuaded by the empresario's excuses. Tariffs were collected without incident in every nation in the world, he replied indignantly, but only on the Brazos River did they provoke a rebellion.[3]

IRRITATED THOUGH HE MAY HAVE BEEN WITH THE UNRULY BEhavior of a small group of Anglo colonists, Terán still regarded the events along the Texas coast as a sideshow. The commandant of the Eastern Interior Provinces was about to be overwhelmed by a far more important crisis at the national level. Santa Anna, biding his time since the fall of Guerrero, initiated a revolt against the government a few weeks later, accusing President Bustamante of seeking to undermine the Constitution of 1824. The rebellion spread quickly across Mexico, as garrisons stationed in cities and towns abandoned the Bustamante regime and joined the insurgency. The renegade general's loyal comrade-in-arms, José Antonio Mexía, was among the first high-ranking officers to defect to the rebels, joining Santa Anna in Veracruz. Federalist and centralist armies took to the field, plunging the country into a civil war that would see the bloodiest fighting since the War of Independence. "The fire has been lit," Lorenzo de

Zavala wrote from New York on hearing of the outbreak of the re-volt, "and God Knows where it will stop."[4]

Terán did not defect to the rebels, even though he agreed with their publicly stated goals. Perhaps he suspected, as many did, that Santa Anna's call to restore federalism was merely a pretext intended to lend the revolt an air of legitimacy. Governed at all times by a scrupulous sense of duty, he abhorred civil strife, and wanted nothing to do with men of ambition who used the turmoil to advance their personal agendas. As the conflict dragged on with no end in sight, Mexican leaders from across the political spectrum urged Terán to step forward as a compromise candidate for the presidency. In many ways he was an ideal choice for a divided, war-torn nation. A mod-erate conservative, the general had managed to avoid being drawn into the bitter factionalism of Mexican politics. No less important, he had a reputation for probity, refusing to use his position to enrich himself, unlike so many of the country's military men.[5]

But Terán did not really want the job. Lacking the appetite for the no-holds-barred combat of the political arena, he modestly confessed to a friend that if he were president, he "would com-mit perhaps greater errors" than those in power. An engineer by training, he longed to retire from public life, and dreamed of es-tablishing a museum of natural history. Dismissing any talk of a presidential bid, Terán was convinced he could do more good in the northeast, maintaining order and defending Texas from grasping Americans.[6]

THE COUNTRY'S POLITICAL UPHEAVAL WAS A GODSEND TO FIRE-brands like Wharton and Travis, who were happy to claim the feder-alist cause as their own. There is no evidence that either man knew much about Mexican national politics. Nor did they care to know. Their grievances were entirely local in nature, and they considered any acts of civil disobedience their birthright as Americans, whose fathers had also rebelled against taxation and arbitrary rule. In Ana-huac, Bradburn dismissed the avowed federalist sympathies of Travis and his followers as a sham, convinced that they were nothing more than a fig leaf to conceal a plot to separate Texas from Mexico.[7]

There was probably talk of secession among the malcontents at Anahuac and Brazoria at some point. Their purchase of ammunition left no doubt that they were actively preparing for armed resistance, and they were busily writing to friends in the United States to let them know of their plans. Still, the unrest was limited to a loud minority that lacked a clear set of goals. They were definitely up to something, but with little more than a vague sense that the political crisis in Mexico could be turned to their advantage, Wharton and Travis seemed content, at least for the moment, to seed the storm clouds of rebellion.

On the basis of the reports he was receiving from Texas, Wharton's younger brother John, a lawyer in New Orleans, decided to head for Texas, and he urged the family's longtime friend, Sam Houston, to do the same. The former Tennessee governor had been living in Indian Territory (present-day Oklahoma) with the Cherokees since the breakup of his marriage to Eliza Allen. But even in disgrace, the irrepressible Houston seemed incapable of a life of anonymity. He had recently made headlines during a visit to Washington when an Ohio congressman, William Stanbery, referred to him in a speech attacking the Jackson administration's Indian policies. A chance meeting between the two men on Pennsylvania Avenue led to angry words, then violence. When Stanbery drew a pistol, Houston beat him severely with his cane. Charged with contempt of Congress (though he was a private citizen), Houston agreed to a trial in the House of Representatives, serving as his own attorney. Predictably, the event became a political circus. Reveling in the spotlight, Houston seized the opportunity to showcase his oratorical skill and flair for the dramatic, playing not only to members of the House but to the packed galleries above. The chamber voted to reprimand Houston, a punishment he gladly accepted. The Stanbery affair not only rescued him from political oblivion, it made him a national celebrity.[8]

Now poised to return to public life, Houston received a letter from the younger Wharton, who informed him that an insurgency was brewing in Texas, which he expected to take place in a matter of months. "A fine country will be gained without much bloodshed," he predicted, adding, "Whenever they are ready for action, I will be with them." Houston had been mulling a trip to Texas, but Wharton's letter seems to have convinced him that there was no better place for a man of ambition, eager to make his mark. Forwarding the letter to a colleague, Houston penned a hasty postscript, "It is important that I should be off to Texas!"[9]

In fact, the simmering tensions between Bradburn and the Anahuac hotspurs had already come to a boil. Fed up with Travis's repeated acts of disobedience, the harried Mexican official ordered his arrest. On June 10, 1832, Anahuac settlers responded by skirmishing with Mexican troops to secure his release. Three days later, the rebels withdrew to Turtle Bayou, a few miles away, where they drafted a seven-point statement condemning the "military despotism" of the current regime and invited the people of Texas to join them. Having heard of recent federalist victories below the Rio Grande, they declared their support for Santa Anna.[10]

The Brazos troublemakers quickly endorsed the uprising at Anahuac. Calling a public meeting to decide upon an appropriate course of action, Wharton declared "open war" on all centralist troops in the colony. Organizing themselves into five regiments, the insurgents sent a party of men overland to aid their compatriots at Anahuac, then launched a well-coordinated attack on Fort Velasco, a recently completed circular stockade at the mouth of the river. Flying from the masthead of the schooner was a flag that would have been instantly recognizable to the American rebels, a single star against a blue background, with thirteen red and white horizontal stripes. Incongruously, even as the rebels adopted a modified version of Old Glory as their battle flag, they shouted, "Long Live Santa Anna!" during their assault on the fort. The Velasco commander, Domingo Ugartechea, held out for two days, surrendering only when the garrison exhausted its supply of ammunition.[11]

11. Velasco battle flag, 1832.
Courtesy of Brownsville Historical Society.

Terán received word of the uprisings on the way to Padilla, a lonely, dusty village about 150 miles south of Matamoros. The news was a devastating blow, confirming his worst fears about the future of Texas. But it was only the latest in a series of disasters for the commandant of the northeastern provinces. The groundswell for Santa Anna was gaining momentum, with Tampico and San Luis Potosí having fallen to the federalists that spring. Marching into the interior to deal with the crisis, he now learned that antigovernment forces had also seized Matamoros, the country's principal port in the northeast. No doubt the fact that the federalists were led by José Antonio Mexía, Zavala's point man in Mexico for the Galveston Bay and Texas Land Company, made the news of rebel victories especially hard to take.

Buffeted on all sides, Terán surrendered to feelings of profound despair. The country was descending into chaos, and he blamed its leaders, men like Zavala, Mexía, and Santa Anna, who seemed incapable of putting the national interest above their own. On July 2, he spent much of the day alone, taking long walks, deep in melancholy contemplation. His chief of staff became alarmed at his mental state.

That evening, in a letter full of poignant anguish, he unburdened himself to his friend Lucas Alamán. "Why does man not have the right to put aside his misery and his pains? . . . I am an unhappy man, and unhappy people should not live on this earth."

Many things preyed upon his mind. The war was going badly, and he had not heard from his wife in months. But again and again, he returned to the one issue that had consumed him for more than four years. How could Mexico expect to keep the lands above the Rio Grande "when we cannot agree among ourselves?" he asked. "The revolution is about to break forth, and Texas is lost." For the devout Mexican patriot, the national humiliation was more than he could bear. "En que parara Texas? En lo que Dios quiera." (*What is to become of Texas? Whatever God wills.*)

The following morning, General Manuel de Mier y Terán put on his full-dress uniform and walked behind an abandoned church. Unsheathing his sword, he braced the handle against a stone and placed the tip against his heart, then plunged forward, impaling himself upon it.[12]

For a fleeting moment in early July 1832, there were signs that some Mexicans might finally heed Terán's plea for national unity. His enemy Mexía was one of them. In Matamoros, the federalist leader poured over the official dispatches from Bradburn and Ugartechea, and they painted a disturbing picture. Never questioning the need for American economic development in Texas, Mexía was still a patriot; he would not stand by as Anglo rebels attempted a brazen land grab. Deciding to check out the situation for himself, he asked the commander of centralist forces for an immediate ceasefire and, with a hastily organized expeditionary force of four hundred men, sailed up the Texas coast. Stephen F. Austin, who had been attending the legislative session in Saltillo, agreed to accompany him.[13]

Neither Mexía nor Austin knew what awaited them when they reached the mouth of the Brazos in mid-July. Much to their relief, they found the rebels in a jubilant mood, celebrating their victory. In the village of Brazoria, a few miles upriver, they were greeted with bonfires and a twenty-one–gun salute. The insurgents hosted a dinner and ball for the Mexican colonel, congratulating him on his recent string of victories and offering toasts proclaiming Santa Anna as a new George Washington. They assured him that they were committed *santanistas*, who had taken up arms only in defense of federalist principles. Wharton and Austin both gave speeches; Mexía replied in impeccable English.[14]

The colonists' nothing-to-see-here routine satisfied Mexía. Convinced that the Americans harbored no ill will toward their adopted country, the Mexican colonel lingered a few days, then departed with his troops to continue the war against centralist armies below the Rio Grande. With Texas at peace, he would leave local affairs to Austin's "prudent discretion."[15]

The violence that swept across the province that summer had not yet run its course, however. The largest contingent of centralist troops in Texas was stationed in Nacogdoches under the command of Colonel José de la Piedras, numbering about 350 men. Sometimes going without pay for months, they were a constant burden to the locals. With little assistance from the capital, Piedras was obliged to levy forced requisitions, and often resorted to more imaginative means to keep them adequately fed and provisioned. Area merchants grumbled when Piedras insisted they pay for a military escort to cart their goods along the Camino Real into Louisiana, despite the absence of any real danger. Piedras was especially unpopular among area Anglos. Doing his best to enforce the Law of April 6, 1830, he scoured the roadways for illegal immigrants and tried to expel squatters. The news that he would soon be awarding land titles to the Cherokees did nothing to improve his standing with the white community. Accustomed to the support of federal and state troops in disputes with tribes in the United States, they found it hard to believe that the local commander regarded whites and Indians "as colonists on the same footing."[16]

At first, Piedras's close relationship with the immigrant tribes prevented Nacogdoches from being swept up in the insurrection. When word of the unrest at Anahuac and Velasco reached the Piney Woods, the colonel called upon the Cherokees and other bands to come to his aid. The Americans wanted to drive all Mexicans from the area, he told them, and their own expulsion would soon follow. Within a matter of days a few hundred Indians rode into town, painted and girded for battle, bringing the crisis to an abrupt end.[17]

The town remained on edge, and a month later violence flared again. Rattled by the disturbances at Anahuac and Velasco, Piedras ordered all residents to surrender their arms, making a confrontation between the garrison and the townspeople inevitable. Leading the uprising was Vicente Córdova, a former alcalde and captain of the local militia, and James Bowie, an American newcomer. Nearby Anglo settlements also joined the insurgents. On August 2 the rebels attacked the garrison, which had taken up positions in the town square. House-to-house fighting continued until nightfall, when Piedras evacuated his troops, marching them north into Indian country to link up with his Cherokee allies. Pursued by the rebels, he made a stand at the Angelina River.

As soon as Bowls learned of the uprising, he again rode with sixty warriors to Piedras's rescue. This time he was too late. Piedras's men had no stomach for a fight; some were laying down their arms and declaring for Santa Anna when the Cherokees arrived. Seeing that the situation was hopeless, Bowls reluctantly chose the prudent course and quit the field, leaving the hapless commander to surrender to the insurrectionists.[18]

Almost as suddenly as it had begun, the rebellion was over. By the time many upcountry farmers learned of the fighting along the coast, the unrest had run its course. With the civil war still raging in the country's interior, Mexico's national leaders were too preoccupied to give Texas much thought, and like Mexía relieved to learn that the rebels had expressed no desire for independence. They were happy enough, for the time being, to take them at their word.

But the turbulent events of the summer of 1832 marked a watershed moment for the peoples of Texas. For the Cherokees and the immigrant tribes, the collapse of Mexican political authority in the region dashed any hope of a land distribution program. Piedras was gone, booted from the province before any land titles could be issued. General Terán, their staunchest advocate, had died by his own hand. And they could expect little help from Terán's successor as commandant of the Eastern Interior Provinces, Vicente Filisola. An empresario himself, Filisola had recently been awarded a contract to settle colonists on a piece of land in East Texas—part of it claimed by the Cherokees. At least the Indians still had a sympathetic ear in Saltillo, the state capital. But in September Governor Letona too would be dead, a victim of yellow fever. There seemed to be no end to the Cherokees' misfortunes.[19]

The Anglo-American rebels, of course, had much to celebrate, the uprisings having succeeded beyond their wildest expectations. After the surrender of the garrisons at Anahuac, Velasco, and Nacogdoches, Colonel Ugartechea withdrew to San Antonio, leaving the most densely populated part of the province—from the Piney Woods to the Brazos River valley—in American hands. With the custom houses closed, residents along the coast no longer had any reason to complain about the government's arbitrary tax policies. After the revolts, Texas seemed to one settler nothing less than "a terrestrial paradise." As he recalled some years later, "A live mastodon would not have been a greater curiosity than a tax collector."[20]

But the most important consequence of the rebels' actions was an unintended one. The absence of Mexican troops brought an abrupt end to the government's efforts to hold the line against illegal immigration. Now, with the Texas-Louisiana border completely undefended, settlers from the United States crowded the roadways. As peace returned to the province in the summer of 1832, a new phase in the Americanization of Texas had begun.

EIGHT

SUSPENDED OVER THE ALTAR OF SACRIFICE

E VEN AS WHARTON AND THE LOOSE BAND OF MALCONTENTS savored their victory, they knew there were many Anglos who disapproved of their actions. Longtime colonists tended to follow the lead of Stephen F. Austin, an unwavering advocate for good relations with Mexican officials no matter which party was in charge in the nation's capital. But now the men who had led the uprisings were emboldened, and they were in no mood to extend an olive branch to those who publicly opposed their actions. During the drunken festivities in Brazoria held to celebrate the surrender of the Velasco garrison in July, a mob of local rowdies hanged in effigy three men who had tried to quell the uprising, one of whom, Samuel May Williams, was Austin's business partner. The "tories," William Wharton remarked acidly, would need to be horsewhipped into line.[1]

The readiness of some Anglo-Texans to defy the national government would test the limits of Stephen F. Austin's leadership of the Anglo-American community. Cautious and non-confrontational, the empresario had thus far managed to safeguard both his own interests and those of the colony he represented. Working within official channels and relying on the contacts he had cultivated among local and national leaders, he had masterfully navigated the ever-turbulent waters of Mexican politics. But as tensions between the colony and

109

Mexican officials mounted, he came to be seen by many settlers less as a champion of their interests than as part of the problem.

No one would do more to challenge the empresario's authority than the master of Eagle Island. William Wharton had never really gotten along with Austin, although both men claimed to be ignorant of the cause. They once squabbled over a land deal, but the animosity between them lay much deeper. Temperamentally, they could not have been more different. Almost a decade younger than Austin, Wharton tended to be impetuous and quick to anger. As one of the wealthier men in the Brazos district (and the son-in-law of the wealthiest, Jared Groce), Wharton never received a land grant from the empresario, and felt no obligation to treat him with deference. But the most important source of the rift between the two men seems to have been the most obvious one: Austin's consistent efforts to placate Mexican officials did not sit well with Wharton. A member of the planter elite, he was accustomed to getting his way in the United States, and saw no reason why that should change now that he was a citizen of Mexico.[2]

Often termed the "radical party," the men who had orchestrated the uprisings and who now assumed a more belligerent posture toward Mexico defied easy categorization. They ranged widely in age and economic status. A few, like Wharton, were well-established Brazos planters. But most were newcomers, including a handful of itinerant lawyers, merchants, and speculators, who had yet to put down roots in the province. By nature fiercely independent, the radicals did not have a unifying, charismatic figure to rally around. Wharton was too cerebral for such a role, though he was widely regarded as the group's mastermind and moving spirit.

They were bound instead by a set of shared values, rooted in the patriarchal culture of the white American South. Embracing a code of male honor, they exhibited a combative masculinity, one in which dueling, a practice falling into disrepute elsewhere in the United States, was the preferred recourse to a perceived slight. Wharton's best friend, Branch T. Archer, a forty-one-year-old Virginia doctor, had killed his cousin in a contest with pistols at fifteen paces before coming to Texas. Wharton's younger brother John had only just arrived in the colony when he provoked a duel with a member of the Austin clan. He lost, never entirely regaining the use of his right hand. And James Bowie made his way to Texas after being severely wounded in a bloody, much-publicized affray on the Mississippi River, the "Sandbar Fight," that left two men dead.[3]

They shared, too, a deeply held Americanism. As Terán noted during his inspection tour, Anglo settlers sought to recreate a familiar world in a foreign land, one in which they expected to enjoy all the rights and privileges of their country of origin. The radicals were especially insistent on defending these rights, and would not hesitate to resort to armed force to do so. Buried deep in their ideological muscle memory was the American republic's own struggle for independence. Like Haden Edwards and the Fredonians five years earlier, they were quick to see signs of tyranny in the actions of the Mexican government, drawing analogies between their disputes with local officials and those of an earlier generation that had fought against the British. "Centralism," William Barret Travis would later write, "is but another name for monarchy."[4]

And, like their forefathers, they held strong views on the meaning and obligations of citizenship. On this point they were not alone; even settlers who did not share the radicals' suspicions of the Mexican government regarded as sacred their right to petition for the redress of grievances. As a result, many colonists agreed with civic leaders in San Felipe, who called for a convention in the wake of the uprisings at Anahuac, Velasco, and Nacogdoches. Some saw a convention as an opportunity to reaffirm their loyalty to the Mexican republic; others hoped to draw attention to the problems that had sparked the recent unrest.

It seemed a perfectly reasonable idea to Americans, well-versed as they were in their own history of colonial resistance. Some Hispanos, those with close ties to the Anglo community, also endorsed the call for a convention. But the proposal was controversial. Political chief Ramón Músquiz refused to sanction the meeting on the grounds that it had no precedent in Mexican civil procedure. Ordinarily, local grievances were presented to the ayuntamientos, which would then issue a remonstrance to the political chief of the province, who would in turn forward the petition to the state legislature for action. With Músquiz firmly opposed to the convention, San Antonio declined to send delegates, while two Hispano delegates from Victoria failed to reach San Felipe in time to participate in the proceedings. The convention would be an all-American affair.[5]

Cautious as always, Austin had his misgivings, worried about the optics of holding a meeting that did not have the strong support of prominent Mexican Texans. Still, he may have believed he had no choice but to participate, hoping to use his authority to temper the passions of the radicals. Serving as chairman, he succeeded—at least up to a point. In a statement drafted, strangely enough, by William Wharton, the delegates proclaimed their commitment to the Mexican federal republic. There was not an Anglo-American in Texas, Wharton averred, who did not "devoutly pray" that Mexico should "remain united to the end of time." Whether these declarations of national loyalty were genuine or a tongue-in-cheek effort to deceive Mexican authorities, there could be little doubt that the reforms the delegates proposed had but one purpose: to Americanize the province of Texas. Accordingly, they called for the repeal of immigration restrictions from the United States. They wanted tariff exemptions that would continue to allow them to import US manufactured products. Finally, they requested that Texas be allowed to separate from Coahuila, a proposal that would have created an American state within the Mexican republic.[6]

No sooner had the delegates concluded their business than they began to have second thoughts about presenting their grievances to Mexican authorities. Since the meeting had been ruled illegal by the political chief of the province, there was little chance that their deliberations would receive a favorable hearing in Saltillo. They could expect an even frostier reception in the nation's capital, where President Bustamante still clung to power, although a federalist victory was considered imminent. A consensus emerged among the delegates

12. San Antonio de Béxar. Courtesy of Special Collections,
University of Texas at Arlington Libraries.

that they should wait to present their petitions to the state and national governments.

When the convention adjourned, Austin paid a visit to Ramón Músquiz in San Antonio, anxious to reassure the province's highest-ranking official that the meeting was not intended as a challenge to his authority. The political chief had long been for the colony a reliable and important ally. In 1829, he withheld publication of President Guerrero's emancipation edict and successfully lobbied to exempt Texas slaveholders from the decree. Two years later, at the empresario's urging, he worked to thwart Terán's efforts to establish a permanent homeland for the immigrant tribes in East Texas. Now he informed Austin that he would gladly help to advance the colonists' reform goals, but only if they would present them through the proper channels.

Matters of protocol were not the only reason behind Músquiz's unwillingness to endorse the Anglo-Americans' calls for reform. Like many well-to-do Hispanos, he remained a committed federalist,

whose views had always dovetailed neatly with those of US immigrants. But as whites became the region's dominant ethnic group, the
political chief began to detect among some of Austin's colonists a troubling belligerence. A turning point in his thinking toward the Americans had come earlier in the year, when five enslaved people escaped
from a plantation on the Brazos and made their way to San Antonio,
where they asked for protection. Sympathetic to their plight, Músquiz
never got a chance to help the runaways. Their owner sent a posse of
slave-catchers after them, who rode into town and brazenly seized the
group. Furious, Músquiz ordered the arrest of the men and demanded
they be returned to San Antonio for punishment. Anglo officials on the
Brazos simply ignored him. The incident may have contributed to his
reluctance to side with white settlers in the disturbances that summer.
Although the uprisings had ostensibly been undertaken as a repudiation of the centralist regime, the political chief did not declare for Santa
Anna until the insurgency had run its course and the outcome was no
longer in doubt. Músquiz was beginning to distance himself from the
Americans, perhaps realizing that he had made a Faustian bargain. In
dutifully supporting an Anglo agenda at every turn, he had only emboldened the newcomers, whose calls for statehood, he now suspected,
concealed a secret drive for independence.[7]

Not all Bexareños shared Músquiz's growing doubts about the
Anglo-Americans. Austin could still count on his friends on the San
Antonio town council, men like twenty-six-year-old Juan Seguín,
the scion of one of the town's most well-established families. Juan's
father, Erasmo, had been among the first Hispanos to welcome the
empresario to the province. Austin stayed with the family whenever
he was in San Antonio, and sent his brother to live with them for a
year to learn Spanish. Despite a reputation as something of a hot-
head, Juan was beginning to assume a prominent role in local affairs.
In December, the ayuntamiento drew up a statement echoing many of
the grievances of the Anglo settlements. Bemoaning their community's impoverished condition, which they attributed to the destructive
raids of the Plains tribes, they too called for the repeal of immigration
restrictions from the United States. A steady flow of American settlers,

they argued, would be the "most efficient, quick, and economical" way to defend the northern frontier and improve its fortunes. Tellingly, however, the council stopped short of requesting statehood, asking instead for more representation in the Saltillo legislature.[8]

While Músquiz and other Bexareños were beginning to reevaluate their relationship with the Americans, the radicals offered further evidence that they were prepared to go their own way. Austin was still trying to mend fences in the Mexican districts when the Wharton faction called for a second convention, to be held at San Felipe the following spring. The empresario saw the move as a deliberate attempt to embarrass him, undercutting his efforts to win Hispano support for reform.

Managing a colony of independent-minded frontier folk had never been an easy task for Austin. For more than a decade the forty-year-old empresario had devoted every waking moment to its affairs, scrupulously attending to every minor detail as it grew to become a thriving American community. But now he was exhausted. He detested the radicals, whom he judged to be an "unprincipled, brutal and ungenerous and ungrateful" lot, and he was troubled by their anti-Mexican prejudices. He talked wistfully about withdrawing from public life. His younger sister Emily had recently moved to Texas with her family, and he looked forward to settling on a farm nearby, perhaps with "a jolly old widow to comfort me in my old age."[9]

Despite Austin's misgivings about a second convention, the decision to wait for a more favorable opportunity to formally present the colonists' grievances turned out to be wise move. There was still resistance from San Antonio; Músquiz still refused to sanction the meeting, and the town again declined to send delegates. But at the national level the political outlook for reform had brightened considerably. Santa Anna entered the capital in triumph in early January, and though some centralist forces continued to fight on, the year-long civil war was coming to an end. The new regime could be expected to take a very different attitude toward Texas and the American immigration problem. José Antonio Mexía, promoted by Santa Anna to the rank of general for his services in the northern campaign, had emerged as a major figure in the corridors of power in the National Palace, and was now being mentioned as a possible candidate for the presidency. Recently elected to the Senate, he assured Austin that he was "as interested in the welfare of Texas as any of its inhabitants." Mexía even managed to broker a peace of sorts between Lorenzo de Zavala and Santa Anna, no easy task given the large egos of the two men. At Mexía's urging, Zavala returned to Mexico from exile and renewed contact with his former ally. The two leaders were probably both to blame for their earlier falling out, Zavala admitted. "Men are not made of vices and virtues," he wrote to Santa Anna, "but a mixture of both." Zavala would also return to congress as a member of the Chamber of Deputies, and with Mexía looked forward to working toward the repeal of the Law of April 6, 1830.[10]

When the second convention met at San Felipe in the spring of 1833, the Wharton crowd dominated the proceedings. Their influence was no doubt enhanced by the presence of a new member of the group, who was well-known to all the delegates, at least by reputation. Wharton's old friend from his Nashville days, Sam Houston, had arrived in Texas three months earlier. The famous Tennessean quickly inserted himself into the province's political affairs, winning election as a delegate from Nacogdoches. Powerfully built and standing more than six feet tall, Houston would have commanded attention under any circumstances. But his penchant for extravagant dress—he could often be seen wearing a broad beaver hat and a "complete Indian costume made of buckskin and ornamented with a profuse variety of beads"—made him an especially striking figure among the fifty or so delegates who had left their farms and ranches to attend. One awestruck settler described him as "the finest looking man I ever saw."[11]

With Wharton serving as chairman, the convention reiterated the reform goals of the first meeting, calling for a repeal of the hated Law of April 6, 1830. This time the delegates took a firmer stand on the question of Texas statehood. Houston chaired a committee that drafted a state constitution, drawing from the Massachusetts charter of 1780, which happened to be on hand.

Still mindful of the fact that the meeting lacked the sanction of local authorities, the delegates chose three men to submit their reform petition to the government in Mexico City whose national loyalties could not be questioned: Stephen F. Austin, San Felipe physician James Miller, and Erasmo Seguín. The latter's appointment may have been wishful thinking on the convention's part, since neither he nor any other Mexican Texan had attended the meeting.

But at the last minute Dr. Miller could not go. Spring brought torrential rains to that part of Texas, causing the Brazos River to overflow its banks. The floods inundated farms and plantations with silt and debris, fouling the water supply and creating a breeding ground for cholera, which was then sweeping much of the American South. By the time the convention adjourned in mid-April, the first cases of the disease had been reported in Brazoria. Soon the pandemic was ravaging coastal lowlands, carrying off young and old, men and women, free and enslaved alike. With Miller too busy attending to the sick, Austin settled his affairs for what he told everyone would be his last service on behalf of Texas. He expected to be gone four months.[12]

Stopping first in San Antonio, the empresario detected an unmistakable coolness toward the convention's proposals. He was convinced that the province would have more success in its efforts to win concessions from Mexico City if it presented a united front, but growing mistrust of the Americans among Bexareño leaders made that impossible. During three lengthy and presumably heated meetings to discuss the memorial drafted by the convention, they refused to endorse it, reiterating their belief that a petition of grievances could only come from the state legislature. There was little enthusiasm for the Americans' call for Texas statehood. Only his old friend Erasmo Seguín favored the measure, though not strongly enough to accompany Austin to Mexico City. Citing pressing personal business, Seguín politely declined to make the trip. Austin would have to present the colonists' case to the Mexican government alone.[13]

And perhaps it was fitting that it should be so. The alliance that Austin had painstakingly crafted between the Anglo and Mexican

communities in Texas was disintegrating, leaving both groups unhappy and wary of the empresario. He blamed the radicals, and not
just for pursuing a course that seemed calculated to alienate Hispano
leaders. He was acutely aware of his own loss of standing among a
growing number of Americans who disapproved of his conciliatory
role. As a friend to the Mexicans, they suspected, he was not fully
committed to their agenda. "He is closely watched," one longtime
settler wrote. Should the empresario fail to achieve the convention's
objectives in Mexico City, he would be "a Ruined man in Texas."
Ever sensitive to his reputation, he complained that he had been
"suspended over the altar of sacrifice" by his enemies.[14]

Austin had worked tirelessly to build bridges between the
Anglo-American and Hispano communities. By 1833, however, he
had become a forlorn, solitary figure, whose task more accurately
resembled a delicate, high-wire balancing act, with both groups looking upward, and many expecting—some, perhaps, even hoping—
to see him fall.

NINE

YOU HAVE TORN THE CONSTITUTION TO PIECES

AUSTIN ARRIVED IN MEXICO CITY IN JULY. HE WOULD MAKE little headway in his mission for the first few months, having barely settled in at his hotel when the cholera pandemic that had wreaked such havoc along the Brazos River valley appeared in the capital. The disease had already made landfall "with the violence of a hurricane" in the country's principal port cities, prompting local authorities to implement a strictly enforced street-sweeping and cleanliness campaign. Such measures proved entirely insufficient to forestall the ravages of cholera in Mexico's most densely populated urban center. The victims initially experienced acute vomiting and diarrhea, causing dehydration and, in severe cases, shock and death. In the space of a month, as many as twenty thousand people died, paralyzing the city and bringing government functions to a complete halt. One resident recalled a city of deserted streets, of "churches with their doors wide open and their altars covered with a thousand lights, people kneeling down with their arms forming a cross and weeping . . . And far off in the distance the dismal high-pitched squeal of wagon wheels as they bore off loads of corpses."[1]

As the weeks dragged by, Austin, weakened by illness himself and dispirited by the news of the effect of the cholera outbreak in Texas, grew impatient. He had learned to his chagrin that Wharton and the radicals in Texas were planning yet another unauthorized convention, a move that was certain to draw the ire of Mexican authorities. Sensing that he was again being outmaneuvered by the radical faction, the empresario in early October penned a letter to the Béxar town council, urging its members to take the lead in organizing a local government independent of Coahuila. It was a decision Austin would soon have reason to regret. The letter smacked of sedition to some San Antonio leaders, who forwarded it to the state capital.[2]

Congress quickly took up the Texas question when it reconvened in September. With Mexía serving in the Senate and Zavala in the Chamber of Deputies, Austin could rely on a solid bloc of support for Texas interests. The Mexican Congress repealed the more objectionable provisions of the Law of April 6, 1830, with little debate. In addition to lifting the ban on immigration from the United States, the legislative body gave further evidence of its willingness to accommodate its American citizens, recommending the temporary suspension of customs duties and even the revision of the judicial system in Texas to allow trial by jury.[3]

The colonists' request for statehood, on the other hand, was a nonstarter. The representatives from Coahuila balked at the proposal, unwilling to give up control of the province's public lands. Vice President Valentín Gómez Farías, then serving as acting president in Santa Anna's absence, was one of a growing number of federalists who saw statehood as a dangerous first step toward Texas independence and vowed that Anglo-Americans should not be allowed to seize "a single inch of Mexican soil." A private meeting with Austin on the matter had gone badly, with the vice president interpreting the empresario's remark that the colonists would not be denied statehood as a threat. Even Zavala, who had supported the idea at first, came to favor a plan that would grant Texas territorial status, giving the national government control over its unoccupied lands. In the end, congress took no action, deferring the matter to the state government in Saltillo.[4]

With the Texas question settled, at least for the time being, Zavala turned his attention to other pressing national issues. A zealous foe of the power and wealth of the Catholic Church, the liberal federalist helped to spearhead a wide range of anticlerical reforms, passing bills that abolished mandatory tithing, secularized Catholic educational institutions, and allowed the government to appoint clerics and seize church property. The reforms elicited outrage from the clergy, and may have been too controversial even for the liberal Gómez Farías. Soon afterward, the acting president tapped Zavala to serve as Mexico's minister to France. It was an honor Zavala could hardly refuse; it may also have been a tactful means to ease him out of the way. By the end of November, he would leave Mexico City with his family and a small entourage. En route to Paris the couple stopped in New York City, where Emily gave birth to their first child, a girl.[5]

Austin also headed for home after four months in the nation's capital. While his push for statehood had been stymied, he could point to the repeal of the ban on American immigration as a significant achievement. Reaching Saltillo in early January, he found Mexican authorities waiting for him with orders for his arrest. Gómez Farías, who had been informed of Austin's letter to the San Antonio council, angrily ordered the Texas leader returned to Mexico City to await trial on charges of treason.

Austin would spend the next three months in a dank, windowless room in the Palace of the Inquisition, a building that had held political prisoners since the War of Independence. Concerned that his arrest might lead to antigovernment protests in Texas, the empresario quickly wrote to the San Felipe ayuntamiento, urging his colonists to remain calm. He need not have worried. While many residents were distressed to learn of his incarceration, in some quarters the news was not exactly met with an outpouring of grief. The Whartons, in fact, were happy to have the empresario out of the picture and did not mind saying so. John A. Wharton penned an editorial suggesting that Austin had himself to blame for his predicament, adding that Mexican leaders in the capital should "hold onto him until he undergoes a radical change." Still, some effort to protest the government's action against the most prominent man in the colony needed to be made. The Texas ayuntamientos dutifully

drafted memorials calling for Austin's release, but the Brazoria
council, which did little without the Whartons' approval, did not
get around to issuing a formal protest until August. The memorials
would arrive in Mexico City in October, more than nine months
after his arrest.[6]

Under normal circumstances, Austin might have been able to
expect some assistance from the US minister to Mexico. Unfortunately for the empresario, the representative of American interests in the capital was Anthony Butler, a man Austin knew all too
well. Austin's father, Moses, had once been business partners with
the diplomat back in Missouri, but the relationship soured, leaving
Stephen to cover the debt when Moses died. Butler believed the
empresario still owed him money, and now felt no compulsion to
act on his behalf, even though the US State Department expressly
ordered him to do so. Like his predecessor, Joel Poinsett, Butler
had spent the last few years pestering Mexican leaders to sell Texas,
making himself obnoxious to just about everyone in the nation's
capital. His private life had also become the subject of unfavorable comment. The US consul in Mexico City was so angered by
the minister's sexual advances toward his two wards, both Mexican
girls in their teens, that he wrote directly to the secretary of state
in Washington, informing him: "Butler is unworthy of and a disgrace to the office he now holds, and ought to be recalled by his
government."[7]

Butler's standing among Mexico's leaders was so abysmally low
that he could have done little on Austin's behalf even if he wanted
to. Still, the US minister found a way to make a difficult situation
worse. To his friends in Texas he penned two anonymous letters,
denouncing the empresario's arrest as the cowardly act of "an ignorant, fanatical and arrogant race." Butler's motives in writing the
letters had nothing to do with the empresario's welfare, but were instead a cynical attempt to stir up Anglo hostility toward the Gómez
Farías government. A revolt in Texas, he reasoned, might induce
Mexico to finally sell the province. Butler's authorship of the letters
soon became public knowledge in the capital, making him persona

non grata as far as the Mexican government was concerned. "He is the worst enemy I have in this Country," the empresario lamented.[8]

Austin had never been a stranger to self-pity, and while the conditions of his confinement began to improve—in June he was moved to a prison on the outskirts of the capital—his mood did not. As the months dragged by, he felt abandoned, despondent from what he considered to be a general indifference in Texas to his plight. As his case moved with snail-like speed through the courts, he came to believe that his enemies back home, and the Whartons in particular, were working to prolong his confinement. Word of the empresario's suspicions became public knowledge along the Brazos, prompting the elder Wharton to author a scathing—and given Austin's predicament, extraordinarily mean-spirited—rebuttal. In a public letter dripping with invective, he reproached the empresario for his "disgusting self-conceit" and "inconsistent stupidity." It was not Wharton's finest moment, and he would later apologize. But the letter laid bare the utter contempt with which Austin was held by the radicals, who no longer regarded him as the colony's leader.[9]

While Austin languished in a Mexico City prison, acting president Gómez Farías worried that the empresario's letter to the San Antonio council might be evidence of a larger pattern of Anglo-American disloyalty. Soon after Austin's arrest, he ordered Colonel Juan Almonte, a diplomat fluent in English, to conduct a fact-finding mission of the province. For two and a half months in the summer of 1834, Almonte traveled across Texas, covering much the same ground as General Terán and the Boundary Commission six years earlier, making a detailed study of its political and economic conditions. He did not find a province on the verge of rebellion. Quite the opposite; the Anglo settlements, he concluded, on the whole seemed satisfied with Mexican rule. There were, to be sure, some rowdy troublemakers, but they did not appear to represent the opinion of the majority. At the very least, he expected to get an earful from colonists angered by Austin's imprisonment. To his surprise, the matter rarely came up.[10]

Anglo-Texans had good reason to be content; the province was in the midst of an economic boom. Since driving Mexican troops from the coast two years earlier, Texans paid no customs duties, nor taxes of any kind. Even more important, cotton prices reached a fifteen-year high in the mid-1830s, fueled by a global demand for textiles. From 1831 to 1835 the province's cotton exports soared a staggering 600 percent. With land cheaper in Texas than in the American South, thousands of small farmers pulled up stakes and headed west for the Sabine River. Almonte estimated that the white population had actually doubled since the passage of the Law of April 6, 1830, and now exceeded twenty thousand, about five times the number of Hispanos.[11]

Prosperity, however, was no guarantee of peace. Indeed, the very economic success of the white settlements ensured that clashes with Native American peoples would occur. As Anglos began to push farther up the Colorado River, into the area that would become known as the Texas Hill Country, they encountered Comanche raiding parties for the first time. The woodland Wichitas once again posed a serious threat to isolated farms and homesteads, the Wacos and Tawakonis having returned to their villages on the Upper Brazos and Navasota rivers when Mexican troops withdrew to San Antonio in 1832.

Indian raids for horses and mules were all but unknown in East Texas, where the Cherokees and their associated bands wanted only to be left alone to farm and hunt. But there were signs that the uneasy peace between settlers and the immigrant tribes would not last much longer, as Anglo-American squatters moved into the forests above Nacogdoches, clearing the tribes' hunting lands of brush and timber, and even stealing Indian cattle by marking them with their own brands. The Jackson administration's Indian policy also increased the likelihood of conflict in East Texas. Ever since Bowls led his people below the Red River in 1819, Mexico's northern frontier had been a destination of choice for Native American refugees. With the passage of the 1830 Indian Removal Act, many more would move to Texas. Forced to sign treaties ceding their lands, several southeastern tribes began to make their way to US Indian Territory, but some groups crossed the Sabine River into Texas instead. In 1834,

Almonte found several hundred Choctaws living above Nacogdoches who had only just arrived. Caddo bands from Louisiana and Chickasaws from Mississippi would soon follow.[12]

The Brazos River valley was also experiencing important demographic changes that belied the appearance of stability and order. Eager to take advantage of the rise in cotton prices, area planters needed more labor to put their undeveloped land into cultivation. Under the workaround reached with Mexican authorities, colonists could bring enslaved people into Texas, but they had few opportunities to acquire additional manpower as their labor needs grew. A lucrative and illegal slave traffic emerged to meet the demand, with so-called blackbirders smuggling large numbers of men and women into Texas from Cuba. Purchased in the slave pens of Havana, most were Yoruba-speaking Africans from the Niger River delta who had only recently endured the horrors of the Middle Passage. Many were deposited at the mouth of the San Bernard River, a few miles down the coast from the Brazos, then herded up to a remote spot known as African Landing, where local planters gathered for clandestine slave auctions, out of sight of local authorities. "They were so destitute of clothing, mother would not permit us children to go near them," nine-year-old Dilue Harris later recalled. One American visitor found "about fifty of those poor wretches," ranging in age from ten to twenty-five, "living out of doors, like cattle." Starving, they fought over scraps of food and had to be whipped back by an African American overseer "to prevent their pulling the raw meat to pieces." After bathing in a nearby creek where their heads were carded for lice, they were given new sets of clothes, and the bidding began.[13]

During the mid-1830s, planters along the Lower Brazos would buy up as many as one thousand smuggled Africans, who would soon constitute as much as half the area's enslaved population. Cotton production increased, but so too did whites' anxiety about the world they had made. It was one of the great ironies of the "peculiar institution" that planters lived in fear of the enslaved, even as they vowed to defend their right to own them. And they were doubly afraid of the "wild Africans" who spoke no English, their faces scarred according to Yoruba tribal custom, a people who had little in common with the men and women born and raised in bondage in the American South. More prone to run off and quick to resist, they were an intractable source of labor, exhibiting the sullen, willful defiance of the newly enslaved.[14]

William Wharton did not attend the auctions at African Landing. Although an ardent defender of slavery, he felt only contempt for those who engaged in the illegal trade. Cultivating the persona of the gentleman planter, like many of his class he preferred to think of the "peculiar institution" as a well-ordered world of benevolent masters and obedient slaves. If Eagle Island fell well short of that ideal, it nonetheless presented a sharp contrast to the nightmarish, dystopian conditions on the plantations of many of his neighbors, who shared neither his scruples nor his sensibilities.

In the space of a little more than a decade, Anglo-American settlers had transformed Texas, creating a vibrant economy that appeared, at first glance, identical to the one they had left behind. But they had succeeded in recreating the American South only up to a point. Mexico was not the United States, and not even its benign neglect of the northern frontier could make it so. In East Texas, whites found a region populated by thousands of Indians, many of them with a long history of conflict with Anglo-Americans, and a government that had no interest in removing them. Meanwhile, in the Brazos River valley, planters increasingly came to rely on an alien and hostile labor force, and felt the need to employ ever more violent means of social control. For all its prosperity, Texas had become a tinderbox, requiring only a spark to set it ablaze.

LIKE TERÁN FIVE YEARS EARLIER, ALMONTE FOUND THE POLITICAL scene in the nation's capital much changed during his absence. Zavala's recent anticlerical reforms had infuriated the Church, as well as the country's propertied classes, the *hombres de bien*. When the federalist Congress turned its attention to the reform of the army, the nation's generals decided it had gone too far. In what had become a familiar pattern, the commander of the Cuernavaca garrison, General José María Tornel, issued a *pronunciamiento* against the government. Almost certainly acting with Santa Anna's consent, Tornel demanded the repeal of all reforms passed under acting president Gómez Farías and called for the president to return to the capital and restore order.[15]

At first, the army's opposition to Gómez Farías seemed to be just the latest in a series of storms to pass across Mexico's political landscape. The country had grown accustomed to such convulsions, which invariably resulted in a new government less stable and less effective than the last. But the Plan of Cuernavaca signaled a much broader dissatisfaction with the republic's existing political institutions. Weary after years of turmoil, the *hombres de bien* had begun to lose faith in the federal system, viewing the Constitution of 1824 as a root cause of the country's chronic instability. While support for federalism could still be found in the country's outlying areas, hundreds of town and regional councils endorsed Tornel's *pronunciamiento*, issuing their own pro–Santa Anna declarations in the months that followed.[16]

In June 1834 Santa Anna returned to Mexico City, where he was greeted by tumultuous crowds. Armed with emergency powers, he dismissed Gómez Farías and the cabinet, locked the doors of the two chambers of congress, and ordered new congressional elections. Another year would pass before a series of laws formally abolished the Constitution of 1824. But for all intents and purposes, the First Mexican Republic was dead.[17]

Santa Anna's actions left his former federalist allies in a state of stunned disbelief. Only a few months earlier, José Antonio Mexía had joined the general-president in defeating what remained of Bustamante's centralist armies in Guanajuato. Now, the *santanistas* implemented a sweeping purge of officeholders, in many cases replacing liberal federalists with the very conservatives they had been fighting against. Mexía was furious; had the civil war that had roiled the country for the past two years been for nothing? Serving as commander of the garrison at Guadalajara, he quit his post in disgust and made plans to leave the country with his family. Upon his arrival in the port city of Veracruz, a letter from Santa Anna was waiting for him with a five thousand dollar bribe. He returned it with a curt reply, stating he would rather "beg for alms than incur infamy by accepting this gift."[18]

In Paris, happily removed from the *Sturm und Drang* of Mexican politics, the Zavalas were making the most of their sojourn in the city. They took leisurely promenades along the Champs Elysées and attended the daytime concerts in the Tuileries Garden. When Lorenzo and Emily were not taking part in the whirl of diplomatic social engagements, they could be found at the opera or the theater. It must have been an exhilarating experience for the country-bred Emily. It was a heady time for Zavala as well, his two-volume history of Mexico having earned him a reputation as his country's first man of letters. In Paris he continued his literary and intellectual endeavors, publishing a memoir of his travels in the United States and delivering a paper in French at the Royal Academy of Painting and Sculpture on the Mayan ruins at Uxmal.

Zavala also devoted his energies to another favorite project: transforming Emily into a lady of elegance and taste. It was not common for ministers to take their families on diplomatic assignments; most opted to forgo the expense. But Zavala was proud of his new wife, and eager to introduce her into Paris society. He secured the services of a French tutor and bought her expensive clothes and jewelry. She sat for her portrait in the gown she wore when presented to the court of Louis Phillipe. The education of Emily did not impress Zavala's snobbish private secretary, however, who evidently knew something of her past. Though loyal to his boss, Joaquín Moreno did not approve of his American wife, whom he found intelligent enough but humorless, a woman lacking in charm and social grace. Convinced that Zavala had married beneath his station, he referred to her contemptuously in his diary as that "*miserable puta norteamericano*."[19]

At first Zavala could scarcely credit the reports he was receiving from Mexía and others about the political situation back home.

He was stung by Santa Anna's newfound opposition to his reforms of the Catholic Church, though in his more reflective moments he was willing to allow that he might have gone too far. The president's readiness to undermine the authority of congress, on the other hand, he regarded as an unpardonable sin. By the end of the summer there could be no doubt about Santa Anna's intentions. On August 30, Zavala dictated to Moreno an even-tempered letter of resignation. Now that it had become clear that his political principles "are in opposition to the existing Government," he could no longer fulfill his diplomatic duties, Zavala informed the foreign minister. Moreno confided to his diary that evening, "Today Zavala resigned, with the dignity of a man who loves freedom. I approve."[20]

But Zavala was not done burning his bridges. Deciding to sever his ties with the new regime in the most public and dramatic way possible, he had Moreno write another letter, this one addressed to Santa Anna himself, which he sent not only to the National Palace but to opposition newspapers in Mexico. Here Zavala pulled no punches. The decision to dismiss congress and hold new elections constituted nothing less than "an insult to public reason and the national conscience." Making his break with the government a deeply personal one between the two men, he raged, "You have torn the Constitution to pieces."[21]

The response from the National Palace was hardly unexpected; Santa Anna ordered him to return to the capital. Zavala had no intention of obeying, since it was a safe bet that only imprisonment awaited him there. Remaining in Paris for several months until his ministerial replacement arrived, Zavala had time to consider his options. From the deal he had made with the directors of the Galveston Bay and Texas Land Company, he still owned a large tract of land at the mouth of the San Jacinto River. Writing to the foreign minister, he explained that he intended to move to Texas, where he could tend to his business affairs. He would retire from politics, and take up the peaceful life of a country squire.[22]

Only the first part was true. Sending his son Lorenzo Jr. on ahead to find a suitable home for Emily and the children, he began to map out his future, one that, if successful, would keep him squarely at the forefront of Mexican political life. He continued to correspond with leading federalists such as Gómez Farías and Mexía, who had both fled to New Orleans, sounding them out on a possible way forward. At this stage his plans were unclear. Certainly the best case scenario was to mount a counterrevolution that would topple the Santa Anna regime. But if that could not be accomplished, Zavala was also willing to consider placing himself at the head of a movement that would bring about the secession of Mexico's northern states. One thing was certain: Texas, so far removed from the nation's capital and so long ignored by its leaders, was about to become a new front line in the battle for the nation's future.

TEN

THE BLOOD OF OUR ANCESTORS
FLOWS WARM IN OUR VEINS

ZAVALA AND MEXÍA SHOULD NOT HAVE BEEN SURPRISED BY Santa Anna's political about-face in 1834; there had always been telltale signs of the general's ideological flexibility. Alone among his contemporaries, he possessed a remarkable ability to sense and seize the moment, adjusting as needed to the slightest shift in the prevailing political winds. He would dominate the national stage for more than a quarter of a century, and though his career would be marked in equal measure by triumph and disgrace, he remained a consummate survivor, a political acrobat who could stumble and still land squarely on his feet. Loved or reviled, he was, for better or worse, Mexico's indispensable man.

He was also an enigmatic figure whose reputation as a tyrant has been greatly overstated. Relentless in his pursuit of power, he exhibited a surprising disinterest in wielding it. He seemed bored by the day-to-day duties of running a country, often relinquishing control of the executive branch to loyal subordinates. He preferred to remain above the political fray, away from the capital, spending his time at the head of an army or raising gamecocks at Manga de Clavo, his vast estate near Veracruz.

Even if Santa Anna had opted for a more hands-on approach to governance, he was not a dictator, at least not in the modern sense of the term. Mexico lacked the most basic levers of state power needed

for authoritarian rule. The country was a patchwork of distinct cultural regions; perhaps as much as one-third of its population consisted of unassimilated Indians who spoke no Spanish. On Mexico's
central plain, a cash-strapped bureaucracy functioned as best it could,
but as the roads disappeared into dense jungles to the south, miles
of empty desert to the north, and high mountain ranges to the east
and west, so too did the national government's authority. As president some years later, he would make an effort to tighten his grip on
power, but in 1834 there was no police force to silence opposition
newspapers or to keep recalcitrant citizens in line. Even the army,
Santa Anna's only real instrument of power, was an unreliable one,
the loyalties of garrison commanders in the past having proved fickle
in the extreme.

Lacking a set of firm principles, the Mexican president viewed
politics in intensely personal terms. He demanded absolute loyalty
from his friends, though he rarely repaid it in kind. Vindictive toward
his enemies, he never forgave an insult. Following the overthrow of
the Bustamante government, Santa Anna personally drew up a list
with the names of more than fifty conservatives to be sent into exile.
But the caudillo could also be magnanimous when it suited him, bestowing favors upon those whose cooperation he considered useful.
True to form, he had expressed up to this point only a passing interest in the thorny Texas question. But he had met Austin in the capital
in the fall of 1833, and decided to take a personal interest in the case
against the empresario. It was rumored that Santa Anna's reasons
for involving himself in Austin's legal battle had much to do with
the influence of a "very sprightly young lady," whose family was on
close terms with the Mexican president. Upon his return to power,
the conditions of Austin's confinement improved. The empresario
was transferred to the Accordada prison outside the city in June, and
allowed to post bail on Christmas Day 1834, with orders to remain
in the city until a verdict in the case could be reached.[1]

With a new congress installed that was more to his liking, Santa
Anna returned to his estate, leaving the executive branch once again

13. Antonio López de Santa Anna (1794–1876), circa 1853. The Mexican president's move to abolish the Constitution of 1824 infuriated federalists like Lorenzo de Zavala and José Antonio Mexía, sparking a series of revolts against centralist rule after 1835. Courtesy of DeGolyer Library, Southern Methodist University.

in the hands of a loyal subordinate. As reactionary as its predecessor had been radical, the legislative body restored the privileges of the Church and, in an attempt to deny federalist governors the means to resist the centralist regime, sharply reduced the size of local militias. The governor of Zacatecas refused to obey the new militia law, prompting Santa Anna to lead an army of thirty-five hundred men into the central highlands in May 1835. Determined to crush the federalist insurgency before it could spread, he decided to make an example of Zacatecas (a tactic he would later employ in Texas), allowing his troops to sack the city and loot the silver mines at nearby Fresnillo.[2]

After this show of force, only Coahuila y Texas refused to fall into line behind the new regime. The political situation there was chaotic. The turmoil in the capital had led to a power struggle between Coahuila federalist and centralist leaders, with each claiming to be the state's legitimate government. When the new commandant of the Eastern Interior Provinces, Martín Perfecto de Cos, sought to remove the federalist governor, Agustín Viesca, in June, Viesca called on Texans to come to his aid.[3]

The response to Viesca's plea was tepid at best. Hispano civic leaders in San Antonio, despite their long history of opposition to centralist rule, opted to stay neutral, hoping to avoid the same fate as Zacatecas. Having recently stepped down as political chief of the district, Juan Seguín managed to raise only two dozen men and set off for Monclova, the federalist state capital. Centralist troops arrested and imprisoned the governor before he arrived. There was even less appetite for an insurrection to defend Mexican federalism in the American settlements, where Viesca's call for volunteers was completely ignored. Most Anglo radicals had no interest whatsoever in collaborating with their Hispano neighbors, and when Seguín reached out to Anglo leaders to join the fight against the *santanistas*, his appeals were met with deafening silence.

The only serious signs of unrest occurred in Anahuac, where a new garrison had arrived to reestablish the port's customs office. The troops under the command of Captain Antonio Tenorio—forty men who lacked the proper arms and ammunition—hardly represented a serious military threat. Like Bradburn before him, Tenorio came quickly to the conclusion that Anglo-Texans had no intention of submitting to Mexican authority. Goaded once again by the irrepressible William Barret Travis, whose antics had earned him a reputation as something of a local *enfant terrible*, they soon ran off the customs agent, and in May set fire to the lumber that had been sent to rebuild the fort. In late June, Travis and a group of rowdies captured the garrison, much to the anger of many Anahuac residents. Condemnation of the assault on the garrison was so swift and widespread that Travis promptly released Tenorio and his men. Sensing the public mood, even the Whartons suggested that a public apology was in order. A chastened Travis would soon write to James Bowie: "Had we better not be quiet and settle down for awhile?"[4]

In San Antonio, Colonel Domingo Ugartechea, military commander of Texas, took the signs of civil unrest in the Anglo settlements seriously. It had been three years since his surrender to the Brazos rebels at Fort Velasco, and he had followed their activities with a wary eye ever since. The Fourth of July celebrations held in the American communities along the Brazos one week after the Ana-huac incident only increased Ugartechea's concerns. As in the United States, the American colonists commemorated the occasion with elaborate banquets, accompanied by toasts and rollicking speeches on the meaning of independence. At San Felipe, a particularly incen-diary address by a newspaper editor, Robert M. Williamson, not only denounced the centralist government but called for a preemptive strike against the garrison at San Antonio.

As worrying as these isolated acts of Anglo resistance appeared, Mexican authorities were far more alarmed by reports that the country's leading federalists intended to make Texas a beachhead of opposition to the Santa Anna regime. As early as March, even be-fore Zavala left his ministerial post in Paris, Mexican officials were reporting that he and Mexía were plotting to separate Texas from Mexico. In San Antonio, Ugartechea received instructions from General Cos to be on the lookout for the pair (and Gómez Farías too) and arrest them on sight. Despite Zavala's claim that he wanted to retire from politics, the government was under no illusions about his real intentions.[5]

Its fears were not unwarranted. Leaving Emily in New York, Zavala sailed for Texas in June, stopping first in New Orleans, where he met with Mexía and Gómez Farías to hatch the broad outlines of a plan to topple Santa Anna's regime. Zavala would work to incite a rebellion in Texas, while Mexía would raise money and volunteers for a military expedition on the Mexican coast. Gómez Farías would coordinate the resistance from New Orleans.[6]

The famous federalist sailed from New Orleans to Velasco during the first week in July. It was a risky undertaking, for he was now the focus of a manhunt, and the two Mexican vessels that plied the waters of the Texas coast enforcing customs laws had received orders to arrest him. Zavala arrived safely at Velasco, then char-tered a sloop to take him up the coast to his new home. As the craft approached Galveston Bay, the armed schooner *Correo* appeared. Quickly disembarking in a small rowboat, Zavala barely managed to avoid capture.[7]

Eventually making his way to Columbia, a village on the Brazos River, he began quizzing local residents about the prospects for an insurrection. Zavala did not get the response he expected. The man who had helped draft the Mexican constitution, who had dined with three American presidents, and who had been presented to the French court was met with indifference by some, icy suspicion by others. The farmers of the Lower Brazos did not have the faintest idea who he was. Said one dismissively: "We must depend on ourselves and not upon an aspiring Mexican."[8]

The news that Zavala had arrived in Texas elicited a very different reaction from Mexican authorities. Ugartechea promptly dispatched a courier to alert General Cos in Matamoros, who in turn notified Minister of War Tornel in the capital. Within a few weeks, Santa Anna, then residing on his estate near Veracruz, learned that his former ally and now bitter rival was in Texas plotting to overthrow him. As the news reverberated across Mexico, the unrest on the northern frontier took on a more threatening aspect for the Santa Anna regime. While William Barret Travis and Robert M. Williamson certainly made the Mexican government's most wanted list, General Cos's dispatches to Ugartechea left little doubt that Zavala was public enemy number one.[9]

Deciding that the situation in Texas required a more robust military presence, the commandant of the Eastern Interior Provinces now resolved to rush as many troops into the area as he could spare. A determined show of force, Cos reasoned, would stop the rebellion before it had a chance to take root, serving as a deterrent to anyone thinking about taking up arms. It turned out to be a serious miscalculation. In an effort to stop a war, Cos set a course that would guarantee that very result.

By August the first contingent of troops from Matamoros disembarked at the mouth of the San Antonio River and marched inland. During the next several weeks, Cos would send five hundred troops into South Texas, a force composed of regular infantry and artillery units, as well as militia companies from the towns along the Rio Grande. In San Antonio they quickly began to put a strain on local resources, as Ugartechea's garrison swelled in size to about one quarter of the town's population. While the young girls of Béxar, as one resident put it, "do not appear much displeased at some attention being paid to them," the troops posed a heavy burden for the town. Prosperous ranchers and merchants found the presence of the army especially inconvenient. Called upon to provide lodging for the officers, as well as to supply the troops with beef, grain, and other necessities, they had little hope of being repaid. Aware of the garrison's unpopularity, Ugartechea kept a watchful eye on those with known federalist loyalties, ordering two of his men to follow Juan Seguín.[10]

IF BÉXAR RESENTED THE ARRIVAL OF MEXICAN TROOPS, THE response in the Anglo-American settlements was nothing short of apoplectic. Recalling their forefathers' struggle for independence, they exhibited a deep and unabiding aversion to military occupation. Public statements by Cos and Ugartechea meant to allay colonists' fears had little effect amid reports that the government aimed "to flood the country with troops" and impose martial law. Inevitably, the wave of hysteria that swept the Anglo-American communities included dark scenarios of sexual defilement. "Behold your wives and daughters," one member of the Wharton faction shrieked, "are you prepared to yield them up to the embraces of a brutal soldiery?"[11]

Racial anxieties aggravated the colonists' growing sense of alarm. Migrants from the United States hailed overwhelmingly from the South and West, regions that vividly recalled British efforts to weaponize nonwhite peoples during the American Revolution and the War of 1812. On the cotton plantations of the Lower Brazos, settlers worried that the Mexican army might use the unrest to incite the enslaved population and "let them loose upon their families." In East Texas, hardscrabble farmers believed the forests would soon ring out with "the Indian yell, mingled with the Mexican cry." Such frightful scenarios seemed all the more plausible given the mixed-race character of the troops that were now landing along the Texas coast.

Drawn from Mexico's poorest classes, the rank and file consisted almost exclusively of dark-skinned Indians. One Anglo resident in San
Antonio reported that the Morelos Battalion included several blacks,
one of whom was a first sergeant, describing its commander as "a
complete hog with the exception of the tail."[12]

It did not help matters that the white settlements of Texas were
already on edge as a result of growing racial tensions in the United
States. In July, Brazos planters were rocked by the news of an elaborate plot to incite a slave rebellion along the Mississippi River. The
hysteria had sparked violence in Vicksburg, Memphis, and Natchez,
where lynch mobs hanged thirty-five blacks and their suspected
white co-conspirators. That same month, East Texas Anglos learned
of reports, later found to be false, that five thousand Alabama Creeks,
among the most warlike tribes of the Lower South, had refused to
relocate to the US Indian reserve created for them by the federal
government above the Red River and intended to make new homes
in Texas.[13]

Unfounded rumors and conspiracy theories aside, East Texas
whites actually had some reason to fear the prospect of a Mexican-
Indian alliance. In recent months relations between white settlers
and the East Texas tribes had deteriorated, resulting in the deaths of
four Indians, one of them a popular Caddo chief. Hoping to exploit
the situation, Ugartechea met with Chief Bowls in San Antonio and
dispatched agents to the villages of the immigrant tribes to recruit
warriors should trouble break out with Anglo colonists. Bowls gave
Ugartechea a respectful hearing, but he had come to regard Mexicans as undependable allies, deeply frustrated by the government's
failure to deliver on Terán's promise of Indian land ownership. Upon
his return to East Texas, the Cherokee leader held a council of local
head men, then sent William Goyens to Nacogdoches to inform civic
leaders of their deliberations. The immigrant tribes hoped to live
in peace with their Anglo neighbors, Goyens told them, but some
younger warriors preferred the path of war. Clearly, the Cherokees
were keeping their options open.[14]

In short, during the summer of 1835 Anglo-Texans labored under a farrago of fears, some real, some imagined. That did not mean, of course, that rebellion was inevitable. Most colonists would have certainly preferred to do nothing, wanting only to be left alone to tend to their crops and livestock. It would take a determined group of men to exploit those fears and to mobilize public opinion on behalf of a more confrontational policy—the same men who had organized the uprisings against the Bustamante government three years earlier.[15]

This time, they would be better organized. From their headquarters in Brazoria, William Wharton and his brother John ran the colony's only printing press, which published not only a weekly newspaper, the *Texas Republican*, but single-sheet broadsides that were circulated widely throughout the province. An able polemicist, the elder Wharton framed the growing crisis as a titanic battle against tyranny, a struggle worthy of the "sons of '76." Even more important, the Whartons used the press to promote a disinformation campaign designed to inflame the crisis. The mood of general anxiety gave way to unbridled panic as it was reported that three Mexican warships were anchored at the mouth of the Brazos (they turned out to be merchant vessels from New Orleans) and that the Mexican army had brought eight hundred sets of iron chains to enslave the colonists.[16]

The radicals also exhibited their political savvy at the grassroots level, working to gain control of the local committees formed during the summer to articulate colonists' grievances and share information. During the month of August the Wharton faction attended meetings in towns up and down the Brazos. Their message of resistance was not always welcomed. When the group showed up at a San Felipe meeting, a heated brawl ensued, and the gathering broke up amid threats of violence. More often than not, however, the radicals dominated the meetings, taking advantage of poor turnout and the colonists' general ignorance of political affairs. One eyewitness, decidedly unimpressed by these displays of the popular will, observed that those who attended "retired as ignorant as they came," adding, "They are dammd stupid & easily ruled by Demagogues and factions."[17]

Within the space of a little more than a month, the Whartons managed to rouse an indifferent Anglo community to action. Taking a defiant stand, the Columbia committee called for a new convention, or "Consultation," and further declared that it would not surrender Zavala, Travis, or anyone else to military authorities. Convinced that armed conflict was inevitable, by August they began purchasing powder and lead in New Orleans.[18]

As Texas drifted toward a violent rupture with Mexico, its most important advocate of peaceful compromise, Stephen F. Austin, was on his way home, having won his freedom under a general amnesty for political prisoners. The empresario's views regarding the colony's best way forward had changed during his involuntary sojourn in the nation's capital. Frustrated by the country's chronic political turmoil, he had abandoned any hope of statehood and now talked openly of an independent Texas. But Austin was still a cautious man; the time had not come to force the issue. Continued immigration from the United States, he believed, would allow the region to become fully "Americanized," as it continued to grow and prosper. "A gentle breeze," he wrote to a cousin upon his arrival in New Orleans, "shakes off a ripe peach."[19]

But the situation in Texas had changed dramatically since the empresario's almost two-and-a-half-year absence. Signs that the province teetered on the brink of war could be seen even before he left New Orleans. Boarding the schooner *San Felipe* on August 25, he found the ship laden with arms and munitions and outfitted with cannons manned by experienced artillerymen. Reaching his destination one week later, Austin and the other passengers had just disembarked at Velasco when the *Correo* approached. The two ships traded cannon fire until nightfall, as anxious residents watched along the beach. With its captain and several crew members seriously wounded, the *Correo* surrendered the next morning. The Texas Revolution had claimed its first casualties.

Austin, his past sins as an agent of compromise all but forgotten by the radicals, returned to a hero's welcome. At Brazoria, stronghold of the Wharton clan, citizens honored him with a lavish dinner and ball. The empresario delighted his hosts with a speech placing the blame for the unrest squarely on the political turbulence in the nation's capital. Going further, he endorsed the radicals' call for the Consultation, scheduled for mid-October. A few days later he rode up to San Felipe, where he moved into an unfurnished cabin. As if he had never left, he threw himself once again into the colony's political affairs. Upon learning that General Cos had sailed for the Texas coast and planned to take command of military operations in San Antonio, Austin, as chairman of the local committee of safety, issued a circular calling upon his colony to organize its militia and defend the Constitution of 1824. "War," the empresario now declared, "is our only resource."[20]

To Austin's stalwart supporters, his celebrated return to Texas marked a pivotal moment in the conflict with the Santa Anna regime. In his customary role of peacemaker, according to this view, he masterfully healed the divisions within the community, rallying hesitant settlers behind the cause of armed resistance. In fact, the radicals had already seized control of the narrative, and there was little he could do about it. As the naval battle between the *Correo* and the *San Felipe* made clear, the time for appeasement was over; the rebellion had already begun. To be sure, they were happy to have Austin's endorsement, which would help to bring wavering colonists to their side. "All eyes are turned towards you," William Barret Travis gushed in an ingratiating letter to the empresario. The destiny of Texas "is now completely in your hands." But the events of recent weeks left little doubt, as he wrote to fellow radical Henry Smith several days earlier, that "the tories are routed, horse and foot."[21]

ONE HUNDRED FIFTY MILES TO THE WEST, IN SAN ANTONIO, the tensions between Mexican Texans and military authorities were set aside, at least temporarily, as the town prepared to celebrate the nation's Independence Day, September 16. The *fiesta patria* had been in the planning stages for more than a month, with civic leaders and garrison officers all working together on half a dozen organizing committees. The day-long celebration opened at dawn with the pealing of church bells to signify the Grito de Dolores, Miguel Hidalgo's revolutionary call to arms in 1810. A series of carefully orchestrated events followed, including a thanksgiving mass at the San Fernando church, speeches by town elders, and a parade with decorated floats featuring a *reina* (beauty queen), all capped off by fandangos in the town's two main plazas, which were festooned with bunting and patriotic banners for the occasion.[22]

Mingling with the crowd, looking completely out of place, was a thirty-two-year-old South Carolinian, Samuel Maverick. He had arrived in town only a week before, taking lodgings at the home of one of San Antonio's two white residents. The son of a prosperous planter and merchant, Maverick had been educated at Yale, where he cultivated a taste for art and music. Trained as a lawyer, he seemed to be on a glide path to a bright future as a member of the state's planter elite. But Maverick, a loner who did not always bend to the dictates of convention, would follow his own course. When his father gave him a plantation to run in Alabama, he found that he did not like managing large numbers of slaves. Eager to find success on his own terms, he abruptly left and made tracks for Texas, with enough capital to set himself up in the land business.[23]

At first, the South Carolinian scouted real estate opportunities along the coast and in the Anglo-American settlements that dotted the river valleys of central Texas. It took him several months to make his way to San Antonio, but he seems to have quickly resolved to make it his permanent home. Never in robust health, Maverick was drawn to the dry climate, which offered an escape from the cholera and malaria that frequently ravaged the coastal lowlands. Despite its dangers as a target of Comanche raids, the town offered certain attractions for the farsighted investor. Though not as fertile or well-timbered as the lands that lay to the east, the surrounding countryside was eminently suitable for stock-raising and—most

14. Sam Maverick (1803–1870).
A native of South Carolina, Sam
Maverick arrived in Texas on the
eve of the Revolution. He would
eventually make San Antonio
his permanent home, becoming
one of the largest landowners in
Central and West Texas. Courtesy
of Legislative Reference Library,
State of Texas.

important, as far as Maverick was concerned—had not yet been
awarded to empresarios.

Still, his choice of San Antonio as a final destination was a curious one. Speaking no Spanish, and with little interest in learning, he
was not a man who could get a feel for another culture. The languid
rhythms of Hispanic life, so different from the mercenary world of
Jacksonian America, held no attraction for him. Offering no hint
of his impressions of San Antonio or its people, his journal entries
consisted only of prosaic musings on land values in the surrounding
area. Purchasing two tracts of land east of town soon after he arrived, Sam Maverick was singularly focused on the task at hand—to
make money.[24]

His timing could not have been worse. Mexican troops were still
landing on the coast and marching up to San Antonio as Ugartechea
fortified the garrison's position in the town. A crisis appeared to be
imminent. In late September the commander learned that the residents of Gonzales, on the Guadalupe River seventy miles to the east,
were in possession of a cannon the army had loaned the village for
defense against the Karankawa Indians. When the townsfolk refused
a request to surrender the ordnance, Ugartechea dispatched a one-
hundred-man cavalry unit to retrieve it. Reluctant to provoke armed

conflict, at least until Cos arrived to take charge of the situation, he instructed the captain in command of the detail to withdraw if he encountered resistance.

A handful of Gonzales settlers, eighteen in all, turned out to defy the order and sent riders to other Anglo communities for assistance. They were soon reinforced by some ranger companies that had just returned from a search-and-destroy mission against the Wichitas. The rangers searched but found little to destroy, spending two frustrating months scouring the upper reaches of the Brazos and Trinity rivers. Knowing little of the events that had brought the Anglo settlements to the brink of war during their absence, they nonetheless needed little persuading to join the growing crowd of settlers that refused to give up the cannon. Like so many Americans, they tended to frame all conflicts against perceived symbols of authority in historical terms, and stood ready to prove their worthiness as the heirs of their colonial forefathers.

The stand-off with Ugartechea's troops seemed especially well-suited to evoke parallels to the American revolutionary experience. Even their battle flag, a crude image of a cannon with the legend "Come and Take It," made from a silk wedding dress by the women of Gonzales, was a nod to the generation of their forefathers (Continental troops in Georgia had issued the same cry of defiance to Lord Cornwallis's forces in 1778). Lest there be any doubt about why they were fighting, a Methodist minister arrived that night and gave the men a rousing speech: "The same blood that animated the hearts of our ancestors of '76 still flows warm in our veins," the minister cried. "Let us go into battle with the words of the immortal Patrick Henry . . . deeply impressed upon our hearts . . . Give me Liberty or Give me Death!"[25]

With the memory of the American Revolution permeating the discourse of Anglo resistance, it was no wonder that the Texans' behavior began to take on a weirdly performative character. The men gathered along the banks of the Guadalupe River had become, for all intents and purposes, historical re-enactors in a struggle against tyranny and military despotism.

Early the next morning, for the third time in less than a decade, Americans claiming Mexican citizenship took up arms in open rebellion against their adopted country. Two soldiers were reported killed in the fighting, and Ugartechea's men soon withdrew, heading back up the road to San Antonio.

The Americans of Texas now had their Lexington.[26]

ELEVEN

SOLELY, PURELY, SIMPLY AMERICAN

A RUBICON HAD BEEN CROSSED ON THE GUADALUPE RIVER, but Colonel Ugartechea did not yet know it. When his troops returned to San Antonio with news of the skirmish, he penned a polite letter to his "esteemed friend," Stephen F. Austin. He had always conducted himself "like a gentleman" in his dealings with the Anglo-American colonists. He asked the empresario to use his influence to have the cannon returned.[1]

But there was no turning back for the province's white settlers, who were now arming themselves and heading for Gonzales. For the Whartons, the moment they had been waiting for had finally arrived. When word of the clash reached Brazoria, William Wharton was busy printing off broadsides, calling on area residents to take up arms against Mexican troops. Within seventy-two hours he dashed off two more, one of which offered a bounty of $5,000 for the death or capture of General Cos. He then set out with his brother John for the town on the Guadalupe, 120 miles away. Recognizing the seriousness of the situation, Stephen F. Austin came down from San Felipe, so sick with fever that he had to be lifted onto his horse to make the trip.[2]

In Gonzales they found three hundred men milling about, ready to engage the Mexican army and waiting only for someone to lead them. A mutual friend of Wharton's and Austin's arranged a meeting between the two leaders, where they agreed to put an end to their long-simmering feud. The reconciliation would not last, but in the exuberance of the moment the Whartons placed Austin's name in nomination to command the army, which promptly elected him by acclamation. In high spirits, the throng of farmers and ranchers then headed west, to lay siege to General Cos's garrison in San Antonio.[3]

The Anglo-Americans on the Guadalupe River were not the only Texans eager for a fight with the Mexican army. When Juan Seguín heard the news of the clash at Gonzales, he quietly slipped out of San Antonio and rode to nearby ranchos, rustling up a few dozen volunteers, young Hispano men known to him since child-hood. They joined Austin's growing army on the outskirts of town. Anglos and Hispanos also banded together in South Texas. The area's most prominent ranching clan, the De León family, enjoyed close economic ties with the Americans and were staunch federalists. After seizing the presidio at Goliad, where General Cos had left a small contingent of troops to guard his supply line to the coast, De León son-in-law Placido Benavides rode to San Antonio with thirty men. Skilled horsemen, Texas Hispanos led by Seguín and Benavides would play an important role in the weeks that followed, serving as scouts and foraging for Austin's army.

Even as Anglo settlers and Mexican rancheros prepared to fight centralist troops outside San Antonio, they could not ignore the region's many other inhabitants. Not long after Austin's volunteers made camp, a Comanche raiding party stampeded their horses. Along the Gulf Coast, the Karankawas, who had rarely bothered Anglo residents in recent years, exploited the unrest to test the limits of white authority, committing a rash of thefts and murders. And from East Texas came the troubling news that a party of white surveyors caught trespassing on Cherokee lands had killed three Indians. Fear-ing reprisals, some anxious settlers suddenly had second thoughts about joining the rebel army, opting to stay home to protect their families.[4]

Most alarming of all were the reports from Brazoria. On the way to San Antonio Austin received word that an enslaved uprising had broken out on the plantations of the Lower Brazos. Little is known about the revolt, or even if there really was one. With slaveholders already on edge, especially now that "wild Africans" made up such a large part of their workforce, the plot may well have been the product of overheated imaginations. Their response, however, was all too real. Planters seized as many as one hundred bondsmen suspected of involvement in the uprising. Alleged ringleaders were hanged; many were whipped "nearly to death."[5]

AMID THE GROWING INSTABILITY, THE REBELS TURNED TO THE United States for aid. News of the fighting reached Louisiana in a matter of days, followed by urgent calls from Texas leaders for men and supplies. Characterizing the recent arrival of General Cos's troops as an "invasion," such appeals all but ignored Mexican sovereignty over the region, stressing instead the common heritage that the colonists of Texas shared with the people of the United States. Acting on his own authority, Sam Houston published a public letter in the Louisiana newspapers as soon as he heard of the fighting, offering "liberal bounties of land" to any man who came with "a good rifle and one hundred rounds of ammunition."[6]

In the barrooms and hotels of New Orleans, and anywhere young men gathered in the Crescent City, all the talk was of Texas. A community of Mexican exiles led by Mexía and Gómez Farías had already held public meetings and generated some interest in the federalist cause. But the news of the skirmish between American colonists and Mexican troops on the Guadalupe River truly electrified the Crescent City. Local businessmen now began to take the lead in support of the rebels, pledging money, manpower, and material aid. Their motives were not purely altruistic. A Texas free of centralist rule, they reasoned, would open the door for the commercial exploitation of the region. And a Texas free of Mexican control entirely, preferably as part of the United States, offered the prospect of even greater financial rewards.

On October 13, civic leaders held a raucous, pro-Texas meeting at the Banks Arcade on Magazine Street. Hundreds of young men crowded into the block-long coffee house and emporium, where they roared their approval as civic leaders exhorted them to make the Texas cause their own. In flagrant violation of US neutrality laws, the meeting's organizers promised to arm, outfit, and pay the expenses of all who volunteered. More than 120 men signed up on the spot. Within a few days a regiment calling itself the New Orleans Greys, dressed in smart-looking grey uniforms and sealskin caps, was en route to Texas.[7]

Mexía attended the meeting at the Banks Arcade, but he was not invited to address the crowd. He could not have failed to notice that the speakers that evening said little about federalism or the restoration of the Constitution of 1824. It was not an oversight. Privately, the event's organizers admitted that they wanted nothing to do with the Mexican exiles. As one put it, the outpouring of enthusiasm for the Texas cause was "solely, purely, simply American."[8]

Despite these warning signs, Mexía's eagerness to join the rebellion remained undimmed. He had always gotten along well with the Americans, and he did not share the suspicions of some federalists that US support for the Texas insurgency might conceal a hidden agenda. Three years earlier, when he visited Austin's colony after the attack on Fort Velasco, William Wharton and the Brazos radicals assured him that they were loyal Mexican citizens. He had probably read Wharton's public statement after the 1832 unrest, in which he declared the colonists' desire to see Mexico united until "the end of time." It seems never to have occurred to him that the struggle of Anglo-Texans and Mexican liberals might not be one and the same.[9]

By the end of October, even Colonel Ugartechea must have realized that the minor fracas over a small cannon in the village of Gonzales had triggered a series of reverberations felt across Texas and beyond. And yet what the rebels were actually fighting for remained very much a matter of opinion.

There were, broadly speaking, three points of view. Mexican federalists, whether they were local leaders like Seguín or men of power and influence like Mexía, saw the conflict in strictly national terms. For more than a year, they had angrily watched the Santa Anna regime attempt to strip away the powers of the states, and they were determined to restore the principles enshrined in the Constitution of 1824. Stephen F. Austin occupied a middle ground. Caution had always been his default position, and he was reluctant to endorse secession, at least for now, knowing that such a drastic step would alienate Mexican allies, and possibly lead them to support the government's effort to put down the revolt. Wharton and the radicals favored an immediate declaration of independence. If they had ever taken their obligations of Mexican citizenship seriously—and certainly, many never did—that time had passed. Having always regarded Mexico's claim to Texas as tenuous at best, they were determined to sever their attachments to their adopted country once and for all.[10]

For the present, these divergent goals would be set aside as Texas rebels faced their first major test: ridding the province of the centralist forces under General Cos in San Antonio. But it was now mid-October, and they were ill-prepared for a prolonged campaign, few having brought tents or even cold-winter clothing. Without siege guns, the rebel army's options were limited; it could either storm the town or wait until Cos ran out of provisions.

Putting Austin in command turned out to be a mistake, and Wharton quickly regretted it. Even the most charismatic leaders found Anglo-American volunteers to be an unruly, insubordinate lot, and the challenges Austin faced were especially daunting. Always in delicate health, he lacked any formal military training or experience, and had little in common with his senior officers—loud, ambitious firebrands like James Bowie, William Barret Travis, and James Walker Fannin—who held strong opinions of their own about tactics and strategy and did not hesitate to share them.

Their confidence in Austin was further eroded when Sam Houston made an appearance in the rebel camp in late October. Astride a yellow Spanish mustang that was so small his feet almost touched the ground, Houston had come over from San Felipe, having been elected to serve as a delegate from Nacogdoches to the Consultation. Mingling easily with his friend Wharton, James Bowie, and Austin's other senior officers, he pronounced the ragtag force totally inadequate to engage the Mexican army and recommended that it fall back to Gonzales until cannons, supplies, and reinforcements could arrive from New Orleans.[11]

Houston's military assessment was undoubtedly valid. At the same time, he had his own reasons for discouraging the siege. With some battlefield experience to his credit, having fought under Andrew Jackson in the Creek Wars, Houston was widely seen as a likely candidate to head the Texas army, a post he badly wanted. He did not stay long in the rebel camp—just long enough to sow doubts about Austin's leadership. A few days later, a detachment under James Bowie clashed with Ugartechea's troops at the Concepción mission, three miles south of San Antonio. As the Mexicans retreated, Austin ordered his troops to pursue their advantage, hoping to bring about a quick end to the siege. Bowie and other officers overruled him, insisting that the town was too well fortified.[12]

The empresario may have been even more upset by the fact that as commander of the rebel forces outside San Antonio, he could do little to influence the deliberations of the Consultation in San Felipe. The meeting, which had been scheduled before the fighting at Gonzales, now assumed heightened importance and would set the course of the rebellion in the months ahead. As a check on the radicals, Austin endorsed his friend Zavala to chair the proceedings, but when the delegates achieved a quorum in early November they chose Branch T. Archer, a close friend of the Whartons, instead. Despite this initial setback, Austin's friends were well-represented at the Consultation, which took up the issue of independence as its first order of business. To the empresario's relief, the measure was rejected by a 33–14 margin, the delegates opting for a vague declaration of loyalty to the Constitution of 1824.

The vote was not the defeat for the radicals that it appeared, however. Some delegates viewed the decision to reject secession as a prudent but temporary measure, reasoning that it would take time for volunteers to arrive from the United States. A formal Declaration of Causes, drafted by John Wharton, made it clear that the rebels' allegiance to the Mexican republic was purely conditional. Texas was not morally "bound by the Compact of Union" under the current government, the Declaration stated, and would only remain part of Mexico if federalism was restored.[13]

The extent of the radicals' influence at the meeting would become clear in other ways. The group easily secured the election of Sam Houston as commander-in-chief to lead the regular army. Turning to the matter of a provisional rebel government, the delegates created a General Council made up of representatives from each district, and chose as governor another Wharton crony, Henry Smith, over Austin by a comfortable margin. The Consultation also took actions that could only be made by an independent government, offering land to American volunteers, and appointing a three-man commission (later naming Austin, William Wharton, and Branch T. Archer) to travel to the United States to secure loans and recruit men for the war effort. In short, the delegates affirmed their loyalty to Mexico and the Constitution of 1824 in principle, but they had set a course that could lead to only one outcome: Texas's eventual separation from Mexican rule.[14]

WHILE ANGLO-AMERICANS IN TEXAS WERE INCHING TOWARD SEcession, in New Orleans José Antonio Mexía was still fighting for Mexican federalism. For several weeks he had been recruiting and arming men at his own expense to launch an attack on Santa Anna's regime. Details of the expedition were shrouded in secrecy. Some of the volunteers may not have known their destination and simply assumed they were bound for the Texas Gulf Coast—or so they would later claim. In fact, the first major engagement of the antigovernment revolt in the northern provinces would not take place in Texas at all, but at the port of Tampico, 250 miles below the mouth of the Rio Grande.

Why Tampico? A veteran of the country's civil wars, Mexía was following a well-tested playbook, and knew that control of the customs houses held the key to any successful effort to overthrow the government. As Mexico's second largest port on the Atlantic, Tampico collected revenue that the cash-strapped army needed to pay its troops. Having been informed that some officers in the Tampico garrison were ready to join the rebellion, Mexía intended to seize the town, then march north to the smaller port of Matamoros on the Rio Grande. With both customs houses in federalist hands, Cos would be unable to supply his army in San Antonio. A major campaign to recover the province would also be out of the question. With all of northeastern Mexico in federalist hands, Gómez Farías, Zavala, and Mexía would then be free to plot their next move against Santa Anna's regime.[15]

On November 6, Mexía sailed out of New Orleans with 160 adventurers, most of them Americans. The expedition arrived at Tampico eight days later, but things had already begun to go wrong. Unbeknownst to Mexía, the garrison commander had been tipped off to the plot and arrested the ringleaders, putting down the mutiny before it could take place. Landing under cover of darkness, Mexía's schooner ran aground off the bar in the Tampico harbor. After several hours trying to dislodge the vessel, the filibusters waded ashore, their firearms water-logged, their gunpowder ruined, the element of surprise lost.

Mexía attacked the Tampico garrison shortly after midnight the following day. With little ammunition, his raw recruits failed to take the town, abandoning the assault after two hours of fighting. Several filibusters lay dead on the streets, and more than thirty had been captured, many of them seriously wounded. Retreating to a stockade at the mouth of the harbor, Mexía and his followers waited for local troops to rally to the federalist cause. None did, but the Tampico garrison showed little interest in pressing its advantage. Twelve days later, with no help in sight, Mexía used his remaining funds to charter another vessel and sailed north. Setting a course for the Texas coast, he would join the Americans in the fight against centralism.[16]

Most Anglo-Texans gave little thought to Mexía's Tampico expedition, if they thought of it at all. But it was anything but a sideshow as far as Santa Anna was concerned. Already angry that Zavala was in Texas fomenting rebellion, the president was furious to learn that the assault on the port town had been led by Zavala's closest friend, a man whose career he had done much to advance. While Santa Anna seethed over what he regarded as a personal betrayal, his minister of war, José María Tornel, saw a wider conspiracy at work. Having paved the way for Santa Anna's return to power as the author of the Plan of Cuernavaca, Tornel had emerged as the president's chief adviser and confidant. Deeply suspicious of the United States, he had been warning for years that American immigration would lead to the eventual loss of Texas, and he now believed that the Jackson administration not only approved of the insurgency, but was actively orchestrating it.

There were plenty of disturbing signs of Washington's complicity in the Texas crisis. Officially, the Jackson administration insisted that it would take no part in Mexico's internal struggles. Yet it had done nothing to tamp down public enthusiasm for the insurgency, or to stop Americans from using the port of New Orleans as a rebel launching pad. Nor could Santa Anna and Tornel fail to notice the rebel government's appointment of a Jackson protégé, Sam Houston, to lead the Texas army. But if Mexico's leaders wanted evidence of Washington's involvement in stirring up unrest on the country's northern frontier, they needed to look no further than Jackson's minister to Mexico, Anthony Butler. The American diplomat had been at his post for five years, and his tactless and increasingly desperate efforts to buy Texas for the United States, not to mention the fact that he stood to profit from the deal as one of Zavala and Mexía's business partners, had won him no friends at the National Palace. Now, in the fall of 1835, Tornel was stunned to learn that the US minister, having traveled to Washington earlier in the year, had stopped off in Texas on his way back to the capital, where he was urging Anglo colonists to declare their independence! While there is no evidence that the freewheeling Butler was acting on the orders of his government, Tornel harbored no doubt that Washington was now ready to acquire Texas by force if necessary—aided and abetted, of course, by two willing Mexican conspirators—Zavala and Mexía.[17]

Determined to put a stop to American interference in what was clearly a domestic matter, Tornel announced a new policy that would set the tone for the government's response to the rebellion in Texas. Known as the Tornel Decree, the order promised no quarter for American filibusters. Armed foreigners found on Mexican soil "will be deemed pirates and dealt with as such," since they were "fighting under no recognized flag." As an example to other Americans who might have thoughts of joining the insurgents, the government held a hasty trial and executed the Tampico prisoners by firing squad.[18]

AT THE REBEL CAMP OUTSIDE SAN ANTONIO, THE SITUATION continued to deteriorate. After almost a month in the field and with no end to the siege in sight, the army grew restless. As morale sagged, some of Austin's men deserted. Those who stayed got drunk, slept through reveille, and refused to line up into company formations. By the first week in November the army was so disorganized that there was some doubt that it could even maintain a siege of the town.[19]

Sam Houston was not helping matters. As commander-in-chief of the regular army, which did not yet exist, he had no authority over the volunteers camped outside San Antonio and tried to undermine Austin at every turn. From San Felipe he corresponded with Wharton and some of Austin's officers, who kept him apprised of the mood in camp. When not engaged in the business of the Consultation, he spent much of his time carousing and denouncing the "little Gentleman," as he called the empresario, to anyone who would listen.[20]

A forlorn figure, Austin knew about the whisper campaign against him and was stung by the criticism. More important, he knew that his enemies were dominating the Consultation, and he desperately wanted to lend his voice to the moderates in San Felipe. In a plaintive letter full of the self-pity his critics found so annoying, he offered to resign his post if a "more competent" commander could be found, reminding the delegates that he had never "pretended to be a military man." That same day, a disgusted Wharton packed up and left, tendering his resignation with a curt letter stating that "no good will be achieved by this army except by the merest accident under heaven."[21]

Austin had other problems, too: the fragile alliance with Mexican federalists was quickly unravelling. Juan Seguín, a close personal friend of Austin's, never wavered in his commitment to the rebellion. But to the southeast many Hispanos were having second thoughts. At Goliad, the rebel commander, Phillip Dimmit, a longtime resident who had married into the De León family, initially supported federalism, but soon antagonized the Mexican community, allowing his Anglo volunteers to steal horses, loot stores, and ransack homes. Within a matter of days, several hundred Mexican residents abandoned the town, fleeing to the relative safety of nearby ranchos.[22]

Dimmit made things worse when the federalist governor of Coahuila y Texas, Agustín Viesca, showed up shortly afterward. Having escaped from a prison in Monterrey, he fully expected to take charge of the rebel movement in Texas. Dimmit had other ideas, refusing to acknowledge him as the duly elected governor of the state, a snub so offensive to the Mexican townspeople that it almost provoked a riot. Viesca proceeded to San Felipe, where an equally cold reception awaited him from Governor Smith, who made no secret of his opinion that all Mexicans, regardless of their political persuasion, were "inimical and treacherous."[23]

Austin did his best to minimize the political fallout. The empresario ordered Dimmit removed from command, and the same day issued a proclamation to remind Texas Hispanos that the rebels were still fighting to restore the Constitution of 1824. But in San Felipe the newly formed General Council saw nothing wrong with Dimmit's insult to the state's governor; it overruled Austin and restored his command. Barely a month after declaring its loyalty to the constitution, the rebel government had made it abundantly clear that it did not need or want any help from Mexican federalists.[24]

Beset on all sides, Austin finally received one bit of good news. A detachment of the New Orleans Greys, resplendent in their new uniforms, marched into camp, bringing two cannons with them. Deciding to make one last attempt to break the siege, the empresario drew up a plan of attack to storm the town in the predawn hours of November 22. But once again he found his leadership thwarted by

his senior officers. Two hours before the assault was scheduled to begin, several captains who had been in contact with Houston refused
to take part. A deeply frustrated and disappointed Austin resigned
two days later.[25]

Command of the rebel army now passed to Edward Burleson, a
hardened, semiliterate Indian fighter. He would have no better luck
keeping his troops in line than Austin. As temperatures plummeted
below freezing, many volunteers began to drift away. They were
done for the winter, and would be back when—or if—the Mexican
army mounted an expedition into Texas in the spring. By early December Burleson's army had dwindled to about three hundred men.
Many were Americans, who had come to Texas for a fight and had no
other place to go; about half were Hispanos, for whom San Antonio
was home.

Just when it looked as if there would be no battle, Sam Maverick appeared in camp, accompanied by the other two Americans
living in San Antonio. Placed under house arrest when General
Cos occupied the town, they had been put to work alongside Mexican soldiers clearing brush, erecting breastworks, and fortifying
the Alamo mission. Assuring the Mexican commander that they
would return to the United States, they instead rode straight to the
rebel camp, bringing vital information. The garrison was running
desperately low on supplies, they told Burleson, and some of Cos's
men were beginning to desert. They urged an immediate attack.
But the Texans' morale was not much better, and even Burleson
now favored calling off the siege. Only an inspirational appeal from
Ben Milam, a grizzled adventurer and entrepreneur who had been
kicking around Mexico since the War of Independence, rallied the
dispirited troops. At last, the bickering came to an end. After six
weeks outside San Antonio, a consensus to attack the town had finally been reached.[26]

In the darkness before dawn on December 5, with Maverick
and one of his companions leading the way, the rebels silently stole
into town from the north, bypassing the Alamo mission, where a
large contingent of Mexican troops was garrisoned. Cos's artillery

batteries in the main plaza stalled their advance, forcing them to seize a block of houses near the river, where they battered down walls and dug trenches to secure their position. When a cannon ball ripped into the leg of one of the New Orleans volunteers, Maverick helped drag him to safety, then assisted in an impromptu amputation as the battle raged around them. The wounded man begged for a pistol to end his life, but would survive, rejoining the Texas army five months later.[27]

The battle for the town now became for the rebel army a slow, grinding slog toward the city center. Fighting house to house, then room to room, the volunteers pried open doors and tore holes through the walls of residents' homes, inching closer to the square. As terrified Hispano residents fled, Cos's cannons pummeled the buildings where the rebels had taken refuge. During a lull in the battle on the third day, Ben Milam was killed by a Mexican sniper's bullet. As the Texan fell backward, his skull shattered, Maverick caught the lifeless body in his arms. It would take four full days of fighting before the Texans finally succeeded in capturing strategic positions on the main plaza. Cos ordered his troops to abandon their positions in town and retreat to the Alamo mission, but all knew the battle was lost, four companies of cavalry deserting that night. As the sun rose over the town on December 9, the attackers spotted a white flag flying over the mission walls.[28]

The Texas rebels could claim an impressive victory against a much larger Mexican army, one that had been achieved with Anglos and Hispanos fighting together. It would be the only time Mexican Texans lent their support to the cause in significant numbers. Juan Seguín and a cadre of young Bexareño men stood ready should Mexican troops return, but a large number of their friends and neighbors were tired of war. The siege had exhausted San Antonio's food supplies and caused enormous damage to the town. And it was becoming clear that the contest had little to do with restoring Mexican federalism. The rebel government's refusal to acknowledge Viesca as the legitimate leader of the insurrection angered many Hispanos, especially in the southeast. With more volunteers arriving daily from the United States, the conflict began to assume an entirely different character, one many Mexican Texans refused to support.

Mexía knew nothing of these developments when he landed with his bedraggled followers on the Texas coast in early December. Exhausted and penniless, the federalist leader nonetheless remained undaunted and ready to fight on. The abortive attack on Tampico had been a serious setback, but he was at least encouraged by the news of Viesca's escape to Texas. Writing immediately to the deposed governor, Mexía told him he intended to recruit a new force and attack Matamoros. He was stunned to learn that the federalist leader was not directing the rebellion after all. Setting aside his growing misgivings, he placed himself at the disposal of Governor Smith. For three weeks Mexía waited for an answer on the Lower Brazos. He never received a reply.[29]

If Mexía had any doubts about the intentions of the Texas colonists, they would soon be dispelled when Dimmit's Goliad garrison, ignoring the Consultation's vote against secession, issued a declaration of independence of its own. Although disavowed by the General Council, the document confirmed for wary federalists what had long been obvious: the rebellion would now be a fight to separate Texas from Mexican rule. Tearing aside the veil of racial cooperation, Dimmitt assumed a tone of condescending benevolence toward the Mexican people, who were "strangers to the blessings of regulated liberty." It was now up to "the North-Americans of Texas" to show them the way.[30]

Mexía had seen enough. It was apparent, he wrote in a remarkably restrained letter to the General Council, that his services in Texas were neither "desired or necessary." Making his way to Velasco, he would wait for the next ship to take him back to New Orleans.[31]

TWELVE

TWO ARMIES

T HE DAY BEFORE CHRISTMAS, MEXÍA BOARDED THE *WILLIAM Robbins* at Velasco. Already despondent over the direction the revolt had taken, he was not looking forward to the trip. The passenger list included Stephen F. Austin, William H. Wharton, and Branch T. Archer, the three men delegated by the Consultation to solicit aid for Texas in the United States. At least Mexía could commiserate with Austin, one of a dwindling number of Americans who still believed that Anglos and Hispanos needed to work together to defeat Santa Anna's regime. But Wharton and Archer were both dedicated secessionists, as was another passenger, Wharton's brother John, who was on his way to New Orleans to purchase war materials for the rebel army.

Austin may have been dreading the voyage even more than Mexía. He was pretty sure the elder Wharton and Houston had conspired against him to undermine his command during the siege of San Antonio. And the brothers were still scheming to promote independence, in defiance of the Consultation's vote on the issue. As usual, he took it personally, convinced that their efforts were "more devoted to injure me than to serve the country." The five men would be sharing close quarters on the sixty-foot schooner. It was going to be an awkward seven days.[1]

The voyage only confirmed for Mexía how wrong he had been about the Americans. United in their hostility toward the *santanista* regime, they had little else in common. The Whartons and Archer, a close friend of the brothers who for a time lived at Eagle Island, no longer bothered to hide their disdain for the Mexican people. And though Austin made every effort to be civil, the fact remained that even he saw an alliance with northern federalists as a tactical strategy, a temporary marriage of convenience until Texas was ready to go its own way.

Mexía disembarked at the port of New Orleans and disappeared into the crowd. For the past fourteen years—all of his adult life—his fortunes had been inextricably linked to Texas. The young translator who accompanied Richard Fields and Chief Bowls to Mexico City in 1822 had been one of the first Mexicans to see the enormous profits to be made in Texas lands, profits that could only be realized by foreign immigration. He had ignored the warnings of some Mexican leaders who saw the obvious danger in allowing the northern frontier to be populated by settlers from the United States. Perhaps, in his more reflective moments, he could admit that he had played no small part in the chain of events that led to Texas's separation from Mexican rule.

Mexía would have nothing more to do with the rebellion, but Santa Anna had not seen the last of him. He remained committed to the overthrow of the centralist regime, and he would return to Mexico three years later to lead yet another federalist revolt against his former mentor. Captured after a bloody battle at Puebla in May 1839, he was told that he would be executed in three hours. According to one account of his capture, possibly apocryphal, Mexía replied, "Santa Anna is very generous. If I had made him prisoner, I would not have given him fifteen minutes."[2]

A VERY DIFFERENT RECEPTION AWAITED THE THREE TEXAS COM-missioners in New Orleans. Kicking off their public relations tour of the United States with a pro-Texas meeting soon after their arrival, they were given a welcome that by all accounts was even more enthusiastic than the earlier ones held in the port city. Deeply impressed, Austin decided that Wharton had been right all along;

American business leaders were ready to support the Texas cause, but only if the goal was complete separation from Mexico. "*I go for independence*," he wrote emphatically to his cousin the following day. "I have no doubt we shall get aid, as much as we need and perhaps more." The empresario's sudden conversion to the radical agenda left his friends in Texas baffled and angry, prompting some to wonder if the indecisiveness his critics attributed to him might have some basis in fact. Austin, Wharton, and Archer soon split up, traveling the country to promote the Texas cause. The wild reception accorded the commissioners in New Orleans would be repeated everywhere they went.[3]

A few Northern editors attempted to throw cold water on the pro-Texas mania. Any Americans who joined the rebellion, they argued, would not only be involving themselves in the affairs of a foreign country, but acting to expand the slave empire. "What would we say," asked a New York newspaper, "if in Haiti a public meeting decided to arm and equip a body of troops to be sent against us for the purpose of helping our colored population to shake off the yoke of slavery?"[4]

There would be no lack of enthusiasm in the South, where support for the rebellion came to be known as the "Texas Fever." Scores of towns held pro-Texas meetings similar to those in New Orleans to raise money and recruit volunteers for the rebel cause. Georgia, Kentucky, Alabama, and Mississippi all organized regiments, while recruiting stations quickly appeared in major cities on the Mississippi River and the Gulf Coast. Most of the volunteers were armed and outfitted through private donations, though in Georgia public support for the rebellion was so overwhelming that the legislature supplied the Georgia Battalion with muskets from the state arsenal. Whole communities were caught up in the groundswell of martial fervor. Women's leagues designed and sewed flags, sashes, and uniforms for the volunteers, who were given a rousing send-off with parades and banquets. Greeted by cheering crowds in the towns they passed, the regiments picked up new volunteers along the way. "The Texas fever has treated us worse than the cholera," one Georgia editor observed. "Journeymen, apprentices, men and boys, devils and angels, are all gone to Texas!"[5]

Though eager to fight, the volunteers knew little of war. While the regiments were often led by older men who could claim a modicum of military experience, the overwhelming majority of enlistees were so-called holiday soldiers. Their ranks included farm boys, shop clerks, carpenters, and schoolteachers. They had grown to manhood in an agrarian South, a pastoral world very different from that of the previous generation, which had seized the land, often violently, from indigenous peoples. Some may have belonged to local militia units which, absent the need for civil defense, had become little more than male social clubs. Many had no military training at all.

The volunteers did not know much about Texas, either. "They did not stop to inquire from what causes sprang the Revolution," one American later wrote. "It was enough for them to know that it had already begun." Aside from New Orleans, which was home to a large Latin American community and the main commercial hub between the United States and the former Spanish colonies, the American press had devoted little attention to political affairs in Mexico. As a result, Americans who learned of civil strife in Texas for the first time in 1835 were generally ignorant of the decade-long power struggle between federalists and centralists. Press coverage of the events in Texas presented the conflict as one of moral absolutes, a struggle between peaceful American settlers and a brutal, despotic regime.[6]

Few paused to consider the larger implications of a conflict that would expand the limits of slavery. Rather, they saw themselves engaged in a noble mission to rescue their countrymen from foreign "thralldom." For some, casting the struggle as a holy crusade allowed them to give purpose to their own lives. John Sowers Brooks was an ambitious Virginia native who longed to do something of consequence. Twenty-one years old, he had yet to find himself, his career path thus far having brought him only frustration and disappointment. Starting out as an apprentice in the newspaper business, he lasted only a few months, finding the work dull. A brief stint as an officer in the US Marines proved similarly unfulfilling. After less than a year, he was so homesick and miserable that his father had to pull strings to secure an early discharge, a minor family scandal that left him burdened by feelings of shame. Employed as a bartender when the rebellion broke out, he urged his family to "forget all my errors and follies," and expressed the hope that he might one day be worthy of their esteem.[7]

Convinced that a greater destiny awaited him, Brooks jumped at the opportunity to enlist when he heard of the fighting in Texas. Without consulting his family he booked passage on the first ship he could find bound for the Gulf Coast, and in December 1835 he washed up, quite literally, on Velasco beach, the schooner on which he was traveling having run aground in a thunderstorm. He lost most of his belongings in the shipwreck, but with letters of introduction from prominent Virginians he secured a position as adjutant of the Georgia Battalion, which had also just arrived. Tedious though he found the task of drilling raw recruits, he looked forward excitedly to the struggle ahead, boasting that it would end at the capital of "Santa Anna's iron ruled dominions." His letters to his family left little doubt that he believed he had embarked upon a cause worthy of his ambition. "We are all animated by one spirit," he wrote to his father, "defiance to tyrants."[8]

Others took a less romantic view, motivated purely by their own self-interest. The offer of land bounties for military service was a significant draw for many, the chance to establish a stake in a rapidly expanding agricultural economy. For men of substance, Texas presented the lure of even greater wealth, an opportunity to parlay a modest capital investment into a fortune. In an age of rampant speculation, when white American men threw themselves headlong into all manner of get-rich-quick schemes, few were more relentless in their pursuit of the main chance than Thomas Jefferson Green. Thirty-four years old in 1835, with a prominent nose and hair that curled around unusually large ears, Green was a whirlwind of entrepreneurial activity. He had spent his adult life dashing from one land deal to the next, only to move on to some new undertaking that held the promise of even greater reward. A zealous self-promoter who seemed to know everyone, or at least pretended to, Green had married a cousin of the Wharton brothers before moving to the Florida territory, where he owned a cotton and sugar plantation and a racetrack. But land speculation offered the quickest route to wealth, and Texas had been on his radar for some time. Back in 1830 he formed the Tallahassee-Texas Land Company, in violation of the Mexican government's anti-immigration law, and claimed to have acquired more than one hundred thousand acres of prime cotton growing land below the Red River. When the rebellion broke out, Green, convinced that land prices would now "rise tenfold," mortgaged his holdings in Florida and beat a path for Texas, placing his four-year-old son in the care of the Whartons in Nashville. "Now is the time," he wrote to an acquaintance, "for enterprize and honor and fortunes."[9]

Green had political aspirations, too, and for Jacksonian American males a career in public life often began on the battlefield. Before the rebellion had run its course, it would provide countless examples of men plucked from obscurity by acts of valor. Green's elevation to the ranks of Texas's leading men, however, had more to do with connections than courage. Arriving in Texas in the spring of 1836, he found the rebel government in temporary residence at Jared Groce's plantation on the Brazos River. Offering to return to the United States and recruit volunteers, he was rewarded with a brigadier general's commission, despite the fact that his military experience consisted of a four-month stint at West Point in his teens. Though he would take no part in the fighting, he would be known as "General" Thomas Jefferson Green for the rest of his life.

Even prominent Americans were swept up in the "Texas Fever." In early January 1836, there appeared in Nacogdoches a company of armed volunteers led by one of the most famous men in the United States, former Tennessee congressman David Crockett. Almost fifty years old, his rise to national celebrity had been an improbable one. Born in what is now eastern Tennessee, like many his military career had been brief. He had served as a scout in the campaigns against the Creek Indians in 1813, and by his own account had little taste for military service. Later, he pursued careers as a farmer and a businessman, with little success. But his affable, outgoing personality served him well in the boisterous world of local politics, especially at a time when many rural voters were inclined to favor men of their own class rather than traditional elites. Though he cultivated a backwoods public image that emphasized his humble origins and lack of formal education, Crockett was hardly a rube. Winning election to Congress in 1827 as a Jacksonian Democrat, he took his legislative duties seriously. Following his own conscience, he gained national attention as a champion of the oppressed, voting against the Indian Removal Act and defending the land claims of poor squatters in his district. His stand on these issues put him at odds with the Jackson political machine, which secured his defeat after two terms in office.[10]

Crockett might well have faded into obscurity had his homespun wit not caught the attention of James Kirke Paulding, a New York playwright and author. Paulding's 1831 stage play, a broad farce titled *The Lion of the West*, featured a backwoods character named Nimrod Wildfire that loosely resembled the former congressman. At first Crockett was reluctant to be associated with the play, concerned that it might make him look ridiculous. And with good reason—the actor playing the buckskin-clad Wildfire wore a dead possum as a hat, much to the delight of audiences. But there was little he could do about it. *The Lion of the West* became a smash hit, the country's most popular play for a quarter of a century, securing Crockett's place in American popular culture. It would make him the first American celebrity—a man famous simply for being famous.

Tennessee voters returned Crockett to Congress in 1833, this time as a member of the Whig Party, whose cosmopolitan leaders were happy to claim him as an authentic "common man." But fame had changed him. He no longer took an interest in legislation, spending much of his time cashing in on the Crockett craze. With the help of a friend he wrote *A Narrative of the Life of David Crockett*, a breezy memoir larded with folksy humor, which soon spawned several knock-offs, and later a series of wildly popular illustrated

15. David Crockett, Tennessee congressman (1786–1836). David Crockett was one of the most famous men in America when he was swept up in the "Texas Fever" in 1835. Intending to rebuild his political career and speculate in land, he spent just nine weeks in Texas before dying at the Alamo. Courtesy of City of Fort Worth, Texas, Log Cabin Village.

almanacs. Defeated in his bid for reelection by the Democrats, Crockett embarked on a lucrative, Whig-sponsored speaking tour of eastern cities, then headed west, looking for a fresh start in Texas, where he hoped to revive his political career.[11]

Lost in all the hoopla was a fundamental paradox: the cult of the frontiersman that Crockett embodied had its roots in urban, not rural, American life. Then, as now, popular culture was produced in large population centers to suit the tastes of urban audiences. The playhouses and publishers that promoted the Crockett craze never claimed to present an accurate representation of life in the west. It was always a form of humor, though it did serve a serious purpose. A veritable parade of foreign travel writers had made their way to the United States, penning memoirs that more often than not portrayed Americans as uncouth bumpkins. In celebrating Crockett, Americans good-naturedly turned their flaws into virtues. Here, in exaggerated form, was a frontier hero who allowed them to take pride in their country's reputation for rustic simplicity, a useful foil against the withering disdain of foreign critics. Rural Americans were not always in on the joke, however. When Crockett arrived in East Texas, some residents were disappointed to find not a larger-than-life figure dressed à la Nimrod Wildfire, but a middle-aged man dressed in the drab attire of a country squire. City dwellers knew better. The avatar of the Anglo-American frontier had always been a comedic invention for eastern audiences, and no one was more conscious of that fact than the Tennessee congressman himself.

Crockett's arrival in Texas highlighted the growing divide between Anglo and Hispano Texans opposing Santa Anna's regime. Traveling in the company of a dozen Tennesseans, the former congressman caused a sensation, feted by American settlers wherever he went. His presence signaled that Americans had not just involved themselves in the struggle of Mexican federalists against centralist rule. They had coopted it entirely, making the rebellion uniquely their own. A rather poignant example of the extent to which Mexican insurgents were unceremoniously shunted aside occurred in Nacogdoches, as civic leaders were preparing to host a banquet for Agustín Viesca, the former governor of Coahuila y Texas. They quickly extended an invitation to the famous American, who now became the star attraction of the evening. Seizing the spotlight, Crockett delivered a well-honed, rollicking speech, regaling the banqueteers with stories of his bear-killing days back in Tennessee. Viesca, who did not speak English, could only nod and smile uncomfortably.[12]

Predictably, the surge of Anglo-Americans into Texas, almost none of whom had ever had any contact with Mexicans, injected an ugly racial dimension to the conflict. Whether such sentiments had always existed, percolating below the surface, or were served up as a rhetorical device to rally American support, the virulent racism that spewed out into the open was a new feature in the contest between Anglos and Hispanos. Addressing his troops on January 15, Houston averred that "the descendants of the sturdy north" could never mix with "the phlegm of the indolent Mexicans, no matter how long we may live among them." Speakers at the pro-Texas meetings across the United States did not fail to invoke racial difference as they laid out their arguments for Anglo-American conquest. The three commissioners on their tour of American cities helped to stir these passions as they crossed the country drumming up support for the Texas cause. "We separate from a people one-half of whom are the most depraved of the different races of Indians, different in color, pursuits and character," William Wharton told a crowd in Kentucky. Even Stephen F. Austin, his mind-meld with Wharton now complete, became a full-throated white supremacist, describing the conflict to an audience in New York City as "a war of barbarism . . . waged by the mongrel Spanish-Indian and Negro race."[13]

AFTER PUTTING DOWN THE REVOLT IN ZACATECAS IN MAY 1835, Santa Anna took a victory lap through several towns in central Mexico before returning to the capital. He stayed only a few weeks, and by June he was back at Manga de Clavo, his estate in the Veracruz lowlands, with a new vice president, Miguel Barragán, governing in his absence. But as the summer wore on, the troubling reports out of Texas could not be ignored, and by the fall—perhaps even before he learned of the fighting at Gonzales—the decision to launch a major offensive into the northern province had been made.[14]

As president, Santa Anna could have delegated the campaign to any one of his senior generals. He never considered doing so. Always happiest in the field, he seems to have welcomed this particular challenge. Supremely confident after his recent victory over Zacatecan militia forces, he was drawn to any contest that allowed him to burnish his reputation as national savior. He had successfully defended the country against foreign enemies at Tampico in 1829; he believed he would do so again in Texas. And perhaps most important of all for the man who saw his greatest struggles not in abstract, political terms but in deeply personal ones, he surely relished the prospect of capturing Lorenzo de Zavala, who had broken with the regime in such a dramatic and public manner the year before.

The challenges the army faced were indeed formidable. Logistically, this would be by far the most ambitious campaign ever undertaken by a Mexican army. From San Luis Potosí, where the army would be organized, the route to the Rio Grande traversed four hundred miles of sparsely populated scrubland; from the river to San Antonio de Béxar the terrain was even more desolate. A small navy planned to ferry some supplies up the Texas coast, but the main army would be on its own, carrying what it needed. And the president would have to conclude the campaign quickly, for a prolonged absence would embolden his political enemies, who were alert to any sign of weakness on the part of the new regime. Above all, there was the question of money. The recent civil war had left the national treasury depleted, without funds to purchase supplies or pay its soldiers. Given these obstacles, the British minister Richard Pakenham informed his superiors in London that there was little the regime could do about the rebellion on the northern frontier; he regarded the independence of Texas as a foregone conclusion.[15]

Yet Santa Anna seems to have brushed off these concerns. He had read the 1834 report by Juan Almonte, who would serve as his aide-de-camp on the march into Texas, and who no doubt told him that the unrest was the work of a handful of troublemakers. Prosperous colonists had too much to lose by a rebellion; they would surely remain peaceful. An experienced campaigner, having fought in Texas as a young officer in the royalist army during the War of Independence, he knew the challenges of a winter march into a remote and inhospitable part of the country. But he was convinced that the army could be resupplied by the towns along the Rio Grande, where it would also find fresh recruits for the final leg of its march into Texas. Expecting to make short work of the insurgency, he anticipated a two-month campaign—a wildly optimistic estimate. His greatest concern was the Jackson administration's response to the crisis. Would Washington abandon its official posture of neutrality and intervene to protect American settlers? In public, at least, Santa Anna appeared defiant, informing the British minister that he actually welcomed a war between the two countries.[16]

Santa Anna returned to the capital for a few days in November, long enough only to obtain permission from the government to mount a Texas offensive. Then he headed north, to San Luis Potosí, where the expeditionary force that would come to be known as the Army of Operations had begun to assemble. Before the general could think about a campaign, however, he first had to find a way to pay for it. He had already imposed a forced loan on the country's foreign merchants, but little money had been raised. Just to cover the costs of feeding the army in San Luis Potosí required a 10,000 peso loan from the town council, which Santa Anna personally guaranteed. Not until the president negotiated a loan of 400,000 pesos could the serious work of procuring supplies and provisions for the army actually begin. Congress balked at the loan's high interest rate, but by the time it voted down the measure, the expedition was already on the march.[17]

An empty treasury was symptomatic of even more fundamental problems. As a developing country, Mexico lacked wartime industries, and had stocked its arsenals with antiquated firearms and equipment of European manufacture, much of which had not been properly maintained. The regular infantry (*permanentes*) and National Guard units (*activos*) tended to be seasoned, battle-tested veterans of Mexico's incessant civil wars. But for the Texas campaign, their ranks would be supplemented by raw, untrained recruits, including many who had been conscripted into service. For these men, there was no time even for the most rudimentary training; most "scarcely know how to carry a musket on their shoulder," one officer complained. They would take up the line of march wearing muslin shirts and pants, the customary dress of the peasant class. Even less attention seems to have been paid to the medical corps, which lacked the necessary equipment for an adequate field hospital.[18]

Over the course of several days at the end of December, the army began to file out of San Luis Potosí, lumbering slowly northward to the Rio Grande. Santa Anna, dressed in a plain frock coat, departed with an aide and a private secretary in a mule-drawn carriage shortly after the first of the year. In all, the Army of Operations numbered more than six thousand men under arms, accompanied by almost as many civilians. Nonmilitary personnel served in a support capacity for the army, as muleteers, cattle drivers, and sutlers, but wives and children of the enlisted men followed along as well. Officers grumbled that families slowed down the march, but acknowledged that their presence tended to reduce desertion rates. The camp followers performed vital roles for the Army of Operations, working as cooks and seamstresses, with some serving as *curanderas* in the absence of professional medical staff. Herds of cattle and long trains of pack animals brought up the rear of the caravan, clogging the roadways and kicking up immense clouds of dust.[19]

Once so confident of victory, Santa Anna arrived in Saltillo, roughly the midway point on his march to the Rio Grande, in a foul mood. The loan he had negotiated had been woefully inadequate to fund the campaign, and money was quickly running out. He berated his quartermasters, demanding they do more to cut costs. The troops were put on half rations, and the bonus pay officers traditionally received for campaign duty was suspended. The general angrily refused to pay the muleteers or give them army rations, relenting only when some deserted during the night, taking their animals with them. When local merchants and stock-raisers presented the army with bills for goods and services, Santa Anna simply referred them to state authorities, then hastily continued his march to the Rio Grande.[20]

Above Saltillo, the route would take the army through the semi-arid Coahuila desert, part of the vast *mezquital* that extended into Texas as far as the Nueces River. As conscripts began to slip away, the army sent patrols along the roadway to search for deserters. The Comanches may have been more effective in keeping soldiers in line, for the route was a main artery for raiding parties driving down into the Mexican interior. Although they stayed well clear of the army, the Indians were in the habit of scavenging through abandoned campsites, killing stragglers and deserters when they found them.[21]

Then the weather turned ugly. Freezing rains were soon followed by a two-day snowstorm that threatened to derail the campaign entirely. Military objectives became secondary to the need to stay warm and keep the animals alive. Having brought no firewood, the troops scoured the desolate landscape, now blanketed in two feet of snow, for thornscrub and mesquite. Cavalry officers stripped the straw from their bedding to feed their horses, but there was not enough forage for the oxen and mules, and many died. "Officers, soldiers, women, and boys, all shivering, gathering around the fires," wrote one colonel. "Circumstances had made equals of us all." In fact, the peasant conscripts and their families suffered the most, the leather *huaraches* on their feet offering little protection from the bitter cold.[22]

By mid-February, the vanguard of the Army of Operations reached the Rio Grande. The staging area for the main army, which Santa Anna would lead personally into Texas, was Guerrero, the northernmost of the half dozen towns strung out along the lower section of the river. General José de Urrea, a seasoned Indian fighter from the Sonoran frontier and one of the most capable officers in the Mexican army, had been dispatched to Matamoros with orders to assemble a smaller force of about fifteen hundred men. The plan to quash the rebellion called for the Army of Operations to pacify the Mexican districts of Texas first. Santa Anna would occupy San Antonio de Béxar, the province's largest population center, while Urrea would move up the coast, taking control of the predominantly Mexican towns of Goliad and Victoria in the southeast.

Logistical problems continued to plague Santa Anna's army as it prepared to move into the settled areas of Texas. All the villas del norte, with the exception of the largest, the port town of Matamoros, had been picked clean long ago by Comanche raiding parties. Army quartermasters searched frantically for even the most basic supplies, while the local militia units proved to be of limited value. They saw their role primarily in terms of community defense and had little interest in serving as scouts for the army on a campaign far from home. Tasked with finding able-bodied men to fill the ranks, a frustrated General Vicente Filisola, Santa Anna's second-in-command, reported that the male citizens of the towns along the river "would rather hide in the woods . . . than take up arms as soldiers."[23]

As he prepared to march into Texas, Santa Anna was not preoccupied with military matters alone. He had also given some thought to what the province might look like after the rebellion, once the Americans were expelled. In a long, thoughtful letter to Secretary of

War Tornel, almost certainly written with considerable input from his aide-de-camp, Juan Almonte, Santa Anna discussed the possibility of a massive land giveaway program to settle the region with Europeans and Mexican citizens. Soldiers in the Army of Operations could also be given lands in Texas as a reward for their service. The Cherokees, too, deserved land for refusing to join the Fredonian Rebellion, Almonte no doubt reminding the general that almost a decade had passed, and the Indians were still waiting for the government to fulfill its promises to the tribe. Finally, Santa Anna opined on the fate of the people of African descent who had been brought into Texas against their will. "Shall we permit those wretches to moan in chains any longer in a country whose kind laws protect the liberty of man without distinction of caste or color?" he asked. If Santa Anna could hardly be termed a dedicated foe of slavery on moral grounds, as a Mexican nationalist he could certainly appreciate the stark cultural differences that set his country apart from the white republic to the north, which now threatened to expand the slave empire at Mexico's expense.[24]

It would take the better part of two months for the Army of Operations to make the trek from San Luis Potosí to San Antonio de Béxar. For many it had been a death march, an estimated four hundred men perishing along the route. Troops numb with cold and fatigue could be heard to grimly remark as they passed the graves littering the roadway that another Mexican soldier had taken possession of Texas. No one knew how many women and children had succumbed to the rigors of the march, but the small crosses left behind at every camp suggested that the death toll was considerably higher.[25]

In the early months of 1836, two very different armies converged on Texas, each attempting to mimic a military tradition of days gone by. The American volunteers who poured into the area fancied themselves as colonial minutemen, republican citizen-soldiers engaged in a noble struggle against a despotic regime. Santa Anna and his generals, meanwhile, followed a European blueprint in vogue in the late eighteenth and early nineteenth centuries, as they sought to recreate the triumphs of Napoleon's *Grande Armée*. The reality fell far short of these aspirations, as an unruly, boisterous rebel force with little regard for authority prepared to meet a Mexican army that had been hastily cobbled together on the cheap. The result would be a shambolic tragicomedy of errors, a catalog of folly, rank amateurism, and ineptitude on both sides.

THIRTEEN

MORE COMMANDERS-IN-CHIEF THAN ONE

IN HIS MEMOIR OF HIS TOUR OF THE UNITED STATES, PUB-lished one year before he arrived in Texas, Lorenzo de Zavala offered a telling prophecy. His deep admiration for the American republic stemmed from the belief that it had managed, far more successfully than Mexico, to root out the vestiges of its colonial past. For this reason, he had welcomed and encouraged Anglo immigration to Texas, convinced that Mexico could only benefit from its exposure to the republican ideals of its North American neighbor. Yet he was under no illusion that the comingling of the two peoples would occur peacefully. The legacies of Spanish rule were so deeply etched in the Mexican character, he believed, that only brute force could eradicate them. Migrants from the United States would take up arms before they would submit to a government so alien to their own. They would resist and, in the end, prevail. "The American system," he predicted, "will obtain a complete though bloody victory."[1]

Now that such a conflict had come to pass, Zavala was certain he had chosen the right side. Like many observers, he believed the logistical challenges for the Mexican army of a winter campaign in hostile country, far from home, were insurmountable. An expedition to subdue the province could have but one outcome—military disaster, and the demise of Santa Anna's centralist regime.

Only one thing stood in the way of a rebel victory, he believed. Could Anglo-Texans set aside their differences and work together toward a common goal? Given their innate hatred of "despotism"— which often meant opposition to any form of authority at all—Zavala worried that a provisional government might not be able to rein in its fractious citizens. In a society in which every man believed himself born to command, there could be "individual patriotism" but no "unified patriotism," Zavala wrote to Stephen F. Austin. "They will defend their private rights until death," he told the empresario, "but still they do not realize the necessity for cooperation."[2]

Zavala proved to be a shrewd judge of the American character, but even he could not have imagined the utter chaos that followed. Almost immediately, serious disagreements arose between Governor Smith and the General Council over military policy. The defeat of General Cos in San Antonio had emboldened the insurgency's war hawks, who now called for the government to press its advantage and attack Matamoros. Neither Governor Smith nor Houston favored the plan, but the General Council forged ahead, authorizing Francis Johnson and James Grant, two men who had recently helped to defeat General Cos in San Antonio, to lead a campaign to the Rio Grande. Leaving behind a skeleton crew of eighty volunteers under the command of James Neill, the pair headed south, to the Nueces River. Adding to the confusion over who was in charge, James Walker Fannin, another veteran of the Béxar siege, had also been ordered to recruit men for a Matamoros campaign. At Velasco he gathered up several hundred American volunteers, including the young adventurer John Sowers Brooks, and sailed down the coast. When John Wharton arrived in Texas in late January with army supplies purchased in New Orleans, he received conflicting orders about where to send them. Unable to hide his frustration, he wrote, "I perceive that there are more commanders-in-chief than one."[3]

The debate over the Matamoros campaign would bring the basic functions of government to a grinding halt. Knowing that Houston was opposed to an offensive, the General Council undermined his efforts to organize the regular army. When the irascible Governor

Smith attempted to dismiss the council, it responded by drafting articles of impeachment, replacing him with the lieutenant governor, James Robinson. Smith refused to step down, with the result that both men claimed executive authority. But at that point it hardly mattered. By mid-January the General Council did not have enough members for a quorum. Resigned to the political dysfunction, rebel leaders looked forward to early March when a new convention would be held at Washington, on the Brazos River, to make a second attempt to establish a stable rebel government.[4]

A general without an army, Houston tried to consolidate the various forces scattered about the western frontier. But he had little authority beyond his own powers of persuasion, and he found that headstrong commanders did pretty much as they pleased. In January he rode to Goliad and Refugio to urge the volunteers to abandon the Matamoros campaign. Some turned back, but the rest headed south to the Nueces River with Johnson and Grant.

In the end, the bumbling, disjointed Rio Grande offensive never took place. As rebel leaders bickered, General José Urrea rushed to Matamoros to fortify the port town, then assembled an army in preparation for a march up the Texas coast. Fannin, Johnson, and Grant now had a choice to make: they could either retreat or wait for the Mexican army to come to them. They decided to wait.

THE REBEL FORCES IN SOUTH TEXAS WOULD STAND THEIR ground in a region overwhelmingly populated by Hispanos. At Goliad, on the San Antonio River, several hundred people lived in jacales clustered around a Spanish mission, now abandoned, and a presidio established in the mid-eighteenth century. On the Guadalupe River twenty-five miles to the northeast lay the smaller town of Victoria, founded in the 1820s by a Mexican empresario, Martín De León. But most of the area's inhabitants lived and worked on large ranchos along the two rivers, many of them sizable communities in their own right, tending to the cattle herds that ranged over the prairies of South Texas.

As in San Antonio, Hispano ranch hands and farmers generally deferred to large land-owning *patróns* in political matters. In the early days of the rebellion, the staunchly federalist De León clan had little difficulty recruiting a few dozen vaqueros in Victoria to fight in the siege of Béxar. The situation was very different in Goliad, however, where any sympathy for the revolt quickly vanished when unruly Anglos led by Phillip Dimmit occupied the town, prompting many Hispanos to flee to Carlos Rancho, twelve miles away. Not yet thirty, Carlos de la Garza was a popular and well-respected figure whose family had lived in the area for generations. His sprawling property on the San Antonio River had long been an important part of local civic life, serving as a refuge during Indian raids. He operated a ferry service on the property, and built a chapel (later, he would open a boys' school) for his ranch hands and the residents of Goliad. He was equally welcoming to non-Hispanos who had recently begun to settle in the area. When a small colony of Irish settlers arrived at nearby Refugio in the early 1830s, de la Garza developed close friendships with his new neighbors, providing much-needed assistance as they adapted to the ranching culture of South Texas. Although he had never shown much interest in national politics or in the bitter debate between federalism and centralism, de la Garza now found himself forced to take sides in the upheaval sweeping across Texas. Unlike the Seguíns and the De Leóns, the Hispano leader saw an Anglo-American victory as a far greater threat to his community than Santa Anna's centralist rule.[5]

Any doubts de la Garza may have had about his decision to oppose the rebellion were put to rest in the early weeks of 1836. Although Dimmit resigned his command at Goliad in January, more volunteers passed through town on their way to join Johnson and Grant, and on February 12 James Walker Fannin and his army arrived, hunkering down behind the imposing limestone walls of the Presidio de la Bahía. Almost all were Americans. The companies under Johnson and Grant had been formed in New Orleans and Mobile during the first bout of "Texas Fever" after the skirmish at Gonzales. Most of the men under Fannin's command were newcomers, too,

Georgians and Kentuckians who had landed at Velasco at the start of the year. Out of an army of more than four hundred men, Fannin counted only five colonists. For all intents and purposes, South Texas was now under American occupation.[6]

Like Dimmit before him, Fannin made no attempt to win local hearts and minds. Having brought little in the way of supplies, he ordered the volunteers to take what they needed, seizing horses and corn, and rounding up herds of cattle from nearby ranchos. Some of his men got drunk and terrorized the Hispanos that had not already left town. Frightened townsfolk again fled to the safety of the Carlos Rancho, to tell of American volunteers assaulting women and turning families out of their homes.

De la Garza responded in the weeks ahead by organizing a volunteer army of his own. According to some estimates, the rancher assembled a force of up to two hundred of his ranch hands and neighbors. Known as the Guardia Victorianos, they would be the only sizable group of Texas Hispanos to take up arms against the Anglo rebellion. De la Garza would soon make contact with General Urrea as he began his march up the coast, sending out patrols to perform scouting duties for the Mexican army before it arrived in the area. Fannin twice sent men to the Carlos Rancho, now the largest community in South Texas, to make a few arrests, but for the most part kept his distance. Reluctant to provoke a clash with the powerful *patrón*, he preferred to focus his energies on building up the defenses at the presidio and wait for his inevitable rendezvous with Urrea.[7]

John Sowers Brooks seems to have had little inkling of the hostility that the presence of Fannin's army had aroused among the locals in the Goliad area. One of the few men at the fort who could claim any formal military training, he spent much of his time drilling the volunteers and fortifying the presidio's defenses. He found particular satisfaction in the latter, building a half-moon artillery battery and experimenting with what he called an "infernal machine," a contraption that allowed one hundred rifles to be fired simultaneously. He spent his evenings reading the Bible and writing to his family, taking advantage of an express rider who carried the mail up the coast to

Velasco. The bitter cold and lack of provisions had not dampened his
spirits, but he was growing increasingly anxious about the rebellion's
chances for success. The little news he received at Goliad distressed
him. The governor and the General Council were not speaking to
one another, and the American colonists, as far as he could tell, had
yet to turn out in large numbers. "Something," he wrote to his father,
"must be done to relieve our Country."[8]

EFFECTIVELY SIDELINED BY THE GENERAL COUNCIL, HOUSTON
could do nothing to stop Fannin, Johnson, and Grant from confronting General Urrea in the south. So he rode north, to the Piney
Woods, to deal with a potential threat that he took almost as seriously
as the Mexican army. Since the outbreak of the rebellion, Houston
had been haunted by a nightmare scenario: that the immigrant tribes
would join the Mexican government in a war to expel the Americans
from the province. Relations between the Indians and East Texas
whites had gotten so bad in recent months that Nacogdoches residents feared an attack from the Cherokees and their associated bands
even before the skirmish at Gonzales. Living in villages within striking distance of the Camino Real, one of the only roads leading out
of Texas, the several thousand Native Americans scattered about the
Piney Woods were well-situated to cause chaos. Should Houston's
rebels fail to defeat the Mexican army, Anglo-Americans would find
themselves pinioned between two enemies, with no means of escape.

For the first time in his tribe's seemingly endless quest for a
permanent homeland, Chief Bowls found himself in a strong bargaining position. He intended to make the most of it. Despite a lifelong hostility toward white Americans, the Cherokee leader made
a calculated gamble and signaled his willingness to open talks with
the rebel government. He had become deeply frustrated with Mexico's failure to make good on its promises. Even so, it is unlikely
that Bowls would have been willing to negotiate with any white
man other than Sam Houston. Their paths may have crossed at
some point, but the chief certainly knew him by reputation. Highly

regarded by the Western Cherokee chiefs in US Indian Territory, Houston, Bowls believed, was a man he could trust.

In the third week of February, Houston led a delegation to Bowls's village, where they spent three days negotiating a treaty with the Cherokee leader and other tribal head men. William Goyens, who often served as a go-between and translator for the tribe and area whites, did not attend the meeting. On this occasion, the duties of translator were performed by Fox Fields, the young son of Richard Fields, who had become a well-respected member of the tribe. Although the Cherokees declined Houston's offer to serve as auxiliaries in the Texas army, the chiefs pledged on behalf of all the immigrant Indians to "a firm and lasting peace forever" with the provisional government. In return, they received from the Texas commissioners everything they had wanted and been unable to secure from the Mexican republic—the promise of an Indian homeland in East Texas, the grant to be held in common by the tribes, not divided into two-hundred-acre parcels according to the Terán plan. The treaty created, in effect, a semiautonomous state in the Piney Woods, one that would not be subject to Texas laws. It remained to be seen whether both parties would abide by the agreement. The treaty still required the approval of the rebel government, and the Cherokees might not be so willing to stay on the sidelines if the tide of war shifted in Mexico's favor. Nonetheless, Houston could now devote his full attention to the advancing Mexican army. At the signing ceremony on February 23, he presented Bowls with a saber, vest, and silk sash; Bowls reciprocated by giving the Texas leader a pair of moccasins made by his sister.[9]

As rebel leaders spent the winter months preparing to meet Santa Anna's armies, Anglo settlers were left to deal with the prairie tribes on their own. In February, a group of Comanches attacked the Hibbins family as it was traveling along a road near the Navidad River. They killed Sarah Hibbins's husband and her brother on the spot, making off with the woman and her two boys. Sarah's infant son they killed soon afterward as the party made its way northwest, following the course of the Colorado River. Bad weather delayed their journey, and at one point, far off in the distance, Sarah heard what she thought was the rumbling of cannon fire. One cold night she untied the leather cords that bound her hands and feet and slipped out of the camp alone, not daring to take her six-year-old son with her for fear she might rouse her captors. Heading south along the banks of the Colorado River, the distraught woman stumbled upon a small detachment of rangers and begged them to rescue her son. The rangers caught up with the Comanches a few days later near present-day Austin, and after a brief skirmish managed to retrieve the child unharmed. Only later did Sarah Hibbins learn that the booming cannons she had heard during her captivity had come from San Antonio. It was the siege guns of the Mexican army on the outskirts of town, firing upon an abandoned mission called the Alamo.[10]

UNLIKE THE GOLIAD PRESIDIO, THE ALAMO HAD NEVER BEEN intended for use as a fortress. A large complex of dilapidated limestone buildings and corrals covering ten acres on the east bank of the San Antonio River, the mission had recently been put into service as housing for the Mexican garrison during the siege of Béxar. General Cos left behind twenty cannons when his troops evacuated the town, which Colonel James Neill had put to good use. Dragging the guns into the mission, Neill's volunteers built an impressive network of earthen breastworks and ramparts to give the artillery batteries a commanding view of the town.

As a result of Neill's hard work, the General Council came to view San Antonio as an important first line of defense against a Mexican attack on the western frontier, once again ignoring the advice of Sam Houston, who wanted Neill to abandon his position and fall back to the Colorado River. After the start of the new year, small groups of Anglo-Americans began to drift into town to reinforce the garrison. James Bowie arrived in mid-January with thirty men. William Barrett Travis rode in a couple of weeks later. They were soon joined by David Crockett and his party of Tennesseans, the former congressman once again obliging the rebels with a stump speech that was no doubt similar, if not identical, to the many he had given since his arrival in Texas.[11]

The residents of San Antonio watched the arrival of the Anglo-Americans with growing trepidation. During the past six months, the town had been occupied by the Mexican army, besieged by rebel forces, and served as a battlefield. Now, just as life was beginning to return to normal, Bexareños once again found themselves on the front lines of conflict. Juan Seguín and his company of about twenty Hispanos remained fiercely committed to the rebel cause, but local support for the rebellion was clearly waning. Civic leaders refused to allow the American volunteers to vote in the election for delegates to serve in the upcoming Convention, so the garrison held its own election, choosing Sam Maverick and another man to represent them. And like Fannin's men at Goliad, the volunteers did little to endear themselves to the local population. When Colonel Neill left on a furlough, the Americans at the Alamo elected James Bowie, a swashbuckler with an especially notorious reputation, to serve as co-commander with William Barret Travis. Bowie proceeded to get "roaring drunk," and encouraged his men to do the same.[12]

Throughout the month of February, there were disturbing reports that a Mexican army was massing below the Rio Grande. Travis dismissed the rumors, attributing them to Bexareños hostile to the rebel cause. Unaware that preparations for a major Texas campaign had begun three months earlier, he found it inconceivable that Santa Anna could mount an offensive until the spring, making no effort to stock the fort with provisions, or even with enough powder and ammunition to withstand a long siege. He remained oblivious to the danger even when Juan Seguín's cousin rode into town on February 20 and claimed to have seen the army crossing the river at Guerrero two days earlier. The rebel commander would spend the night of February 22 carousing with other Americans at a fandango to celebrate George Washington's birthday, convinced that Santa Anna's army was nowhere near San Antonio.[13]

If Travis refused to believe Seguín's cousin, the Mexican townsfolk clearly did. The next morning, the Americans awoke to find

Bexareños "hurrying to and fro," loading their belongings onto wagons and carts as they prepared to leave en masse. Only then did Travis dispatch two scouts (both Anglos) to reconnoiter along the roadways south of town. They were soon racing breathlessly back into the main plaza, having stumbled upon Santa Anna's advance guard a few miles away. In the mad scramble that followed, the Americans frantically gathered what supplies they could and rushed into the Alamo. They commandeered a herd of cattle from an unlucky drover who happened to be in town, but in their haste they left fifty rifles behind. Travis barely had enough time to send a rider galloping off to Fannin at Goliad, ninety miles to the southeast, to plead for reinforcements.[14]

On the day the Mexican army marched into town, a few dozen Hispanos—most of them members of Juan Seguín's militia company and a few women and children—followed Travis into the mission. But as many as half of the defenders were American newcomers, and when Travis and Bowie attempted to negotiate a surrender, they were bluntly informed that "the Mexican army cannot come to terms under any conditions with rebellious foreigners." Lest there be any doubt that Santa Anna viewed Americans as the real enemy in Texas, he offered a general amnesty to the Bexareños who had sought refuge within the mission walls. Many took advantage of the opportunity.[15]

William Barret Travis also saw the rebel cause as an American one. A prominent member of the radical party, he had spent much of his time ginning up Anglo hostility toward Mexican authorities since coming to Texas four years earlier. Despite his reliance on Seguín's men as scouts and couriers during the siege, he regarded the local population as "public enemies" whose property should be confiscated to pay for the war. He would address the most famous of several letters from the mission, written one day after the Mexican army arrived, to "The People of Texas and all Americans in the World," calling upon them to come to the aid of the Alamo defenders "in the name of Liberty, of patriotism, & every thing dear to the American character."[16]

WHEN FANNIN RECEIVED WORD THAT SANTA ANNA HAD TAKEN San Antonio, he acted decisively—the first and last time he would do so in his brief, ill-starred military career. With three hundred men he marched out of Goliad the next morning. The relief mission quickly became a fiasco, a sad testament to the inexperience of the volunteers. One of the wagons broke down within sight of the presidio; two more became unusable as the little army tried to cross the San Antonio River two miles away. Finally reaching the other side, the exhausted army camped for the night, only to awake the next morning to find that some of the oxen had wandered off. The entire affair, Brooks wrote, was "embarrassing in the extreme." While Fannin and his officers debated what to do next, an express rider appeared with the grim news that Urrea's advance guard had attacked Colonel Johnson's camp at San Patricio on the Nueces River. Only Johnson and five others managed to escape. The intelligence dashed what little martial enthusiasm remained among Fannin and his officers, and the dispirited army straggled back to the presidio.[17]

The rescue mission debacle weighed heavily on Fannin. He suspected—correctly, as it turned out—that he would be roundly censured for failing to come to the aid of the Alamo defenders. In his correspondence to the General Council he stressed that the decision to turn back had not been his alone, but rather a collective one made by a council of the army's senior officers. Never an especially popular commander, he could not have failed to notice that the grumbling in the ranks now grew louder. The army received more bad news when it returned to the presidio: Urrea's main force had also surprised and routed Grant's party at Agua Dulce. Morale among the volunteers now began to collapse.[18]

John Sowers Brooks did not blame his commanding officer for the abortive rescue mission. Perhaps he was still grateful to Fannin, who had shown such confidence in the young man's ability. But he shared the garrison's darkening mood. He had not heard from his family in months, and did not know if they approved of his decision to come to Texas; he was not even sure if they had received any of his letters. But he kept writing, his correspondence full of poignant self-reflection and mounting dread. "My life has indeed, been a wayward and useless one," he confided to his sister. Still, he clung to the belief that it had not all been in vain. He was ready, he told her, to perish "on the field of battle, with the shout of victory in my ears," comforted by the knowledge that "if I die . . . it will be in a good cause."[19]

In San Antonio, Travis made another appeal to Fannin on February 28, sending Juan Seguín with a companion out of the Alamo under cover of darkness. The two men crawled along the muddy *acequia* that provided water to the mission, dammed up by Santa Anna's troops when the siege began. Finding horses at a nearby ranch, they rode toward Goliad. Along the way, they learned that Fannin had abandoned the effort to reinforce the San Antonio garrison, and headed instead to Gonzales to join the rebel force gathering there.[20]

The Army of Operations would spend the next several days testing the Alamo's defenses, moving artillery batteries and trenches closer to the mission walls. Even as the Mexican cordon tightened, Travis continued to send out couriers with urgent pleas for aid. On March 1, thirty-two colonists from Gonzales managed to dash through enemy lines to enter the Alamo compound. Sam Maverick, who had been elected to serve as a delegate to the Convention, left the Alamo the following day. On the night of March 4, when it became clear that no further help would be forthcoming, Travis wrote one final letter—to Santa Anna himself. Sending a Mexican woman into the general's camp, the Alamo commander again offered to surrender on the condition that the lives of the defenders would be spared. But it was too late; the decision to storm the mission had already been made.[21]

In the predawn hours of March 6, more than eighteen hundred Mexican troops crossed the river and approached the mission in four columns. The Texan picket guards, asleep at their posts, were bayoneted before they could sound the alarm. When the defenders were awakened by the shrill sound of a Mexican bugle from the sapper battalion, the attackers had already reached the outer walls of the mission complex. The Texans replied with cannons loaded with bits of scrap metal, tearing gaping holes in the tightly formed Mexican ranks. In the dark, with the Alamo enveloped in thick clouds of gunpowder smoke, it became impossible to distinguish friend from foe; General Filisola later estimated that three-fourths of the Mexican casualties were the result of friendly fire. "The tumult was great, the disorder frightful; it seemed as if the furies had descended upon us," Colonel Enrique de la Peña later recalled. The air was filled with "the sharp reports of the rifles, the whistling of bullets, the groans of the wounded, the cursing of the men, [and] the sighs and anguished cries of the dying." Twice the Mexican assault was beaten back, and Santa Anna sent in two battalions of reserves. By daybreak, the battle was over. The handful of defenders left alive tried to surrender, including, according to some accounts, Tennessee congressman David Crockett. At Santa Anna's command they were hacked to death with swords and bayonets.[22]

There were survivors. Although one woman was killed accidentally as Mexican troops stormed the mission, more than a dozen women and children managed to escape the carnage, having taken refuge in the chapel. The soldiers also spared two African Americans, one of whom was Travis's own enslaved manservant, a twenty-one-year-old man named Joe. All were brought before Santa Anna, who interviewed each of them at length. In keeping with his self-image as the stern *caudillo*, who could be merciless or merciful, as it pleased him, he gave to the women blankets and two silver dollars. He seemed to take a particular interest in Joe, quizzing him on the strength of the rebel forces. The general also wanted to know how many Americans had joined the Texas army. If Joe could not provide a precise answer, Mexican troops found a partial clue as they sifted through bodies and debris after the battle: the fringed, blue silk battle flag of the New Orleans Greys. Santa Anna would include the flag with his account of the battle in his dispatches to the Ministry of War that morning.[23]

Assembling his army in a grand review after the battle, Santa Anna delivered an impassioned speech; his troops responded with hoarse and exultant *vivas*. In a grisly coda intended to signal his determination to crush the rebellion, he ordered the bodies of the defenders dragged beyond the mission walls. Heaped into three enormous pyres, they were doused with grease and set alight. It would take two days for the flames to consume the bodies.[24]

The assault was a costly one for the Mexican army, although just how costly has long been a matter of debate. Viewing the Alamo defenders as martyrs in a heroic cause, the American press eagerly gave credence to astronomical figures of Mexican casualties, creating an impression that the siege dealt a crippling blow to Santa Anna's forces. According to the more realistic reports of Mexican officers, however, the army suffered about three hundred killed and wounded, with only sixty killed on the morning of March 6. A precise figure remains elusive, for the simple reason that the Mexican wounded, without proper medical attention, were dying of gangrene and sepsis long after the battle ended. When an American doctor arrived in San Antonio six weeks later, he found a scene of almost unimaginable horror: about one hundred soldiers in a field hospital so poorly equipped and staffed that few operations had been performed. "There has been scarcely a ball cut out as yet," he wrote, "almost every patient carrying the lead he received on that morning."[25]

Purveyors of a heroic Anglo-Texan myth would also assert that the thirteen-day siege bought valuable time for the rebel army. But in late February and early March, something akin to anarchy prevailed among the rebellion's political and military leaders. The largest concentration of troops remained holed up at the Goliad presidio, where Fannin seemed paralyzed with indecision, waiting to be told what to do. He would wait in vain; in recent weeks the General Council had stopped meeting, unable to achieve a quorum. Some colonists had gathered at Gonzales, but there was no one to lead them, Houston having gone to the Convention at Washington after signing the treaty with the Cherokees. The Alamo defenders had delayed the advance of the Mexican army, but in the absence of a functioning government, their sacrifice had accomplished little.

WHEN HOUSTON ARRIVED AT WASHINGTON, A CRUDE SETTLE-ment of a dozen or so shanties, he found about sixty delegates crowded into an unfinished building that served as a meeting hall. Someone tacked cotton cloth over the open windows and doorway to keep out the bitter cold. Lodgings were equally spartan; Lorenzo de Zavala, one of the delegates from Harrisburg, slept in a carpenter's shop that he rented with three other men. Despite rumors of Mexican troop activity around San Antonio, 150 miles away, the delegates felt little cause for alarm. Fannin and the colonists in the western settlements would surely come to Travis's aid. "It is believed the Alamo is safe," one member noted in his diary, unaware that the siege was already well underway.[26]

On March 2, the day after the meeting was called to order, the delegates drafted a declaration of independence, one that echoed in style and substance the document drafted by American colonists in 1776. Few of the signers could claim roots in the province. A majority had come to Texas illegally, after the Law of April 6, 1830, while one-third had been in Texas a matter of months, arriving after the Battle of Gonzales. Many owed their election to American volunteers, who had demanded the right to take part in the balloting. Only two were native Texans: San Antonio delegates José Antonio Ruíz and José Antonio Navarro. Both had close ties to the American community, as did the third Hispano delegate at the Convention, Lorenzo de Zavala. With his abiding hatred of Santa Anna, Zavala put his signature to the document without a moment's hesitation. But Navarro balked at the thought of being forever associated with the dismemberment of his country. He would later insist that he felt pressured to do so by the clamor of the assembled Anglo delegates. His hand trembled as he signed his name.[27]

The delegates were busy in the days that followed, as they began the work of drafting a constitution. They also resolved the military command issue that had so badly hamstrung the war effort, giving Sam Houston authority over all rebel forces. Their deliberations took on a somber tone when Sam Maverick and another Alamo defender brought the latest news from San Antonio on March 6. Crowding into the assembly hall, they listened intently to a letter from Travis—his final message from the doomed mission. He had heard nothing from Fannin at Goliad, and unless he received more men and ammunition—and quickly—he fully expected to be "sacrificed to the vengeance of a Gothic enemy."[28]

Appealing for calm, Houston urged the delegates to remain in session, then saddled up and rode to Gonzales. He reached the town five days later, where he found less than four hundred men with enough provisions to last only a few days. He initially planned to march to the relief of the Alamo defenders, but no sooner had he arrived when his scouts brought in three shell-shocked survivors of the siege: Susanna Dickinson, her two-year-old daughter, and Travis's manservant, Joe. Aware that his small force was in no condition to meet the Mexican army, he decided to withdraw to the more densely populated interior of Texas. To Fannin at Goliad, Houston sent orders to destroy the presidio and fall back to the Guadalupe River, while he retreated to the Colorado, torching the village of Gonzales before he left.

FANNIN HAD AT LAST RECEIVED A DIRECT ORDER FROM HIS GOVernment, but he could not comply with it, at least not right away. A retreat from Goliad required wagons, and he had just sent them to Refugio, twenty-five miles to the south, to assist in the evacuation of some of the Irish colonists in the area. The delay proved costly. Upon reaching the village, Fannin's men were attacked by Carlos de la Garza's experienced horsemen and forced to take cover in the Refugio mission. Compounding his error, Fannin then sent a larger force to their rescue. It fared no better, and wound up joining the rebels behind the mission walls. When about two dozen rebels tried to escape, the Guardia Victorianos quickly ran them down. De la

16. James Walker Fannin (1804–1836). Georgia-born James Walker Fannin moved to Stephen F. Austin's colony in 1834, where he operated a plantation and supplemented his income by smuggling African slaves into Texas. Courtesy of Dallas Historical Society.

Garza discovered a few local Mexicans and Irish colonists among them, including one of his neighbors, an Irishman named Nicholas Fagan. These he released unharmed; the rest he led back to Urrea's camp. In accordance with the Tornel Decree, Urrea dispatched a squad of infantrymen to take them to a grove of post oak trees, where they were bound and summarily executed.[29]

Having divided his force and squandered valuable time, Fannin now scrambled to evacuate the town as Urrea's army closed in. Rustling up what few carts and oxen they could find, the volunteers needed two days before they were finally ready to move out. Spiking the largest cannons, they demolished the fortifications that had taken them six weeks to build, and destroyed everything of value, including Brooks's "infernal machine." The provisions they could not take with them they set alight, burning the dried meat of several hundred cattle seized from surrounding ranchos. On the morning of March 19, they marched out of the fort, burning the Mexican jacales as they went, the fires sending an enormous plume of black smoke into the sky that could be seen for miles.[30]

Fannin's evacuation of Goliad was no less chaotic than the abortive attempt to relieve the Alamo garrison three weeks earlier. Slowed by unruly oxen and undependable wagons, by late afternoon the army had covered a distance of ten miles. Alerted to Fannin's withdrawal by de la Garza's scouts, Urrea hurried forward, intercepting the American force near Coleto Creek. Inexplicably, Fannin ignored the advice of his officers, who begged him to fight from a line of timber along the creek. Instead, he chose to make a stand in open country, using the wagons to form a square on an acre of tall prairie grass.

Given the rank ineptitude that had characterized the American occupation of South Texas, Fannin's little army performed surprisingly well at the Battle of Coleto. During the course of the day Urrea ordered three charges with cavalry and infantry, and each time they failed to breach the American lines. That afternoon Mexican snipers crawled forward in the tall grass, picking off Fannin's men and their animals until darkness enveloped the Coleto prairie. The untested volunteers had fought Urrea's seasoned troops to a stalemate. By daybreak, however, it became clear that their position was untenable, Urrea having brought up additional troops and several pieces of artillery from Goliad during the night. Though only ten Americans lay dead, more than sixty were wounded, most of them seriously, including John Sowers Brooks. His first combat experience had been cut short when a Mexican musket ball thudded into his left thigh, shattering the bone. The agonizing, unremitting groans of the wounded had a chilling effect on morale. The army was out of water, and with most of the horses and oxen lying dead on the battlefield, an orderly retreat with the wounded was impossible.

Urrea had just ordered his men to resume the attack when a white flag went up from the American ranks. Meeting midway between the two camps, Urrea and Fannin discussed terms of capitulation. The Mexican commander refused to accept anything less than an unconditional surrender, though the final document stipulated that the rebels would be accorded the rights of prisoners of war and the wounded treated "with all consideration possible." Urrea's translator assured them that they would be repatriated to the United States in a matter of days.[31]

By the third week of March the rebellion in Texas appeared to be all but over. The province's largest town, San Antonio,
was once again in Mexican hands, while Urrea, with the help of
de la Garza's partisans, had made short work of the rebel forces in
the south. The Convention delegates at Washington-on-the-Brazos
learned of the fall of the Alamo on March 16. Working through
the night, they completed their work on a constitution and created
a new interim government. To serve as president, the delegates
elected David G. Burnet, an East Texas land speculator. Lorenzo
de Zavala was the unanimous choice as vice president, a post he
accepted with some reluctance, having not entirely abandoned his
hopes for a comeback in Mexican politics. The Convention then
hastily adjourned, and within a matter of hours the town was almost
completely deserted. Sick with fever, Sam Maverick was one of the
few stragglers left behind, but after a few days he mustered enough
strength to saddle his horse and ride east, just ahead of Santa Anna's
advancing army.[32]

In what was hardly a vote of confidence for Houston and the
troops under his command, the new government decided to recon-
vene in Harrisburg, as far away from the theater of war—and as close
to the United States—as possible. Situated on Buffalo Bayou, which
emptied into the San Jacinto River a few miles above Galveston Bay,
the town offered easy access to the coast should Burnet and his cabinet need to make a hasty exit.

Zavala approved of the change of venue. He had recently purchased a small, three-bedroom house on a strip of land on the bayou
at Lynchburg, a few miles east of town. Emily and the children were
there, having arrived in December, with an Irish maid, a black servant, and three French laborers in tow. Astride a mule, the vice president of the new Texas Republic set out for Harrisburg, which he
reached in five days. He had been confidently predicting the defeat
of the Mexican army and Santa Anna's downfall since the rebellion
began. Now, as the Army of Operations began driving eastward
across Texas, that prospect seemed very far away.[33]

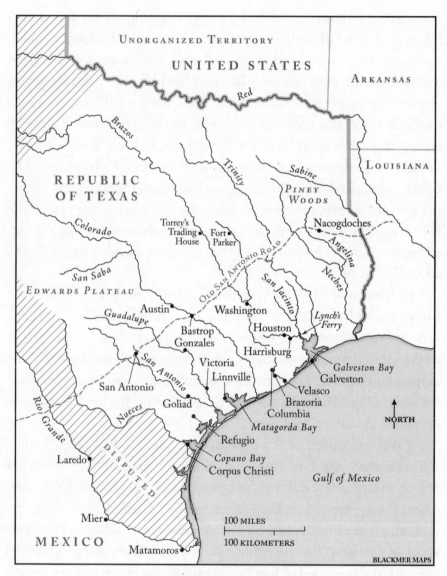

UNORGANIZED TERRITORY

UNITED STATES

ARKANSAS

Red

REPUBLIC
OF TEXAS

Brazos

Trinity

Sabine

LOUISIANA

PINEY
WOODS

Colorado

Torrey's
Trading
House

Fort
Parker

Nacogdoches

Angelina

San Saba

OLD SAN ANTONIO ROAD

San Jacinto

Neches

EDWARDS PLATEAU

Guadalupe

Austin

Washington

Lynch's
Ferry

Bastrop
Gonzales

Houston

San Antonio

Harrisburg

Victoria

Galveston Bay

San Antonio

Linnville

Galveston

Nueces

Goliad

Velasco
Brazoria
Columbia

Rio Grande

DISPUTED

Matagorda Bay

NORTH

Laredo

Refugio

Copano Bay
Corpus Christi

Gulf of Mexico

Mier

100 MILES

MEXICO

Matamoros

100 KILOMETERS

BLACKMER MAPS

Texas Republic, 1836–1845

FOURTEEN

TO THE LYNCHBURG FERRY

"ON THE COLORADO I MAKE MY STAND," HOUSTON WROTE to a friend from his camp on the east side of the river, on March 24. He was encouraged by the fact that over the past several days hundreds of colonists had rushed to join the army, and though they were no better trained or equipped than the volunteers at the start of the rebellion, they seemed eager for a fight with the Mexican forces that were preparing to cross the river above and below his position at Beason's Ford, near present-day Columbus. But later that same day came word of Fannin's defeat at Coleto Creek, and with it the realization that Houston's force now stood alone against Santa Anna's Army of Operations. As quickly as it had swelled in size, Houston's army now began to melt away. Men who a short time earlier boasted loudly of victory abruptly decamped, to find their families and lead them to safety. Amid the growing sense of panic, Houston gave the order to fall back to the Brazos River, thirty miles east.[1]

News of Fannin's defeat and the retreat of the rebel army triggered a mass exodus of the civilian population, known later as the Runaway Scrape, as Anglo settlers and enslaved African Americans headed pell-mell toward the Louisiana border. They would take two principal routes: through the Piney Woods along the Camino Real, and along the southern road that wound its way through the bogs and marshes of the Gulf Coastal Plain. The gathering throng would grow in size in the days ahead, ultimately becoming one of the greatest sudden dislocations of people ever seen on the North American continent. Many settlers hid their silverware and other valuables before setting out, while one family took the time to bury all their household items—wash tubs, pots, kettles, cooking utensils, even an old secretary desk. Others fled in a panic, leaving cabins "standing open, the beds unmade, the breakfast things still on the tables, pans of milk molding in the dairies." Driving their livestock, they took to the road in every conveyance imaginable, in hand-barrows, sleds, carts, and wagons crammed with their belongings, astride burros and horses and on foot. As one enslaved man later recalled, "The children were crying, the women praying and the men cursing. I tell you it was a serious time."[2]

IN SOUTH TEXAS, THE HISPANO RESIDENTS OF GOLIAD RETURNED to find the town a smoldering ruin. After Fannin's surrender at Coleto Creek, Mexican troops escorted the main body of prisoners back to the presidio, where they were crammed into a small chapel, with little food or water. It would take three days to transport the wounded back to the fort. John Sowers Brooks, his shattered leg bound by an axe handle that served as a crude splint, screamed in pain as he made the trip by oxcart. The wound was so serious that Fannin requested that he be kept in a house outside the fort that served as a field hospital for Mexican troops, in the hope that he might receive better medical attention. After a few days the able-bodied prisoners were moved to a courtyard in the presidio, where they were joined by some of the men sent by Fannin on the ill-fated rescue mission to Refugio. When Carlos de la Garza rode in with his Guardia Victorianos, he was surprised, and perhaps not a little irritated, to find among the prisoners the redoubtable Irishman Nicholas Fagan, whom he had saved from a firing squad a few days earlier. Once again, Garza succeeded in winning the release of his Irish neighbors.[3]

Urrea did not stay long in Goliad. Leaving a small force under the command of Lieutenant Colonel José de la Portilla to guard the prisoners, he continued his rapid march up the coast. At Copano, a frequent drop-off point for ships bringing in supplies to South Texas, he captured more Americans, a regiment of about eighty volunteers from Nashville. Having just landed, they were swimming in the bay as Mexican troops appeared on the scene, and had not even had time to bring their weapons and belongings ashore. There could be no doubt about their intentions, but Urrea chose to regard them as non-combatants and sent them back to Goliad with orders to keep them apart from the other American prisoners.

One week after Fannin's surrender, a dispatch for Portilla arrived from Santa Anna, reminding the officer that American mercenaries were to be shot in accordance with the Tornel Decree (a copy of which he included in the orders). Although Portilla found the directive "repugnant to my feelings," he dutifully made arrangements to comply the next morning. Several women attached to the army were horrified by Santa Anna's orders. One, Francita Alvarez, secreted away a few of the prisoners later that night and convinced a colonel to intervene on behalf of the recently captured Tennesseans. Portilla also exempted from the order some twenty others—doctors, carpenters, and other artisans—who could be of use to the Mexican army.[4]

Shortly before dawn the following morning, March 27, the main body of American prisoners was assembled in the parade ground of the presidio under various pretexts. Some were told that they would be marched to the coast where a ship was waiting to carry them back to the United States, others that they were being sent to forage for firewood and water. Portilla's officers divided the prisoners into three groups, then escorted them out of the presidio in separate directions. They were oblivious to any imminent danger, but as they marched away Francita Alvarez could be seen standing "in the street, her hair floating, speaking wildly, and abusing the Mexican officers, especially Portilla. She appeared almost frantic."[5]

Fifteen minutes later, alone in the sacristy of the mission chapel, Fannin heard a succession of distant volleys. Then more volleys, as Portilla's men executed the wounded prisoners along a wall of the presidio courtyard. At length they came for Fannin. Unable to walk on his own, he limped out of the chapel, supported by an American doctor, to a bench in the courtyard, where he was blindfolded and shot at close range. In the Mexican field hospital beyond the presidio walls, John Sowers Brooks escaped notice, but not for long. He was discovered by an officer and two soldiers with bayonets affixed to their muskets, who dragged him into the street. "He extended his arms towards me," the doctor attending him later recalled, "imploring my assistance, until his voice was silenced forever."[6]

It is unlikely that Santa Anna gave much thought to the consequences of his decision to countermand Urrea's order to spare the prisoners. His "no quarter" policy was intended to cause panic and sap the morale of the rebels, and to deter other Americans from joining the insurgency. And so far he had reason to think the strategy was working. Since Fannin had surrendered "at discretion," the order was not technically a violation of the rules of war. Nor was the policy new; the Mexican government had been summarily executing American prisoners—at Tampico, San Patricio, Agua Dulce, Refugio, and the Alamo—since the rebellion began.

But the sheer size of the mass execution at Goliad—almost 350 men—was an entirely different matter, and the political fallout was both immediate and severe. The British and French ministers in the Mexican capital met with the acting president, Miguel Barragán, to lodge a formal complaint. Within a matter of days, congress passed a new law amending Tornel's decree, which mandated a sentence of banishment or ten years in prison to foreigners captured under arms. But as a public relations matter, the damage had been done. In the United States, the executions fed an emerging narrative, popular among the country's jingoistic press, that the rebellion was not only a struggle against Mexican tyranny, but Mexican barbarism. Newspapers that had heretofore tried to take a more balanced view also found the slaughter indefensible, noting that Fannin's men became lawful combatants once Texas declared its independence, and therefore should have been given the protections of prisoners of war. Even in the northeast the episode was condemned as a war atrocity, silencing antiwar critics who had censured the young men of the

South for rushing to join a rebellion led by slaveholders. With one fateful decision, Mexico had lost its claim to the moral high ground.[7]

ALONG THE BRAZOS RIVER, HOUSTON'S ORDER TO RETREAT HAD caused a panic among the general population, but at least it gave him some breathing room. Marching his men up to Jared Groce's plantation, twenty miles above San Felipe, he set about the task of turning them into something that resembled an organized army. By this time he was facing mounting criticism for his inaction from some of his officers, as well as from the newly installed interim government. President Burnet was so angered by Houston's withdrawal from the Colorado that he briefly thought about replacing him with the secretary of war, Thomas Jefferson Rusk. From the relative safety of Harrisburg, Burnet ordered his top general to retreat no farther.

For ten days Houston concentrated his forces and drilled his troops on the west bank of the Brazos River. But many Texans— perhaps as much as three-fourths of the adult male population—did not answer his call to join the rebel army. Some were too old or too young to take part in the fighting. Others wanted to escort their families to safety. After the stunning defeats at the Alamo and Goliad, many believed the rebellion was over. Along the Camino Real near Nacogdoches on his way to join Houston's army, one Mississippi volunteer encountered three hundred armed men heading the other way. Well-to-do Texans were also quick to abandon the rebellion. A disgusted William Wharton would later remark, "The planters were taking care of their cattle and slaves and the merchants were minding their goods." Those who chose to evacuate, as one female settler recalled with some bitterness, were "panic stricken and wild with excitement."[8]

Amid the chaos of the Runaway Scrape, the perennial specter of slave unrest added to the anxieties of Texas whites, especially along the coastal route taken by the planters of the Lower Brazos. With her husband in Washington, Sarah Wharton fled Eagle Island on horseback with her seven-year-old son, an adopted teenage daughter, and a black servant, leaving the family's field hands with an overseer to make their way east on their own. For those planters who had purchased "wild Africans" from Cuba, the collapse of white authority raised new fears of a racial bloodbath. But even amid the tumult of revolution, with all its talk of freedom from oppression, Southern whites refused to abandon the system of bonded labor on which their way of life had been built. On the day that Convention delegates declared Texas's independence from "the most intolerable of all tyranny," slave smugglers unloaded a coffle of 170 Africans at the mouth of the Brazos and herded them inland.[9]

There would be no revolt, though some enslaved men and women took advantage of the confusion to make their way to Mexican lines. Most accompanied their owners on the trek eastward, while a few African American bondsmen helped to supervise the evacuation of individual parties. Eleven-year-old Dilue Harris later recalled with gratitude an elderly enslaved man, "Uncle Ned," who put the white women and children in a canvas-covered wagon, the black women and children in open carts, then guarded the group as it made its way toward the US border.[10]

Along the Nacogdoches-Natchitoches corridor to the north, fleeing Anglo settlers were preoccupied with a threat of a different kind: an uprising by the Indians of East Texas. Acting on the orders of Mexican authorities, some local Hispanos were urging the tribes to take up arms, giving rise to wild rumors that the Indians intended to launch a war of extermination. In the mass hysteria that ensued, no report was too far-fetched to be dismissed. According to one, Mexican troops had linked up with a force of Cherokees and Caddos and seized Nacogdoches, driving off the town's white residents. On the Red River, visitors to the Shawnee and Delaware villages found them deserted, stoking fears that the Indians were en route to the Piney Woods to join their Cherokee allies. Perhaps the most sensational reports came from the upper Midwest, where one thousand Fox and Sauk warriors were said to be on the march to East Texas. "Idle rumors," said one Georgia volunteer, "have done more to the injury of Texas than the horde of Mexicans have done."[11]

Though not one to panic, Sam Houston did worry that the news of rebel defeats at the Alamo and Coleto Creek might cause Bowls to renege on the agreement the two men had made in February. As his army began crossing the Brazos River, he dashed off a letter to the Cherokee chief, gamely trying to put the best face on things. "Our army are all well, and in good spirits," he wrote. Reassuring Bowls that the Indians would receive the lands the rebel government had promised them, he strained to end the letter on a note of cheerful optimism. He was still wearing the moccasins the chief's sister had given him at the treaty signing, and he hoped to see the chief "before they are worn out."[12]

As the situation continued to deteriorate, rebel leaders clung to the hope that the United States government would save them. When he learned of the fall of the Alamo, Houston floated the absurd, desperate suggestion that the government should simply declare that Texas was not a part of Mexico after all, but had been acquired by the United States in the 1803 Louisiana Purchase. Burnet had a more realistic plan to draw the United States into the conflict. Even as he urged Houston to stand and fight Santa Anna's army, he sought to draw attention to the danger from the East Texas tribes. Although the Jackson administration was anxious to maintain a policy of strict neutrality, an 1828 treaty between the United States and Mexico authorized both governments to send troops into the other's territory in the event of an Indian threat. Washington had already dispatched General Edmund Gaines, a crusty Indian fighter, to the Louisiana-Texas border to monitor the crisis, and Burnet begged him to intervene to prevent the imminent slaughter of civilians who had, until only recently, been citizens of the United States.[13]

Gaines could hardly be considered a neutral observer. His brother, a resident of Nacogdoches, had just signed the Texas Declaration of Independence; his cousin operated the Sabine River ferry on the US-Texas border. Most important, Gaines did not view the rumors of a wider conflagration as wild-eyed hysteria. Only weeks before, he had been stationed in Florida, where hundreds of escaped slaves from the sugar plantations around St. Augustine joined the

Seminoles in their second war against the federal government, some daubing their faces with war paint in a sign of solidarity with their indigenous allies. His last assignment before assuming his new post at Fort Jesup had been to bury the mutilated bodies of more than a hundred US troops ambushed in a palmetto grove in the central part of the territory. Edmund Gaines knew firsthand the horrors of all-out race war.[14]

When Gaines arrived at Fort Jesup in early April, Anglo refugees were already crowding around the ferry landing on the west bank of the Sabine. Lacking specific instructions from Washington as to how far he could go to protect American lives, Gaines ordered US troops to aid in the evacuation, but to remain on the US side of the river. He called upon the governors in the Southern states to provide him with additional manpower, and even dispatched couriers into East Texas to warn Bowls and other chiefs that the US Army would take swift, punitive action in the event of an attack on the white settlements. But for the time being, US troops would not cross the river onto Mexican soil.[15]

SANTA ANNA REACHED THE BRAZOS RIVER BY THE FIRST WEEK in April, twenty miles below Houston's camp at Jared Groce's Bernardo plantation. Feeling reasonably confident that the insurgency was over, he considered returning to Mexico City, leaving General Filisola to engage what remained of the rebel army. He had already spent longer in Texas than he intended, and worried about the political situation in the capital, having recently learned that acting president Miguel Barragán had died. In the end he decided against it. Up to this point Mexican troops could claim victories against rebel forces composed mostly of foreign mercenaries. Houston's small army of colonists had yet to be defeated.[16]

Any thought of returning to the capital vanished when Santa Anna reached the other side of the river. There he received news that would change the course of the rebellion: Lorenzo de Zavala and the other members of the Texas government were at Harrisburg, wholly unprotected, only forty miles to the east. Santa Anna did not hesitate. He would capture the rebel government and return to Mexico City in triumph, with the traitor Zavala in irons. Houston's army he could deal with later. Blinded by a desire to punish his inveterate political enemy, he now made the gravest error of his career. With most of his army still on the west bank of the Brazos, he took the seven hundred men who had already crossed the river and pushed on toward Harrisburg. His bitter rivalry with the country's leading federalist, forged in the maelstrom of Mexican politics, would be settled on the marshlands of coastal Texas.[17]

Houston was puzzled by Santa Anna's decision. Believing that the Mexican general planned to come up behind his position at Bernardo to block his retreat, he began ferrying his troops to the east bank of the Brazos. The decision did not sit well with the hotspurs in Houston's army, some of whom had disapproved of the order to retreat from the Colorado. Serious opposition to his leadership among some of the senior officers now began to emerge, with his old friend John Wharton among the loudest advocates for engaging the enemy. The grumbling grew louder as the army headed east, with his critics convinced that Houston did not intend to fight, but planned to head north to Nacogdoches to await the intervention of General Gaines and the US Army. In fact, Santa Anna's decision to divide his forces emboldened Houston, who now saw a chance to engage the enemy on relatively equal terms. When the army came to a fork, with one path leading to Nacogdoches, the other to Harrisburg, Houston took the Harrisburg road.[18]

JUST AHEAD OF THE TWO ARMIES, THE RUNAWAY SCRAPE WAS quickly becoming a full-blown humanitarian crisis. For several days in mid-April, all of East Texas was drenched by torrential spring rains, turning the coastal road into a muddy quagmire. Measles, whooping cough, and congestive fever broke out among the refugees, and several children died along the way. Wagon wheels sank up to their hubs in the bog, causing settlers to discard clothing, furniture, and other goods as they went. Anarchy reigned as squads of army deserters, Mexican troops, Indians, and runaway slaves scoured the country-side, plundering empty cabins. Men with orders from Houston to impress all available horses into military service seized them at gun-point, leaving families to make their way on foot. And through it all, "the wet earth and angry sky offered no relief."[19]

By the time the throng reached Lynch's ferry landing on the San Jacinto River, some ten miles east of Harrisburg, the evacu-ation had devolved into complete chaos. Fights broke out as five thousand people waited for three days to take a single flatboat across the river. Stranded on the west bank, some families made their own rafts of driftwood and fallen logs. Twenty miles beyond the San Jacinto, the scene of mass confusion was repeated at the rain-swollen Trinity. One woman watched in horror as an alligator dragged her husband beneath the black waters. "The river was rising and there was a struggle to see who should cross first," Dilue Harris later recalled. Some enterprising Alabama-Coushatta Indians, tak-ing advantage of the pandemonium, bartered with the refugees, who were happy to part with their goods in exchange for help getting across.[20]

In the Piney Woods, the presence of Gaines's troops on the east bank of the Sabine ensured that the evacuation of white settlers along the Camino Real would at least be an orderly one. Thousands of ter-rified white families swarmed the ferry landings, expecting an Indian attack at any moment. The fears of an Indian attack never materi-alized. In fact, when panic-stricken Anglos evacuated Nacogdoches, some Cherokees abandoned their villages and headed north toward the Red River, thus embarking on a runaway scrape of their own. But most of the immigrant Indians remained in their forested enclaves in the Piney Woods, far from the routes taken by fleeing colonists.[21]

When Sam Maverick arrived at Nacogdoches, he found the town abandoned. Still suffering from what was probably a case of pneumonia, he stayed there for two weeks, not knowing what to do next. The American cause now seemed lost. Having fought in the siege of Béxar, helped to defend the Alamo, and cast his vote for independence at the Convention, Maverick may have felt he had done what he could for his adopted country. When he was well enough to travel, he mounted his horse and, like thousands of others, found a ferryboat that would take him back across the Sabine River and to the safety of the United States.[22]

AFTER A FORCED MARCH IN PURSUIT OF THE REBEL GOVERNMENT, Santa Anna reached Harrisburg on the night of April 15. Burnet and Zavala were gone, and so was almost everyone else. From the two residents who remained, the general learned that the Texas leaders and the townspeople had been evacuated on the steamboat *Cayuga* only a few hours earlier. Burnet and Zavala, they told him, were on their way to Galveston Island to supervise the evacuation of refugees. Actually, they were much closer than that. Burnet and his family had gotten off the steamboat a few miles downriver at New Washington, a strip of land jutting out into upper Galveston Bay. The Zavalas were even closer, having disembarked at Lynch's Ferry near their home to retrieve a chest of silver and other valuables. A furious Santa Anna sent Juan Almonte and fifty dragoons racing ahead in search of the two men, then ordered his troops to torch Harrisburg, helping to set the fires himself.[23]

Almonte reached Lynch's ferry landing the next morning, the scene of such pandemonium a few days earlier. Now the place was deserted, save for the Lynch family, who lived near the Zavalas at the mouth of the San Jacinto River. Lorenzo and Emily were in a small boat rowing toward their house just as the cavalrymen approached. Spotting Almonte's men on the west bank, Fanny Lynch gathered her children and fled, crying, "The Mexicans are upon us!" Hearing the commotion, Lorenzo guided the boat into the high reeds along the banks of the bayou. With no way to cross to the opposite side, Almonte and his men wheeled around and headed south, thundering past the hidden couple. Just as they reached New Washington they spotted Burnet, his wife and children, and a few of his neighbors pushing off in a skiff into Galveston Bay. Although only forty yards distant, well within range of Mexican muskets, Almonte ordered his men to lower their weapons, as there were women and children on board.[24]

Santa Anna followed Almonte to New Washington, but he had missed his chance to capture Zavala and soon headed north, toward Lynchburg. In the meantime, the rebel army reached the charred remains of Harrisburg, where Houston learned for the first time that the Mexican army he was stalking was commanded by Santa Anna himself. He now hurried his men forward, arriving at the ferry landing on the morning of April 20, making camp in a grove of trees near the confluence of Buffalo Bayou and the San Jacinto River. That afternoon, Santa Anna' scouts discovered Houston's position, and after some skirmishing the Mexican army retired to higher ground a short distance away.

April 21 dawned clear and bright, a welcome respite from several days of unremitting rains. Early that morning General Cos arrived with five hundred men, bringing Santa Anna's force to about twelve hundred. They were exhausted, having not slept or eaten in twenty-four hours. The Mexican general intended to attack the following day, but his decision to divide his army and go in pursuit of Zavala meant he no longer had the advantage of overwhelming numerical superiority. The rest of his army was far behind, slowed by bad weather as it tried to get across the floodwaters of the Brazos.

For the first time since the earliest days of the rebellion, a large majority of the men who would engage the Mexican army in battle—about two-thirds—consisted of Anglo-Texan settlers. The remainder was composed of volunteers from the United States, as well as a few US troops, deserters from Gaines's army on the Louisiana border. There were still a few Mexican Texans in Houston's army; Juan Seguín commanded about twenty of his friends and neighbors from the ranches around San Antonio. But most of the Hispanos who supported the rebellion in the fall of 1835 had long since drifted away.[25]

Houston and some of his senior officers would later give varying accounts of the decision to stand and fight at Lynchburg. The arrival of General Cos's troops once again gave the general's critics grounds for complaint, who argued that he had already waited too long to engage the enemy. As the morning wore on, a frustrated John Wharton visited every mess in camp, telling the volunteers to prepare for a battle whether Houston issued the order or not. At noon the general held a contentious but inconclusive council of war with his senior officers that lasted two hours. Afterward, Houston walked alone through camp, stopping to talk to his troops, gauging their willingness to fight. It was only fitting that an army of volunteers should have some say in the matter. But in the end, the decision was Houston's alone.[26]

By late afternoon the order to attack had not been given, and Lorenzo de Zavala Jr. assumed there would be no fighting that day. Making his way down to Buffalo Bayou, the vice president's twenty-two-year-old son had recently joined the army and was serving as Houston's aide-de-camp. Finding a canoe he rowed over to the north bank, where his family's home had been converted into a field hospital, intending to visit a friend who had been seriously wounded in the skirmish the day before. As he walked up the bluff to his house, he suddenly noticed activity in the Texas camp across the bayou. The rebel army was forming in two parallel lines, about five hundred yards from the Mexican picket lines. A fifer began to play "Yankee Doodle," the unofficial national anthem of the United States at the time. "My heart leaped for joy," one volunteer recalled as the rebel army, given the order to advance, moved slowly across the open prairie. "I felt that I was an American citizen, and . . . no harm could befall me." Then Lorenzo heard the loud boom of the Texans' two six-pound cannons echoing across the water. Stopping to fire a single volley at the Mexican camp, the rebels broke into a mad run.[27]

Lorenzo started running, too, back down to his boat at the water's edge. By the time he got across, the Texans had overrun the Mexican breastworks. Santa Anna's poorly trained troops broke in total confusion. In a complete rout, blue-coated soldiers fled toward the San Jacinto River, described by one Mexican officer as "a bewildered and panic-stricken herd." It was all over in less than twenty minutes.[28]

The slaughter lasted much longer. For the next three hours, the battleground became a killing field, with nine hundred Texas troops shooting, clubbing, and stabbing Mexican soldiers in an orgy of bloodlust fueled by the desire to avenge the Americans who had fallen at the Alamo and Goliad. Most of the killing took place at Peggy's Lake, behind the Mexican line, where rebel marksmen easily picked off floundering infantrymen, weighed down by their heavy woolen uniforms, as they tried to swim across.

Seeing the Mexican troops throwing down their arms, Wharton attempted to put a stop to the carnage. He pulled a Mexican soldier onto his horse, only to have him promptly shot off. He gave one volunteer a direct order to cease firing; the man stepped back and menacingly cocked his rifle. Juan Seguín and his Hispano volunteers, who had placed white cards in their hats so as not to be confused with the enemy, also tried to end to the slaughter. When a voice in Spanish called out to him from a thicket, Seguín gave the order to stop firing. Juan Almonte and a group of officers emerged from the tall grass. Seguín's men rounded them up, and also took charge of some of the women accompanying the Mexican army. As darkness fell, six hundred Mexican soldiers lay dead, their bodies covering ten acres of blood-soaked ground. Incredibly, only eight Texans had died.[29]

WHEN THE SMOKE CLEARED, THE FULL IMPORT OF SAM HOUSton's lop-sided, logic-defying victory had yet to come into view. Although Santa Anna's entire senior command staff had either been killed or taken prisoner, the Mexican leader was nowhere to be found. The bulk of his army, meanwhile, far removed from the fighting, was still very much intact on the Brazos River. But in the days that followed it would become evident that the battle at Lynchburg represented a dramatic coda to the chain of events that had begun more than six months earlier at Gonzales, and Americans and Mexicans would craft starkly contrasting narratives to make sense of it all.

In Mexico City flags were flown at half-mast, and though Santa Anna bore no small amount of blame for the defeat, few Mexicans believed that the Army of Operations had been bested by an undisciplined mob of Anglo colonists. In their view, the rebellion had been outsourced to mercenaries from a hostile power, with the tacit approval and support of its government. The reaction in the United States did little to dispel this impression. Throughout much of the American republic, and particularly in the slaveholding South, the news was greeted with frenzied jubilation. Pundits found themselves at a loss for historical parallels in the modern era, and likened the contest to the battle between the Athenians and Persians at Marathon in 490 BC, to the Norman defeat by the Saxons at Hastings in 1066. Their breathless accounts portrayed a motley band of "Texians" as an Anglo-American David, which had triumphed against insuperable odds over a tyrannical Mexican Goliath.[30]

Such extravagant comparisons aside, the significance of the battle could hardly be overstated. What began as a Mexican story had morphed into an American one; a decade-long internal struggle between federalists and centralists had opened the way for the United States' rapid advance across the continent. But on a granular, human level, the rebellion represented a transnational and transcultural moment for the peoples of North America, one that drew Mexicans, Anglos, disparate groups of Native Americans, and people of African descent into the vortex of violent conflict. Either as actors or bystanders, and whether they knew it or not, all could claim a stake in the outcome. A multiracial nation had lost control of a vast swath of its territory to a people with a very narrow definition of citizenship and liberty. Life for those who called Texas home would never be the same again.

FIFTEEN

THE PRISONERS OF VELASCO

T HE NEXT MORNING, HOUSTON DISPATCHED SQUADS OF MEN
to scour the countryside for any Mexican soldiers who had escaped the Texan fury at Lynchburg. In the afternoon a search party
discovered a middle-aged man hiding in some sedge grass about
eight miles west of the battlefield. He was incongruously dressed in
a blue cotton jacket, leather cap, and pointed red slippers, clothing
he had found in an abandoned cabin, and a silver-buttoned, white
linen shirt. He told them he was an aide to Santa Anna, but as they
led him into camp they soon realized that the man in their custody
was no common prisoner. Despite his strange attire, Santa Anna's
officers recognized him immediately. Claiming to have important
information on the Mexican army, the man asked his captors to take
him to General Houston. They found him lying underneath a large
oak, nursing an ankle wound he had received during the battle. It was
only then that the prisoner announced that he was Antonio López
de Santa Anna.[1]

As word of his identity spread among the Texans, a crowd gathered, all jostling for a glimpse of the general, with more than a few
men demanding that he be executed on the spot. Houston sternly
ordered them away. Santa Anna was much more valuable alive than
dead. More mindful of public opinion than the captive caudillo,
whose "no quarter" policy had cost Mexico so much international
goodwill, he felt strongly that an independent Texas must follow

"every rule of humanity and morality." With Almonte serving as translator, the two men quickly worked out the details of a cease-fire. In dispatches to Filisola and Urrea to inform them of his capture, Santa Anna directed his generals to abandon their push into Texas and await further orders. At one point the Mexican leader paused to inquire the name of the field where the battle had taken place. "Lynchburg," Houston replied. Wharton, who had a more lilting name in mind, quickly suggested an alternative: "San Jacinto."[2]

Zavala came up from Galveston a few days after the battle. As the steamboat *Cayuga* chugged up to Lynch's Landing, it fired off a cannon to announce his arrival. Details of the first meeting between the vice president and Santa Anna since their dramatic falling out are sketchy, but Zavala was in no mood to be charitable. He was appalled by the slaughter all around him, and shaken by the news that one of his closest friends, General Manuel Castrillón, had been among the Mexicans killed in the fighting. Siding with the majority of the men in camp, he demanded that Santa Anna be executed immediately, a view he later attributed to "the heat of passion." Once his anger had subsided, he could see that Houston was right. "Here we do not use firing squads," he wrote a few weeks later, "like the semi-barbarous Spaniards and their imitators."[3]

After a few days, the stench of rotting corpses on the battlefield became oppressive, so the army packed up and moved camp, taking Santa Anna and his small entourage—his personal secretary, an aide, and Juan Almonte—with it. Stopping briefly on Galveston Island, then little more than a barren sandbar, the prisoners were taken by steamboat down the coast to Velasco. Houston sailed to New Orleans for medical treatment, leaving command of the army in the hands of Thomas Jefferson Rusk, who marched south to monitor Filisola's withdrawal. Conditions at Velasco were only marginally better than those at Galveston. Consisting of a dozen shanties, a two-story hotel, and a tavern, the village nonetheless bustled with activity as a rendezvous point for the hundreds of volunteers who were still arriving from the United States.[4]

Huddled in a small cabin, with the waves of the Gulf lapping along the beach, Santa Anna and Burnet negotiated a formal peace treaty. Declaring an end to hostilities, the so-called Treaty of Velasco provided for an exchange of prisoners and required all Mexican troops to withdraw south of the Rio Grande. In a separate, secret agreement, to be made public only after the terms of the public treaty had been met, Santa Anna promised to use what remained of his political influence to establish formal relations between the two countries. In what appeared to be a stunning concession, he acknowledged the Rio Grande as a boundary line, although the Nueces River had been the official border between Texas and Coahuila since the formation of the state more than a decade earlier.[5]

In truth, Santa Anna was eager to see the last of Texas, and would probably have signed anything Burnet put before him. Besides, he lacked any real authority to negotiate on his country's behalf, having relinquished executive power upon taking command of the army for the Texas campaign. What was more, the Mexican Congress could hardly be expected to endorse an agreement made by a captive under duress, who had just suffered the most ignominious defeat in the nation's history.

To represent Texas's interests, Zavala agreed to serve as a peace commissioner and accompany Santa Anna back to Mexico. It was a bold decision, one fraught with potential hazards, since he was now deeply unpopular in his homeland. But as a Mexican he wanted nothing more than to see his country return to the principles of liberalism, and Santa Anna's disgrace had surely given Zavala reason to hope that the ship of state could be righted. He may have also wanted an excuse to go home. He had always enjoyed a close relationship with Stephen F. Austin, who was still on his diplomatic mission in the United States. But he found Burnet to be an incompetent ass, and believed the new country's future was bleak with such men at the helm. And as much as he liked Americans, he may have come to realize that they would never accept him as an equal. They had been happy to embrace him during the rebellion, but with the onset of peace Zavala was not spared their racial prejudice, especially when it became known that the Mexican leader's wife was an Anglo-American.[6]

Zavala was also having a change of heart toward Santa Anna. After their tense meeting at San Jacinto, a reconciliation between the two men hardly seemed possible. But in the days that followed, signs of their old friendship began to emerge, and they dined together frequently. While the substance of their conversations is unknown, both men were nothing if not pragmatic. For more than a decade, their political fortunes in Mexico had been tightly intertwined, and their strange, on-again, off-again collaboration had, at times, worked to their mutual advantage. It is not unreasonable to suppose that Zavala and Santa Anna, as they surveyed the wreckage of their careers, plotted their return to public favor. In the dizzying tumult of Mexican politics, anything was possible.

But many Texans did not want Santa Anna to escape punishment so easily. Some members of Burnet's cabinet vigorously opposed the treaty, believing that the Mexican general's execution of the Goliad prisoners merited his imprisonment or death. The army of men camped on the beaches at Velasco felt the same way. The hostile mood among the volunteers only intensified when the schooner *Invincible* appeared offshore at the end of May to transport the prisoners and Zavala to Veracruz. In an effort to calm tensions, someone suggested that Santa Anna issue a public farewell, to which he readily agreed. "You shall never have cause to regret the kindness shown me," he told the people of Texas. On June 1 the Mexicans said goodbye to those who had befriended them during their captivity. John Wharton, who had grown particularly close to the prisoners, accompanied Santa Anna and Almonte by rowboat to the *Invincible* to see them off. Just as the ship was preparing to weigh anchor, a storm came up, delaying the voyage until the following day.[7]

The next morning, a storm cloud of a different sort appeared, in the form of one of the republic's newly minted generals, Thomas Jefferson Green. Since receiving a commission from President Burnet to raise troops for the Texas cause, Green had not been idle.

Drawing on his personal funds, he purchased powder and lead and recruited some 250 men in Natchez and New Orleans. Green learned of Houston's victory at San Jacinto as he was preparing to leave the Crescent City for Texas. With the Mexican government vowing to continue the war, he saw no reason to change his plans. Chartering a steamboat in Galveston, he brought with him his small army of volunteers.[8]

Green quickly took stock of the situation, and within a matter of hours managed to turn the sullen opposition to Santa Anna's release to his advantage. That night, he and other rabble-rousers held a public meeting to protest the Mexican leader's imminent departure. Only the Texas Congress, which had yet to be elected, possessed the authority to decide Santa Anna's fate, Green declared. In the morning he led a crowd of armed men to Burnet's cabin to demand that the Mexicans not be allowed to depart. Burnet pleaded with the crowd to honor the terms of the treaty. No one listened. Even Wharton, who was related to Green by marriage, failed to persuade the adventurer and his men to stand down. Zavala was furious and threatened to resign if Santa Anna was delivered up to the mob. The terms of the treaty must be honored, he insisted, for "a government that takes orders from armed masses is no longer a body politic." But Burnet saw no other way out. By this time, even the captain of the *Invincible* sided with the angry crowd, refusing to set sail unless ordered to do so by Green himself. Unnerved by the rowdies, some of whom were threatening violence against him and anyone else who might stand in their way, Burnet relented, and ordered Santa Anna and his aides returned to shore.[9]

Rowing out to the *Invincible*, Green and a group of men found Santa Anna in an agitated state below deck. Convinced that he would be lynched the moment he set foot on land, he refused to leave the ship, only relenting when local merchants proposed to take him and the other prisoners to a warehouse across the bay. A large crowd gathered on Velasco beach to laugh and jeer as the humiliated Mexican leader was escorted from the *Invincible*. "I was taken ashore and shown as a spectacle," Santa Anna later recalled bitterly. He would

17. Thomas Jefferson Green
(1802–1863), from Green's *Journal
of the Texian Expedition Against Mier.*
Arriving in Texas too late to take
part in the fight for independence,
"General" Thomas Jefferson Green
would become one of the most vocal
agitators for continuing the war
against Mexico after the Battle of San
Jacinto. Courtesy of North Carolina
Museum of History.

write an angry note of protest to Burnet, specifically blaming Green
and his volunteers "for the abuse to which I have been exposed." The
president may have been less concerned with the Mexican leader's
bruised feelings than the fact that he now had a major diplomatic
headache on his hands. In caving to an armed mob, Burnet was in
violation of the peace treaty he had just signed. Clearly, Santa Anna
was not the only hostage on Velasco beach.[10]

Still worried for the safety of the prisoners, the government
moved them upriver to Columbia a few days later. But they were
still in danger. Soon after they arrived, a drunken soldier fired a pistol at Santa Anna through the window of the cabin where they were
being confined. Not long afterward, their guards arrested a Spanish
saloonkeeper for an attempt to free them. Details of the plot, and
Santa Anna's role in it, were sketchy, but the evidence was deemed
strong enough to keep the general and Almonte chained together
by the leg to an iron ball, which they wore for several weeks. Time
passed, and they slowly settled into the monotony of their confinement. Several prominent Texans called on them, including Sam
Houston and Stephen F. Austin. The prisoners especially looked
forward to regular visits from John Wharton, who brought fresh

vegetables, butter, and other provisions from Eagle Island. They spent their days playing checkers and dominos, sometimes wagering their meager dinner rations, allowing the winner the luxury of a more adequate meal.[11]

Green's stunt at Velasco was yet another example, albeit an extreme one, of the almost compulsive inability of Anglo-Texas males to accept authority. It was this kind of behavior that had at times reduced the rebel army to an unruly mob, and which would continue to bedevil the republic's political and military leaders in the years ahead. Determined to make a name for himself, Green joined a cohort of loud, self-aggrandizing men, all jostling for pole position in the new republic. After the Velasco incident, he marched his volunteers south to Victoria to join Rusk's army. At first he refused to serve under Rusk, insisting that his own commission was the senior of the two. Upset that he had missed all the fighting, he conspired with Felix Huston, a Mississippi firebrand who also arrived after San Jacinto, in an effort to pressure the government to renew hostilities against Mexico. Thirsting for glory and plunder, the two men called for a new campaign against Matamoros and the villas del norte, but Rusk refused to endorse the scheme. Green's bombastic behavior and constant maneuvering to advance his career quickly grew tiresome. Said one Texan: "God help the work when the army of Texas is commanded by such a man."[12]

EVEN AS GREEN AND HUSTON CLAMORED FOR A CHANCE TO prolong the conflict with Mexico, the war-torn region would experience a dramatic escalation in violence involving Native Americans. The spring of 1836 saw a noticeable uptick in Indian raids, and by the summer the wave of depredations became impossible to ignore. Some were the work of familiar enemies like the Wichitas, who resumed their raids on settlements in the Brazos River valley. There were new sources of trouble, too. The Caddos of western Louisiana had recently signed a treaty with the US government that reduced them to near-starvation. When unscrupulous Indian agents cheated them out of the meager federal subsidies they had been promised, Caddo raiding parties crossed the Sabine River into Texas, sometimes attacking ranches as far west as San Antonio.

Settlers who moved to the margins of Anglo settlement would confront a more formidable adversary than the Wichitas and the Caddos. In the mid to late 1830s the Penateka Comanches were at the height of their power, pillaging the towns along Rio Grande with virtual impunity. And when there was nothing left to steal, they kept riding, venturing ever deeper into Mexico in an unending search for horses, mules, and captives. In the winter of 1835–36, several hundred well-armed warriors rode down off the Low Plains, fanning out across the region. Large Comanche raiding parties briefly occupied Laredo and, after the siege of the Alamo, San Antonio, in both towns driving off livestock, stealing horses, and demanding food and supplies from frightened residents. In the spring, as the rebellion was grinding toward its conclusion, Penatekas attacked a group of English colonists near the Nueces River, only a few miles from the Gulf Coast. And in May, when Anglo-Texans were still savoring their victory at San Jacinto, a combined force of Comanches, Caddos, and Wichitas descended on Fort Parker, a stockaded settlement on the Navasota River, in one of the most sensational of all Indian raids on the Texas frontier. Among the captives was six-year-old Cynthia Ann Parker, who would be raised by the Comanches until recaptured by Anglo-Texans twenty-four years later. In short, as Mexican armies retreated across South Texas, a new struggle for control of the lands above the Rio Grande—between Anglos and Native peoples—was just beginning.[13]

THAT SUMMER, THE PUBLIC'S ATTENTION TURNED TO THE COUNtry's first elections. Urged to run by William Wharton, Stephen F. Austin appeared to be a shoo-in for the presidency. Since their diplomatic mission to the United States, the two men had again become fast friends, this time for good. Austin enjoyed far better name recognition than the other candidate, Henry Smith, the controversial governor who had been impeached by the General Council after only a few weeks in office. But many radicals had never trusted Austin, not as an empresario when he tried to mediate conflicts with local authorities, nor as a rebel leader when he sought to bring Mexican federalists into the fight against Santa Anna's regime. His political enemies reminded voters that some of his closest friends had been engaged in questionable land deals before the rebellion. They even found fault with his role as a member of the three-man delegation to the United States, claiming he had done little more than "eat fine dinners and drink wine" while Texans fought for independence. Sam Houston waited until August to announce his candidacy, then won in a landslide, with Austin polling a distant, humiliating third. The empresario would accept the post of secretary of state in Houston's cabinet, but it was small consolation for a man who never found much love from the people he had labored so dutifully to serve.[14]

As might be expected in a new country still reeling from the trials of war, there were voting irregularities. And more often than not, they came at the expense of the Hispano population. In Nacogdoches, many Americans, some of whom had not been in Texas long enough to meet the six-month residency requirement to vote, tried to disqualify native-born Mexicans on the grounds that they had not taken part in the rebellion. The most brazen case of Hispano disenfranchisement occurred in Bexar County, a district consisting almost entirely of Mexican Texans. Passing through San Antonio with the army when the balloting took place, Thomas Jefferson Green announced his candidacy for a congressional seat. With the support of his troops, he won handily.[15]

When the new government met at Columbia, an insignificant village on the Brazos River, one of its first orders of business was to find a way to deal with the Santa Anna problem Green had created. The Mexican leader had become a political embarrassment for the new administration. Houston had no interest in a show trial, but Anglo-Texans' emotions were still too raw to send him home. So the president bundled him off to Washington, DC, to meet with Andrew

Jackson, ostensibly to discuss the possible annexation of Texas by the United States. The disgraced general departed in November, happy to leave Texas behind him. But Santa Anna was, if nothing else, a consummate survivor. His humiliation at San Jacinto did not spell the end of his political career, only an ignominious chapter of it. He would return to power in Mexico three years later, vowing to reclaim the country he had lost.

As Texas embarked on a new chapter in its history as an independent republic, it would do so without two men who had helped make its nationhood possible: Zavala and Austin. Zavala had found his seven-month stint as interim vice president to be a joyless task, and he was happy to return to private life. At his home near Lynch's Ferry, he succumbed to pneumonia on November 15, his forty-eighth birthday, a few days after his boat capsized in Buffalo Bayou. Austin, whose health had always been fragile, would die a month later, also of pneumonia, at the age of forty-three.

Longtime friends, the two men had much in common. In an age of rising nationalism, Austin and Zavala remained firm believers in a republicanism that transcended borders. Austin devoted his adult life to serving as an intermediary between white settlers and Mexican authorities. Zavala had labored no less diligently to remove all obstacles to American immigration as one of his country's most influential politicians. Both men, too, rose to prominence at a time when hyper-masculinity was considered to be an essential qualification for civic leadership. Behind his back, Austin's enemies derided the empresario as "a perfect granny," while Zavala, ever the cosmopolitan intellectual, saw his path to the presidential chair in Mexico closed to him as the strong man cult of *santanisma* took hold.[16]

Their legacies, however, could not have been more different. The news of Zavala's death was greeted with unmixed satisfaction in the Mexican press, which denounced him as a traitor to the nation. His seeming infatuation with American institutions, his unwavering support for the rebellion even as it became a war for independence, would earn him the enduring scorn of a people who would increasingly come to define their "Mexicanness" in opposition to the United

States. For their part, Anglo-Texans in the years that followed came to view him as a peripheral figure, unaware of his unstinting support for American colonization in Texas or his role as a furious opponent of Santa Anna's centralist regime.

Austin's reputation, by contrast, gained new luster after his death. Always eager to validate their creation story with comparisons to the American experience, Anglo-Texans promptly anointed him the "Father of Texas." With a single-minded sense of purpose, the empresario had blazed a trail in Texas that thousands followed, making his frontier community on the banks of the Brazos a beachhead for white settlement in the West. But in the end, Austin was no Washington. His apotheosis in death belied the fact that he had been out of step with Anglo public opinion for several years. Ironically, this was due in no small part to the fact that Austin's greatest contribution lay in his ability to bridge the cultural divide between his colonists and Mexican authorities. But as Texas became more American, Austin became less relevant. As Wharton's radicals began to push for a more confrontational policy toward the Mexican government, and as they came to insist on a complete separation from Mexico, he had been more follower than leader.

SIXTEEN

THE BARNYARD REPUBLIC

A NGLO-TEXANS ASSUMED THAT THEIR REPUBLIC WOULD BE nothing more than a stop-gap measure, a brief interlude before it could be annexed to the United States. If there had ever been any doubt as to their feelings on the matter, the recent fall elections included a referendum on the question, which passed by a convincing 3,277 to 93. And no one was more keen to see the Lone Star Republic annexed than its new president, Sam Houston. The constant threat of Indian depredations, rumors of a new campaign by Mexico, and the rank insubordination of the Texas army had convinced him that the fledgling nation could not long survive on its own. In a letter to President Jackson, Houston fairly begged his mentor to act quickly to shepherd Texas into the Union. "I look to you, as the friend and patron of my youth," he wrote, "to interpose on our behalf and save us."[1]

To serve as the new government's minister to the United States, Houston appointed his old friend William Wharton. The master of Eagle Island was a natural choice for the important assignment, having been a member of the three-man commission that toured the United States earlier in the year to seek aid on behalf of the rebel government. Wharton's instructions were simple enough: persuade Washington to recognize the Lone Star Republic as an independent state and open talks with the Jackson administration that would, Houston hoped, ultimately lead to a treaty of annexation.

Nine months earlier, Wharton had been greeted by rapturous crowds, not only in Southern cities but in Cincinnati and New York. Now, as he traveled by steamboat up the Mississippi on his way to Washington, he could not fail to notice the shift in public mood on the Texas question, which had become enmeshed in the increasingly bitter debate over slavery. A speedy union of the two North American republics, once seen as a foregone conclusion, looked increasingly unlikely.

In Washington, Wharton found President Jackson in an inhospitable frame of mind. Old Hickory was eager for the United States to acquire Texas, but only if it could be done without disrupting relations with Mexico. Indeed, Jackson was annoyed that the question had been put before the voters of Texas at all. The referendum had infuriated Mexican leaders, confirming their suspicions that Washington intended to annex Texas all along. Domestic political concerns were another, no less important, reason for Jackson to tread lightly on the Texas question. In three months, he would leave the White House to his successor, Martin Van Buren. Any attempt to acquire Texas was bound to be controversial, and Jackson preferred to let the incoming administration tackle the issue later, when passions had cooled.

Despite Jackson's concerns, pro-Texas Democrats pushed a bill through Congress recognizing Texas as an independent, sovereign state, which the president signed as he prepared to leave office. Wharton stayed in Washington long enough to attend Van Buren's inauguration, then headed for home. His mission only partly accomplished, he left the capital more convinced than ever that "if Texas is annexed at all it will not be until after the question has convulsed this nation for several sessions of Congress."[2]

The future of the new republic would not be decided by Anglo-Americans alone, however. The centralist government in Mexico City refused to concede the loss of its former province, and though it lacked the resources to launch another major offensive, a blockade of Texas ports remained in effect. On his way home to Eagle Island, Wharton boarded the *Independence*, bound for Velasco. The schooner was in sight of land when a pair of Mexican warships hove into view and gave chase. A four-hour naval battle followed, as an anxious crowd watched along the beach, until the Texas vessel, out-gunned and disabled, struck its colors. All aboard were captured and taken to Matamoros. "I do not pity him," Stephen F. Austin's sister Emily wrote when she heard the news that Wharton was a prisoner in Mexico, recalling his lack of sympathy following the empresario's arrest in 1834. "I hope they will keep him until his Proud Spirit is completely Humbled."[3]

As it turned out, they did not keep him long. In an attempt to secure his brother's release, John Wharton chartered a vessel and sailed to Matamoros with thirty Mexican officers captured at San Jacinto, hoping to arrange an exchange of prisoners. But the ship ran aground in a storm at the mouth of the Rio Grande, and local authorities hauled him off to jail, where he learned that his brother had already escaped (according to family lore, in the garb of a priest). A well-placed bribe secured the younger Wharton's release a few days later, and by the end of the summer the brothers were back home at Eagle Island, just in time to stand for election to the next session of Congress. The citizens of Brazoria celebrated their return by electing William to the Senate and John to the House of Representatives.[4]

THE SO-CALLED CITY OF HOUSTON, THE NEW CAPITAL OF TEXAS, did not exist when William Wharton left on his diplomatic mission to the United States a year earlier. The change of venue was at best a marginal improvement over the miserable accommodations at Washington-on-the-Brazos. Though touted by its enterprising founders as "handsome and beautifully elevated," where residents could enjoy the "sea breeze in all its freshness," Houston sat on a flat, treeless prairie about twenty miles west of Galveston Bay. The town was accessible to the Gulf by a stagnant waterway, Buffalo Bayou, which was so narrow in some places that steamboat passengers often needed to get out and remove fallen trees and other detritus blocking the boat's path. Until recently the town had been little more than a collection of tents, which one visitor likened to a revival campground or a traveling circus. But in the summer of 1837, Houston was a boom town, with two hotels filled to capacity, a few stores, and numerous grog shops. Its unpaved streets, which turned into ankle-deep, muddy bogs when it rained, thronged with immigrants from the United States, speculators and gamblers, volunteers recently discharged from the army, and large numbers of "floaters," rootless young men with no discernible livelihood in search of opportunities.[5]

The rise of Houston from the swampy lowlands of the Gulf Coastal plain was emblematic of the explosive growth which the country had experienced during Wharton's absence. Literally scores of town-building projects appeared along the country's many waterways, all vying to provide goods and services to the influx of settlers from the United States. Most would remain undeveloped, though the savvy entrepreneur was not always the poorer for it. Little capital was required to have a town site surveyed and platted, and the demand for town lots was so great after independence that land titles often served as the principal medium of exchange.

Speculators invested heavily along the coast, especially in areas they thought would serve as ports of entry. Thomas Jefferson Green and the Wharton brothers bought up land in Velasco, which seemed for a time destined to become the great commercial emporium of the new republic. As president of the Velasco Association, Green spent lavishly to promote the town. He operated a horse track and bought a newly constructed hotel, where he held grand balls during racing season, shipping in food and liquor from New Orleans. By all accounts the galas were a tremendous success, attracting visitors from the plantations along the river and as far away as Houston. The fare failed to meet the exacting tastes of one English traveler, however, who thought the sherry tasted like chili vinegar and bilge water.[6]

Green's dream of founding a Gulf Coast metropolis might well have succeeded if not for the sandbar at the mouth of the Brazos, which proved so treacherous that the port was littered with the hulks of vessels that had run aground. Faced with prohibitively high maritime insurance rates, shippers looked for safer ports of call. They found one on Galveston Island, a barren, thirty-mile-long sand bar farther up the coast. By 1838 the island's eastern edge had become a bustling town of three thousand.[7]

For all this frenetic economic activity, the fact remained that after a decade and a half of settlement, whites had managed to establish at best a foothold over the region. The Camino Real, now known as the Old San Antonio Road, still formed a rough western frontier line for citizens of the republic, who in the immediate aftermath of the rebellion constituted just over half the population. The villages of the Cherokees and other immigrant tribes occupied much of the northeast, whereas the Upper Brazos and Trinity rivers were home to the Wichitas. To the west, on the Edwards Plateau above San Antonio, lay the hunting grounds of the Penateka Comanches. South Texas, the enormous wedge of land between the Nueces and Rio Grande, also lay beyond the reach of Anglo-Texan rule. "Of this section of country very little is known," the first official map issued by the Texas government noted. That would have come as a surprise to the people who lived there, the Hispano residents of Laredo, who for generations had worked ranches on both sides of the river and considered themselves citizens of the Mexican state of Tamaulipas. But the white republic claimed it all. Declaring the Rio Grande to be its southern and western boundary, it would insist that its domain encompassed all of modern-day Texas and half of New Mexico, and sizable chunks of present-day Colorado, Kansas, and Wyoming, as well.[8]

Just as Anglo Texans liked to draw parallels between their struggle for independence and the American Revolution, their new government presented a rough facsimile of American political institutions. Yet despite its similarities to the US Constitution, the charter drafted by the delegates at Washington-on-the-Brazos in 1836 reflected the fervently democratic impulses of its times. Whereas its American antecedent had been drafted by men seeking to create a political mechanism that would protect the landed gentry, the Texas Constitution fully embraced the ideas of white male democracy and popular sovereignty. It explicitly eliminated property requirements for voting and abandoned the Electoral College. All offices were to be filled by direct election, with the exception of judges, who served not for life but four-year terms. As a check on the power of the executive branch, separate ballots were required for president and vice president, who served three-year, nonconsecutive terms. Opposed to the idea of a professional political class, the framers of the Texas Constitution reduced the terms for officeholders to half that of those in the United States: one year for representatives, three for senators.[9]

As earnest Jacksonians, the delegates were equally concerned with the concentration of economic power. Reflecting the era's anti-elitist mood, the constitution barred imprisonment for debt, endorsed the idea of free public education, and explicitly forbade the creation of corporate monopolies—an issue the United States government would not begin to seriously address for another fifty years. Most important of all, the document guaranteed the republic's citizens—that is, whites and Hispanos—access to land, the cornerstone of an agricultural republic. Thus the constitution came with a promise: that each family living in Texas at the time of the rebellion would receive title to 4,600 acres of land (single men would receive one-third that amount)—no strings attached.[10]

In the years that followed, the republic's political leaders would exhibit the same brand of pioneer populism. In one of his first Senate speeches, William Wharton censured many planters, calling them out by name (including his own in-laws, the Groces), who had chosen to flee with their slaves during the Runaway Scrape rather than defend the homeland. Similarly, an aversion to the so-called money power became evident when a group of businessmen sought to obtain congressional approval to build a network of roads, railroads and canals, the profits of which it proposed to use to assume banking operations. Congress initially gave the green light to this ambitious scheme, then abruptly reversed course and revoked the company's charter amid growing criticism that it had created a financial behemoth that would manipulate land prices and stifle competition.[11]

The Texas Congress would give statutory teeth to these economic principles. In an effort to clear away the obstacles that blocked the path to prosperity for white Americans, it passed the Homestead Exemption Act in 1839, barring creditors from seizing an individual's home, the tools of his trade, and fifty acres of farmland for payment of debt. Intended to allow debtors the means to regain their financial independence in hard times, the act proved so successful in luring settlers looking for a fresh start that it would be copied by several Southern states. Education offered another pathway to economic mobility, prompting Congress to pass a bill requiring each county to set aside land to fund public schools.[12]

These legislative achievements appear all the more impressive given the crude conditions and rowdy atmosphere that prevailed in the Texas Congress, both of which tended to discourage sober deliberation. When legislators convened for their first session in Houston, they met in a building without a roof. Visiting Congress when it moved, briefly, to Washington-on-the-Brazos in 1842, one traveler found the honorable members "seated on candle boxes and sugar casks, in short, on any thing they could find; and each man was *whittling* away without intermission." Proper decorum often gave way to angry, and occasionally violent, confrontations. The Surgeon General of the army resigned after he assaulted the president pro tem of the Senate in the gallery with his buggy whip. In the Fourth Congress, the appointment of a new Postmaster General so infuriated another aspirant for the job that the two men, both senators, exchanged angry words on the floor of the chamber, then came to blows. A recess was called, and the contest resumed on the street outside the capitol. Friends of the two men also weighed in, and the fight degenerated into an ugly free-for-all. There were at least three cases of gunfire in the capitol or its immediate vicinity involving lawmakers. On one such occasion, the congressman from La Grange drew a derringer and shot the former Speaker of the House twice, though not fatally. Violence in the halls of Congress became so commonplace that one frustrated legislator complained that members would no longer speak their minds "for fear of being murdered."[13]

Houston generally managed to avoid such affrays, notwithstanding a unique ability to goad his enemies into fits of rage. By his own count, possibly exaggerated, he was called upon to settle affairs of honor on the dueling ground no less than twenty-four times. All of them he brushed aside, usually with a sense of humor, telling his antagonists to wait their turn. In response to a challenge from the much shorter David G. Burnet, he begged off with the excuse, "I never fight downhill."[14]

One of the most common indictments leveled by critics of the president was his overweening vanity. Gregarious and charismatic, the hero of San Jacinto enjoyed a cult-like following among a broad swath of the voting public. But the new country's boisterous men of ambition deeply resented the long shadow cast by the president, who was often accused of claiming for himself the "credit that was due others." Certainly there can be little doubt that Houston felt a compulsive need to be the center of attention. Cultivating the persona of eccentric showman, he delighted in flouting conventional forms of behavior. He drank heavily, often to spectacular excess. "He has not drawn a sober breath since he has been here," one man who lodged with the president in a Nacogdoches boarding house observed in 1837. Forgoing the drab black frock coat that was the fashion of the day, he dressed outlandishly, and could sometimes be seen in full Cherokee dress, complete with moccasins and brightly colored turban. When the ornithologist John James Audubon met him in 1837, he found the forty-four-year-old president, who was then living in a small, log cabin dogtrot, attired in "a fancy velvetcoat, and trowsers trimmed with broad gold lace."[15]

Houston's critics also found fault with the president's policies, especially his refusal to sanction an offensive war against Mexico. Many saw the continuation of hostilities as the surest means to advance their own careers. For all his prodigal flamboyance, Houston continued to exhibit the caution that had characterized his leadership during the war for independence. A policy of restraint was needed, he believed, if Texas was to have any hope of coaxing Washington into making an offer of annexation. Unfortunately for Houston, he

18. Sam Houston (1793–1863), by Martin Johnson Heade in 1846. Although many prominent Texans were angered by his flamboyant personality and cautious policies, the "Hero of San Jacinto" enjoyed strong support among the voters, who twice elected him president of the Lone Star Republic.

inherited from the interim government a rowdy and restless army that had been camped in southeast Texas for several months, whose firebrand commander, Felix Huston, was chomping at the bit to lead a campaign to the Rio Grande. When the administration tried to install a more compliant general, Huston insisted that his honor had been sullied by the decision to supersede him and challenged his successor to a duel. The two men drew pistols at dawn, Huston wounding his rival so seriously that he was unable to take command. The president finally managed to check his insubordinate general by issuing furloughs to all but a few hundred troops, just enough to protect the frontier but dashing the war hawks' dreams of glory, at least for the time being.[16]

Houston had even more trouble with his secretary of the navy, S. Rhoads Fisher. The president believed the two ships that constituted the Texas navy should guard the Texas coastline, but Fisher wanted to retaliate for the attack on the *Independence*, a course strongly endorsed, not surprisingly, by the Wharton brothers. Ignoring Houston's orders, the secretary not only dispatched the fleet to the Yucatán, but decided to tag along as a "volunteer." For three months in the summer of 1837, the fleet attacked enemy vessels, burned fishing villages, and even raised the Texas flag on the island

of Cozumel, an act that was met with the "acclamations" of the inhabitants—or so Fisher later claimed. The secretary returned to
Galveston with the fleet to a hero's welcome. Houston promptly
fired him.[17]

The matter did not end there, since the constitution, in another
check on executive power, barred the president from dismissing
any cabinet member without the advice and consent of the Senate.
Houston's enemies rushed to Fisher's defense, and for three days the
chamber deliberated, with John Wharton serving as one of the secretary's lawyers. For Wharton, one of Houston's sharpest critics during
the San Jacinto campaign, the president's decision to dismiss Fisher
was the final straw. He condemned Houston's conduct in a blistering
speech, described by one observer as "the bitterest invective I have
ever heard uttered by man." Recalling the heroism of the men who
had given their lives for Texas independence, Wharton contrasted
their sacrifice with the current occupant of the presidential chair,
whom he described as a "bloated mass of inebriety and insanity, of
hypocrisy, vanity and villainy, . . . sitting like an incubus, and weigh-
ing down the hopes and paralyzing the energies of our infant republic." The Senate ultimately confirmed Houston's decision to replace
Fisher, but the president's longtime friendship with the Wharton
brothers had come to an ugly end.[18]

With Houston barred by the constitution from serving a second
consecutive term, his political enemies were confident of victory in
the next presidential election. Casting about for a candidate, they
settled on Vice President Mirabeau Lamar, a former newspaperman
from Georgia. Lamar had name recognition, but he was no match
for the "Hero of San Jacinto" in the charisma department. The two
men were a study in contrasts. An intense, brooding figure, the vice
president at times seemed lost in a world of his own, oblivious to
those around him. As careless in his dress as Houston was flamboyant, he could usually be seen wearing pleated baggy pants cut so
short that they barely covered the tops of his shoes. And whereas the
president possessed a clear-eyed view of the country's challenges and

weaknesses, Lamar imagined a new American republic stretching as far as the Pacific Ocean. His "mind is altogether of a dreamy, poetic order," said one acquaintance, who believed he was "wholly unfit" for the "realities of his present station."[19]

Lamar's rather limited people skills extended to affairs of the heart. He wrote poems and bits of verse, a collection of which he would later publish, almost all of them about women he had known. Having lost his wife to tuberculosis, he courted at least two women in Texas, both of them recently widowed. The attractive Emily Zavala caught his eye, from whom he bought some land on Buffalo Bayou. "V.P. Lamar has gone up there to settle some business with her," wrote one of his friends. "'Tis *whispered* he has some *other business*," he added confidentially, though he doubted, correctly as it turned out, that the vice president would meet with success so soon after her husband's death. Lamar pursued James Walker Fannin's widow, still grieving over her husband's execution at Goliad, with a similar want of tact. Paying a visit to raise the issue of matrimony, the vice president suddenly got cold feet. Finding that "her mind was not in a state" to discuss "the intended subject," he wrote, "I withdrew without an interview." Minerva Fannin withdrew to Georgia a short time later.[20]

With the socially maladroit Lamar as its standard-bearer, the anti-Houston faction would never be more than a loosely organized bloc, a cabal of angry men united only by their hatred of Sam Houston. The Wharton brothers, seasoned political operatives who had done so much to steer Texas toward independence, might have lent the group much-needed organizational leadership. But fate would take a hand, and both men would die before the end of the decade. Thirty-two-year-old John succumbed to yellow fever late in 1838. He lingered for a time, and a story circulated that he asked to see Houston on his deathbed. His friends hotly denied the rumor. Enormously popular with the men who served with him during the rebellion, he was buried with full military honors, eulogized as "the keenest blade" at San Jacinto. Three months later, older brother

William would meet an untimely and painful end in a freak accident when one of his pistols discharged as he was mounting his horse. The bullet sheared away two fingers and lodged in his abdomen. At first there was hope of a recovery, but tetanus set in, and he died three days later. With his prickly temperament and aristocratic bearing, the master of Eagle Island never received credit as the driving spirit of the radical movement. Anglo-Texans owed him more than they knew.[21]

FACED WITH AN ARRAY OF SEEMINGLY INSURMOUNTABLE CHALlenges, the Texas experiment in nationhood during its first couple of years had gone about as well as one might have expected—poorly. Not that it mattered. After all, the Texas government was just marking time until a treaty of annexation could be negotiated with Washington.

Or so Houston thought. Disappointed by Jackson's decision to leave the issue to his successor, he still expected the Van Buren administration to take quick action on the measure. But the rumblings of anti-Texas feeling in the North were growing louder. At the center of the debate over whether to annex Texas was Benjamin Lundy, a Quaker who had been quietly preaching the antislavery gospel for more than two decades. Less radical than his protégé William Lloyd Garrison, who demanded immediate abolition, Lundy favored the gradual emancipation of African Americans in bondage. With the encouragement of José María Tornel, he had visited Texas in the early 1830s to explore the possibility of establishing a colony of free blacks on Mexico's northern frontier. Red tape and a shortage of funds delayed the project, however, which was finally shelved when the rebellion broke out.[22]

Little known outside antislavery circles, Lundy suddenly burst onto the national scene after San Jacinto, authoring a series of articles on Texas that were later published as a widely read pamphlet. He made a startling allegation: the uprising in Texas had not been a struggle for freedom against a tyrannical regime, but a plot to seize the area by Southern slaveholders, with a little help from New York land speculators. Ignoring the long history of friction between American colonists and the government in Mexico City, Lundy offered little in the way of concrete evidence to support his claims. The antislavery advocate was on firmer ground, however, when he looked to the future, describing a Union in which Texas, subdivided into as many as half a dozen slaveholding states, would tilt the balance of power in Washington in the South's favor. Lundy's charges of a dark conspiracy by the "slave power" found a forceful champion in John Quincy Adams, the former president, now a seventy-one-year-old congressman from Massachusetts, who began submitting to Congress scores of petitions from Northern voters urging the Van Buren administration to forswear any intention of bringing Texas into the Union.[23]

As a New Yorker, Van Buren always had qualms about the South's system of bonded labor. In the interests of party unity, as well as a desire to remain in Jackson's good graces, he had kept them to himself. But it was now clear that rising antislavery sentiment threatened to drive a wedge between the Northern and Southern wings of the Democratic Party. The fact that Texas seemed hell-bent on continuing the war against Mexico also gave the president pause. As a result, when Texas diplomats in Washington submitted a formal request for annexation, Van Buren's secretary of state gave them little reason for optimism. Acquiring the infant republic would be a violation of the United States' treaty with Mexico, they were told. Indeed, the secretary of state questioned whether the United States had the legal right to annex a foreign state at all.[24]

In the summer of 1838, the geriatric but indefatigable Adams staged a twenty-two-day filibuster to prevent a resolution on annexation from coming to a vote. In a voice trembling with sulfurous rage, Adams held the House floor each morning, drawing upon Lundy's writings to rail against the American slaveholders who would stop at nothing to perpetuate their institution. An exhausted Congress adjourned without taking any action on the matter, but for Van Buren the message was clear: Texas was far more trouble than it was worth.

The Houston administration quietly withdrew the annexation proposal a few months later.[25]

If American slavery did not father the new republic as Lundy claimed, it had certainly made it an orphan. Left to fend for itself, Texas now became a country by default—something none of its citizens expected and few wanted. It was one thing for Texas to declare itself a republic, one British visitor noted, but that did not make it a nation. As the likelihood of annexation dimmed, land prices fell and immigration slowed. Mounting debts left the government unable to field an army, and therefore vulnerable to an angry southern neighbor that vowed to erase the stain of San Jacinto. And through it all, the chaos that had characterized the rebellion showed no sign of abating, fueled by a class of noisy, swaggering men who, a frustrated Houston complained, seemed incapable of submitting to "any rule but their passions, nor to any government but their will." With no little understatement, one immigrant from Virginia wrote in his diary as he mulled these challenges, "The prospect before us is anything but cheering."[26]

SEVENTEEN

HE IS UNFORTUNATELY
A MAN OF COLOUR

LONGTIME RESIDENTS OF NACOGDOCHES REMEMBERED BEN-
jamin Lundy. Three years before the outbreak of the rebellion,
in the summer of 1832, he had walked into town from Louisiana—he
could not afford a horse—on his first trip to explore the possibility
of establishing a colony of emancipated African Americans in Texas.
Although he arrived under an assumed name, he quickly dropped the
pretense and made his intentions known to local officials. They were
immediately receptive to the plan and introduced him to Nacogdoches's most prominent free person of color, William Goyens.

Lundy was impressed by Goyens. Convinced that slavery could
only be eradicated by showing Southern whites that African Americans possessed the capacity for self-improvement, he was delighted to
find a free person of color who had clearly prospered under Mexican
rule. Indeed, the Nacogdoches businessman was a living testament to
Lundy's belief that the debased condition of enslaved people in the
American South stemmed not from an inherent inferiority, but from
the "peculiar institution" itself.

Encouraged by what he had seen, Lundy returned to the United
States to raise funds for the venture. He was back in Nacogdoches
two years later, staying more than a fortnight. He spent some of the
time with Goyens and his wife, Mary, at their home on Goyens Hill,
where the Quaker abolitionist had a chance to bring him up to date

on his colonization project. One evening, Goyens took Lundy to a fandango in the Mexican quarter, and two of Mary's brothers, who were visiting from Louisiana, tagged along. Evidently they enjoyed themselves, Mary's siblings confiding to Lundy that they were "well satisfied with their coloured brother-in-law."[1]

Lundy's notoriety as the author of a damning polemic against slave owners after the Texas Revolution could not have been welcome news to Goyens. His friendship with the now-famous antislavery champion must have confirmed for Nacogdoches's white residents what they had long suspected: that unenslaved African Americans, even the very few like William Goyens who owned slaves themselves, represented an insidious threat to the stability of the social order.

Not that they lacked reasons to resent Goyens already. He was more prosperous than most whites, and his marriage to Mary Sibley flouted sexual conventions. What was more, he was well-known as a friend and advocate of the Cherokees, a group many feared almost as much as their slaves. Perhaps most galling of all, Goyens refused to assume the deferential posture that his white neighbors, most of them dirt-poor farmers from the Lower South, expected of a free person of color. "There are some quarreling kind of people in this country that cusses Goin [Goyens] in every direction," one resident observed. The Nacogdoches businessman could hardly have been oblivious to these sentiments, yet he carried himself proudly, as someone "who felt his consequence."[2]

At the time of the rebellion, William Goyens was one of only three or four hundred unenslaved African Americans in Texas, most of them adult men. While a few may have joined Santa Anna's army, far more is known about those who fought alongside Anglo-Americans. Swept up in the tumult of rebellion, and with the promise of land bounties for military service, they volunteered with their white neighbors, often serving with distinction. A few days after the skirmish at Gonzales, Kentucky native Samuel McCullough was wounded in the attack on the Mexican garrison at Goliad, and thereafter became known as the first Texan to shed blood in the fight for independence. Greenbury Logan, a blacksmith in Stephen F. Austin's colony, fought alongside Sam Maverick in December at San Antonio, where he, too, was severely wounded, losing the use of his right arm. Far more unusual was the case of Peter Allen, a middle-aged Philadelphia musician who inexplicably joined the throng of white Americans that made their way to Texas when the rebellion began. Joining a regiment of Alabama volunteers, he would be captured at the Battle of Coleto and executed at Goliad. None played a more important role than Goyens, however, whose diplomatic service as a liaison and interpreter helped maintain peace between the rebel government and the Cherokees.[3]

From the outset of the conflict with Mexico, there were unmistakable signs that free men of color would not share in the benefits of an Anglo-American victory. Fears of slave unrest prompted the General Council to prohibit free blacks from immigrating to Texas. A few months later, as Santa Anna's army was moving across the province, the status of free blacks was very much on the minds of delegates who met at the Convention at Washington-on-the-Brazos. The constitution not only upheld the immigration ban, but required that free people of color already living in Texas receive permission from Congress to stay. An early draft granting citizenship to free blacks was quickly scuttled. In its final form, the document recognized "all persons" living in Texas as citizens, "Africans, the descendants of Africans, and Indians excepted." Though some free black veterans eventually did receive headrights for their military service, it was small consolation for their loss of liberty. In the new white republic, racial lines snapped taut, and the rights and privileges they had taken for granted as residents of mixed-race Mexico abruptly disappeared.[4]

For most Texans of African descent, their lives after San Jacinto changed not at all. Abandoning the legislative sleight-of-hand that winked at de facto slavery under the Mexican system of debt peonage, the delegates to the Convention wrote into the constitution language that made the "peculiar institution" a cornerstone of the new republic. Unlike the United States, where political leaders had wrestled with the slavery issue since the country's inception, in Texas

the government was barred from abolishing the labor system or cur-
tailing it in any way. Its slaveholders needed an act of Congress to
emancipate their human property, and even then had to bear the
costs of removing them from the republic. In rebelling against the
tyranny of Mexican rule, Anglo-Texans acquired a new inalienable
right: the freedom to own slaves. It was a cosmic irony that, almost
without exception, they preferred to ignore.[5]

After San Jacinto, cotton farmers streamed into the region,
bringing their bonded labor with them. While the majority of enslaved people could still be found on the plantations of the Lower
Brazos River valley, the Piney Woods that Goyens called home
would see a dramatic increase in its chattel population. Ayish Bayou,
a collection of shanties near the Louisiana border only a decade earlier, now known as San Augustine, would become a flourishing emporium for the cotton trade. Farther north, American settlers poured
onto the open prairies below the Red River. The area had long been
ignored by westward-moving whites because of the "Great River
Raft," a logjam stretching for more than a hundred miles that made
commercial traffic on the waterway impossible. In the 1830s the US
War Department began to clear the river, driving specially outfitted
boats through the dense snarl of cottonwoods, post oaks, and other
trees that fell into the river each spring during flash floods. Inhabited
largely by Shawnees and Delaware Indians before the rebellion, by
the end of the decade far northeast Texas was home to several thousand people, one quarter of whom were enslaved.[6]

Yet try as they might, slaveholding Texans could never fully
replicate the institution they had known in the American South.
Although the new republic followed the United States in writing
into its constitution a provision barring the importation of slaves,
the Brazos River continued to be a destination for slave ships from
the Caribbean. Texas's most prominent merchant and entrepreneur,
Thomas McKinney, built slave pens for "newly landed Africans" at his
warehouses at Velasco. The traffic in human cargo was so lucrative
that some ships dropped anchor at the mouth of the Sabine River,
where smugglers drove enslaved men and women into Louisiana.

With no letup in the trade after San Jacinto, the Texas government requested help from the US Navy to patrol its coastline. Concerned that the republic's reputation as an illegal market for Caribbean slaves would scuttle its chances for annexation, William Wharton wrote to Stephen F. Austin from Washington, "For God's sake and for our country's sake, crush these new projects for introducing Africans, and put to death all concerned." But the piracy continued, with the last known slave ship from Cuba landing along the Texas coast in 1840.[7]

Sitting on the western edge of the cotton empire, Texas also differed from the Lower South by offering a range of potential safe havens for enslaved people intent on making a bid for freedom. Some men of African descent found refuge among the immigrant tribes of the Piney Woods and often took part in clashes with Texas whites. One slave, thought to have entered Texas on a slave ship from Cuba, simply disappeared into the post oak bottomlands of the Navidad River. Venturing out at night to rob chicken coops and dairies of isolated farmhouses, he managed to avoid capture, giving rise to folktales about the "Wild Man of the Navidad" that would persist for generations. Along the Brazos and Colorado river valleys, most enslaved people seeking freedom naturally set their sights on Mexico. As one former slave put it many years later, "There was no reason to *run* up north. All we had to do was *walk* south, and we'd be free as soon as we crossed the Rio Grande." Actually, it was quite a bit harder than that. Some died crossing the more than one hundred miles of bleak chaparral; others were killed by roving gangs of cattle rustlers or Comanche raiding parties.[8]

It is impossible to know how many people escaped lives of bondage, but Texas newspapers were filled with runaway notices placed by owners seeking to reclaim their property, or by sheriffs who had apprehended men and women they believed to be escaped slaves. Recently enslaved Africans were especially prone to escape, judging by the number of runaway notices describing slaves with tribal scars who spoke little or no English. In one notice, Leander McNeel, a neighbor of the Wharton family who was actively involved in the illegal slave trade, offered a reward for two escaped Africans, one of whom had run away "five or six times," twice when he was in irons.[9]

$200 REWARD.

I WILL give the above Reward for the delivery to me of two African Negroes, named GUMBY, and ZOW, who absconded from my plantation, Oyster Creek, county of Brazoria, some time since. The above slaves are about 30 years of age—one about 5 feet 10 inches, the other 5 feet 8 inches—the largest has a broad face, the other a very wild look.

EDWIN WALLER.

September 27, 1837.   9–tf

19. Runaway African Slave Notice, *Matagorda Bulletin*, 1837. Courtesy of Dolph Briscoe Center for American History, University of Texas at Austin.

Most fugitives were adult males, though whole families sometimes attempted the hazardous journey. A party of eleven enslaved people escaped from a plantation on the Brazos River that included women and two small children. Runaways also coordinated their flight with those from nearby farms, making daring escapes that must have been well-planned in advance. Seven slaves on three different plantations near the Brazos Falls ran away in December 1844, absconding with supplies and more than two dozen horses. A month later, twenty-five escaped from farms in the Bastrop area, most of whom were recaptured near the Guadalupe River, seventy miles to the south. More often than not, runaways were held in local jails until their owners could be found and came to collect them, though in very rare cases whites simply shot them on sight, leaving their bones "to bleach upon the soil."[10]

But many did find their way to safety. As the cotton economy became more deeply entrenched in Texas, more and more fugitives—several thousand over the next two decades—would make new lives for themselves in the towns along the Rio Grande. They blended easily into the mixed-race communities along the border, with some marrying into prominent families. Even two of Sam Houston's slaves, Tom and Esau, escaped to Mexico. One became a barber in Matamoros, the other joined the Mexican army. Taking their loss in good humor, Houston described them as "smart, intelligent fellows," who would help to "civilize and refine Mexico." After all, he noted dryly, "their associations in Texas had been remarkably good."[11]

In one important respect, Texas slavery was identical to the system of labor in the American South: it fostered a deep distrust of outsiders bordering on paranoia. When slaves ran off, Texas planters were quick to assume they had help, eyeing with intense suspicion anyone who did not have a direct stake in the institution. Some town councils passed ordinances attempting to isolate enslaved people by limiting their contacts with the community. Critics of the slave system usually had the good sense to keep their opinions to themselves. Some did not. Benjamin Lundy was threatened with violence during a stopover at San Felipe on his second trip to Texas. When Stephen Pearl Andrews, a Massachusetts lawyer, attempted to deliver a public address on abolitionism on Galveston Island in 1843, a band of armed men escorted him down to the wharf and put him on a boat back to the mainland. The controversy followed Andrews to Houston, where a mob brandishing a rope appeared at his house. Andrews got the message and hastily left the country.[12]

Outside agitators were few and could usually be identified without too much difficulty. But as in the American South, free people of color seemed to represent a particularly serious threat. Some had taken enslaved women as common law wives, giving them access to the slave quarters. Even if they were not actively working to undermine the institution, unenslaved African Americans challenged the natural order of things, whites believed. "A family of free Negroes," explained one newspaper editor, "will render the slaves of the plantations near which they are situated, dissatisfied, disobedient, restless, thievish and corrupt."[13]

At first, Anglo-Texans tolerated the small number of free blacks in their midst, but in 1840 Congress passed a draconian law requiring all unenslaved black people to leave the country within two years. Those who remained would be arrested and sold. Slaveowners supported the legislation in principle, apparently giving little thought to how it might impact their own communities. As soon as the law went into effect, Congress was inundated with memorials from whites on behalf of free persons of color they knew to be productive and law-abiding.[14]

William Goyens had little trouble lining up prominent citizens to endorse his exemption petition. Realizing that his success depended on making himself useful to the white community, he continued to serve as Sam Houston's link to the Cherokees, and on at least one occasion helped slave owners reclaim runaways who escaped to Indian Territory. Thomas Jefferson Rusk, major general of the Texas militia and a Nacogdoches congressman, drafted the memorial testifying to the good character of Goyens, who "has conducted himself as an honest industrious citizen, has accumulated considerable property in lands etc. and has been of great service to the country in our Indian difficulties."[15]

Nonetheless, the Texas Congress sought to sharply restrict the freedoms of unenslaved African Americans, following the lead of state governments in the South. Free people of color found guilty of using insulting or abusive language to a white person could receive from twenty-five to one hundred lashes. A free black could not preach the gospel unless at least two slaveholders were present. Cities and towns also passed a raft of ordinances limiting the freedom of mobility of free blacks, setting nighttime curfews and travel restrictions that differed little, if at all, from those imposed on slaves. And while the courts upheld the right of free blacks to sue, they could not testify against whites, and were obliged to hire white attorneys to handle their cases. Most decided to forgo the expense.[16]

Whites who took African Americans as marriage partners also saw their lives disrupted after independence. Congress forbade the legal union of whites and blacks, although, as in the 1840 expulsion act, it lacked the power or the inclination to enforce it. More significant in discouraging such unions was the policy of the Land Office, which routinely rejected the headright petitions of men known to be married to women of color. Racial prejudice also forced mixed marriages onto the margins of society. Two of Stephen F. Austin's early colonists brought African American women with them to Texas, settling on the Colorado River several miles away from the closest settlements. One of them, a Vermont doctor named John Webber, established a homestead with his common law wife and their eleven children on a horseshoe bend in the river, east of present-day Austin. As more whites settled in the vicinity of Webber's Prairie, some began to speak out against the couple, forbidding the woman from fraternizing with their slaves. Ultimately, community pressure forced the family to relocate to the lower Rio Grande valley, an area almost uninhabited by white Texans.[17]

FAR MORE THAN MOST FREE BLACKS, WILLIAM GOYENS WOULD consistently push against the formal barriers that suddenly appeared between whites and nonwhites after independence. He left no letters or writings of any kind, yet the broad outlines of his life in Nacogdoches can be pieced together from court and tax records. His loss of citizenship does not seem to have curbed his entrepreneurial spirit— or his litigious nature. Goyens's business deals, almost byzantine in their complexity, often wound up in the courts, and he did not hesitate to employ the services of white lawyers (since he could no longer represent himself) to protect his interests. When the economy went into a tailspin in the years after independence, Goyens thrived, buying up densely wooded acreage around Nacogdoches at rock-bottom prices. By the early 1840s, as many local whites struggled, he had amassed more than four thousand acres of improved land, two town lots in Nacogdoches, fifty head of cattle, and nine slaves.[18]

There were, of course, limits to how far even a successful free person of color could go in challenging the social order. And as a businessman, what bothered Goyens most of all were the restraints his loss of status placed on his personal fortunes. He found it especially galling to be shut out of the government's enormous land giveaway program. His diplomatic service with the Cherokees did not entitle him to one of the headrights given to men who had taken up arms against Mexico, and as a noncitizen he was ineligible to receive the league of land given to any Anglo or Hispano who could prove residence in Texas at the start of the rebellion. But he could prove that he had once been a citizen of the Mexican republic, which had awarded one-league grants to Texas settlers under the original Colonization Act. Perhaps, he believed, the new government might recognize his years of loyal service by giving him a land certificate on the basis of the earlier law.

The legal hurdles that stood in the way of a satisfactory judgment were daunting, to say the least. Before his case could be reviewed by the board of Land Commissioners, he would need approval from Congress. In 1838, his lawyers lobbied for a bill on Goyens's behalf, offering a poignantly ingratiating argument. Although "he is unfortunately a man of colour," the petition read, "he has ever been identified with the feelings and interest of the Anglo American population and has born his humble part in their struggles."[19]

Approved in the Senate, the bill failed to pass in the House, effectively settling the matter. Undaunted, he tried again two years later, this time presenting his claim directly to the board of Land Commissioners. Without congressional approval, Goyens could hardly have been surprised when the Land Office rejected his petition. Still determined to pursue all legal avenues, he then sued the land commissioners in district court. In 1841, a Nacogdoches jury ruled against him, bringing his three-year legal battle to an end. Finding the suit frivolous, the jury added insult to injury and billed him for court costs.[20]

Goyens would have little time to dwell on this legal setback. That summer, Nacogdoches was rocked by the news that several members of a white family had fallen violently ill, under circumstances that seemed suspicious. An investigation revealed that they had been poisoned by a pot of coffee laced with jimson weed (also known as nightshade). The evidence pointed to a female house servant, and then to her common law husband, Jake, one of Goyens's slaves. Jake confessed to the crime and was hanged a month later. Quoting scripture before a large crowd, he "stood it like a hero," said a witness at the execution, his body writhing at the end of the rope for a full minute before he finally expired.[21]

The attempted murder shocked the white community, once again bringing Goyens much unwanted scrutiny from his neighbors. Some local slaves had escaped around the same time, giving rise to fears that the affair might be part of a broader conspiracy. Soon, anxious residents came forward to state that they had seen signs of suspicious activity in their own slave quarters. Allowing their imaginations free rein, the townsfolk of Nacogdoches and other East Texas villages held tense public meetings, convinced that a full-blown revolt was imminent. For several weeks, nighttime vigilance patrols thundered along forested roads in a hunt for runaways, and strict curfews and an area-wide crackdown on slave activities were imposed. No further incidents came to light, and by summer's end, the crisis—or the fear of one—had passed.[22]

Goyens fades from the public record until the following year, when tensions with his white neighbors finally came to a head with an attempt on his life. The specific cause of the affray is unclear, though the shooting may have been the result of a drunken frolic that had taken place in town the night before. Many whites may have seen the affair as a long overdue comeuppance for the local businessman. Certainly the local magistrate, Adolphus Sterne, saw it that way. Two years earlier, Sterne had signed the petition with other prominent civic leaders exempting Goyens from the expulsion act. But in 1842 Sterne could no longer be counted among his defenders, perhaps irritated by the businessman's frequent appearances in his court. The day after issuing an arrest warrant for Goyens's assailant, a white man, the judge scribbled in his diary, "Goyens . . . is but slightly wounded." And with a hint of wry satisfaction, he added, "Not enough to [do] any good."[23]

The fact that Sterne ordered the arrest of one of his neighbors for assaulting a black man suggests that Goyens was still a figure of some standing in the community. More fortunate than other free men of color, he nonetheless occupied the same liminal space on the margins of white society, neither enslaved nor truly free. Former citizens of Mexico, they were now outcasts, regarded with contempt and suspicion by the white majority, and threatened with expulsion by the government many had fought to create. Though their economic circumstances were quite different, Goyens would have surely agreed with the disabled veteran Greenbury Logan, who considered himself to be "more a freeman than in the States," when Texas was a province of Mexico. After the rebellion he fell on hard times, deeply in debt and facing the confiscation of his land for back taxes. "But now look at my situation," he reflected bitterly. "Every privilege dear to a freeman is taken away."[24]

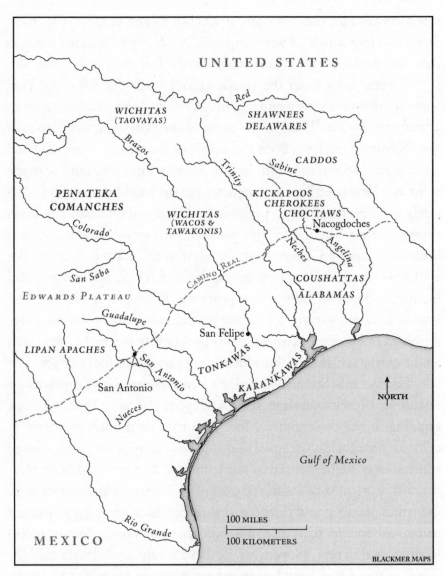

Native Peoples and Immigrant Tribes of Texas, 1821–1839

EIGHTEEN

I HAVE NEVER TOLD YOU A LIE

WHATEVER HIS WHITE NEIGHBORS MAY HAVE THOUGHT OF him, William Goyens enjoyed the confidence of Sam Houston. In one of his first official acts as president, Houston appointed Goyens as Indian agent to the Cherokees, and he already had an assignment for him in mind. The Comanches and the Wichitas had stepped up their raids against the settlements on the western edges of the republic, and the administration lacked the means to subdue them. The president wanted Goyens to ride up to Cherokee country and relay a message to Chief Bowls. Would the Indian leader be willing to meet with the prairie tribes and inform them that the new government was ready to negotiate a permanent peace? Houston's predecessor, David G. Burnet, had already sent a white Indian agent to meet with the Comanches and the Wichitas, who failed to impress upon them the advantages of better relations with the Anglo-Americans. Perhaps, the president reasoned, a Cherokee chief would have better luck.[1]

Now in his early eighties, the chief was happy to be of service, even though it would involve an arduous trek across Texas that would take the better part of three months. Bowls probably would have done anything the president asked of him. The tribe had never been closer in its years-long quest to establish ownership of the land it occupied in the Piney Woods. For Bowls the years under Mexican rule had been maddening, to say the least. Again and again Mexican officials, all seemingly well-intentioned, had led the Cherokees to believe that a land grant would be forthcoming. And each time they failed to deliver. But in Sam Houston they at last had an advocate with deep personal connections to the tribe. As far as Bowls was concerned, the new government was already committed to protecting Cherokee land claims above the Angelina River. The terms of the treaty signed by the two men the year before required the tribe to take no part in the struggle against Mexico. Having fulfilled their part of the agreement, the Indians now waited for a boundary line to be drawn that would clearly demarcate the Cherokee homeland. Sam Houston's election to the presidency surely dispelled any doubts that the whites might renege on their promise.

What Bowls did not know—Houston had not told him—was that the treaty still required Senate ratification, and that was by no means a sure thing. No doubt the president thought there was no need to enlighten the old chief on this important point. Anglo-Texas settlers could not move into Cherokee lands, at least not legally, without valid titles, and Houston had bought some time by vetoing Congress's first attempt to establish a Land Office. Sending Bowls on a sensitive diplomatic mission was one way to allay the concerns of wary whites, who had not forgotten the hysteria caused by rumors of an Indian attack during the Runaway Scrape. The president even floated the idea in Congress that the Cherokees and other immigrant bands could be enlisted to police the frontier against the Comanches, although nothing came of the suggestion. Houston knew the senators would never share his affection for the tribe. If the treaty was to have any hope of ratification, they would need to see the immigrant Indians as valuable members—though not, of course, citizens—of the Texas Republic.

Sometime in March 1837, Bowls headed northwest with a ten-man Cherokee delegation to relay Houston's message of peace to the prairie Indians. Goyens furnished supplies and arranged for horses and guides for the group, accompanying them at least part of the way. At the headwaters of the Trinity River, near present-day Dallas, Bowls conferred with several Wichita and Caddo leaders, who seemed only vaguely interested in the president's proposal. Riding west onto the Low Plains, he met with Comanche chiefs who were even less encouraging. With little fear of the new Texas government, the prairie tribes did not want peace, Bowls concluded. The trade in stolen horses and mules was simply too lucrative to give up.[2]

That summer, Bowls journeyed to Houston with Goyens and several dozen Cherokees to brief the president on his mission. The Indians erected a camp of deerskin tipis on the east bank of Buffalo Bayou, where they performed a dance for bemused locals. Goyens also attracted attention, described by one resident as "a large Negro" who was treated with great respect by the Indians "and seemed to hold undisputed dominion with the chief."[3]

If the president was disappointed to learn that Bowls had made little headway with the prairie tribes, at the moment he had a much bigger problem on his mind: the fate of the Cherokee treaty. The three men on the Senate Indian Affairs Committee tasked with reviewing the agreement were not friendly to the president's Indian policy. One was an East Texas land speculator who stood to profit by expelling the immigrant tribes. Another was Thomas Jefferson Green, one of his most vocal critics. Yet there is no evidence that the president gave Bowls any reason to think that the treaty might be in jeopardy. Houston, who invariably assumed the tone of benevolent father in his dealings with the Indians, assured him that all would be well. By this time the president must have been having his doubts about the treaty, but he kept them to himself.

The committee's report, issued in the fall, was worse than Houston could have imagined. A scathing indictment of the administration's entire Indian policy, the report concluded that the treaty was invalid, because the land the Cherokees occupied had been awarded to empresarios by the Mexican government. Mindful of the fact that the immigrant tribes were sitting on prime East Texas real estate, the committee went on to make the extraordinary and wholly baseless assertion that the "most savage and ruthless of our frontier enemies" were not the Comanches or the Wichitas, but the Indians of the Piney Woods. The Senate followed the committee's recommendation and rejected the treaty, handing Houston the biggest defeat of his presidency. Texas had land in abundance, an angry president lectured the legislators afterward, but it was the improved Cherokee lands, with "their blooming peach trees, their snug cabins, their well cultivated fields," that speculators and settlers wanted most.[4]

Congress dealt Houston's Indian policy another body blow the following month when it passed (over the president's veto) a bill to finally establish a Land Office. The office now proceeded to issue headrights to over a league of land (4,600 acres) to adult male citizens who could prove residency in Texas at the time of the rebellion. By year's end it passed another bill authorizing the Land Office to award 640-acre headrights to veterans of the fight for independence. What the government considered to be public domain, of course, was land the Indians either occupied or used as hunting grounds. With the arrival of warm weather the following year, surveying parties would start to push aggressively into these areas—including the lands between the Neches and Angelina rivers, home to the Cherokees. Conflict with the Native peoples of Texas now became inevitable.[5]

Bowls returned to the capital in the late spring of 1838, and this time he would not be put off by Houston's vague assurances. A few Anglo settlers had been spotted above the Angelina River in violation of the 1836 treaty, claiming they had every right to be there. Bowls was especially upset that several Alabama families had established a settlement only two miles away from a Cherokee village. Led by Isaac Killough and his four sons, the party had arrived during the winter, clearing land and building cabins, and recently planted a corn crop. Again the president dissembled and tried to convince the old chief that he still had the authority to keep white settlers out of Indian country. He promised to have a boundary line drawn that would formally define the territory occupied by the Cherokees. The meeting between the two men was respectful, and Houston thought it had gone well. Bowls thought otherwise. A boundary line was meaningless at this point, and the chief knew it. He left the capital convinced that Houston, the great friend to the Cherokees, had lied to him.[6]

For Bowls, there was nothing left to do but prepare for war. The old chief wasted little time lining up allies for a campaign

20. *Stick Stock* (or *Surveying in Texas before Texas Annexation
to the U.S.*). By Theodore Gentilz. Courtesy of the
Sheerin family and the San Antonio Museum of Art.

against the white settlements. He sent runners into US Indian Territory to find Dutch (Tahchee), the former war chief of the Texas Cherokees. Several years earlier, Dutch had led Bowls's people to their greatest victories against the woodland Wichitas. Bowls now pleaded with the legendary warrior to come to his aid, urging him to recruit men above the Red River to help defend the Cherokee homeland in Texas.[7]

The Indian leader also looked to the Mexican government, which had been trying to recruit the Cherokees to fight against the whites since the rebellion. After his meeting with the president, Bowls did not return to his village in East Texas, but instead rode to Matamoros, to confer with Mexican officials there. He made no attempt to conceal his movements, and actually seems to have made a point of drawing attention to himself as he journeyed south. When his party crossed the Navidad River, near Lavaca Bay, Bowls made camp near the Spring Hill settlement, where a dance was in progress. The soiree came to an abrupt halt when Bowls made a dramatic appearance, dressed in "a breechclout, anklets, moccasins, feathers and a long, clean white linen shirt." Taking advantage of the stunned silence, he announced to the gobsmacked guests that President Houston "was no longer a Cherokee," but "the Great Father" of the white man.[8] The mood became still more awkward when Bowls tried to dance with the ladies, all of whom refused. Asked to leave, the old chief indignantly stalked out.[9]

A more cordial reception awaited the Cherokee leader in Matamoros, where General Vicente Filisola, commander of the Mexican army in the northeast, was happy to take advantage of the Cherokees' anger. In the two years since San Jacinto, Mexico had been looking for cost-effective ways to continue the war against Texas. While a lack of funds made a second campaign to reconquer the breakaway province unlikely for the foreseeable future, Filisola was ready to provide logistical support and encouragement to any groups willing to wage war on Mexico's behalf. The Cherokees were hardly alone in their opposition to the new government. All the immigrant tribes felt threatened by the sight of surveyors pushing into the country north and west of Nacogdoches, and the town's Hispano population, though small, was being overwhelmed by the influx of Anglo-Americans after San Jacinto. If there was to be a counterrevolution against white rule, it would happen in East Texas.

In late May a small force of one hundred Mexicans, with two dozen Cherokees and Caddos serving as guides, slipped out of Matamoros and crossed the Rio Grande. Led by an army officer, Julián Pedro Miracle, the group made its way through the barren South Texas scrublands undetected. Above the Nueces River it proceeded more cautiously, staying off the main roads to avoid being seen. Somewhere near Refugio, Miracle and his men happened upon an Irish family, whom they killed to prevent local authorities from learning of their movements. Texas whites were still unaware of the secret mission when the party reached the edge of the Piney Woods, having completed a trek of some six hundred miles.[10]

Here, near the Trinity River, Miracle made contact with the leader of the Hispano resistance, Vicente Córdova. Like many

Mexican Texans, the former Nacogdoches alcalde and militia captain had once welcomed the Anglo-Americans, sharing their distrust of the centralist government in Mexico City. He had joined with James Bowie and other white newcomers to defeat Colonel de las Piedras in the 1832 revolts and considered throwing in his lot with the rebels against Santa Anna three years later. He quickly changed his mind when Nacogdoches became a principal point of entry during the revolution for rowdy American volunteers, who overran the town and behaved badly toward the Mexican inhabitants. The situation had gotten worse for local Hispanos after San Jacinto. Barred by whites from voting or serving on juries, they found themselves reduced to second-class citizenship. When Córdova complained to the Houston administration about their mistreatment, he received no response. Now he was a committed partisan, ready to give his life in the fight against white rule.[11]

A few days later, Bowls and a party of Cherokees arrived at the Mexican camp on the Trinity. Miracle expected to be greeted warmly by the Indians, who had been so eager for war in the spring. To his surprise, they seemed to have cooled on the idea of an attack on the Anglo-American settlements. Perhaps Bowls expected a more robust military contribution from Matamoros, though Miracle vaguely promised more troops once the war got underway. The chief's lack of enthusiasm may have also stemmed from the fact that he had just learned that Dutch and the Cherokees in Oklahoma would not be joining the revolt. Now well established in his new home in Oklahoma, Dutch was a prosperous farmer and stock raiser, his days as a warrior well behind him. He wanted no part of Bowls's campaign against the Anglo-Texans, nor did the other Western Cherokee leaders.[12]

Miracle spent the month of July in the Piney Woods, shuttling from one Indian village to another, growing increasingly frustrated as he tried to drum up support for an attack on the white settlements. Torrential summer rains and a lack of competent translators did not make his task any easier. Confusing caution with indolence, he concluded, "These cursed Indians are as lazy as the devil."[13]

Finally he headed north, to the open prairies below the Red
River, to recruit warriors among the Shawnees and Delawares.
There, resistance to white rule was already underway. After living
unmolested in the area since the 1820s, the two tribes found themselves locked in a round of deadly clashes with American settlers after independence. In 1837, the district's leading surveyor launched
an unprovoked attack on a band of Shawnee hunters, killing several
and burning their bodies. The Indians responded in kind, sparking a
vicious cycle of raids and counterraids, forcing many white families
to abandon their homesteads. Taking refuge in more secure, forted
compounds, they ventured out only to harvest their crops in teams,
as armed men stood guard.[14]

Camped on the Angelina River above Nacogdoches, Córdova
began cobbling together a small force of about two hundred of
his Mexican neighbors, runaway slaves, and immigrant Indians. A
large concentration of men and horses could not escape detection
for long, however, even in the dense pine forests of East Texas. On
August 4, the plot was discovered, well before it had a chance to
mature, when some of the town's Anglo residents stumbled upon
Córdova's camp. The insurgents fired on the men and fled. Visiting
Nacogdoches at the time, Houston, sick with fever, issued a proclamation offering amnesty to the rebels if they would return to their
homes. Córdova replied with a hastily drafted manifesto declaring
that Texas was still a part of Mexico. The rebels were "tired of the
injustices and the usurpations of their rights," and would "shed the
last drop of their blood" to defend "the nation to which they be-
long." Then they rode into Cherokee country, deep in the pine
forests above the Angelina River.[15]

Houston sensed both the gravity of the situation and the need
to tread carefully. A show of force by the government was clearly
needed to discourage the tribes from joining the rebellion. At the
same time, the president feared that a heavy-handed response would
provoke the Indians, plunging the region into chaos. Luckily for
Houston, he was in a position to act quickly. The country's top military commander, Thomas Jefferson Rusk, also happened to be on the

scene when the crisis broke. The president ordered Rusk to raise a militia force and pursue Córdova into Indian country, but cautioned him against taking any action that might provoke bloodshed. Sending William Goyens along to mediate, he hoped that a violent confrontation might still be avoided.

Torn between his personal feelings and presidential obligations, Houston faced a painful dilemma. He was deeply sympathetic to the plight of the Cherokees, yet as president his primary responsibility was to keep the peace. In his letters to Bowls he tried to conceal his frantic desperation, pleading with him to take no part in the uprising and reminding the Cherokee leader of his friendship. "I have never told you a lie," he wrote. But he had already told him several, and now he proceeded to lie some more. Rusk's militiamen would soon be receiving reinforcements from the US Army in Louisiana, he told the chief, which he knew to be untrue. And even now, with Anglos and Indians on the brink of war, he continued to insist that the terms of the 1836 treaty could still be honored, and ordered a surveying team to mark out the formal boundaries of an Indian homeland.[16]

If Houston's promise of a boundary line seemed to Bowls like a cruel joke, the administration's threat of force was real enough. Within a few days, Rusk assembled an army of several hundred local militiamen and marched north, camping on the edge of Indian country. He then sent Goyens, the only man the Indians still trusted, into Bowls's village to urge the Cherokee leader to stand down.

Bowls probably needed little persuading at this point. He was already having serious doubts about his alliance with the Mexicans. With a large Texas army only a few miles away, he stepped back from the precipice on which he found himself, and sent word to Córdova to leave the area immediately. The fugitive rebel leader had no choice but to obey. Riding northwest, Córdova and his followers would find a safe haven among the Kickapoos, a few miles below present-day Tyler. Goyens returned to Rusk's camp to tell the Texas commander that he could expect no trouble from the Cherokees.[17]

A much relieved Houston ordered Rusk to return to Nacogdoches. He had always been more afraid of a pan-Indian uprising than

Córdova and his few dozen Mexican followers. The worst seemed to be over.[18]

But early September brought another round of bad news, with the report that Miracle had been killed on the Red River. Papers found on the Mexican officer's body revealed the full scope of his government's plans, and the first concrete evidence of Indian collaboration. The cache of papers included correspondence from the commander in Matamoros to tribal leaders, as well as Miracle's journal, scrawled in pencil, detailing his negotiations with Bowls and his visit to the villages in Indian country. Houston tried to downplay the significance of this bombshell revelation, arguing that the documents proved only that Mexican officials had tried to recruit the Cherokee leader. Chief Bowls, he insisted, stretching the truth considerably, "was too much our friend to be influenced by them."[19]

By this time, many Anglo Texans were growing exasperated with Houston, who seemed more concerned with his "pet Indians" than the protection of the white settlements. General Rusk, a longtime friend, found Houston's conduct "unaccountably strange," a view shared by the secretary of war, Bernard Bee. The government's response to the crisis in East Texas was complicated by the fact that the presidential campaign was now underway. Frustrated by Houston's caution, Rusk and Bee began to look to Vice President Lamar for leadership, who was all but certain to win the election.

The Houston faction had struggled to put forward a viable presidential candidate, turning first to Attorney General Peter Grayson. But Grayson had long battled mental illness, and in a fit of melancholy two months before the balloting, he shot himself in a Tennessee inn, after penning a letter to the innkeeper apologizing for the inconvenience. The president's followers then threw their support to James Collinsworth, chief justice of the Supreme Court, an equally infelicitous choice. An alcoholic, Collinsworth fell off a boat and drowned in Galveston Bay after a weeklong drinking binge. Running virtually unopposed, Lamar won with a whopping 96 percent of the vote.[20]

Events were spiraling out of control in East Texas, and the lame duck Houston was powerless to do anything about it. From his new base of operations in Kickapoo country, Córdova sent out skirmishing parties to harass Rusk's militia units. No one in Nacogdoches knew how many nonwhites had joined the insurgency, though the Hispano leader seemed content to wage a guerilla campaign, suggesting he lacked the manpower to risk a major confrontation with Rusk's army.

But as Houston feared, the immigrant tribes posed the greater threat to peace in the region, and they were angry, whether they joined Córdova or not. Bowls now found himself in much the same predicament as the president, striving to maintain the peace as many of his tribesmen clamored for war. While only a handful joined the Hispano rebels, others seethed as surveyors continued to move into tribal hunting grounds and settlers cleared land near their villages. The presence of the Killough settlement so deep in Cherokee country was especially galling. In early October Bowls showed up at the farmhouse of Isaac Killough and urged him to leave the area. He refused. One afternoon a few days later, a burst of gunfire erupted from the woods on the edge of the settlement's cornfield, riddling Killough with bullets. A band of Cherokees then swept through the little community, firing as they went. They killed eighteen people, torching cabins and barns and carrying off everything of value, obliterating any trace of the Killough settlement by the time they were done.[21]

Unable to stay the fury of his own tribesmen, Bowls commanded even less authority over the Kickapoos, who had never fully acknowledged Cherokee leadership of the immigrant Indians. On the same day as the Killough Massacre, a surveying crew of about two dozen whites encountered a large encampment of Kickapoos on a buffalo hunt on the prairies west of the Piney Woods, near present-day Corsicana. The first two days passed without incident, as the surveyors and chain bearers ran their lines, often glimpsing small groups of Indians in the distance. On the third day the Kickapoos, armed with bows and arrows and American-made rifles, attacked without warning. Taking refuge in a shallow ravine, the surveyors managed to beat back repeated efforts by the Indians to dislodge them throughout the day. That night the men tried to make their escape, but the Kicka-poos picked them off by moonlight. Only a handful survived, most of them seriously wounded.[22]

News of the two attacks reached Nacogdoches in mid-October, prompting angry calls for retribution. While Córdova's men do not appear to have been involved in either episode, his insurgency had clearly emboldened the immigrant tribes, triggering acts of resis-tance to white rule. Convinced that East Texas was about to be en-gulfed in a bloody race war, General Rusk took decisive action. This time, he would not be restrained by a president who preferred the olive branch to the sword.

Taking the field once again, Rusk followed an old Indian trail deep into the forest to an abandoned Kickapoo village. When the army arrived on October 15, the rebels were nowhere to be seen, Córdova's men having taken up positions in the woods surrounding the Texan camp. At dawn the following day, the air was suddenly filled with war whoops and the crack of gunfire. Rusk could never ascer-tain the size of Córdova's force, which was concealed by thick under-growth and towering pines. But as the early morning mist gave way to a drizzling rain, the rebel fire began to slacken, and Rusk ordered his men to charge into the woods. Córdova's followers fell back, then scattered. Within minutes, the Battle at Kickapoo Town was over.[23]

Most of Córdova's Indian allies deserted him after Kickapoo Town, leaving the rebel leader with a core group of a few dozen Mex-ican partisans and some runaway slaves. The Kickapoos dispersed, some moving north into US Indian Territory above the Red River, others heading south, to make new homes below the Rio Grande. As they made their retreat they torched an East Texas farmhouse, with three women and four children perishing in the flames.[24]

Rusk was not finished. For good measure, he now embarked on a campaign to clear the northeast corner of Texas of the Caddos who had drifted into the area from Louisiana. He sent militia units against their villages on the Trinity River, driving them onto the northern prairies, and pursued their warriors in the east across the Sabine River. Rusk gave his officers a simple order: "When you fight," he told them, "exterminate." Only the onset of winter put an end to the bloodshed.[25]

As 1838 drew to a close, an uneasy peace settled over the republic's northern frontier. No one expected it to last. Córdova had gone to ground since the battle at Kickapoo Town and was thought to be hiding out somewhere in the Piney Woods. But the rebellion had clearly failed, and the Hispano residents of Nacogdoches soon felt the wrath of the white majority. Local authorities rounded up three dozen men and charged them with treason, none of whom appear to have been actively involved in the revolt. But East Texas Hispanos, numbering only about five hundred people, were never a serious threat, and all would be acquitted save one, whose death sentence was later commuted. Faced with reprisals that included land seizures and vigilantism, many Hispano residents quietly gathered what property they could and fled the area into Louisiana, never to return.[26]

Most of the immigrant tribes remained in their villages scattered across East Texas, however, and Anglos wanted the army to finish the job Rusk had started. Though only a few Indians had joined Córdova's revolt, to the white majority the spasms of violence in the fall of 1838 were all connected. Citizens of the Texas Republic often did not distinguish between one tribe and another. Indians were Indians, and together they appeared to pose a single, existential threat to white rule. In the wake of the insurgency, Anglo-Americans saw the immigrant tribes as a fifth column within the nation's borders, waiting only for the signal from Mexico to descend upon their communities. For the Cherokees, judged guilty if only by association, there would be a reckoning. And with a new president, Mirabeau Lamar, at the helm, it would not be long in coming.

NINETEEN

WILD CANNIBALS OF THE WOODS

Mirabeau Buonaparte Lamar had been working on his inauguration speech for several days, showing various drafts to close friends and making countless revisions. The poet and former newspaperman fancied himself something of a litterateur, but public speaking was not his strong suit. He was uncomfortable in large crowds, and fretted about making a good impression. At least he could rely on a friendly audience. The throng of people who gathered outside the capitol, a new, peach-colored clapboard building, in Houston on December 10, 1838, were mostly supporters of the president-elect. It was rumored that Sam Houston would not even bother to attend.

But at the appointed hour a murmur of astonishment spread through the crowd. The outgoing chief executive strode confidently to the dais, and he was dressed in a manner deliberately calculated to steal the spotlight away from his successor. Wearing knee breeches, silk stockings, and a powdered wig, à la George Washington, he proceeded to deliver his "Farewell Address." For the next three hours, the audience was treated to a self-referential discourse on the achievements of the past administration, as Lamar fidgeted nervously in his seat. Thoroughly discombobulated by Houston's showboating, the president-elect refused to follow him, handing the speech instead to his private secretary, who delivered an uninspired reading of it to the audience.[1]

The inauguration crowd probably paid little attention, exhausted by Houston's performance, and disappointed that the man of the hour would not be making a speech after all. Had they listened carefully, they would have heard a breathtakingly bold expression of the president-elect's Southern nationalist credo. A staunch states' rights advocate in his native Georgia, Lamar had long maintained that states had the right to leave the Union, an extreme view even for Southerners at the time. And if states could secede, it was but a short step to imagine an entirely different geopolitical destiny for the North American continent, one in which the United States was not the only white republic. Born an American, Lamar could nonetheless declare that Texas, "the land of my adoption," claimed his highest allegiance. While most Texans still looked hopefully to the United States, Lamar saw the recent collapse of annexation talks as a blessing in disguise. He had been greatly alarmed by the rapid rise of the antislavery movement in the United States, convinced that Northern agitation on the subject threatened to undermine the plantation economy and the slaveholding way of life. An independent Texas, he believed, presented an extraordinary opportunity to reinvent the American republic along Southern lines. Rather than go begging for admission to the United States, Texas should embrace its newfound nationhood, devoting itself to safeguarding the South's "peculiar and essential interests"—i.e., slavery.[2]

In their more exuberant moments—which were not infrequent—Texas nationalists like Lamar could envision an empire that would one day rival the United States. It was this kind of thinking that prompted Thomas Jefferson Green to sponsor the 1836 bill declaring the Rio Grande to be the republic's boundary with Mexico. Green and Lamar saw the river as a new Mississippi and a potential gateway to the Far West, with railroads linking Texas to California. With ports on the Pacific, Texas would be close enough, as Green colorfully put it, to "converse with the people of China through a speaking trumpet," giving the republic access to the lucrative markets of Asia. The fact that their fledgling republic could not yet claim a population of fifty thousand citizens did little to dampen their imperial ardor.[3]

Mirabeau Lamar said little about the Indians in his inaugural address, but they were not far from his mind. A few days later, in his first message to Congress, the president made his feelings on the subject abundantly clear. Determined to remove all impediments to white progress, he vowed to do everything in his power to ensure that Native Americans would have no place in his slaveholding republic. Angered, like so many Texans, by the recent attacks by the immigrant tribes, he singled out the Cherokees for special condemnation. They were "wild cannibals of the woods," he declared, who massacred settlers "with the ferocity of Tigers and Hyenas." There could be no compromise on the Indian question; any attempt on the part of the tribes to resist white settlement would lead to "their total extinction or total expulsion."[4]

At first glance, Lamar's call for the removal of the Cherokees echoed the policies of Democratic administrations implemented in the United States. In 1835, Andrew Jackson's Indian negotiators had signed with the Eastern Cherokees the Treaty of New Echota, by which a handful of chiefs, over the objections of many Cherokees, agreed to cede tribal lands east of the Mississippi in exchange for land in the West and a payment of five million dollars. As Lamar delivered his message to Congress, Van Buren's War Department was forcibly removing the Indians from their homes in the southeastern states and marching them on a grueling, one-thousand-mile trek in the dead of winter to US Indian Territory. More than two thousand people would succumb to disease, exposure, and malnutrition along the way, earning for the Trail of Tears a well-deserved place as one of the darkest chapters in the history of American race relations. But while Washington felt obliged—for the sake of appearances, if nothing else—to acquire Indian lands by treaty, Lamar regarded the Cherokees as "strangers and intruders." The new president refused to recognize any prior agreements they might have made with Mexico and Texas, and rejected out of hand the suggestion that they should be compensated for the lands they occupied. Lamar had given little thought to the logistics of removal, or where they would go. He just wanted the Indians gone.[5]

Indian-hating came naturally to the new president. Early in his career, as the private secretary to Georgia governor George M. Troup, he had cut his teeth as the protégé of one of the country's most vicious opponents of Indian rights. Troup evicted the Creek Indians in 1825 in open defiance of the federal government, mobilizing the state militia when President John Quincy Adams attempted to intercede on the Indians' behalf. The governor then distributed the vacated lands by a lottery system, becoming a hero to Georgia's upcountry farmers. Viewing all Indians as obstacles to civilization and progress, the new president needed only a pretext to complete the work of expulsion begun during the Córdova rebellion the year before.[6]

SAM HOUSTON NOW FOUND HIMSELF IN AN UNFAMILIAR ROLE, a private citizen out of the limelight. After Lamar's inauguration the ex-president traveled to the United States, to visit old friends and to find investors for a new town project he was involved in at the mouth of the Sabine River. Houston did his best to promote the project during the trip, but he never fully embraced the speculative mania that absorbed so many Jacksonian Americans. An innocent in financial matters, he "neither saved nor made a dollar," and even at the height of his career found himself in such difficult straits that local merchants were unwilling to sell to him on credit. He remained, at heart, a political animal, and his US tour offered an opportunity to bask in the attention and applause of Americans who were eager to see the hero of San Jacinto. But he was still drinking heavily, and according to one report managed to make a spectacle of himself on the voyage to New Orleans.[7]

Charming when sober, he made a more favorable impression in Mobile, attending a party in his honor at the home of a wealthy merchant, William Bledsoe. He stayed at the Bledsoes for several days, ostensibly to persuade his host to invest in his town-building scheme. His attentions, however, seem to have quickly turned to more personal matters. At the advanced age of forty-six, Houston was an eligible bachelor, though not quite as eligible as he would have liked. Gossip surrounding his brief, ill-starred marriage to Eliza Allen ten years earlier, not to mention his legendary dissipation, had thwarted his romantic forays in polite society. As a citizen of Mexico he had tried, and failed, to dissolve the union with Eliza, finally succeeding when Texas became a republic. Now free to remarry, and perhaps intent on making up for lost time, he embarked on a whirlwind courtship of Bledsoe's sister-in-law, Margaret Lea.

Twenty-year-old Margaret had seen little of the world when she met Sam Houston. Raised in rural Alabama, she received a formal education at two local female academies that catered to daughters of the planter class. Such institutions generally favored what were then known as the "feminine arts," training their students for future careers as wives and mothers. Serious and deeply religious, Margaret did not question the domestic role assigned to her. She took no interest in politics and frankly confessed to Houston that she preferred her "books, music and needle-work." At the same time, Margaret was probably telling him the truth when she informed him that she was not "a romantic star-struck young lady." She does not appear to have been awed by the famous Texan in the least, though she did not discourage his attentions during his stay in Mobile. When he wrote to her from Nashville, Margaret replied with some forwardness the next day. Her letter, she wanted him to know, "was the first I have written to any gentleman," adding, "You must write to me immediately and constantly until I see you."[8]

Houston happily obliged, and a proposal of marriage soon followed. Margaret's mother did not take the news well. She considered Houston to be an inappropriate suitor; the age difference was too great, and she had heard the rumors about his drinking. But Margaret could be headstrong, and on the subject of matrimony she would not be dissuaded. Houston's friends were astonished when they learned of the engagement, one noting that he had never in his life met a man "more totally disqualified for domestic happiness." "Will it last?" shrugged another, skeptically. "I always hope for the best."[9]

BACK IN TEXAS, MANY ANGLOS HAD ALMOST FORGOTTEN ABOUT Vicente Córdova. Lying low since the battle at Kickapoo Town, he drifted down to south-central Texas around the start of the year with a few diehard followers, hoping to regroup and attract new support among the Hispano population there. In late March, white settlers discovered their trail and tracked them for four days before attacking the group on the banks of the Guadalupe River. Wounded in the arm, Córdova escaped, but three African Americans with him were not so fortunate. The settlers took two of the men to a clump of live oak trees and gave them shovels to dig their own graves. The eldest, a man in his sixties, was unrepentant, defiantly telling his captors that he had killed his master and his entire family and would kill again if returned to slavery. After executing the pair, the volunteers then proceeded to hold an impromptu auction for the third, a wounded teenager, who was sold for 450 dollars.[10]

Though Córdova never managed to lead an effective resistance movement against white rule, Mexican authorities were not unhappy with the results of his guerilla campaign. If the government lacked the resources to subjugate Texas, it could at least cause havoc, and there was no question Córdova had succeeded on that score. So in May the military commander in Matamoros tried again, dispatching a second contingent of armed guerillas into Texas with orders identical to Miracle's the year before. This time, white militia units discovered and routed the small force before it reached the Piney Woods. Among the belongings of their commanding officer, the Texans found a packet of letters addressed to Bowls and other chiefs, with the usual promises of land if they took up arms against the republic.

For Lamar, the mere existence of the letters was evidence enough of the tribe's ongoing collaboration with Mexico. The president now had the justification he needed to expel the East Texas Indians, and he wasted little time putting his removal policy into effect. A few weeks later, in early June, a delegation appeared at Bowls's village with a message from the president. Accusing the Cherokees of being a "secret enemy" of Texas, Lamar informed the

21. Mirabeau B. Lamar (1798–1859). To fulfill his dream of an imperial destiny for Texas, President Mirabeau Lamar called for the expulsion of all Native peoples from the Lone Star Republic. Courtesy of the San Jacinto Museum of History.

chief that his people would now be removed to the lands set aside for the tribe by the US government above the Red River in present-day Oklahoma. The Texas Congress would work out the details when it convened in the fall.[11]

Seated on a fallen tree trunk, the old chief listened intently as a translator read him the letter. A welter of thoughts and emotions crowded upon his mind. Seventeen years had passed since his journey to San Antonio with Richard Fields to ask Governor Trespalacios for a permanent Cherokee homeland in East Texas. As close as the tribe had come to achieving that goal, it had always remained elusive, just out of reach. Bowls had known for some time that the Cherokees' days in the Piney Woods were numbered. He had already contacted tribal leaders in US Indian Territory about the possibility of moving together to California. Perhaps there the Cherokees might finally find a home "out of reach of the white people."[12]

Concerned for the safety of his three wives and children, Bowls was ready to leave. But the decision was not his to make. His authority as a Cherokee "beloved man" had always rested on his wise counsel, and the village chiefs no longer deferred to him. The tribe's younger men, some of whom had taken part in the violence the year before, believed they could defeat the whites. He asked the commissioners for time to consult with his people, but he seems to have already known that they would not go peacefully.[13]

The talks dragged on through June and into July. Lamar and his generals grew impatient, convinced that Bowls was gathering the immigrant tribes in anticipation of a war with the whites. Mobilizing all the troops at his disposal, the president sent militia units and a regular infantry regiment under the command of Edward Burleson into the Piney Woods to take up positions on the edge of Cherokee country. By midsummer Burleson had assembled an army of more than one thousand men, larger than the one Sam Houston had commanded at San Jacinto.

In mid-July the negotiations collapsed. Lamar's commissioners informed the Indian chiefs that they would be compensated for their immovable property, such as crops and storehouses, but as squatters they would get nothing for the land they had lived on and improved. Another stumbling block was the commissioners' insistence that the Cherokee men surrender their gunlocks (firing mechanisms) before embarking on the journey. The gunlocks would be returned, the commissioners told them, when the Indians reached the Red River. Unwilling to place their people at the mercy of the Texas forces that were massing only a few miles away, the chiefs refused. At the final meeting with Lamar's commissioners they arrived carrying war clubs, their faces smeared ominously with black paint.[14]

Determined to leave on their own terms, the Cherokees abandoned their villages and headed north. Burleson's troops followed their trail, and on July 15 exchanged fire with Bowls's tribesmen, who had stopped at a dry creek bed west of the Neches River to give the women and children time to continue their flight toward the US border. The Texans pursued the Indians the following day, catching up with them at a Delaware village a few miles farther north. When the Cherokees took cover in the thick woods of the river bottomlands, Burleson's men dismounted, and after torching the village, formed battle lines. As flames engulfed the cabins and thick columns of black smoke filled the early morning sky, they descended into the steep ravine that led down to the river.[15]

Bowls would make his final stand at the Neches. For his last battle, the aged chief wore a tricornered hat and a red silk vest. The hat was part of the uniform given to him by Mexican authorities in 1827 after the Fredonian Rebellion; the vest was a gift from Sam Houston at the signing ceremony for the treaty the two men had signed in 1836. The Cherokee leader had once worn them proudly. Now they were emblems of the false promises the two governments had made to the tribe. Throughout the battle Bowls could be seen astride a sorrel horse, "a magnificent picture of barbaric manhood," a young volunteer, John H. Reagan, recalled. As the retreating Indians splashed across the shallow river, the old chief remained on the west bank. Shot in the thigh, Bowls dismounted. Another bullet ripped into his back, and he staggered, then fell to his knees, facing the advancing Texans. As Reagan approached, an officer ran toward them, his pistol drawn. "Captain, don't shoot him," Reagan cried out. The officer fired his weapon at close range into Bowls's head, killing him instantly.[16]

A mob of militiamen crowded around the fallen chieftain in a scramble for grisly souvenirs. They stripped the Cherokee leader of his clothes and rifled through his pockets, then mutilated his body. One sliced off Bowls's scalp. Another cut a long strip of skin from his back, which he planned to use as a razor strop.[17]

Lamar's plan—to the extent that he had one—was for Burleson to lead an orderly evacuation of the Indians out of Texas. But Burleson's men had other ideas, turning their attention instead to the abandoned Indian farmhouses, which they plundered before putting them to the torch. The stores of corn and the herds of livestock which the Indians had left behind were said to be enough to feed the army for a year. Left to fend for themselves, the Cherokees dispersed, most heading north to the Red River, a trek of more than two hundred miles. Some refugees journeyed west, to the prairies beyond the Cross Timbers, while others found homes among the pockets of other displaced tribes, such as the Caddo and the Wichita, near the headwaters of the Brazos and Trinity rivers.[18]

Shocked by the government's ruthless assault on the Cherokees, Shawnee and Delaware chiefs quickly sued for peace. Within a matter of weeks they accepted the government's offer of compensation to relocate in US Indian Territory. Only the Alabama-Coushattas were allowed to remain within the borders of Texas. Numbering only a few hundred, they hunted and fished on a patch of densely wooded swampland in southeast Texas, an area wholly unsuited to cotton-growing or other large-scale farming. They remain there today.[19]

In Nashville, where he was visiting his mentor Andrew Jackson, Houston followed the events in Texas with growing fury. Cutting short his trip, he hurried home, stopping briefly in Alabama to see Margaret and her family. By the time he returned he had learned of Bowls's death at the Battle of the Neches, and he vented his rage in a speech in Nacogdoches, delivering a blistering attack on Lamar's Indian policy. Never one to pander to public opinion, the former president did not care that the expulsion of the immigrant tribes enjoyed broad if not unanimous support among East Texas whites, or that many in the audience had participated in the recent military campaign.[20]

Houston's friends had placed his name in nomination as a congressional candidate for San Augustine during his absence, and he would take his seat in the Fourth Congress when the legislative session convened that fall. Still seething over the expulsion of the Indians, he did not miss an opportunity to raise the matter, finding ways to lecture his colleagues on the painful subject even when speaking on issues wholly unrelated to Indian affairs. Addressing Lamar's claim that the Cherokees were living in Texas illegally, he reminded the chamber that Anglo-American colonists and the immigrant tribes had both been invited into the country by the Mexican government. "They were no more intruders than we were," he declared.

Further, he noted, in taking no part in the conflict with Mexico in 1836, the tribe had ensured the success of the Anglo rebellion. In return, "the Cherokees had been treated with duplicity and fraud, . . . driven, unjustifiably, from their country and their homes." His frequent speeches on the Indian question, always lengthy and always impassioned, infuriated his enemies and embarrassed his friends. One army veteran, who had been wounded at the Neches, was so upset by Houston's defense of the Indians that he tried to assault the congressman with an axe.[21]

Houston's tirades could do nothing to help the Cherokees, nor do they seem to have changed any legislators' minds on the subject. Only one question remained: Who owned the lands vacated by the immigrant tribes? In Cherokee country alone, some 680,000 acres now became available to white settlement. The likeliest claimants were the stockholders of the old Galveston Bay and Texas Land Company, which still held the East Texas empresario contracts issued by the Mexican government. Houston saw an opportunity to prevent the stockholders, one of whom was his longtime enemy, David G. Burnet, from reaping a windfall in land sales, and to embarrass the administration in the process. Arguing that private speculators possessed no claim to the area, the former president drafted a bill that put forward a novel argument. The Cherokees, he insisted, had owned the land since 1822, when Richard Fields received permission from Governor Trespalacios to settle the area. All subsequent claims—Burnet received his empresario contract four years later—were therefore invalid, and the lands should now become the property of the republic.[22]

At the very least, Houston's Cherokee Land Bill placed the government in an awkward situation. Lamar's claim that the Cherokees were trespassers in East Texas had, after all, been a primary reason for their removal; Congress could hardly acknowledge the Indians as rightful owners of the land it had just seized. But the war against the Cherokees had been expensive, and the bill offered the government a means to recoup the costs, and a great deal more. By some estimates, the land would bring a total of three million dollars in

additional revenue, and could be used as collateral to obtain foreign loans. In the end, Congress passed Houston's land bill, thereby
recognizing the Cherokees' claim. But the final draft struck out any
explicit reference to Indian ownership. There was, apparently, only
so much hypocrisy the legislators could live with.[23]

For the Indians, of course, it did not matter whether the land
was sold off by the government or private speculators. By this time,
most of Bowls's people had joined the tribe in US Indian Territory
above the Red River. Overwhelmed by the Trail of Tears refugees
earlier in the year, the Western Cherokees did not greet them with
open arms. The Texas bands only aggravated what was already an
acute humanitarian crisis, straining the limited resources of federal
Indian agents. Destitute and denied a voice in tribal affairs, some saw
little reason to stay.

That December, Chief Bowls's forty-three-year-old son, John,
led several families back across the Red River, bound for Mexico.
Braving the winter cold, they stayed well clear of the Anglo settlements, hoping to reach the Rio Grande unmolested. But on Christmas Day the band was suddenly confronted by a force of several
hundred well-armed Texans and Tonkawa scouts commanded by
Edward Burleson, who had fought the Cherokees at the Neches
River six months earlier. On a mission to destroy the Comanches'
winter encampments, they had been unable to find them, and were
spoiling for an Indian fight of any kind. With only a handful of men,
Bowls tried to surrender. Then someone opened fire—Burleson's
official report implausibly blamed the Indians—setting off a furious attack by the Texas troops. Chasing the Cherokees into a cedar
thicket, they killed Bowls and most of the other men, sparing the
women and children, who were returned to the Cherokee Nation
above the Red River.[24]

In the spring, a team of Land Office surveyors rode up from
Nacogdoches to the now abandoned Cherokee villages above the
Angelina River. Setting up their headquarters in Bowls's village, they
spent the next several weeks walking with compass and chain through

the dense timberland that had once been the hunting grounds of the tribe, taking careful notes of its geographical features, and doing the same with the tribe's farm and pasture lands, carving the region up into 640-acre parcels. Anglo settlers soon followed. In a curious nod to its past, the new inhabitants named the area Cherokee County. A decade later it was the third largest county in Texas, home to more than five thousand whites and twelve hundred slaves.[25]

TWENTY

AS FAR WEST AS IT IS POSSIBLE FOR AMERICANS TO GO

F OR THE ENTERPRISING LAND SPECULATOR, THE OPENING OF the Texas Land Office in 1837 presented a once-in-a-lifetime opportunity. Over the next several years, the office would issue headright certificates to citizens of the republic and military veterans totaling more than thirty-six million acres of public domain. Many recipients would never settle the land, but would sell their certificates for cash at a fraction of their value. Savvy investors could make a fortune, and Sam Maverick wanted in on the action.

After joining the throng of refugees in the Runaway Scrape, Maverick had made his way to his family's plantation in northwestern Alabama. He may have felt some remorse, and perhaps even a twinge of guilt, that he had not stayed in Texas to see the fight for independence to its triumphant conclusion. In any case, as the dust settled after San Jacinto, he began making plans to return. He had spent six months in San Antonio and seen little but the chaos of war, but the experience had not changed his mind about the region's economic potential. Even before the Land Office opened, Maverick was selling his Alabama properties to raise money, still determined to build a land empire in the west.[1]

This time, he would not be making the trip alone. On a visit to Tuscaloosa he had met Mary Adams, a country-bred nineteen-year-old whose widowed mother owned a small cotton plantation outside town. Three months later they were married. A big-boned young woman, she was taller than her husband, and fifteen years his junior. She possessed an optimistic, cheerful temperament, inclined, as she put it, to see "the sunny side of life." Maverick seems to have had little difficulty getting Mary excited about a move to Texas. He described the lands beyond the Sabine as "a new El Dorado," speaking with such confidence about the opportunities to be found there that he persuaded her two brothers to relocate to Texas as well.[2]

The couple's parents did not share Maverick's enthusiasm. Mary's mother, Agatha, was inconsolable at the thought of her daughter living on a dangerous frontier seven hundred miles away. Sam's father, who for several weeks believed his son had been among the victims at the Alamo, begged them not to make the trip, offering to deed the couple his plantation in South Carolina if they would stay. But Sam would not reconsider his decision, delaying their journey only long enough for Mary to give birth to their first child, a boy. In the fall of 1837, they set off from Tuscaloosa in a carriage with five-month-old Sam Jr. and Mary's brother, Robert. Ten slaves followed in an open wagon, with four horses loaded with provisions. In tears, Agatha ran after the carriage as it trundled down the road, sensing that this might be a final farewell. Dying four years later of congestive fever, she would never see her daughter again.[3]

After an overland trek that took three and a half months, the Maverick party arrived at Spring Hill, a Navidad River stopover for settlers on their way into the interior. Worried that other speculators were already acquiring the best lands, Sam went on ahead with Mary's brother, leaving her to spend the spring of 1838 at the settlement. In June he returned to take his family on the last leg of the trip to San Antonio. The Mavericks were now "a family of adventurers," as Mary put it hopefully in one of her letters home, on a journey that would take them "as far West as it is possible for Americans to go."[4]

In fact, there were very few Americans where Mary was going. Sitting on the southern rim of the Edwards Plateau, far removed in distance and culture from the Anglo settlements of Texas, San Antonio remained for all intents and purposes a remote Mexican outpost.

The town's only access to the coast was a 150-mile dirt road, the narrow San Antonio River, which twisted and looped like a coiled spring on its way to the Gulf, being unsuitable as a commercial waterway. There was little likelihood that Americans less adventurous than the Mavericks would be pushing that far west anytime soon.

The road from Spring Hill to San Antonio could be a hazardous undertaking in the best of times, a testament to the limits of Anglo control over much of Texas. Though well-armed, the family would have been powerless to fend off a Comanche raiding party, which could number as many as one hundred warriors. Tonkawas and Lipan Apaches also roamed the area, tribes that were generally friendly to whites, though Anglos could not take their friendship for granted. Later that summer, a gang of American cattle thieves would enlist the Tonkawas in a raid against Mexican traders. Instead of dividing the spoils, the whites stole the Tonkawas' horses, prompting the Indians to kill several settlers near the headwaters of the Lavaca River.[5]

Near the end of the trip, the Mavericks were startled one evening when a party of seventeen Tonkawas appeared at their campsite. Dressed only in breechclouts, their faces daubed with war paint, the group was in good humor, having recently skirmished with Penateka Comanches on the Nueces River. The Tonkawas rarely got the better of the Comanches, but on this occasion they had bested their enemies, and carried with them the trophies of war: two scalps, a hand, and pieces of putrid flesh. The Indians would later celebrate their victory with a scalp dance at their village, feasting on a stew that included the remains of their victims. Although often desperately hungry—Tonkawas were known to tie strips of leather tightly around their waists until they could find something to eat—the tribe did engage in ritual cannibalism, attaching special spiritual significance to the limbs of warriors killed in battle.[6]

The Indian visitors professed friendship in broken Spanish, which did little to reassure the Mavericks, who hurriedly started to break camp. As the Tonkawas milled about, inspecting the family's horses, Mary and her infant son took refuge in the carriage. Peering into the window, the Indians expressed an interest in the baby, still less than a year old, which Mary, with no little reluctance, held up for them to see. The Maverick men and their two male slaves, Griffin and Wiley, loaded the wagon in the gathering darkness and set off. The Tonkawas followed at a distance, their silhouettes visible in the moonlight. One by one they began to drift away, allowing the families to reach their destination unmolested.[7]

In San Antonio, Maverick set himself up as a surveyor and land agent, fully expecting that Anglo settlers would abandon the republic's coastal regions for Béxar's drier, healthier climate. Unable to contain his irrepressible boosterism in letters to family members back home, he declared San Antonio to be "the only place in Texas where there is plenty to eat & every body is in good spirits."[8] But the settlers did not come, at least not in the numbers Maverick expected. With little demand for the thousands of acres he had purchased and surveyed, he returned to the practice of law to make ends meet. The couple purchased a three-room stone house on Commerce Street, on the northeast corner of the main plaza. Behind the house stood a shed that doubled as a kitchen and enslaved quarters, with a stable, bath house, and wash place near the bank of the San Antonio River.[9]

The absence of a steady flow of settlers meant that San Antonio would continue to be an easy target for the Penatekas, and Mary quickly learned that her new life required constant vigilance. Small groups of Indians often lurked on the outskirts of the town, waiting for a chance to steal horses and livestock. Soon after the Mavericks arrived, Griffin and Wiley were plowing a parcel of nearby farmland when the sudden appearance of Comanches sent the two men dashing into the river, leaving the Indians to ride off with the work animals. "It seemed they were always on the watch everywhere," Mary recalled, "but only acted at the most favorable moments."[10]

WHILE SAN ANTONIO HAD LONG BEEN A TARGET OF PENATEKA raiding parties on their way to the Rio Grande, up to this point the tribe had pursued a very different course toward the Anglo settlements of Texas. Comanche hunters following the buffalo herds into the Guadalupe River Valley occasionally raided white ranches and homesteads, but the tribe also came to appreciate the Anglo-Americans as trading partners. Far to the north, on the Red River, American merchants supplied them with guns and ammunition in exchange for stolen horses and mules. Closer to home, Comanche men and women were a familiar sight in Bastrop, on the Colorado River, where they came to barter furs and skins for calicoes and tobacco.[11]

Over time, however, Comanche leaders grew increasingly concerned as Anglo settlers pushed farther up the Colorado and Guadalupe river valleys, closer to their hunting lands on the Edwards Plateau. As in East Texas, the opening of the Land Office accelerated the process of white encroachment. Muguara, a prominent tribal elder, and other Penateka head men generally favored a nonconfrontational policy, hopeful that a diplomatic solution with the Texas government could be reached to contain the Anglo advance. Younger war chiefs demanded a more aggressive approach, and stood ready to attack parties of surveyors and settlers that ventured into the Hill Country.

Among the most forceful advocates for hostilities was Buffalo Hump (Potsanaquahip), a war chief celebrated for his devastating raids into northern Mexico. A German settler who met him some years later described a powerful, striking figure, his body decorated with beaded necklaces and copper arm rings. Unlike many Comanche men, who had begun to wear coarse cotton clothing acquired from American merchants, Buffalo Hump proudly spurned Western dress. With only a buffalo hide tied around his waist, he seemed "the genuine, unadulterated picture of a North American Indian."[12]

For the time being, the moderate views of Muguara and other tribal elders prevailed. In the spring of 1838, a group of Comanche headmen met with representatives of the Houston government, and for the first time raised the issue of a boundary line between the two peoples. Ignoring the fact that the Penatekas had pushed Apaches and Tonkawas out of the Hill Country a few decades earlier, they insisted that the land to the north and west of San Antonio was rightfully theirs. Muguara led a delegation to meet with President Houston in May to make the same claim. Houston knew there was little, if anything, he could do to prevent Anglo migration into the area, and frankly told them so. "If I could build a wall from the Red River to the Rio Grande, so high that no Indian could scale it," the president told them, "the white people would go crazy trying to devise a means to get beyond it." He offered to build the Comanches a trading post, but the project never materialized. The Córdova rebellion broke out a few months later, and the unrest in the Piney Woods would preoccupy the president for the remainder of his term.[13]

That fall, Comanche policy abruptly changed. Angry that Houston had failed to honor his promise of a trading post, and with surveyors pushing ever deeper into central Texas, Muguara and tribal elders were less inclined—or perhaps unable—to rein in younger leaders like Buffalo Hump. In mid-October, Sam Maverick spent several days with a surveying team near the Leon River, four miles north of San Antonio. Shortly after he left the group to return home, a party of one hundred Comanches swept through the camp, sparing only a Mexican, who later escaped. When word of the attack reached San Antonio, a volunteer company set off in hot pursuit. It, too, was ambushed by the Indians, who killed fifteen men before chasing the survivors all the way back to town.[14]

The following month, the Penatekas went on the offensive, launching a series of daring raids in the Bastrop area. Then, instead of retreating back to their rancherías in the north, the Indians headed south, to the white settlements along the lower Guadalupe River, a mere fifty miles from the Gulf Coast. In a display of the Comanches' unique ability to terrorize their enemies, the Penatekas seized five young members of the Lockhart and Putnam families as they gathered pecans along the banks of the river, tying them to their horses with rawhide thongs. A sixth, a two-year-old girl, would have slowed them down. She was killed on the spot.[15]

The episode ignited the fury of Anglo settlers, although an initial attempt to rescue the children was stymied by the onset of winter weather. Two months later, Lipan Apaches located Muguara's encampment on the San Saba River, and though the weather had not improved, an expedition of one hundred Anglos, Lipans, and Tonkawas was quickly organized. After a difficult trek in snow and freezing rain, they reached the San Saba undetected, approaching the camp in the cold dawn. Dismounting, the Texans and their Indian allies fired into buffalo skin tipis, killing indiscriminately. In the midst of the carnage and confusion, Andrew Lockhart dashed frantically through the village, calling out for his daughter, Matilda, but Comanche women held her fast, dragging her into the brush on the edge of the camp. When the Texans retreated to a nearby ravine, the Indians drove off their horses, leaving the attackers no choice but to turn homeward, making the long journey on foot.[16]

Buffalo Hump retaliated immediately. Long before Andrew Lockhart and the dispirited Texans made it back home, Comanche warriors were on the move, heading into the Colorado River Valley, where they killed homesteaders, stole horses, and seized captives, including several slaves. Harried Bastrop settlers and ranger companies pursued the Indians as they rode north with their plunder, engaging Buffalo Hump's warriors in a bloody, two-day fight at Brushy Creek, near present-day Taylor.[17]

The Hill Country was beginning to take on the appearance of a war zone. But just six weeks later, to the surprise of many Texans, a five-man commission tasked with finding a site for a permanent capital selected Waterloo, the westernmost settlement on the Colorado River. The far-sighted commissioners explained, with unbounded optimism, that the site would one day be more centrally located. They envisioned Austin, as the new capital would be called, at the intersection of two great roads, one linking Santa Fe, New Mexico, and the Gulf Coast, the other stretching from the Red River to Matamoros. Not surprisingly, the site was also the preferred choice of the expansion-minded Lamar, who visited the area on a buffalo hunting trip the year before. The poet-president had little difficulty imagining the rolling hills and savannas of the Edwards Plateau as a garden spot for enterprising Anglos, a bucolic region dotted with farms and ranches. Here, on the southeastern edge of Comanche country, Lamar saw a great city, "the seat of future empire."[18]

Construction of the new capital began that summer. A nearby pine forest provided lumber, but all tools and other materials had to be carted by oxen from Houston, 150 miles away. To finish the project in time for the opening of the Fourth Congress in the fall, a crew of two hundred men, many of them enslaved, worked around the clock. On a parcel of land that sloped down to the Colorado River they built log cabin government offices, a barnlike structure that passed as a capitol, a two-story whitewashed president's mansion, and a large hotel. For the most part, the Comanches kept their distance, though small parties still prowled the thickets on the edge of town. Looking for horses to steal, they killed two men before construction could be completed.

IN THE OPEN COUNTRY TO THE NORTH AND WEST OF AUSTIN, IT was still an Indian world. A few days before the official opening of Congress, sixty-five-year-old John Webster, a Virginia native, led a party into the dry, post oak region north of the capital, with the intention of establishing a settlement on the San Gabriel River. The group included his much younger wife, thirty-one-year-old Dolly, their two children, and a dozen men. Webster, who had spent the past two years in Bastrop, could hardly have been unaware of the risks involved. Their trek would take them far beyond Brushy Creek, the scene of fierce fighting between Indians and Texas militiamen only a few months earlier. Yet the party seemed utterly oblivious to any danger, and the men amused themselves by shooting at wild game (not very successfully, according to Dolly). Their buoyant mood vanished when, as dusk fell, they realized they were not alone. The sound of chanting could be heard distinctly off in the distance—a Penateka raiding party holding a war dance, Dolly would later learn.[19]

After an anxious night the Websters began to retrace their steps at dawn. Crossing a narrow, post oak prairie, they first spotted a party of Indians a few hundred yards behind them and hurried forward, trying to reach the protection of a timbered creek bed. More than a hundred well-armed and mounted Comanches were waiting for them. Turning the oxen and cattle loose, they huddled behind their two wagons, the only cover available. For a time the group held off their attackers, as arrows whizzed from the cover of a thicket, and squads of Indians galloped past, firing their rifles. Dolly watched in horror as the men fell around her, one by one, the Indians drawing closer, until only she and her two children were left alive. The Comanches proceeded to ransack the wagons and scalp their victims, leaving her husband untouched on account of his gray hair.[20]

Snatching up Dolly and her two children, the raiding party headed northwest at full gallop, riding day and night, stopping only to water the horses, to escape the volunteer companies that would pursue them when the residents of Austin learned of the attack. Linking up with other bands in the area, the Indians made their way across the rugged, rolling hills of the Edwards Plateau. Eight days later they reached Muguara's encampment near the headwaters of the Colorado River, having covered a distance of 250 miles.

Home to more than two thousand people, the Penatekas' principal ranchería was one of the largest population centers in Texas in 1839. Buffalo hide tipis stretched for more than a mile along the river. A world that few whites had ever seen, it was nonetheless a major hub for the flow of contraband on the Low Plains, attracting not only Mexican and American traders but Indians from across the Southwest. Just as Houston and Galveston connected the white republic to the urban centers of New Orleans and Mobile, Muguara's ranchería occupied an important place in a vast commercial network, one that had existed long before whites arrived with Stephen F. Austin to settle the Brazos River valley.[21]

Here Dolly found Matilda Lockhart and the Putnam children, as well as several dozen other captives, most of them Mexicans seized from towns along the Rio Grande. While the abuse of Comanche captives seemed indiscriminate to outsiders, their treatment varied according to their value to the tribe. Eleven-year-old Booker fared better than his mother and sister. It was not uncommon for young Mexican and Anglo males to be accepted as members of the tribe.

22. Mexican boy recovered from
the Comanches, by W. P. Bliss.
Comanche raiding parties captured
hundreds of women and children in
the early decades of the nineteenth
century, most of them Hispanos
like the boy in this photograph.
Courtesy of Gilcrease Museum,
Tulsa, Oklahoma.

One boy, the son of one of Austin's early colonists, had become so
thoroughly assimilated that he seemed to enjoy the plight of the
other captives, informing on them and even joining the Indians in
meting out punishment.[22]

Infants and young girls were not so fortunate; the Comanches
did not hold to the universal Western view of children as symbols of
innocence. Dolly's three-year-old daughter, Patsy, had survived the
attack on the San Gabriel, but her age made her unproductive and
therefore expendable. Indeed, a captive female child had more value
dead than alive. Comanches typically slaughtered animals upon the
death of a warrior, but when the wife of a chief died at the encampment, one of the Putnam girls was killed and buried with her.[23]

As for Dolly, she would join the ranks of a reviled class—
captive women who served as the concubines of Comanche warriors.
Claimed by a member of the war party that had killed her husband
at the San Gabriel, she was put to work alongside the women of the
tribe, who regarded female captives as sexual rivals, subjecting her to
frequent beatings. Stripped of her clothing and dressed in two pieces
of buckskin, she spent her days collecting firewood, skinning and

tanning buffalo and deer hides. Usually separated from her two children, Dolly did not think of escape. Then, one November afternoon,
they found themselves alone gathering the pecans that covered the
dark soil along the bottomlands of the Colorado River. Without hes-
itating, she grabbed them and ran.[24]

Following the course of the river, they slowly made their way
south. Traveling only at night, they survived on nuts, prickly pears,
and berries when they could find them, often going days without
food. As time passed the weather grew colder. Booker fell seriously
ill after eating the red berries of a yaupon bush, and for several days
was unable to travel. Their harrowing ordeal through open country
lasted more than a month, until one day Dolly glimpsed, off in the
distance, a large body of men in Western dress. Her spirits soared
and she called out, scrambling toward them. They were not Anglo
settlers, but a group of Córdova's partisans routed by the Texans near
Seguin earlier in the year. For several days the party argued over
what to do with Dolly and her children. Before a decision could be
reached, a band of Comanches visited the camp, buying them back
for a mule and a horse.[25]

Returned to Muguara's ranchería on the upper Colorado, Dolly
learned there had been an important development in the on-again,
off-again conflict between the Penatekas and the white republic.
Muguara and other tribal elders were not yet ready to abandon diplomacy, still hopeful that they could open a dialogue with the Texas
government. That winter the chief sent a party of Indians to San
Antonio under a flag of truce, with one of the Putnam boys as a
sign of good faith, to announce that the tribe was again willing to
discuss a boundary line between the two peoples. The local ranger
commander told the envoys that the government would negotiate
only under certain conditions. The Indians must restore all stolen
property, he told them, and in an astonishing admission of the government's disregard for the republic's nonwhite citizens, return any
"American" captives. Evidently, the Comanches could do what they
wanted with any Hispano Texans who had the misfortune to fall
into their hands.[26]

Muguara seems to have been confident that an agreement with the white government could be reached. Dolly would later recall that the mood in the camp was buoyant as tribal leaders prepared for their diplomatic mission. The chief questioned her at length about the whites, and she made for him a silk white flag trimmed with white ribbons. But not all the important men of the tribe shared Muguara's optimism. Buffalo Hump would not attend the meeting at San Antonio. A war chief, he preferred to leave diplomacy to tribal elders, and he rode off to take part in a new campaign against Mexican towns below the Rio Grande.[27]

If Dolly had won the old chief's trust, it made little difference to the Penateka women. The beatings at their hands continued, and she decided she could wait for her freedom no longer. Her son Booker was opposed to the idea of a second escape attempt. He had almost died on the first one, and they would certainly be killed if recaptured. Dolly pleaded in vain for him to come with her, but he reassured his mother that he stood a better chance of survival if he stayed, having been adopted by a family that had recently lost a son the same age. Not long after the peace delegation left for San Antonio, Dolly took her infant daughter and stole out of camp in a drizzling nighttime rain.

ON THE MORNING OF MARCH 19, 1840, TWO INDIAN RUNNERS came into San Antonio to announce the Comanches' arrival. A short time later Muguara appeared, riding slowly and with great ceremony at the head of a group of about sixty Penatekas that included chiefs, warriors, and a large number of women and children. Mary Maverick and other townsfolk crowded along the route to see the "wild Indians." Bringing up the rear to tend to the extra horses was fifteen-year-old Matilda Lockhart. Her body covered with sores, the young girl bore visible signs of mistreatment. Her nose had been slashed and burned to the bone, a punishment often reserved for females accused of adultery.[28]

Muguara's first diplomatic overture to the whites, his meeting with President Houston two years earlier, had ended without an agreement on a boundary line. But now he believed he would be negotiating from a position of strength. Since 1838, the Penatekas had made it clear they would protect their hunting grounds on the Edwards Plateau, and demonstrated their ability to strike at will deep into the white settlements. Muguara was so confident, in fact, that he ignored the government's demand that all white captives be returned, bringing in only the Lockhart girl. The others he intended to use as bargaining chips to extract additional concessions from Lamar's commissioners.

If Muguara had reneged on his promise to return the white captives, the Lamar government was also guilty of negotiating in bad faith. The president had no intention of discussing a boundary with the Comanches. "Our citizens have a right to occupy any vacant lands," the commissioners were told, and that was the end of the matter. What was more, Lamar had decided to dispense with the most basic forms of protocol governing diplomacy between Americans and Native peoples. This time, there would be no gifts for the Indians. And while Muguara had been welcomed by the Houston administration two years earlier, he arrived in San Antonio to find the town swarming with soldiers.[29]

Captain George Howard, the leader of the Texas delegation, ushered the chiefs into the Council House, a one-story, flat-roofed stone building just off the main plaza, while the rest of the Comanche party milled about on the street. The Texans wasted little time bringing up the issue of the missing captives. When Muguara replied that they were being held by other Comanche bands, Howard ordered one company of troops to enter the building. Speaking through a Mexican interpreter, he informed the chiefs they would all be detained until the other captives were brought in.[30]

Outside, Mary Maverick and a friend watched through a picket fence as a group of Comanche youths entertained the townspeople with their marksmanship with bows and arrows. Suddenly, she heard a "deafening war whoop" inside the building, a sound "so loud, so shrill and so inexpressibly horrible" that she failed to grasp its meaning. But the Indian boys playing on the street recognized the sound, and without hesitation drew their bows on two men nearby, killing one instantly.[31]

Inside the Council House, all was chaos and confusion. Some chiefs lunged for the Texas delegation, knives drawn, others dashed for the door. Captain Howard gave the order to fire. Muguara died in a hail of bullets, the volley killing several Indians and two whites.[32]

Amid the sound of gunfire and the clouds of powder smoke that billowed from the doorway and windows of the Council House, the large throng of Indians, Mexicans, and Anglos on the street outside suddenly began running helter skelter in a mad dash for safety. Mary picked up her skirts and ran to her house on Commerce Street, passing two Indians, who stopped in their tracks and gave chase. She slammed and bolted the door behind her. Pushing against it for a moment, they ran on.

In one room, Mary found Sam and her brother Andrew inspecting survey plats, oblivious to the commotion outside. Pausing only long enough to shout, "Here are Indians! Here are Indians!," she rushed past them to find her children.[33]

Within minutes of the first shots inside the Council House, Soledad and Commerce streets were littered with bodies. Some Indians tried to escape on horseback, others headed on foot for the San Antonio River. Three Comanche warriors burst into the Maverick's backyard and ran to the water. Andrew felled two with a rifle before they reached the opposite bank. That evening, San Antonio residents found two Indians hiding in an outside kitchen, which they set on fire, killing them as they tried to escape. In all, about forty people, most of them Comanches, died in the melee.

One week later, a woman with an infant tied to her back stumbled down the road on the outskirts of town. Her face creased and weather-beaten, her matted hair cropped short in the Comanche style, Dolly was initially mistaken for an Indian. She was badly dehydrated, her arms and legs lacerated by thorns and briars, but her decision to escape the Comanche encampment rather than wait to be ransomed had saved her life. Furious when they learned that their leaders had died under a flag of truce, the Penatekas tortured and killed thirteen white captives, roasting them over a fire. They spared Booker and one of the Putnam girls, exchanging them a few weeks later for some of the Indians captured at the Council House.[34]

For Buffalo Hump and the Penatekas, the slaughter in San Antonio demanded a dramatic response. While raiding was a part of everyday life, the tribe went to war only on rare occasions, and always to avenge the deaths of kinsmen. Throughout the spring and summer, Buffalo Hump recruited men from the other four principal Comanche bands and may even have received support from Kiowa allies in New Mexico. By August they were ready. Like all major campaigns, this one would have been preceded by elaborate ceremonies lasting several days, in which mock battles were staged in anticipation of the victory to come. The pre-war rituals culminated in a night of war dances accompanied by the sound of chants, drums, whistles, and gourd rattles. At dawn the warriors rode out of the camp in dazzling military array, wearing feather headdresses and buffalo horns, their bodies and horses daubed with war paint. This would be no ordinary raid on the Anglo settlements of Texas.[35]

The army numbered several hundred warriors and their camp followers, perhaps as many as one thousand in all. In what would later become known as the Great Comanche Raid, it followed much the same path the Penatekas had taken two years earlier when they seized the Lockhart and Putnam children, sweeping in a southeasterly direction to Bastrop, then down into the Guadalupe River valley. After burning homesteads and killing settlers near Victoria, the Indians rode on, cutting a swath of destruction to the coast. For the inhabitants of Linnville, a small seaport on Lavaca Bay, their only warning was the distant thundering of horses. In a complete panic, they ran into the water, some escaping in small boats, where they watched as the Indians spent the day looting the town and the warehouses along the waterfront. After torching the buildings, the Comanches gathered their plunder and wheeled about, to make the long ride back to their rancherías on the upper Colorado.[36]

As news of the attack spread throughout the region, the residents of Austin, Bastrop, Gonzales, and other settlements began to organize into units to intercept the Indians as they headed north. They were not hard to find. Driving two thousand horses and mules stolen from the corrals of Victoria and Linnville, the Comanche column stretched for miles, kicking up immense clouds of dust. Upon closer inspection, the throng seemed to resemble a parade of harlequins rather than one of the most feared paramilitary organizations in North America. Flushed with victory, the group danced and sang. Warriors wore black frock coats and beaver hats taken from the Linnville storehouses, their horses gaily caparisoned with bolts of brightly colored calico and bed sheets, as ribbons tied to the animals' manes and tails streamed behind them.

Four days later, at Plum Creek, twenty-five miles south of Austin, the Comanches found their path blocked by a force of two hundred Anglos and Tonkawas. After some initial skirmishing, the mounted Texans charged the Comanches, who retreated to a motte of live oak trees. The Indians soon broke into small parties and the Texans gave chase, the battle quickly devolving into a running fight for several miles, lasting over an hour. Suffering heavy casualties, by some accounts more than one hundred warriors, the tribe scattered, abandoning the stolen horses as they fled north.[37]

The feral ferocity of the battle was shocking even on a frontier that had experienced more than its share of racial violence. When the Comanches saw that the battle was lost, they shot arrows into their white female captives before making their retreat. That afternoon, the Texans scoured the area for Indian wounded, killing them where they lay. One volunteer came upon a dying Penateka woman who had been shot in both thighs. Grabbing the woman by the hair, he pulled her head back and slit her throat, then plunged the knife to the hilt into her chest, twisting it "round and round like he was grinding coffee." As night fell, amid a prairie strewn with bodies and animal carcasses, the Texans built campfires along Plum Creek. So did their Tonkawa allies, who held a victory celebration that lasted until morning. Dancing over a slain Comanche warrior, they cut chunks of flesh from the body, which they roasted and ate.[38]

With the Great Comanche Raid the struggle between the white republic and the Penatekas reached its gory climax. The Texans claimed victory at Plum Creek, which they would follow up with a pair of attacks on Comanche villages later that fall. Chastened, the band moved its rancherías farther up the Colorado. It would never again launch a major campaign against the Anglo settlements, though small parties would continue to prey upon farms and ranches, usually on their way to and from their raids into Mexico.

But the Penatekas' main goal, one shared by tribal elders and younger war chiefs alike, had always been to keep whites from pushing onto the Edwards Plateau, and in that regard Buffalo Hump's summer campaign was an undeniable success. His bold show of force had stunned the Anglo community, allowing the Penatekas to stake their claim to the area north and west of Austin. Mirabeau Lamar could dream of a flourishing capital on the upper Colorado, but few settlers were intrepid enough to follow him there. For the time being at least, the two peoples eyed each other warily, from a respectful distance.

TWENTY-ONE

A FOREIGNER IN MY NATIVE LAND

Aبout a year and a half before the Mavericks arrived in San Antonio—a cold, wintry afternoon in February 1837—Bexareños gathered on the streets of the town to watch a solemn ceremony. As the bells of the San Fernando church pealed, Lieutenant Colonel Juan Seguín and an honor guard filed slowly across the San Antonio River, accompanied by clergy and civic leaders. The soldiers carried a casket draped in the Texas flag (then a large gold star on an azure blue background), on which had been placed a rifle and sword. The procession came to a halt a few hundred yards beyond the Alamo mission's battered walls, where the charred remains of the Alamo defenders still lay a year after the siege in three enormous, blackened heaps. Three musket volleys rent the air, and Seguín stepped forward to give a brief eulogy in Spanish. The martyrs of the Alamo "preferred to die a thousand times rather than submit to the tyrant's yoke," he declared. "With the venerable remains of our worthy companions as witnesses, let us declare to the entire world: Texas shall be free and independent, or perish in glorious combat."[1]

These stirring words may well have been an expression of Seguín's true feelings. But the burial ceremony for the Alamo defenders was also intended to allay white suspicions about the loyalties of a Hispano population that suddenly found itself part of a nation composed largely of Anglo-Americans. Seguín had good reason to be concerned. The American volunteers who had poured into the country during the rebellion regarded all Mexicans with contempt, and their hostility was especially evident toward well-to-do Hispanos "whose only crime," Seguín said, "was that they owned large tracts of land and desirable property." His friends the De Leóns, who had backed the rebellion from the beginning, were among the first to suffer in the transition to white rule. When the Texas army occupied Victoria in the summer of 1836, General Rusk seized the family's cattle and horses and shipped seventy members of the extended family into exile in Louisiana.[2]

Seguín himself came under suspicion, although few Texans could claim a more distinguished record in the struggle for independence. As a veteran of the siege of Béxar and cavalry commander at San Jacinto, he had seen more fighting than just about anyone. But amid rumors that the Mexican government intended to mount a second campaign against Texas, the country's top-ranking general, Felix Huston, tried to have him relieved of duty because "he cannot speak our language." Only a few weeks before the memorial service at the Alamo, Huston, expecting an attack by the Mexican army at any moment, ordered Seguín to evacuate the town and destroy everything of value. Fortunately, the Bexareño leader found a sympathetic advocate in President Houston, who tried to shield Texas Hispanos from the recriminations of vengeful whites and countermanded the order.[3]

Fears of a new Mexican offensive eventually subsided, and by the time the Mavericks moved into their home on Commerce Street, San Antonio was beginning to adjust to its new role as a predominantly Hispano town in the Lone Star Republic. Bexareño leaders welcomed the Mavericks and other Anglo newcomers, allowing them to take an active part in civic life. Given the ever-present danger of Comanche raiding parties, they could hardly do otherwise. All able-bodied men were expected to keep a good horse and a store of provisions on hand, ready to ride in pursuit within fifteen minutes of the sound of the alarm bell in the San Fernando church. Despite their relatively small numbers, whites served on both the town council and as mayor, Sam Maverick winning election to the town's highest office a year after he arrived.

23. Juan Nepomuceno Seguín
(1806–1890), by Thomas Jefferson
Wright. A staunch defender of
Anglo-American interests in the
1830s, Seguín felt he had become
"a foreigner in my native land"
after independence, fleeing Texas in
1842. Courtesy of State Preservation
Board, Austin, Texas.

Still, formidable barriers of language and culture remained.
While politics, commerce, and civil defense required some degree
of cooperation among Anglo and Hispano men, social intercourse
among the two groups, an activity in which women played a more
significant role, was generally limited. Before independence, the few
Americans in town blended easily with the Bexareño community,
some taking Mexican wives. But the Mavericks and other Anglo
families tended to keep to themselves. Like her husband, Mary was
never comfortable with the easy informality of Mexican life. She
disapproved of the Sunday cockfighting in the plaza, and the raucous fandangos where the dancing, gambling, and drinking lasted
well into the night. She frowned, too, on the local custom of allowing children to run about naked. With a handful of other Anglo
ladies she paid the obligatory social calls upon the matriarchs of
the prominent Bexareño clans, but for the most part they preferred
their own company.[4]

Outwardly amicable, the relationship between the two San Antonio communities was at best an uneasy, awkward, and ultimately
fragile one. The news of Vicente Córdova's uprising revived Anglo
fears of Hispano disloyalty, although Bexareños almost certainly
knew nothing of the plot in East Texas. There were inevitable

disputes over land, with some unscrupulous whites taking advantage of the fact that few Mexican Texans could provide legal title to the large ranchos that had been in their families for generations. And while San Antonio was far too remote to attract large numbers of the drifters who flocked to coastal boom towns like Houston and Galveston, the newcomers included a small undesirable element that quarreled, sometimes violently, with longtime residents. One month before the Mavericks arrived, the town was rocked by the murder of José Antonio Navarro's younger brother Eugenio, shot in his dry goods store by an American gambler. The mortally wounded Navarro drew a knife and stabbed his assailant; they both died at the scene.[5]

Above all, in the eyes of many whites, a pall of suspicion hung over the Hispano residents of San Antonio for the simple reason that they continued to maintain close ties with Mexicans below the Rio Grande. Texas independence could not change the fact that family networks had for generations linked Bexareños with the people of the villas del norte. Economic contacts with the Anglo-Texan settlements in the east were generally limited. Far more important was the trade with Laredo, Mier, Reynosa, and Matamoros, with Bexareños driving livestock to the Rio Grande and returning with mule teams of tobacco, foodstuffs, and other trade goods.

In 1838, a new wave of political turmoil below the Rio Grande would draw San Antonio Hispanos even closer into the orbit of northern Mexico, when a dispute between the centralist government and France led to a blockade of the country's Atlantic ports by the French navy. Far from uniting the Mexican people against a foreign enemy, the crisis ignited flash fires of political unrest, as federalists who had been waiting for their chance to restore the Constitution of 1824 rose up in revolt.

The brief war against France also paved the way for one of history's most remarkable comebacks. Santa Anna, then living in retirement at his hacienda near Veracruz, rushed to the coast to take charge of the city's defenses, losing a leg in a battle with French troops. A national hero once again, he was borne on a litter back to

Mexico City, where the ruling junta appointed him president, less than three years after his humiliation at San Jacinto.

In northeastern Mexico, the federalist insurgency was led by a charismatic Monterrey lawyer, Antonio Canales. Angered by Mexico City's utter neglect of the northern frontier, which had long borne the brunt of Comanche raids, Canales and an army of rancheros harassed centralist garrisons across the states of Tamaulipas, Coahuila, and Nuevo Leon. Early in 1840 he organized a meeting of prominent norteños in Laredo to proclaim the formation of a new federal union in the northeast, which would come to be known in Texas as the Republic of the Rio Grande, although the group stopped short of issuing a formal declaration of secession.

Seguín threw himself headlong into the federalist cause. It was, after all, the struggle he always wanted, the one he thought he had been fighting in the early days of the Texas rebellion before it became a war for independence. When Canales made a trip to the Lone Star Republic to drum up support for his revolt, Seguín provided him with letters of introduction. President Lamar declined the rebel leader's offer of an alliance, unwilling to get involved in Mexico's internal affairs. But Seguín, who had always had an impetuous streak, resigned his seat in the Senate and recruited a regiment of Hispanos from the San Antonio area. A citizen of Texas, he was still a proud Mexican, whose national loyalties were nothing if not flexible.

When Seguín and his men reached the Rio Grande, the federalist campaign against the centralist garrisons in the northern towns was already going badly. Deeply superstitious, Canales was handicapped as a military leader by his penchant for making decisions based on astrology and other signs of the supernatural. Federalist morale sagged when his most capable guerrilla commander was captured and executed, his severed head placed on a pole in Guerrero as a warning to the rebels. Most important of all, Canales made the mistake of recruiting several hundred Anglo-American mercenaries, who proceeded to pillage the very towns the federalists hoped to win over to their side. The insurrection soon collapsed, leaving Seguín to bear the cost of the troops he had raised.[6]

The federalists' defeat in northern Mexico dealt a serious financial blow to many Texas Hispanos. Authorities in Matamoros now took steps to put a stop to the trade between San Antonio and the valley towns, commissioning roving bands of marauders to patrol the Trans-Nueces. Armed gangs of American cattle rustlers, many of them mercenaries from the federalist campaign, also roamed the South Texas chaparral. The most notorious was a group known as the Nueces Cow Boys, led by Mabry "Mustang" Gray. Earning his colorful nickname for his talent taming wild horses, he was also a cold-blooded killer, described by a Texan who knew him as a "moral monstrosity." In an effort to quell the violence, President Lamar created a volunteer ranger company, the San Patricio minutemen, but it did more harm than good; its members included some of the same bandits responsible for the area's most vicious crimes. The threat from Comanche raiding parties had always made the desolate Trans-Nueces one of the more dangerous regions of Texas, but now the area between the Nueces River and the Rio Grande became a lawless no-man's-land, where Indians, Anglos, and Mexicans stole livestock, robbed merchant trains, and killed anyone who got in their way.[7]

Meanwhile, the Lone Star Republic was feeling the full effects of a financial panic that had already crippled the American economy. Easy credit fueled the cotton boom throughout much of the 1830s, but when interest rates rose sharply at the end of the decade, agricultural prices tumbled. To rescue the republic's failing fortunes, Lamar in 1841 seized upon the idea of establishing a trade route to Santa Fe, New Mexico. In addition to gaining access to the lucrative commerce that brought yearly revenues of five million dollars to merchants in Missouri, the venture appealed to the president's imperial ambitions. Lamar had been informed that Santa Feans, ignored by a distant government in Mexico City, would happily submit to Texas rule. An expedition to New Mexico, the visionary president reasoned, would secure the republic's claim to the Rio Grande as its western boundary, a major step toward fulfilling his dream to make the Lone Star Republic "the richest and most powerful nation in America."[8]

In May Lamar traveled to San Antonio, an official visit that presented Bexareños with another opportunity to show their allegiance to the government. Recently elected mayor, Seguín ordered a twenty-one-gun salute for the president and his entourage as they entered the town. At a ball held in his honor that night, Lamar opened the festivities by leading Seguín's wife, Gertrudis, in a waltz. Mary Maverick, who did not get along particularly well with the Seguíns, would later write that the mother of ten was so fat that the president had difficulty getting his arms around her waist. She had snarky things to say about Lamar, too, who looked somewhat ridiculous in his unfashionably short, baggy trousers. The president might be a "first rate conversationalist," she recalled, "but he did not dance well."⁹

Lamar had come to San Antonio for a reason: to persuade José Antonio Navarro to serve as one of the commissioners on the expedition to Santa Fe. The forty-six-year-old rancher's first reaction was to reject the idea out of hand. For one thing, Navarro did not share the president's confidence that a large force of Texans would be well-received by the people of New Mexico, and he worried that the mission would more likely be seen as a hostile act. Nor did he feel up to the assignment. A childhood injury had left him lame in one leg, and the seven-hundred-mile journey across uncharted terrain would be hazardous and difficult under the best of circumstances. But Lamar would not take no for an answer. The president desperately needed a prominent Hispano who could explain to the people of Santa Fe the advantages of a union with Texas. Navarro had bowed to pressure once before, signing the Declaration of Independence. Now he did so again, keenly aware that it would reflect badly on all Bexareños if he refused.¹⁰

The expedition set out a few weeks later from Austin—merchants, teamsters, and five companies of infantry totaling more than three hundred men. Heading north, the caravan soon ran into trouble. The days grew hotter, and it wasted valuable time following the course of the Wichita River, mistakenly believing it to be the Red. Deserted by their guides, the Texans did not reach the ridge

24. José Antonio Navarro (1795–1871).
One of only two native-born Texans to
sign the declaration of independence
against Mexico, rancher José Antonio
Navarro remained loyal to the Anglo-
American cause, voting to annex the
republic to the United States in 1845.
Courtesy of Texas State Library and
Archives Commission.

of high bluffs known as the Cap Rock escarpment until the end of
August. Ascending onto the trackless savannahs of the High Plains,
where "not a tree or bush, and hardly a weed could be seen in any direction," they found that the prairie grasses the pack animals needed
for forage had withered in the summer heat. As their provisions ran
out, they wandered aimlessly in search of wild game. Kiowa Indians stampeded their horses and picked off stragglers. The expedition
had already begun to break up by the time it reached New Mexico,
whose residents, as Navarro feared, showed no inclination whatsoever to submit to Texan rule. It surrendered to Mexican troops without firing a shot.[11]

The trek across the Plains had been a grueling one for Navarro,
but his ordeal was only just beginning. Regarding the Texans as prisoners of war, the Mexican government ordered them marched south
to the nation's capital, where they arrived four months later. The US
minister, Waddy Thompson, would secure the release of all of them
the following year—except Navarro, whose decision to sign the

Texas Declaration of Independence ensured for him a much harsher fate. Separated from his companions, he was charged with treason and placed in solitary confinement in the Accordada in Mexico City. A military court sentenced him to death, though the verdict would later be commuted, over the strenuous objections of Santa Anna, to life in prison.[12]

THE SANTA FE EXPEDITION WAS STILL MAKING ITS WAY ACROSS the western plains when Texas voters went to the polls to elect a new president. Now eligible to serve a second term, Houston tossed his hat into the ring early, having made his intentions clear almost from the moment he left office in 1838. To run against him, the Lamar faction turned with no little reluctance to Vice President Burnet, who had never been especially popular with the electorate. With the administration widely blamed for the economic crisis gripping the country, Burnet's prospects for victory were bleak, and his supporters tried to make Houston's alcoholism a campaign issue, with little success. The hero of San Jacinto won handily with more than two-thirds of the vote. "Old Sam H. with all his faults appears to be the only man for Texas," one settler admitted. "He is still unsteady [and] *intemperate*, but drunk in a ditch is worth a thousand of Lamar and Burnet."[13]

Taking the presidential oath of office for the second time in Austin in December 1841, Houston had his work cut out for him. The currency issued by the Lamar government, known as red-backs, was virtually worthless. The public debt—owed in specie—had swollen from less than two million to more than seven million dollars. The foreign loans that Lamar hoped would inject new life into the country's flagging economy had fallen through. Meanwhile, Lamar's aggressive policy toward Native peoples proved not only costly but counterproductive. The Comanches still ruled the Edwards Plateau, and after the Council House fight no longer talked of a boundary line with the white republic. Bands of displaced East Texas Indians roamed the upper reaches of the Trinity River Valley.

Once prosperous farmers, they now raided white settlements just to stay alive. Still another problem confronting the new administration was a bloody feud that had erupted in a northeast corner of the Piney Woods. Amid accusations of forged land titles in Shelby County, on the Texas-Louisiana border, two rival factions had organized into Regulators and Moderators, plunging the region into anarchy and civil war.

But it was the fallout from the failed Santa Fe expedition that would present Houston with the most serious crisis of his second administration. For Mexican leaders the reconquest of Texas was a rallying cry, a matter of national pride, and the desire to erase the stain of San Jacinto had only become an even greater priority with Santa Anna's return to power. The Mexican president vowed a swift response to Lamar's violation of the country's territorial sovereignty, but as always the turbulent state of the country's political affairs precluded a full-fledged military campaign. Stamping out federalist rebellions had become an all-consuming task for the centralist government. A Texas campaign would have to wait.

There was, however, an alternative to a full-fledged invasion. A swift retaliatory strike by the Mexican army above the Rio Grande, Santa Anna believed, would spark national pride and divert attention from the chaotic affairs of state. Since the frontier of Texas was thinly populated and completely undefended, the risks involved in a show of force were negligible. The appearance of Mexican troops could be expected to cause a panic in the western settlements, serving to deter Anglo-American immigration, which could not be allowed to continue if Mexico hoped to one day reclaim its former province. If Santa Anna was in no position to win a decisive victory over Texas, he could at least send a clear message that he was not yet ready to concede defeat.

The threat of a new war with Mexico threw San Antonio into an uproar, inflaming tensions between Bexareños and their American neighbors in the process. As mayor, Juan Seguín had made enemies of some of the Anglos in town, and his frequent trips below the Rio Grande prompted some to whisper, without evidence, that he was in contact with Mexican authorities. Both groups began to evacuate in early March. Bexareños sought refuge at the large ranchos along the San Antonio River, while Anglos packed up their belongings and headed east for the safety of the white settlements along the Colorado and Brazos rivers. Sam and Mary Maverick buried their valuables under a storeroom floor in their house on Commerce Street and, with their three children and two enslaved families, joined the exodus.[14]

A few days later, an expeditionary force of about seven hundred men led by General Rafael Vásquez marched unopposed into town and hoisted the Mexican flag from the San Fernando church. A second, smaller force seized the communities of Refugio and Goliad in the southeast. Although the attack on the republic's frontier had been expected for weeks, the news created a general panic among the Anglo settlements, amid wild reports that the Mexican army numbered in the tens of thousands. In a scene reminiscent of the Runaway Scrape of 1836, Texans en masse abandoned their farms and homesteads and fled eastward.[15]

Vásquez held the town for two days, then retreated back across the Rio Grande. As they had done so often after Comanche raids, the town's civil militia—Bexareños and Anglos—saddled up and gave chase. Numbering only a few dozen men, they pursued the Mexican army across the South Texas chaparral, but they could only follow at a distance, and after a few days rode back to San Antonio.

Seguín was not prepared for the chaotic situation that awaited him upon his return. Finding their homes ransacked, Anglo residents were quick to blame their Hispano neighbors, though Vásquez's troops seem to have been responsible for the pillage. When Seguín refused to make any arrests, long-simmering animosities burst into the open. Armed vigilante groups scoured the countryside for the fugitive mayor. A hunted man, Seguín spent several days in hiding, then returned to Casa Blanca, the family's sprawling rancho on the San Antonio River. Defended by a large number of loyal farm hands, the palisaded compound provided a safe haven, but it was too dangerous for him to show his face in town. After several weeks holed up at Casa Blanca he came to a painful decision. Citing "the turbulent state in which this unfortunate country finds itself," he resigned as mayor of San Antonio and with his large family headed south to the Rio Grande, to begin a new life in exile.[16]

The Vásquez raid sparked angry calls for reprisals, reviving the war hawks' cherished dream of a campaign to seize Matamoros. At first, Houston believed the reports that a full-scale Mexican invasion was underway. Keeping his options open, he ordered militia units to the frontier and issued an appeal for volunteers from the United States, then called for a special session of Congress to enact war legislation. There was more fighting on the frontier in early June, when Antonio Canales, now back in Mexico City's good graces, led a force of five hundred troops across the Rio Grande and attacked the Texas army encamped near Corpus Christi. By this time, the cautious president had come to the conclusion that the best way to deal with these border raids was to remain on the defensive. When the special session convened later that month, Houston stunned the firebrands by vetoing the war bill and sent the army home.

AFTER THE VÁSQUEZ RAID, SAM MAVERICK WAS RELUCTANT TO again expose his wife and children to the dangers of an unsettled frontier. Deciding the family would be safer on the Colorado River, one hundred miles to the east, he bought land in La Grange and sent Griffin, one of the family's enslaved men, to San Antonio to pack up the rest of their belongings from their home on Commerce Street. His father, now seventy years old, was still trying to get Maverick to abandon his dream of building a land empire in Texas entirely. He again pleaded with his son to return to South Carolina to manage the Maverick clan's business affairs. "Should you lose your life" in Texas, he wrote, "it would be fatal . . . to our whole family."[17]

As usual, Maverick followed his own path. He still had extensive land holdings in San Antonio, and with Mary and the children on the Colorado, he was anxious to return to attend to his interests there. Ignoring vague, unconfirmed reports that the Mexican army was planning another attack on the town, Maverick rode back to San

Antonio that summer, leaving his wife at the home of friends near La Grange.

Mary dreaded these long separations from her husband. Only twenty-two, she had already lost some of the vigor and youthful optimism with which she had set out on her Texas adventure four years earlier. Desperately lonely, she sometimes confessed in the pages of her diary to being unhappy with her frontier life. The family was certainly more prosperous than most, but for Mary it was a life of relentless drudgery, in which she felt "almost a hermit at home with sick babies." Above all, she disliked having to oversee the family's slaves in her husband's absence. Left "to struggle with them alone, unaided," Mary felt trapped by what she called "this most unholy system." Although she could speak of Griffin with genuine affection, on the whole she harbored no fondness for the enslaved, and the feelings seem to have been mutual. For the deeply religious Mary, who reproached herself for a lack of Christian charity, the utter disdain she felt for those with whom she shared close quarters in turn gave rise to a sense of guilt. She had "no right to condemn them," she believed. But condemn them she did, writing with more than a little self-pity some years later that not one of the men and women she owned "loves me or cares consistently to please me." Weighed down by the responsibilities of maintaining the household alone, she lamented her lot as *the slave of slaves.*[18]

Like Sam Maverick, many Anglos assumed the danger along the western frontier from Mexico had passed. District court met as scheduled in San Antonio that fall, with Sam defending a client for unpaid fees owed to the city. Early on the morning of September 11, under the cover of a dense fog, a Mexican army of more than a thousand troops under the command of General Adrian Woll approached the town undetected, having taken an old smuggling trail through the hills that lay to the west. Residents were suddenly awakened by the firing of an artillery piece, followed by martial music. In the chaotic minutes that followed, Anglo-Texans grabbed their rifles, taking refuge in Maverick's home on the corner of the main plaza. For half an hour they mounted a spirited defense, but when the fog lifted they saw the hopelessness of their position. In all, more than fifty men surrendered, many of them prominent leaders of the republic, including the district court judge and two congressmen.[19]

Woll's capture of San Antonio revealed just how divided along racial and ethnic lines Texas had become by 1842. To the town's American residents, the Mexican troops were invaders. But most if not all Bexareños saw a liberating army, one that included many nonwhite Texans fighting against white rule. Vicente Córdova, the de facto head of the Hispano resistance in Texas, led a group of Nacogdoches Mexicans and several dozen Cherokees and Coushattas in the attack on the town, the remnants of his own failed revolt three years earlier. Woll's force also included as many as one hundred native-born Hispanos forced from their homes after independence. And perhaps no one under Woll's command felt a greater satisfaction as the army seized the town that morning than the officer of a company of Bexareños, who could be seen urging his men forward into the plaza. It was a man the townsfolk knew well: their former mayor, Juan Seguín.

Word of the attack soon spread to the white settlements along the Colorado River. When a distraught Mary Maverick heard the news, she gave Griffin a gun, a mule, and a money belt with four hundred dollars in gold coins and sent him back to San Antonio, imploring him to buy her husband's freedom or help him to escape.[20]

In the days that followed, the roads to San Antonio were crowded with hastily organized volunteer units from the white settlements on the Colorado and the Guadalupe, all eager for a fight with the Mexican army. Griffin fell in with a company of settlers from La Grange led by Nicholas Mosby Dawson, a veteran of the Battle of San Jacinto. When they arrived on the afternoon of September 18, a battle between Woll's forces and the Texans was already underway at Salado Creek on the outskirts of town.[21]

Drawn by the sound of gunfire, they hurried forward, but were blocked from reaching the Texans' position by Mexican cavalry. Taking cover in a mesquite thicket, they fought off their attackers until two artillery pieces were brought up, cutting most of them down.

Hand-to-hand combat followed, Griffin clubbing Woll's cavalrymen with his gun stock and, when that failed, swinging at his assailants with a limb torn from a mesquite tree. Mexican troops commonly spared men of African descent when fighting against Texans, but Griffin refused to surrender, and in the end they fired on the enslaved man who had been sent to buy his master's freedom. Surveying the carnage after the battle, one Texan reported that "the enemy lay in piles" around the body of "Maverick's large negro."[22]

General Woll evacuated the town two days later and began his long march to the Rio Grande. Like the previous two attacks on the Texas frontier earlier in the year, the expedition was intended only to make a point: six years after San Jacinto, Mexico still regarded Texas as a province in revolt. But the renewal of hostilities in 1842 had very real consequences for the region's Hispanos. Fearing reprisals from angry whites, about two hundred Bexareños accompanied Woll's army on the march south, driving oxcarts loaded with their belongings. In South Texas, Anglo cattle rustlers became a law unto themselves. A few months after Woll's retreat, Mustang Gray's gang murdered Silvestre De León, who had returned from exile to try to salvage the family's ranching business, and several of his ranch hands. When Gray came upon a party of Mexican merchants a short time later, the gang robbed them of their goods, tied them together, and shot them at close range. Anglos also attempted to run off Carlos de la Garza, still hated for leading the Guardia Victorianos alongside General Urrea's forces against Fannin in the Texas rebellion. They were unsuccessful, but only because his rancho remained a safe haven for local Hispanos, a community larger in 1842 than the towns of Victoria, Refugio, and Goliad combined.[23]

De la Garza's Mexican loyalties were well-known; he had never been a supporter of independence or the white rule that followed. But since the earliest days of Anglo settlement, the Seguín family had stood alongside the Americans, defending their rights as colonists and binding their interests to their own. After 1842, "the traitor Seguín" would serve as the face of Mexican treachery, living proof that Texas Hispanos could never be loyal citizens of the republic.

To his credit, President Houston refused to join in the general condemnation of the San Jacinto veteran, writing to Juan's aged father,
Erasmo, to assure him that he did not question Seguín's honor. Mary
Maverick took a less charitable view (as she did of most Mexicans),
describing Seguín as a man "of great pride and ambition," who resented the success of his American neighbors.[24]

In his memoirs written many years later, Seguín would try to
explain his decision to take up arms against his former countrymen.
He claimed that Mexican authorities had given him a choice: imprisonment or service in the army. That may have been true, but
Seguín probably didn't need to be coerced to take up arms against
the nation he had fought to create. Hundreds of Mexican Texans had
already done the same thing. It was a decision Carlos de la Garza
made during the rebellion, Vicente Córdova soon after independence. Seguín had simply taken longer than most. In the end, like so
many Hispano Texans, he believed there was no place for him in the
white republic. He had become, as he would put it poignantly many
years later, "a foreigner in my native land."[25]

TWENTY-TWO

STRIDING WITH GIANT STEPS
TOWARD DISSOLUTION

N OW PRISONERS OF THE MEXICAN GOVERNMENT, SAM MAV-
erick and the fifty Texans Woll had captured at San Antonio did
not know what lay ahead. When the army reached the Rio Grande,
Maverick was able to write a letter to Mary, now pregnant with their
fourth child, to reassure her that he was safe and in good health. He
had learned that Griffin had been killed with Dawson's men at the
Salado, and he was genuinely affected by the loss. "God knows I feel
his death as the hardest piece of fortune we have suffered in Texas,"
he wrote. In the days that followed, a military escort would lead the
prisoners deeper into the interior of Mexico, and Maverick would
take every opportunity to communicate with his wife, entrusting the
letters to anyone who expressed an interest in the Texans' plight in
the hope that they would eventually reach her. The thought of seeing Mary and the children again consoled him, and he urged his wife
to "take care of our jewels and thy precious self." But he could give
her little information about when they would be reunited. It might
be weeks; then again, it might be months. Nor did he know his final
destination. He knew only that each day took him farther south, and
farther from home.[1]

Woll's attack on San Antonio had finally forced Houston's hand.
Although the immediate danger had passed, the hundreds of volunteers who rushed to engage Woll's army did not drift back to their

farms and homesteads. Most stayed in San Antonio, expecting the government to finally authorize an offensive campaign. Houston had furloughed the regular army in 1837, but in the fall of 1842 the western settlers were so hot for war, and so fed up with what they saw as the president's timidity, that there was a strong chance they might strike out for the Rio Grande on their own, with or without Houston's permission. The president may have sensed that he was losing control of the situation when he learned that one of his most stalwart critics, Thomas Jefferson Green, who had been calling for an attack on Matamoros for years, had joined the volunteers. Realizing he could no longer forestall what he derisively called the "campaign of the people," the president ordered General Alexander Somervell to proceed to San Antonio to take charge of the army.[2]

Houston was still hopeful that an offensive campaign might be avoided. The army could not march south without the necessary supplies, and the president seemed unable or unwilling to provide them. Weeks passed, and with the onset of colder, wetter weather, Houston appeared to be playing for time, reasoning that the volunteers would eventually lose interest and return to their homes. The gambit might have worked, but for one problem; with the country's economy in shambles, many of the men had little else to do. Only the prospect of plunder kept them bivouacked on the Cibolo River, east of town, waiting for Somervell's orders. During these lean years, white adult males often found soldiering more lucrative than any other occupation. The volunteer army included Federalist War mercenaries and men who rustled cattle and horses in the Trans-Nueces. Even some of the more upstanding citizens in Somervell's ranks had engaged in officially sanctioned forms of pillage, as members of militia companies in Lamar's wars against the Indians. For Green, the campaign could not have come at a better time. His Velasco real estate ventures had gone belly up, and he arrived in camp "as poor as the poorest," according to one Texan—"*Coat out at elbows* & pockets empty."[3]

Mixed in among the many volunteers in search of plunder was a cohort of young men seeking the raw excitement of the western

25. Samuel Hamilton Walker (1817–1847). Daguerreotype by Matthew Brady. Still boyish-looking at age thirty, Samuel Walker had spent five years fighting Comanche raiding parties and Mexican troops when he sat for this photograph in 1847. Courtesy of Library of Congress, Prints and Photographs Division.

frontier. As a youth, twenty-five-year-old Maryland native Samuel H. Walker had read about "the chivalry and noble deeds of our forefathers" and was no doubt equally familiar with the immensely popular romantic novels of Sir Walter Scott. Trained as a carpenter's apprentice, he dreamed of a life of adventure, running away to join the army in his teens. Stationed in Florida during the Seminole Wars, he chafed under military discipline, finding a culture in which "I had no right to think." He saw no action, spending four miserable years assigned to laundry detail and other menial duties as a result of frequent clashes with his commanding officers.[4]

Walker did not have the look or the temperament of so many of the hard, swashbuckling types drawn to the violent border regions of Texas. Small in stature and boyishly good-looking, his soft features belied a daredevil recklessness. Proud of his working-class origins, he saw himself as a knight-errant for a democratic age, hell-bent on making his mark on the field of battle. Since the war for independence a desire for martial glory had drawn many young men to Texas, and his letters home struck the same confident tone as those written by the unfortunate John Sowers Brooks, who had died, helpless and alone, on a Goliad street six years earlier. "That unextinguishable love of chivalric immortal fame still clings to my heart," he wrote to his sister-in-law, just before setting out for Texas. "The love of fame still urges me on."[5]

Houston had given Somervell a truly thankless task. Green and other administration critics in camp viewed the general as a "Houston man," and distrusted him from the start. They were soon spreading the baseless rumor that Somervell had secret orders to sabotage the campaign. At the same time, many problems seemed to be of Somervell's own making. A good-natured man with a hearty laugh, he did little to inspire confidence among the volunteers at San Antonio. "He was a very nice kind Gentleman," one private observed, "but no more fit to Command an Army of men in those times than a ten year old Boy."[6]

The general mood of the volunteers was already surly when it began to rain. Tiring of the privations of the camp, some ventured into town, turning Mexicans out of their homes to wait out the storms. They took what they wanted, and there were disturbing if unconfirmed reports that some women had been raped. Finally, if only to keep his men from inflicting any further hardship on the people of San Antonio, Somervell ordered the army, now numbering about seven hundred men, to take up the line of march. A campaign into northern Mexico, a cherished dream of Texas hotspurs since the fight for independence, was finally underway.[7]

It got off to an inauspicious start. After weeks of torrential rains, one dirt track looked pretty much like another. Somervell's scouts somehow veered off the Laredo road, and the little army soon found itself hopelessly lost, spending the next several days floundering in the mud. Some of the horses and pack animals could not be pulled from the water-logged, loamy soil and had to be shot. After a difficult, seventeen-day journey that should have taken less than a week, the army reached Laredo.

Having long heard tales about the wealth of the villas del norte, the Texans were surprised to find an impoverished village, whose alcalde could offer Somervell's hungry army little in the way of food and other supplies. Convinced that the Mexicans must be hiding their valuables, more than two hundred Texans left camp against orders and proceeded to sack the town. Green later defended the conduct of the men, but denied taking part in the pillage. Hours later they returned, driving horses and cattle, the backs of the animals piled high with their booty—"coats, hats, trousers, blankets, even nightclothes" and all manner of household items. Somervell made them give most of it back, but the affair amply confirmed Houston's worst fears: a riotous mob masquerading as an officially sanctioned Texas army had descended on the Rio Grande.[8]

It would be a few weeks before Houston would get wind of these unhappy developments. In the meantime, he had a government, or a crude facsimile of it, to run. Citing the dangers of convening Congress on a dangerously exposed frontier, the president ordered the new session to meet at Washington-on-the-Brazos. If Houston hoped that a more centrally located venue would satisfy backcountry settlers, he would be sorely disappointed. Some of the western members of Congress were so unhappy with the president's decision that they arrived several weeks late, and a quorum could not be reached until early December.

The Brazos River hamlet was not without its own disadvantages as a seat of government. With a permanent population of about 250 souls, the village in 1842 was not much bigger than it had been when it hosted the Convention six years earlier, and even Houston had to admit that conditions there were "rather raw."[9] Pregnant with their first child, his wife, Margaret, chose to remain in East Texas, staying at her sister's house during her confinement. The president took lodgings at the home of John Lockhart, a local judge, who found the honor of hosting the president of the republic a decidedly mixed blessing. Each day after the adjournment of Congress the garrulous Houston held court from the porch of the Lockhart home. Expounding on political matters and regaling his audience with amusing stories, the country's head of state interrupted his monologues only long enough to spit tobacco juice onto the gallery, a habit which did little to endear him to the judge's wife.[10]

On the Rio Grande, any enthusiasm Somervell may have still had for the campaign vanished after the sack of Laredo. There were reports that the Mexican army headquartered in Matamoros was now mobilizing against him, and his little force was getting smaller by the day. Some volunteers—those who managed to keep their loot and others who were thoroughly ashamed by the whole affair—started to peel away. On December 19, the general called his men together to tell them that the campaign was over.

The announcement threw the entire camp into an uproar. Given the complete disregard many had shown for their commanding officer up to this point, Somervell could hardly have been surprised when many volunteers refused to obey the order. Most were bent on plunder, unwilling to go home empty-handed after a long and difficult march to the Rio Grande. Others, like Samuel Walker, had only joined the expedition to "stir up the whirlwind of war," and were indignant at the thought of retreating without firing a shot at the enemy. With Walker and Green among Somervell's loudest detractors, two-thirds of the men under his command mutinied and elected William S. Fisher, a veteran of the recent federalist campaign in northern Mexico, to lead them.[11]

Now reduced to about three hundred men, the renegade army marched downriver to another hardscrabble town, Ciudad Mier, where Antonio Canales had gathered the militias of the valley towns to block the Texans' advance. General Pedro Ampudia had just come up from Matamoros with several companies of regular troops, bringing the total Mexican force defending the town to almost one thousand men. During the Federalist War, Ampudia and Canales had been on opposing sides. Whatever bad blood existed between the two men they now put behind them as they prepared to make their stand against the Texan invasion.

Outnumbered three to one, Fisher might have considered retreating. But the victory at San Jacinto had instilled in Texan citizen-soldiers a sense of almost mythical superiority, allowing them to believe they could soundly thrash a Mexican army of any size. Holding a council of war, he proposed to attack the town. His captains agreed without a single dissenting vote.

At nightfall on Christmas Day, Fisher's men charged into Mier. They were quickly disabused of any notions of an easy victory. Meeting heavy fire from Ampudia's artillery in the plaza, they scurried for cover in a block of row houses on the edge of town. The battle began in earnest at dawn the following morning. Ampudia made repeated attempts to dislodge the Texans, and by midafternoon the narrow dirt street was littered with bodies. Calling for a cease-fire, the Mexican general promised to treat the Texans as prisoners of war if they would surrender. Fisher declined the offer, still confident they could hold their position and make an orderly retreat that night. But in the houses at the end of the street, the scene was one of utter pandemonium, as his men argued about what to do next. Thomas Jefferson Green, who had appointed himself second-in-command since the army abandoned Somervell on the Rio Grande, argued that they should fight their way out of town. But many, exhausted and with ammunition running low, were ready to surrender and began walking up the street to lay down their arms. Fisher, not the first Texas commander to lose control of his men, hastily returned to the plaza to accept Ampudia's offer. The Texan invasion of Mexico had come to an inglorious end.

Although Houston had predicted just such an outcome, the Mier fiasco came as a heavy blow to the beleaguered president. The news of the defeat was bad enough, but once he learned that Somervell had called off the expedition days earlier, he worried that he might have another, even more serious problem on his hands. Would the Mexican government still regard Fisher's men as lawful combatants when it found out they were not acting on the orders of their government? Houston was so alarmed by the possibility that the Mier men might be executed as filibusters that he immediately got in touch with the British envoy in Texas, Charles Elliot. Her Majesty's government enjoyed by far the best relationship with Mexico of any major power, and Houston urged Elliot to use his influence to intervene on the Texans' behalf. The president conceded, however, that since the men had crossed the river in defiance of their commanding officer, the rules of war did not apply. The Mier men would eventually learn of his correspondence with the British diplomat, and they hotly denied any suggestion that they were guilty of mutiny. In their minds, they had simply taken the initiative when the courage of their commander had faltered. Many, like Thomas Jefferson Green, blamed Houston for doing everything in his power to prevent an invasion of Mexico. Now, they blamed him for its failure. If the prisoners were harmed in any way, Green raged, the blame would lie with the president, and no one else.[12]

The dispiriting news from the Rio Grande came on the heels of another embarrassment for the administration, this one closer to home. Austin residents, facing financial ruin as a result of the president's decision to move the capital, had for months stubbornly refused to send the government archives to Washington-on-the-Brazos. Matters came to a head when Houston sent a ranger company with three oxcarts to retrieve the state papers in late December. A vigilant innkeeper sounded the alarm, firing a cannon to alert the townsfolk, and the rangers left empty-handed. Everywhere, it seemed, respect for the government had reached its lowest ebb.

So ended 1842, the Lone Star Republic's *annus horriblis*. The year that had begun with the news of the capture of the ill-advised Santa Fe expedition and seen three attacks on the western frontier had ended with the Texan defeat at Mier. Reports of the debacle on the Rio Grande seriously damaged the government's standing abroad, giving rise to concerns that the border war with Mexico was about to explode into a full-blown conflict that Texas might not survive. Exhibiting all the characteristics of a failed state, the Lone Star Republic, one unhappy American investor in Texas lands concluded, "appears to be striding with giant steps and headlong impetuosity toward dissolution."[13]

The country's mounting problems would take a personal toll on the normally unflappable Houston. Congress adjourned in January, leaving the president, his cabinet, and a skeleton crew of government functionaries to handle the republic's official business. Weighed down by the cares of office, which seemed to grow heavier by the day, and deprived of the company of friends and admirers, Houston succumbed to feelings of loneliness and despair. Since his marriage to Margaret, he had curbed his heavy drinking, but in her absence the temptation proved too great. At some point during this dark period the president got hold of a large bottle of Madeira wine and drank himself into a stupor, becoming so thoroughly intoxicated that he called for an enslaved servant to fetch an axe and chop up the four-poster bed in his room in the Lockhart home. Word of the incident was soon the talk of the village. Once he sobered up, an embarrassed Houston rode to his sister-in-law's home in East Texas, where he confessed all to a pregnant Margaret. With her mother in tow she returned with him to Washington. Clearly, he could not be left alone without reverting to his old ways. The Houstons rented a small cabin on the outskirts of town, where Margaret would give birth to a son, Sam Jr., in May. No doubt the Lockharts were relieved to see him go.[14]

The Battle of Mier was a much-needed tonic for Mexico, still suffering from the blunt force trauma of San Jacinto. At each of the towns along the river en route to Ampudia's headquarters in Mata-moros, elaborate ceremonies greeted the Mexican troops and their prisoners. As church bells pealed, Ampudia and Canales escorted the Texans down streets lined with cheering crowds and festooned with paper banners proclaiming the two men as the victors of Mier. For a few days at least, northern Mexico's fraught relationship with the centralist government was forgotten in a jubilant outpouring of national pride.

HUNDREDS OF MILES TO THE SOUTH, HIGH UP IN THE SIERRA Madre Mountains, Sam Maverick's journey was coming to an end. In late December the San Antonio prisoners reached the Fortaleza de San Carlos de Perote, an imposing stronghold on the National Road midway between the capital and the port of Veracruz. At seven thousand feet above sea level, the fort sat in a broad valley in the shadow of the towering Cofre de Perote. A star-shaped bastion of volcanic rock, its fifty-foot walls rising from a dry moat, the fortress had been built by the Spanish in the 1770s to guard the country's principal trade route to the coast. Housing a permanent garrison of several hundred men, it also served as a detention facility for political and military prisoners.

The Texas inmates would be confined in two large, barrel-vaulted rooms and assigned to a work detail with the fort's convict laborers. At first they refused to work alongside men Maverick described as "felons, robbers and murderers." The San Antonio prisoners took offense, too, at the poor quality of their rations and squalid living conditions. Emerging as a spokesman for the group, it fell to Maverick to voice their complaints to the captain of the guard, and he was promptly tossed in solitary confinement for his trouble. Normally reserved, after two months at the fort an angry Maverick vented his spleen in a lengthy letter to the Mexican foreign minister, giving it to the US minister, Waddy Thompson, to hand deliver at the National Palace. Providing a vivid and detailed description of their daily fare, which included a stew of "bone, grissel, and the badly cleaned guts of a poor cow with maggots in them," he demanded the captain of the guard's immediate removal.[15]

The US minister wisely pocketed the missive, knowing it would have anything but a positive effect on the San Antonio prisoners' situation. Like Maverick a native South Carolinian, Thompson had already asked the Mexican government to release him as a personal favor. His lobbying eventually paid off, and on March 30, more than six months after his capture in San Antonio, Maverick received his liberation papers. That same day, in a cabin on the Colorado River, Mary gave birth to their fourth child, a girl.[16]

THE MIER PRISONERS, MEANWHILE, HAVING BEEN PARADED BY Ampudia and Canales through every town along the Rio Grande from Mier to Matamoros, were hustled southward along the road to the capital. Separated from their men, Fisher and Green fared better than the others. Furnished horses and given a light military escort, they stayed in posadas and sometimes even the homes of prominent citizens, while a loan from the US consul in Monterrey allowed them to acquire new clothes and pay for better meals. But for Samuel Walker and the main body of prisoners, the trek was a grueling one of long days on the road, and nights spent in corrals and cow pens thick with manure. As the days turned into weeks, and as the journey took them deeper into Mexico, they began to talk of escape. Soon they talked of little else.

One morning, at the Hacienda el Salado, a remote rancho on Mexico's arid central plain, the prisoners burst through the gates of their corral and overpowered the company of infantrymen guarding them, killing five. Seizing all the weapons, mules, and horses they could find, they split into small groups and fled into the barren Sierra Madre Mountains. Their journey soon became a desperate search for food and water. Lost and disoriented, and already weak and malnourished after six weeks of forced marches, they resorted to drinking the blood of their pack animals, then their own urine. Squads of Mexican soldiers fanned out across the area, rounding them up with little difficulty. Incredibly, four of the escapees managed to make their way back to Texas.[17]

Acting president Nicolas Bravo ordered the execution of the Mier prisoners for the deaths of the Mexican troops killed during the Texans' escape attempt. The US and British ministers lodged angry protests, and the order was countermanded; instead, one out of ten would be executed by lottery. Returned to the ranch where they had made their bid for freedom, the Mier prisoners, their numbers now reduced to 176 men, were made to draw from a large earthen pot containing white and black beans. The seventeen who drew the black beans were given pen and paper to write letters home, then shot by firing squad.

Once again, Mexican authorities had bungled the optics of their struggle with Anglo-Americans. Much like the decision to execute Fannin's men at Goliad, the so-called Black Bean Episode became a public relations disaster. The sack of Laredo and the attack on Mier by an irregular, undisciplined army had briefly allowed Mexico to assume the moral high ground in its border war with Texas.

But the arbitrariness of the punishment was widely condemned in the American press as "the most inhuman piece of butchery ever perpetrated by a government professing to be civilized within the present century." Even some New England papers, never sympathetic toward the slaveholding republic, labeled the episode a "massacre." For Americans, the ongoing conflict on their southwestern border served as a window through which to see Mexico, a distant land about which they had once given very little thought. Even as Northerners and Southerners found themselves increasingly at odds over the future of slavery, a broad consensus existed as to their feelings toward the United States' Latin American neighbor. The growing catalog of perceived Mexican atrocities, sensationalized in the press, formed an indelible impression in the national consciousness of a benighted, barbarous country at war with Anglo-Saxon values.[18]

After the executions at the Hacienda el Salado, the Mier prisoners were marched to Mexico City, where they were chained in pairs and for several months put to work building a road leading to Santa Anna's residence outside the capital. In the fall, they were transferred to Perote. Soon after they arrived a typhus epidemic swept through the fortress. Over the course of several weeks the sick list grew, felling prisoner and soldier alike, until the hospital resembled a madhouse, with feverish patients tied to their cots as they screamed in pain, their bodies covered in blisters.

For all the physical hardship of their incarceration, the Texans may have found the humiliation of their confinement harder to bear. Their freedom they regarded as their birthright as white Americans, and the loss of it touched them deeply, upending the order of things as they were supposed to be. The prison guards "often beat the Texians with sticks with as little ceremony as they would beat negroes," one wrote. "What then must be the deep agony of an American to be struck by these imps of darkness?" complained another to US minister Thompson when a soldier struck one of the men. "Sir, it is insupportable. The blood of an American cannot brook the degradation."[19]

26. *Thomas Jefferson Green's Escape from Perote Fortress.*
By Charles McLaughlin, 1843. Courtesy of Special Collections,
University of Texas at Arlington Libraries.

With little hope of release, they continued to look for ways to escape. The Mexican army was ill-equipped to deal with large numbers of prisoners, and the troops assigned to watch them grew careless as time went on. When the guards stopped chaining the men, Samuel Walker and two of his companions simply wandered off from the iron foundry where they were being held near Mexico City. Passing himself off as an Englishman and traveling only at night, he made his way to the port of Tampico, where he found a ship to take him to New Orleans.

Breaking out of the fortress of Perote proved considerably more difficult. Thomas Jefferson Green threw in with several San Antonio prisoners, who were already at work digging a hole in the exterior wall of their cell when he arrived. Eight feet thick, the porous volcanic rock had become soft in the damp highlands climate, and they made quick progress. One summer night sixteen Texans squeezed out of the opening and with the aid of ropes dropped down into the

dry moat below. Green got home just in time to run for John Wharton's old congressional seat in Brazoria County, and by the end of the
year he was back in the House of Representatives, reprising his role
as one of Houston's principal antagonists.[20]

The men that remained at Perote were prisoners of war in a war
without end. While there had been no attacks on the Texas frontier since General Woll's expedition to San Antonio the year before,
Santa Anna continued to bluster that an invasion was imminent.
Without money in the treasury to fund such a campaign, his threats
of reconquest rang increasingly hollow. Thus the two governments
settled into a war of words that left the Texas prisoners in a state of
limbo. Only Santa Anna held the power to unlock their prison doors
and send all of them home, something he showed little willingness
to do.

Yet the Mexican president did grant special dispensations, as he
had done in Sam Maverick's case. It was a privilege he clearly enjoyed.
Though he could fly into a rage at the very mention of the attack on
Mier, and made no apologies for the execution at the Hacienda el
Salado, he took a curious interest in the Texans, bestowing clemency
on many individuals brought to his attention. Not one to forget past
favors, Santa Anna released two prisoners at the request of Andrew
Jackson, who had received the disgraced general in Washington after his defeat at San Jacinto in 1836. When the Mexican president
learned that one of the Mier men was the son of a Brazos planter
with whom he had stayed after the battle, he sent for the youth, who
arrived in the capital still wearing his red, green, and white prison
stripes and filthy from work on the chain gang. Santa Anna gave him
a room at the National Palace and paid for his passage back to Texas.
The most unusual case was that of John C. C. Hill, a sixteen-year-
old youth from La Grange who had joined Somervell's army with
his father and older brother. Singled out for bravery in General Ampudia's dispatches after the Battle of Mier, Santa Anna not only gave
the boy his freedom but persuaded him to stay in Mexico, paying for
his education at the prestigious College of Mines. Hill went on to
become a successful engineer, dying in Monterrey in 1909.[21]

For Santa Anna the Texas prisoners also represented valuable political capital. The collapse of Houston's efforts to annex Texas to the United States during his first presidential term had been welcome news to Santa Anna. But now Houston was back in office, and there was every reason to think that he would try again. With a second campaign to subjugate Texas out of the question, Santa Anna's options to prevent such a scenario were few. Eager to curry favor with any American leader who opposed annexation, he gladly released a handful of prisoners at the request of John Quincy Adams, Daniel Webster, and Henry Clay, all prominent Whigs. Santa Anna would eventually grant the freedom of the remaining San Antonio prisoners as a favor to Waddy Thompson, and the grateful diplomat returned to the United States a firm friend of Mexico. Her Majesty's government, ever opposed to the expansionist goals of the United States, also succeeded in winning the freedom of incarcerated Texans claiming British citizenship.[22]

For the Mier prisoners who did not have friends in high places—and that was most of them—the months dragged by slowly and uneventfully. They felt abandoned by their government and, with only the rare letter from home, by their friends and families. "I could rite you much but it appears that you like the rest have forgotten a frend in distress," one wrote. Above all, they blamed Sam Houston for the indignities and hardships they had suffered during their imprisonment. Thomas Jefferson Green had always been an inveterate enemy of the president, but his months at Perote had given him time to brood and sharpen his hatred until it bordered on monomania. Determined to prove that Houston was personally responsible for the failure of the expedition and the tribulations that followed, he penned a series of angry editorials and would eventually publish a memoir of his misadventures in Mexico. Samuel Walker felt the same way, and wrote to Houston demanding that he provide a full account of his conduct toward the Mier prisoners, a request the president ignored. The two men happened to cross paths a few months later at a public meeting in Galveston. As Walker descended a flight of stairs, the president greeted him cordially, extending his hand. The young ranger brushed past him, scowling. "I am very sorry you are indisposed, Mr. Walker," Houston called out after him.[23]

In all, more than 650 Texans would find themselves imprisoned below the Rio Grande during Houston's second administration. The string of recent defeats at the hands of Mexico had tarnished the much-celebrated Texan reputation for Spartan heroics won at San Jacinto. More important, it made a mockery of the republic's pretensions as a new American empire in the west. Joseph Eve, the top-ranking American diplomat in Texas, was only one of many observers who did not know what to make of the "young nation just emerging from its cradle" that seemed bent on self-annihilation. Texas, "with a population of less than 100,000 souls [and] without a dollar in its Treasury," and already reeling from a wave of bloody conflicts with Native peoples, had embarked on a war against Mexico, a country of eight million, it could not possibly win. "Strange as it may seem," he wrote incredulously to his superiors in Washington, "such is the fact."[24]

TWENTY-THREE

WE ARE NOT ASHAMED TO CONFESS THAT WE WANT REPOSE

S AM MAVERICK RODE UP TO MARY'S LITTLE CABIN NEAR LA Grange on the Colorado River in early May 1843, after an absence of almost nine months. The overwhelming joy of their reunion was tempered to some degree by the misery of their Fayette County neighbors. When William Bollaert, an English naturalist, passed through La Grange not long after Maverick's return, he found a community still reeling from General Woll's attack on the frontier in the fall of 1842. Consisting almost entirely of "widows and orphans," the town had been devastated by the defeat of Nicholas Dawson's volunteers outside San Antonio, which claimed the lives of more than thirty men, a staggering loss to the small farming community. The rest of La Grange's able-bodied males had joined the campaign to the Rio Grande. Some had died at the battle at Mier, others in the execution at the Hacienda el Salado. Most of the survivors were still languishing in Mexican prisons.

Bollaert found a similarly bleak picture in Austin, which he reached a couple of days later. The former capital lay virtually abandoned, save for a few determined souls who had defied Houston's order to give up the government archives. Grass and weeds choked the empty streets. The President's House was "falling to pieces." Bats nested in the rafters of the capitol building and stray cattle roamed the grounds. Once hailed as the "seat of empire," the town now stood as a forlorn testament to the hubris of Mirabeau Lamar's imperial vision.[1]

And everywhere he went, Bollaert found a longing for peace. "Many of us," one Austin resident wrote, "have spent, or rather wasted, more than twenty years amidst every species of hardship and privation, war, turmoil and confusion, and we are not ashamed to confess that we want repose."[2]

SAM HOUSTON WELCOMED THE SHIFT IN PUBLIC MOOD IN 1843, and there were promising signs that peace with Mexico might, at long last, be possible. That summer, Santa Anna released one of the San Antonio prisoners from Perote and sent him back to Texas to deliver a startling proposal: if Texas agreed to renounce its independence, it could be readmitted as a Mexican state with virtual autonomy. Such an offer was out of the question, of course. Texas had seceded in 1836, and under no circumstances would it consent to a plan that brought it back, even nominally, under Mexican rule. But Houston was reluctant to pass up an opportunity to open a dialogue with Mexico City. At the very least, any negotiations would bring a temporary halt to Mexican attacks along the border; they might even induce Santa Anna to finally send the Mier prisoners home. Deciding that he had little to lose and much to gain, Houston in June 1843 issued a proclamation declaring a one-year armistice between the two countries.

Peace with Mexico was an important first step in bringing stability and prosperity to the western settlements; peace with the Indians was another. Developing better relations with Native peoples would prove to be vastly more difficult, for the Indians' trust in white leaders had been shattered by the brutal policies of the Lamar government. As an initial gesture of goodwill, Houston issued licenses to three merchants to build trading houses along the western frontier, where the Indians could go to exchange furs and hides for corn and other supplies. Establishing an Indian Bureau, he dispatched agents to locate the tribes and win their confidence. Tell the chiefs they had nothing to fear from the new administration, Houston instructed his agents. The white republic was ready to negotiate with tribal leaders to achieve a lasting peace.

Slowly, the Indians began to come in to the trading houses, warily at first, then in greater numbers. The remnants of the immigrant tribes were the most receptive to the overtures of Houston's Indian agents. Having never recovered from their forced expulsion by Lamar, they needed all the government help they could get. The Cherokee leaders were so ashamed of their destitute appearance that at one preliminary meeting they refused to enter the council grounds unless the Indian commissioners provided clothes for their women and children.[3]

A newfound willingness among the woodland Wichitas, the Wacos and Tawakonis, to engage in peace talks also gave Houston reason for optimism. One of the Wacos' principal chiefs, Acaquash, persuaded his warriors to return some of the horses they had stolen from the whites as a sign of good faith. More important, he agreed to serve as a liaison between the administration and the other tribes. Assuming a diplomatic role not unlike the one Chief Bowls had once played, Houston regarded him as "an honest man and a true friend."[4]

But the Penateka Comanches, still deeply embittered by the slaughter at the Council House in 1840, refused to attend any peace talks, sending word that "the bones of their brothers" killed at San Antonio had "appeared on the road and obstructed their passage." When Houston's agents located the Penatekas' main encampment near the Red River in the spring of 1843, the Indians' anger had not yet cooled. A major chief, Pahayuco, listened to what the agents had to say, but in an unmistakable sign of disrespect refused to smoke a peace pipe with them. It soon became clear that this was the least of their problems. Some warriors who had lost family members at the Council House were enraged that the agents were there at all, and demanded they be put to death. Fortunately for the visitors, Acaquash had accompanied the agents to the Comanche village and came to their defense, saving their lives. They left with a promise from Pahayuco that the Penateka chiefs would discuss Houston's peace overtures when the tribe camped on the Upper Brazos over the winter.[5]

Nothing more was heard from the Penatekas until the following spring, when Indian agents arrived at Thomas Torrey's Tehuacana Creek trading post near the Brazos River with important news. Pahayuco had taken his band north, but another tribal elder, Old Owl (Mopechucope), expressed interest in Houston's plan to hold a grand council of the tribes in the fall. Once again, the Comanches wanted to discuss a boundary line between the two peoples. Old Owl suggested as a southern boundary the confluence of the San Saba and Colorado rivers, almost one hundred miles north of Austin—an offer the administration could certainly live with. Assuring the agents that "past times are now forgotten," Old Owl would bring his people down to the trading house for the grand council. It was the breakthrough the president had been waiting for.[6]

HOUSTON'S NEGOTIATIONS WITH THE INDIANS AND THE ARMIstice with Mexico were both promising developments. But they could not hide the fact that the Lone Star Republic still faced enormous challenges in its quest to establish itself as a viable nation-state. The border war with Mexico had scared off foreign lenders, and though the cotton economy was showing early signs of a rebound, the government remained mired in debt, with barter still passing as the principal means of exchange.

The obvious remedy, as always, was annexation to the United States. The flow of capital and settlers across the Sabine would quickly solve the republic's financial woes. No less important, the defense of the frontier would become the responsibility of the US Army. Unfortunately for Houston, this was not an especially good time to retest the annexation waters. Opposition in Washington to admitting Texas into the Union had once been limited to John Quincy Adams and a few New England congressmen. Now, seven years after San Jacinto, the slavery question had become the third rail of American politics, with a large number of Whigs and Democrats from the Northern states unwilling to approve such an enormous addition to the slave empire. And Houston could expect little help from the Whig administration in Washington. In 1840, party leaders had given John Tyler, a states' rights Virginian, the second spot on the ticket to attract Southern votes, never dreaming that he would assume the powers of the presidency. But William Henry Harrison died after only a few months in office, and the party found itself saddled with a chief executive who disagreed with much of its economic agenda. Tyler proceeded to wield his veto pen to block a series of bills on tariffs and banking, and Whig leaders booted him from the party. When Texas diplomats in Washington quietly broached the possibility of reviving the annexation issue in the summer of 1843, Tyler, now president non grata, could give them little encouragement.

In the face of these obstacles, Houston would now embark on an artful diplomatic dance that would occupy much of his time for the remainder of his presidential term. Frustrated by Washington's foot-dragging on the annexation issue, he began to make it known that Texas had other potential dance partners, namely Great Britain. For some months, and especially since the dark days following the defeat at Mier, Houston had cultivated a close relationship with the British chargé d'affaires, Charles Elliot. An armistice with Mexico was well and good, but Texas could only succeed as an independent republic, he told the British diplomat, if Mexico formally recognized its right to exist. Through Elliot he urged the British government to use its influence over Mexico to make diplomatic recognition a top priority. Only then would Texas be secure, free to grow and prosper without the United States—and as an ally of Great Britain.[7]

This was, of course, exactly what Elliot wanted to hear. "This is the first hint I have ever had of the President's ideas upon this Subject," Elliot wrote happily to his superiors in the Foreign Office of Houston's avowed desire for an independent, pro-British republic. Although the diplomat knew Houston well enough to have once observed that he "sometimes says and writes what appears to be capricious and contradictory," it does not seem to have occurred to him that the president was capable of deceiving his friends as well as his enemies. In the months that followed, the British diplomat would work diligently to broker a lasting peace between the republic and Mexico, hoping to remove the single most important obstacle to an independent Texas.[8]

Reports that Houston had a new best friend in the urbane Elliot soon reached Washington, where they had just the effect the president intended. Even Northern congressmen adamantly opposed to the extension of slavery shuddered at the thought of the British gaining a new foothold on the continent. "You would be amused to see their fear of England," wrote one Texas diplomat in Washington, "and that is the secret of our success if we do succeed." Former president and arch-Anglophobe Andrew Jackson, now ailing in retirement at his plantation outside Nashville but still a power broker in Democratic circles, was especially distraught to learn that his former protégé was cozying up to the British. Old Hickory described to Houston in vividly apocalyptic terms the consequences of an alliance with Her Majesty's government. Should Texas succumb to the enfolding embrace of the British Empire, he warned, the United States would confront "an Iron Hoop" on its western border that would cost "oceans of blood . . . to burst asunder."[9]

With these concerns in mind, the Tyler administration was soon signaling its willingness to revive the annexation issue. In the early months of 1844, US and Texas diplomats hammered out a treaty in strict secrecy, a condition Houston insisted upon, knowing that the negotiations would jeopardize the close relationship he had worked so hard to cultivate with Charles Elliot. Even the Senate Foreign Relations Committee was unaware of the talks until an agreement had been reached. When the story finally broke in March, the news was a major embarrassment for the British diplomat, who as late as February had assured the Foreign Office that there was no possibility that Texas would be annexed to the United States.[10]

At first, the Tyler administration tried to quiet Northern fears that the treaty was a Southern scheme to expand slavery. Annexation, it argued, was a matter of national security, to prevent Great Britain from gaining a new foothold on the continent. But just as the Senate was about to debate the issue, Tyler's secretary of state, John C. Calhoun, a Southern ideologue, published a proslavery screed in defense of annexation. Within days, Martin Van Buren, the presumptive Democratic nominee, came out against Tyler's treaty. Southern members of his party were furious, and none more so than Andrew Jackson, who promptly abandoned his former vice president and endorsed a fellow Tennessean, James K. Polk. An avowed expansionist, Polk won his party's nomination on the ninth ballot in a raucous convention in May. When the Senate voted on ratification the following month, Van Buren's allies, looking for payback, sided with Northern Whigs to defeat the measure.[11]

In the early summer of 1844, Houston's Indian diplomacy also looked like it was in danger of foundering. After a period of relative peace, the Comanches abruptly started raiding again. A rash of horse thefts in the San Antonio area led to a bloody encounter between a company of rangers armed with new, five-shot Colt Paterson revolvers and a large body of Comanches on the Guadalupe River. Samuel Walker, still searching for fame and adventure, had joined the ranger company after his escape from Mexico City the year before. With the advantage of superior numbers, the Indians taunted the Texans, daring them to fight. The rangers obliged, firing as they rode the Indians down, until the struggle became hand-to-hand. One Comanche horseman ran Walker through with a lance, knocking him off his mount and pinning him to the ground. The rangers pursued the Indians for another two miles, then doubled back to retrieve Walker's body. When they returned to the scene they found him very much alive, sitting upright, the tip of the spear still protruding from his back. He lingered near death for several days, but was eventually well enough to be transported by wagon back to San Antonio.[12]

Fortunately for Houston, the Comanches on the Guadalupe had not been Penatekas but Yamparikas, a northern branch of the tribe

that rarely raided south of the Canadian River. There were still signs
of discord between Penateka elders and the band's war chiefs, however. When Houston's Indian agents visited the tribe that summer,
Old Owl told them that his plans to attend the council remained
unchanged; he had given his word and he intended to keep it. As for
Buffalo Hump, the agents detected less enthusiasm for the upcoming meeting. The Comanches would only come down to the trading house, he told them, if Houston got there first and prepared the
way for their arrival. A bit taken aback by Buffalo Hump's imperious
tone, the agents reminded the two leaders that this would be their
last chance for peace, then departed. Were the Penatekas coming to
the council or not? No one seemed to know.[13]

In early October an enormous makeshift village of deerskin
lodges and buffalo hide tipis began to emerge on the prairie along
Tehuacana Creek near Torrey's trading house. Most had traveled
hundreds of miles to the trading post, some from the upper reaches of
the Brazos and Colorado rivers, others from as far away as Indian Territory above the Red. All the tribes expelled by Lamar were there—
the Cherokees, the Caddos, the Shawnees, and the Delawares. So too
were the woodland Wichita bands, the Tawakonis and the Wacos.
The Lipan Apaches, who frequently served as scouts for Anglo-Texas
militia companies, came over from their rancherías west of San Antonio. And much to Houston's enormous relief, a large delegation of
Penateka Comanches, led by Old Owl and Buffalo Hump, appeared
shortly before the meeting began.[14]

For the next several days, more than a thousand people mingled
together in a festive atmosphere. All blood feuds were forgotten—or
at least set aside for the moment—as the tribes engaged in trade.
Pidgin Spanish served as the lingua franca for the tribes, and when
that failed, sign language. At night, great bonfires were built, around
which each of the tribes sang and performed ceremonial dances that
lasted until dawn.[15]

For three days, Houston and the chiefs met at the trading house
council ground to formalize the treaty, which the president hoped
would finally bring an end to years of bloodshed and chaos. Fully

27. *Treaty of Peace.* By John O. Meusebach, 1847. Courtesy of
Gillespie County Historical Society, Fredericksburg, Texas.

aware of the significance of the occasion, the tribal leaders set aside
Western dress and adorned themselves with feathers, jewelry, and
trophies of war—accoutrements consistent with their status and
power. What Houston wore at this particular council was not re-
corded, but like the chiefs he understood the importance of these
ceremonial protocols. At an earlier meeting with the Indians he appeared in full military uniform, at another in a purple velvet suit
embossed with figures of a fox's head, with an enormous Bowie knife
tucked into his belt. For this council, the largest gathering of Native
Americans ever held in Texas, he would have dressed to impress.[16]

Houston waited until all the chiefs assembled before he made
his grand entrance. Accompanied by a cohort of Indian commissioners and seven translators, he rode at full canter once around the
encampment before dismounting. After greeting the chiefs in the
traditional Indian manner with a powerful embrace, the president
opened the council with the ritual smoking of a pipe of peace, passed
to each of the dignitaries in solemn silence. Houston rose to address
the group. He apologized for the brutal policies of his predecessor,
a "bad chief" who had made war on the Indians, assuring them that
his administration wanted peace. He then called Acaquash forward

to bestow upon him a special honor. In what was clearly a bid to elevate the chief's standing among his people, the president presented him with a silk scarf, which he wrapped around the old man's head. Fastening it with a gold broach, he proclaimed Acaquash "chief of the Waco."[17]

On the second day it was the Indians' turn to speak, all of whom echoed Houston's desire for an end to the conflict among their peoples. The president produced a formal treaty that was read to them by the interpreters, an impressive document stamped with the seal of Texas, with three colored ribbons attached to the bottom. The white ribbon "denoted peace," Houston intoned, "the blue was like the sky, unchangeable; the green, like the grass and the trees existing as long as the world stands." Most of the provisions were predictable enough; the Indians would return any horses and captives they had taken from the white settlements, and the government promised to build new trading houses where they could go to receive corn and farming implements. By far the most important were the articles defining a boundary line between the Penatekas and the whites. Houston expected no problems on that score; it was, after all, the San Saba boundary that Old Owl had proposed several months earlier.[18]

So far, things were going smoothly. But when the meeting reconvened on the third day, Buffalo Hump rose to speak. "I like the Treaty well enough, all but one thing, the line is too far off; [it is] too far up the country." The war chief wanted the line drawn farther south, well below the San Saba River. "That country is full of bear, deer, wild horses and buffalo for my people to live on." Taken aback, Houston tried to hide his surprise. Then where, he asked, should the line be drawn? "About four day's fast riding below the mouth [of the San Saba]," the war chief replied. That was impossible, the president protested; that would mean Comanche territory extended over an area that included Austin and Bastrop. But Buffalo Hump refused to give ground. With growing desperation, Houston assured him of the government's goodwill, pointing out the benefits of a new trading house closer to the Comanche rancherías. The war chief was unmoved. "I am like the bird traveling through the air. I can travel and am always traveling and can easily come down here." Buffalo Hump did not need a trading house in Comanche country.[19]

There was nothing left to do but delete the boundary line articles from the treaty, which the chiefs then duly signed. The historic gathering of the tribes at Tehuacana Springs did yield some positive results. At the very least, Houston had reopened a dialogue with the Comanches, securing from Buffalo Hump a promise not to attack American settlements. Still, the failure to reach a boundary line agreement with the Penatekas was a bitter disappointment for the president. His hopes for an end to Wichita raiding by giving the peace-loving Acaquash the government's stamp of approval did not pan out either. The old man might be the "chief of the Waco" to the whites, but the young men of the tribe did as they pleased, and within a matter of weeks they were back to stealing horses and mules from farms and homesteads.

HOUSTON DID GET SOME GOOD NEWS AS HIS PRESIDENTIAL TERM drew to a close. In an effort to ease tensions with the United States, Santa Anna finally decided to release the Perote prisoners, and on November 10 the last of the Mier men arrived in Galveston. Only one Texan remained—Santa Fe prisoner José Antonio Navarro. Resisting all entreaties to liberate him, Santa Anna offered the unfortunate Bexareño his freedom if he would renounce his allegiance to the Texas Republic. Navarro refused, and had now spent four miserable years in Mexican prisons, most recently at the imposing San Juan de Ulúa, a fortress at the mouth of the harbor in Veracruz. Over time he managed to gain the sympathy of his guards, who eventually allowed him to roam the fort at will. The conditions of his confinement improved still further when Santa Anna, who for too long had vowed to bring Texas back under Mexican control and failed to deliver, was deposed by the army and exiled to Cuba. Taking advantage of the political turmoil, Navarro quietly slipped out of the fort and was back in Texas by the start of the new year.[20]

There was even more important news from the United States. American voters had gone to the polls and elected James K. Polk, in what was then the closest presidential contest in the country's history. Polk's campaign platform, a pledge to acquire not only Texas but Oregon as well, put the annexation issue squarely back on the table. Tyler, meanwhile, determined to redeem his ill-starred presidency with a major foreign policy achievement, had already announced a new plan to annex Texas when Congress convened in December, this time as a joint resolution, which would require only a simple majority of both houses.

Though momentum for annexation was clearly building, Houston was in no rush to endorse the new proposal. In his presidential valedictory address, he urged his fellow Texans not to "go begging again for admission into the United States," reminding US policy makers that his country still had other options available to it. Houston's insistence on playing his cards close to the vest so late in the game left his friends in the United States concerned and bewildered. Even Andrew Jackson did not know if his protégé's public comments were an expression of his true feelings or merely a bluff.[21]

With or without Houston's support, Washington now moved quickly on the annexation question. The resolution drafted by expansionists in Congress offered Texas significantly better terms than the earlier treaty, admitting the republic as a state rather than a territory. This would allow Texas to keep its public lands, a valuable source of revenue it could use to pay off its debts. The proposal also left the precise boundaries of Texas undefined, assuming that Mexican leaders could be induced to sell the land between the Nueces and the Rio Grande. The resolution passed easily in the House, but the vote was a nail-biter in the Senate, requiring the president pro tem to break a tie.[22]

The holy grail of American slaveholding expansionists now seemed within reach. But the path to annexation had been littered with unforeseen obstacles from the start, and the final stretch would present still more hurdles. Newly elected Texas president Anson Jones hinted strongly that he favored independence, while Houston remained coyly indifferent to Washington's offer, arguing that Texas should hold out for an even better deal. Complicating matters further, the Mexican government finally agreed to recognize Texas's independence in a last-ditch attempt to derail annexation. Charles Elliot rushed down to Mexico City to negotiate an agreement, but his eleventh-hour mission came too late. During his absence, Houston for the first time publicly revealed the diplomatic double game he had been playing, a game in which Elliot had played a prominent if unwitting part. Taking the lion's share of the credit for shepherding the new state into the Union, the former president claimed that his overtures to the British had been intended only to arouse the jealousy of the United States. "If ladies are justified in making use of coquetry in securing their annexation to good and agreeable husbands," he told a crowd in Houston, "you must excuse me for making use of the same means to annex Texas to Uncle Sam." In Nashville, Andrew Jackson heaved a sigh of relief. "*All safe*," he wrote to Polk in the White House. "I knew British gold could not buy Sam Houston."[23]

When Jackson scrawled these lines, he had only a few days left to live. Houston was already en route to Nashville with Margaret and their young son, having learned that the end was near. Their carriage pulled up at the Hermitage only a few hours after Jackson's death. Following the funeral, Southern Democrats held a series of public dinners in Houston's honor. The hero of San Jacinto reveled in the attention, continuing to take the credit for the marriage between the two North American republics. Back in Texas, his enemies lambasted the former president, insisting that he was a tool of the British, who had only endorsed annexation when the issue was no longer in doubt. Even out of office, Houston possessed a unique ability to make himself the center of attention, driving his critics into fits of apoplectic rage.

He had told Margaret, or at least led her to believe, that he would retire from politics when he stepped down from the presidency.

28. Margaret Lea Houston (1819–1867). Twenty-six years younger than her famous husband, Margaret defied her mother and accepted Houston's proposal of marriage after a whirlwind courtship in 1840, when this photograph was taken. Courtesy of Dolph Briscoe Center for American History, University of Texas at Austin.

His enslaved laborers were building for the family a house on a tract of land near Huntsville, and he seemed ready to take up the life of a gentleman farmer. But now there was talk of a run for the US Senate—perhaps even the White House—and Houston would do nothing to discourage the rumors.

Margaret abhorred the rough-and-tumble public arena in which her husband thrived, but bore his passion for the limelight without complaint. Since their marriage she had been busy carving out for herself a more private, domestic role. Like many middle-class women of the period, she was concerned with her husband's spiritual well-being and considered it her Christian duty to bring the famously profligate Houston back to God. The untimely deaths of friends and family members in recent years had made her more aware of the fleeting nature of human existence, and the need to attend to a life eternal. Her husband's accomplishments in the political realm would avail him nothing, she liked to remind him, "if your soul is unprepared." Houston had resisted her entreaties early on in the marriage; he "had no time to think of these things," he told her. But Margaret persisted, imploring him repeatedly to "lift your thoughts and affections with mine to that Heavenly country where all our sufferings and sorrows shall be forgotten."[24]

During their stay in Nashville, Houston's old friends could not have failed to notice Margaret's influence over him. He had lost weight, and now drank only in moderation, if he drank at all. The couple did not dance, nor did they engage in "worldly employment" on the Sabbath. A dedicated student of the Bible, he read the scriptures daily, committing long passages to memory. "You have, I doubt not, heard that my wife controls me, and has reformed me, in many respects? This is pretty true," Houston wrote to a friend. Margaret, he noted, "gets all the credit for my good actions," while he had to endure "all the censure of my bad ones." But he was still a man of towering vanity, who reveled in the attention and acclaim of public life. Margaret's campaign to reform her husband could only go so far.[25]

Though Texas annexation was now assured, Mexican leaders struck a warlike pose, angrily insisting they still had some say in the matter. It had been three years since General Woll's seizure of San Antonio, and Texans took such saber-rattling with a hefty dose of skepticism. Washington, however, believed that Great Britain might now goad Mexico into a war with the United States. Convinced that an attack was imminent, President Polk sent General Zachary Taylor and an army of fifteen hundred men into Texas, with orders to take up positions at the mouth of the Nueces River.

The following month, a convention was held in Austin to consider the annexation proposal. Accepting the US offer with only one dissenting vote, it then set about the task of drafting a state constitution. At year's end, Texas voters went to the polls to elect the state's first governor, James Pinckney Henderson.

Few Texans mourned the passing of the Lone Star Republic. Utterly dysfunctional, it had always been something of a geopolitical curiosity, a madcap experiment in nationhood bordering on the burlesque. Shunned for much of its brief existence by the United States, the republic was nonetheless a purely American creation, exhibiting all the unbridled impulses of the Jacksonian id. Hovering near anarchy at times, it embraced a boisterous, almost manic populism. It mimicked, too, the imperial swagger of its country of origin, laying claim to enormous swaths of land with a grasp that far exceeded its reach. Above all, as a nation forged in the crucible of racial conflict, it was defiantly and unapologetically committed to the ideology of white rule. Sam Houston may have spoken out passionately against the expulsion of the Cherokees, and condemned the mistreatment of the republic's Hispanos. But such voices were dispiritingly few. In attempting to create from scratch an entirely new American nation-state, Anglo-Texans had created not a mirror image of the United States, but a magnified, exaggerated reflection of its virtues and vices.

The Mavericks learned of the convention's vote on annexation on Matagorda peninsula, where they had moved the year before. A treeless sandbar extending for fifty miles along the Gulf, it was far removed from the dangers of life on the western frontier. Mary expressed the feelings of many with this entry in her diary: "July, 1845. Thank God, we are now annexed to the United States, and can hope for home and quiet."[26]

TWENTY-FOUR

TO CONQUER A PEACE

N O ONE EXPECTED SAMUEL WALKER TO SURVIVE THE LANCE wound he had received in the Indian fight on the Guadalupe River in the summer of 1844, much less return to duty. But after six months convalescing at an American boardinghouse in San Antonio, where a friend of Mary Maverick's nursed him back to health, he was well enough to ride a horse and rejoin his old ranger company, pursuing Comanches in the Trans-Nueces. In the Tehuacana Springs treaty, Buffalo Hump had promised not to raid American settlements, and for the most part he was true to his word. But Penateka bands still had to pass through the area on their way to Mexican villages below the Rio Grande. Horse thefts and murders of white settlers occasionally occurred, and each time the rangers took off after them. In a skirmish with Comanche horsemen in the spring of 1845, Walker was wounded again, this time not seriously. "Walker had no sense of fear," one of his friends later recalled. He "seemed to seek danger; to love it for itself."[1]

The arrival of US troops at the mouth of the Nueces River that summer would mark a new chapter in Samuel Walker's relentless quest for adventure. Calling itself the Army of Observation, it eventually swelled to four thousand men. The Mexican press continued to thunder loudly against annexation, but the war scare that had prompted Polk to send Taylor into the area never materialized. The Gulf Coast heat proved to be the most serious enemy the army

had to contend with, dysentery and malaria rendering more than
10 percent of the troops unfit for duty. Needing skilled horsemen
familiar with the terrain, Taylor asked the Texas government to allow one of its ranger companies to be mustered into federal service,
and by the fall Walker was stationed on the Nueces, performing
scouting and foraging duties for the US Army.

Since the terms of the annexation agreement left the border
between the two countries undefined, Polk grew impatient as the
months passed, alternating between bullying and brinksmanship to
resolve the issue. Naturally, the president accepted the Texas claim to
the Rio Grande, ignoring the fact that the republic had never made
the slightest effort to extend its authority south of the Nueces River.
In December, Polk sent a diplomat, John Slidell, to Mexico City with
an offer of compensation for the Trans-Nueces. Then, acting on the
wholly misplaced belief that this might be a good time to press for
additional concessions, he instructed Slidell to broach the possibility
of acquiring California as well. Entertaining either suggestion would
have been political suicide for the government of President José Joaquín Herrera, already unpopular after failing to prevent annexation.
With public anger toward the United States reaching a fever pitch,
he refused even to recognize Slidell's diplomatic credentials. The
army deposed him anyway, installing as president a hawkish conservative, General Mariano Paredes. Angered by Mexico's unwillingness to negotiate, Polk ordered Taylor to march south and take up
positions on the Rio Grande.

In so doing, the president activated a trip wire that made a Mexican military response all but inevitable. For all their bellicose rhetoric,
Mexico's leaders had never seriously considered an invasion of Texas.
But the Paredes government could hardly ignore the US occupation
of the Trans-Nueces, and rushed troops to Matamoros to meet the
American challenge. Mexicans regarded Polk's claim to the region as
an absurd fiction, and with good reason. The only landowners in the
area held land grants from New Spain dating back to the eighteenth
century. As residents of the state of Tamaulipas, they were governed
by Mexican officials and subject to Mexican laws. If Polk did not want

to start a war, he was certainly doing everything he could to goad Mexico into one.[2]

Even had cooler heads in the two capitals prevailed, it would not have mattered. Festering hatreds between Mexican and American borderlanders made for a combustible situation once the two armies came within striking distance of one another. After a decade of conflict, men on both sides nursed deeply personal grievances and were looking for any opportunity to act on their desire for blood revenge. Samuel Walker and some of the other Texas rangers under Taylor's command had been prisoners in Mexico. The group also included a more unsavory element—men like Mustang Gray and members of the cattle-stealing gangs that for the past few years had roamed the chaparral below the Nueces. On the other side of the river, Antonio Canales, who had last fought Texans at the Battle of Mier, commanded the *defensores* of the villas del norte. Juan Seguín was there, too, leading a company of Hispano men from the San Antonio area. Everyone, it seemed, had scores to settle.

Now renamed the Army of Occupation (a term that belied Polk's claim to the territory), Taylor's force set up camp directly across the river from Matamoros, its artillery batteries within easy range of the town plaza. The standoff lasted only a matter of days, as Canales's guerillas began to pick off Americans who ventured beyond Taylor's picket lines. They grew bolder when Mexican infantry regiments arrived, attacking a party of dragoons on April 25. Polk learned of the skirmish two weeks later. Diplomacy could still have resolved the border crisis, but for the president the time for negotiation had passed. Convinced that the United States would prevail in a military contest with Mexico, he was already looking ahead to the territory that could be gained in the event of an American victory, and promptly asked Congress for a declaration of war.[3]

The outbreak of hostilities unleashed a primal fury that would become a permanent, ugly feature of the war in northern Mexico, which commanders on both sides struggled to control. Within days, Mexican guerrillas attacked a group of teamsters carting supplies to Taylor's army. They shot two men and slit the throats of the others, some of whom were women and children, dumping the bodies in an arroyo. Retaliation for what would be known as the Rogers Massacre was swift. When he learned of the attack, Mustang Gray rode at the head of a group of Texans to a nearby rancho and murdered its male inhabitants. The two countries had yet to fight a major battle, but a brutal war between the peoples of the border was already underway.[4]

As South Texas devolved into a death spiral of retribu- tive violence, the Polk administration stepped up its effort to reach some kind of settlement with the state's Indians. It was especially eager to sign a treaty with the Penateka Comanches, concerned that the tribe might disrupt the military supply lines in South Texas. After some initial parleys, another grand council was held at Torrey's trad- ing house in May 1846. The commissioners explained to the Indians that Texas had been acquired by the United States, and they were now under the protection of the federal government. Once again, no substantive agreement on a boundary line could be reached, although at Buffalo Hump's insistence the US commissioners did insert a provision by which Washington promised to prevent any further encroachment on Comanche hunting grounds. Believing he had won a major concession, Buffalo Hump and other Penateka leaders signed what would become known as the Council Springs Treaty and accepted the commissioners' gifts, pleased that they were far more extravagant than anything Houston's cash-strapped admin- istration could afford.[5]

With treaty in hand, the commissioners accompanied an Indian delegation of fifteen Texas chiefs and some two dozen followers to Washington. The purpose of the trip to the capital was to impress upon the Indians the sheer size of the nation to which they now be- longed. It could hardly have failed to do so. The large group traveled by steamboat to New Orleans, then up the Mississippi en route to the nation's capital. The fifteen-hundred-mile journey took the better part of a month. In each town they passed, large crowds assembled along the wharf to gawk at the Indian delegation. In Washington they attended the theater and took in the sights. Senator Houston, who knew them all from his earlier negotiations with the tribes, gave the visiting dignitaries a tour of the Capitol Building. Dressed in Western clothing, they were received by President Polk at the White House, who presented them with silver medals. Afterward, they attended a performance of the Marine Corps band, slipping out of their shoes to feel the grass of the South Lawn on their feet.[6]

After three weeks in the capital they were ready to go home. For some, old tribal feuds resurfaced, and they began to quarrel with one another. One chief fell ill during the trip, while another got publicly, riotously drunk. When Polk learned that the excursion had cost four times more than originally budgeted, the pennywise president was happy to see them go. But the visit had achieved its goal, the administration believed. Surely the Indians would make peace, now that they had seen, as one told the president, that the Americans were "more numerous than the stars, and he could not count them."[7]

Polk was wrong about the Indians. Impressed though they may have been with the overwhelming numbers and resources of the people who were steadily crowding in on their domain, they soon realized that the promises of the US government were as empty as the Texas Republic's had been. The US Senate gutted the Council Springs Treaty, striking out the one article that Buffalo Hump cared about most, the promise to keep whites from trespassing on Penateka hunting lands. Adding insult to injury, it rejected the clause that guaranteed the Indians a steady supply of gifts, and for good measure noted that the federal government would not be paying for any more trips to the capital. Angered by Washington's failure to honor the terms of the treaty, Buffalo Hump refused to acknowledge American sovereignty. When told that the president of the United States was now the Great Father of the Indians, he replied indignantly, "I have no father but Heaven, and no mother but Earth."[8]

POLK TURNED OUT TO BE WRONG ABOUT MEXICO, TOO. IN MAY, General Taylor scored two impressive victories on the Rio Grande, at Palo Alto and Resaca de la Palma. The president assumed the war was over, and so it might have been, but for the absence of a stable government in Mexico to negotiate with. By the summer, Paredes had been overthrown, paving the way for the return of the one man Mexicans always seemed to turn to in times of crisis—Santa Anna. From exile in Cuba, the Mexican leader informed the Polk administration that he was prepared to negotiate for the sale of New Mexico and California. Taking him at his word, it arranged to have his vessel pass unmolested through the US blockade of Veracruz, whereupon Santa Anna rushed to the capital to take control of the war effort. An end to the conflict was nowhere in sight.

During the early months of the war, the Polk administration could rely on strong public support. To be sure, antislavery Whig leaders grumbled that the conflict was another attempt by the South to expand the slave empire, and their protests would grow louder as the war dragged on. But the fighting on the Rio Grande produced a groundswell of martial enthusiasm across the country, as thousands of young men rushed to enlist. To satisfy the nation's hunger for news from the front lines, the American press gave the crisis with Mexico extensive coverage, making the war the first to be widely reported. Several big city dailies sent correspondents into the field to provide eyewitness accounts of the action. With the telegraph connecting most major American cities by 1846, their wartime experiences could be read by millions across the country.

As the only troops with prior experience fighting Mexicans, the Texas volunteers attracted national attention. Often deployed as scouts and engaged in small, targeted missions, the rangers made especially good copy, allowing them to rise above the anonymity of troops engaged in set piece battles. Public interest in the state's volunteers was so great that no fewer than four New Orleans newspapers hired correspondents who doubled as members of Texas Ranger companies. They were anything but unbiased observers. The *Picayune* correspondent, George Wilkins Kendall, had been a member of Lamar's ill-fated Santa Fe Expedition, and he would file more than two hundred stories portraying the Texans as heroic, frontier archetypes who represented the best of American manhood.[9]

No Texan would get more press than Samuel Walker. Tasked with guarding the thirty-mile route between Taylor's headquarters at Fort Brown, opposite Matamoros, and Point Isabel, the army's supply depot on the Gulf Coast, Walker found himself in the thick of the fighting. Two days after the outbreak of hostilities, a large Mexican force crossed the river to sever Taylor's supply lines, overwhelming Walker's company, which was almost entirely wiped out. Galloping back to Point Isabel, Walker then volunteered to alert Taylor at Fort Brown of the Mexican advance, successfully dashing through enemy lines with half a dozen men. Two weeks later, at the Battle of Resaca de la Palma, the Texas Ranger again distinguished himself when his horse was shot out from under him. Walker coolly shot a Mexican lancer, then grabbed the reins of his horse and swung onto the riderless mount to continue the battle.[10]

Mentioned prominently in early dispatches, the Ranger captain quickly became front page news. The "gallant Walker" was seemingly everywhere, wreaking havoc in clashes with Mexican troops along the river. The ranger's earlier exploits fighting Comanches and as a member of the Mier Expedition soon came to light, adding more luster to his reputation. To the public, his working-class origins made him a uniquely appealing figure, a welcome contrast to the well-born leaders who occupied the nation's martial pantheon. Above all, it was the story of Walker's encounter with the Mexican lancer at Resaca de la Palma that captured the national imagination. Civic leaders in New Orleans purchased a war horse, Tornado, and had it sent to him at the front. The noted western artist Charles Deas was inspired to recreate the scene of the now-famous encounter in a painting titled *The Last Shot*. By the summer, a play loosely based on his adventures opened in New York City, and a short, illustrated biography, *The Brave Ranger*, was rushed into print. Almost overnight, Walker had become a national hero.[11]

There was, however, a less romantic side to the exploits of
Walker and his Texas Ranger company. After the battle at Resaca de
la Palma ended in a rout of the Mexican army on the Rio Grande,
Walker and his men ignored orders to retire, calmly shooting frantic infantry regulars as they tried to swim across the river. When
Taylor seized Matamoros a week later, drunken Texans shot up the
town, killing half a dozen citizens in cold blood. Commenting on the
many affrays attributed to the rangers, one reporter observed, "It is
no novel sight to see a Mexican laying in the streets at daylight, shot
or stabbed to the heart." A squad of rangers descended on Mier, the
scene of the Texas defeat in 1842, and, though they met with no resistance, executed several prominent citizens. After a three-day battle for Monterrey in September, Texas volunteers ran amok on the
streets of the city, murdering scores of unarmed civilians.[12]

The Texans were hardly alone in perpetrating acts of brutality.
To supplement the regular army, the War Department relied on volunteer regiments from several states with little training or discipline.
The Arkansas regiment committed the most infamous atrocity of the
campaign when, in retaliation for the murder of a volunteer accused
of rape, it herded more than two dozen civilians into a cave and shot
them. But none of the troops under Taylor's command could claim
the notoriety of the Texans, who viewed the conflict simply as an
extension of the decade-long border war. Often actuated by personal
vendettas, Taylor's Texas scouts spent much of their time scouring
the countryside for Antonio Canales and Juan Seguín. Both managed
to elude capture.[13]

The bad behavior of the Texas volunteers posed a dilemma for
Taylor. Sensitive to the country's new role as an occupying power
and mindful of Whig opposition to the war, the Polk administration repeatedly urged the commander of US forces to do nothing
to alienate the civilian population. But the Texans made it difficult
for Taylor to win Mexican hearts and minds. Local officials lodged
furious protests; even members of his own staff complained about
them. Amid reports that Texans were scalping the bodies of Mexican
troops, one disgusted officer wrote: they "act more like a body of

savage Indians than of civilized whites." The general admitted that some of the Texas volunteers were little better than "robbers and cut-throats," but during the early months of the campaign he believed he could not do without them. Sending those accused of more serious crimes to the rear, Taylor would eventually request that no more Texans be mustered into service.[14]

The US Army managed to impose some semblance of order when it gained control of northern Mexico with the fall of its largest city, Monterrey, in September. A military tribunal, which would remain in place for the duration of the war, levied punishments on the more egregious violations committed by American troops against the civilian population. But in the countryside the atrocities continued. Mexican partisans harassed US supply lines, sometimes killing teamsters by lassoing them and dragging their bodies through the cactus-covered chaparral. As always, such episodes prompted equally vicious reprisals. Following a particularly bloody attack by Canales's guerrillas on a supply train near Saltillo, Mustang Gray's rangers once again went looking for revenge, descending on the community of Rancho Guadalupe, where they rounded up and summarily executed two dozen unarmed men.[15]

Walker's company of Texans disbanded after the fall of Monterrey, their terms of enlistment having expired. But the war for Walker was far from over. Offered a captain's commission in the US Mounted Rifles, he returned to the United States as part of a recruitment effort, where the slightly built, unassuming ranger was feted wherever he went. In New Orleans, a ladies' civic group presented him with an engraved sword. In Washington he received an interview with President Polk and led an honor guard in a memorial service for men killed in the war. Traveling to New York, he sat for the famous photographer Matthew Brady and met with gun manufacturer Samuel Colt to discuss modifications to the five-shot revolver, the weapon of choice of the Texas Rangers. Parlaying his newfound celebrity into political influence, he convinced the War Department to purchase one thousand new six-shooters, which the grateful arms maker named the "Walker Colt."[16]

Thus far, the war had gone astonishingly well for the United States. Mexico had suffered an uninterrupted string of defeats in Texas and below the Rio Grande, and New Mexico and California had fallen quickly to US troops. Yet the country hovered on the brink of political anarchy, making a negotiated settlement impossible. Though advised by some members of his cabinet to simply declare the war over—the US Army had already seized what Polk wanted anyway, access to the Pacific Ocean—the president decided to ramp up the war effort, opening up a new theater of operations in the heart of Mexico. It was a bold gamble. Up to this point US forces had subdued the most thinly populated regions of the country, where years of opposition to the government had weakened national allegiances. An invasion of central Mexico could expect much stiffer resistance. But Polk forged ahead. Following his instincts and guided by an unwavering faith in the superiority of American arms, he was determined, as he put it, to "conquer a peace."

Under the command of General Winfield Scott, the US Army made an amphibious landing at Veracruz in March 1847. Scott's forces inched their way toward the capital, winding through valleys and mountain passes of the volcanic region that spanned the nation's midsection. Defeating Santa Anna's army at the Battle of Cerro Gordo, they soon captured Perote, where so many of the San Antonio and Mier men had been imprisoned. Walker arrived a month later and was again assigned the task of safeguarding army supply trains, effectively clearing out the guerilla bands that lurked in the forests along the National Road.[17]

But the former Texas Ranger had always had a problem with authority, going back to his days as a private in the US Army in Florida, and he was even less willing to bend to the rules of military discipline now. Regarding all adult males as enemy combatants, he was dogged by allegations of brutality. Though he vigorously denied that he had hanged a local alcalde and shot seventeen villagers, his reputation for ruthlessness appears to have been well-deserved. "God help them," one soldier said of the guerrillas Walker encountered on his scouting patrols, "for he seldom brings in prisoners."[18]

At the same time, Walker could not be lumped in the same category as Mustang Gray and others who cut a bloody swath through Mexico, much as they had done in South Texas before the war. Governed by his own moral code, he refused to allow his men to engage in looting, a practice common among US troops. From the start of the campaign he quarreled with his commanding officer, Colonel Francis Wynkoop, and the two men engaged in a test of wills that became more acrimonious as the regiment proceeded up the National Road. Ordered by Wynkoop to destroy the picturesque and militarily insignificant town of Jalapa, Walker refused on the grounds that it would bring dishonor to his company. During an expedition into the mountains to hunt for guerrillas, Walker became so incensed when Wynkoop's men sacked a village that they almost came to blows. The colonel had finally had enough of his insubordinate officer and ordered Walker arrested and stripped of command.[19]

Walker spent a frustrating summer at Perote, as the war went on without him. To relieve the boredom he led a team to climb the fourteen-thousand-foot Cofre de Perote, where he planted the American flag. Meanwhile, Scott's army pushed forward to Mexico City, and after a series of hard-fought battles at the gates of the capital, Santa Anna evacuated the city in mid-September. An American victory now seemed imminent; Polk's offensive strategy to carry the war to the "halls of the Montezumas" had paid off.

But Santa Anna refused to concede defeat, even as his army slowly started to melt away. Marching eighty miles east to Puebla, he laid siege to the American garrison there, hoping to score an eleventh-hour victory that would rally the country around him once more. At Perote, General Joseph Lane hurriedly assembled a three-thousand-man army to lift the siege. In need of experienced scouts to clear the way along the National Road, Lane decided that Walker's court-martial could wait and ordered the Texas captain returned to active duty. There would be one more battle in the war against Mexico, and for Walker, a final chance to achieve "immortal fame."

Walker rode out of the fortress with Lane's army on October 5. Four days later they reached the outskirts of the village of Huamantla,

29. *Death of Samuel Walker*. By R. Magee, 1847. Courtesy
Special Collections, University of Texas at Arlington Libraries.

with Walker and his mounted company at a brisk trot, well ahead of
the main relief column. Spotting a large force of Mexican lancers
entering the town, he did not bother to wait for Lane. His blood
up, Walker ordered his men to draw sabers and spurred his horse,
leading them on a wild charge into the village, where they quickly
dispersed the lancers and seized an artillery battery in the central
plaza. In the space of only a few minutes, they took possession of the
town, but the lull in the fighting proved only temporary. At Santa
Anna's orders the cavalry counterattacked, sending Walker and his
men racing down narrow side streets in confusion. They eventually
regrouped, doubling back to take cover behind the walls of the San
Luis Obispo church on the town square.

There were various accounts of what happened next. Early reports described a Mexican soldier spearing Walker off his horse with
a lance. Other eyewitnesses would later come forward to add more
colorful detail. According to one, Walker had been slain by a noted
guerilla leader; according to another, by a man seeking vengeance

for a son Walker had killed in battle. The myths surrounding Walker's death also came with the obligatory famous last words. "Boys, forward, and don't flinch a foot," he was said to have cried. "I know I am dying but don't give way." His second-in-command remembered it differently. The Texan had been felled by a sniper's bullet, and could only mumble that Lane's troops would soon arrive before he expired.[20]

Just as one of the first heroes of the war had become one of its last casualties, the contest against Mexico would end much as it began, in a paroxysm of racially fueled bloodlust. After driving Mexican troops from Huamantla, Lane allowed his men to sack the town to avenge Walker's death. A frenzied rampage followed, with "drunken soldiers, yelling and screeching," committing "every species of outrage," one horrified officer in Lane's Indiana regiment wrote in a letter to his father. "Old women and girls were stripped of their clothing" and raped; dozens of men were shot in cold blood. "Such a scene I never hope to see again," he confessed. "It made me for the first time, ashamed of my country."[21]

With the death of "the gallant Walker" dominating the headlines, the sack of Huamantla got little coverage in the press. Walker's body was brought back to the United States with full military honors. Funeral processions for the Texas Ranger were held in New Orleans, Galveston, and Austin before his body was laid to rest in San Antonio.

Americans had grown tired of war, but the appeal of the Texas Rangers would endure. Tales of their exploits in Mexico, a land that seemed exotic and mysterious to most Americans, continued to capture the public imagination. Dime novels of the rangers' adventures, the stuff of adolescent heroic fantasy, would become a cottage industry in the years that followed, with storylines featuring virile alpha males who were often called upon to rescue dark-eyed senoritas from the clutches of lascivious Mexicans. Even Mustang Gray became the subject of a popular romance, the Trans-Nueces bandit and cutthroat absurdly reinvented as an intrepid Texas Ranger, a violent man on a noble quest: to avenge the honor of his beloved Inez. It was a body of literature disconnected from the bitter debate that had preceded Texas's entry into the Union and the sectional strife between North and South that would embroil the nation in the years ahead. The rangers came to be seen as a warrior elite, a border breed credited with taming not only a frontier, but a foreign land. Whatever their views on slavery, Americans were happy to claim them as their own.[22]

TWENTY-FIVE

A DECENT PLACE IN WHICH
A WHITE MAN COULD LIVE

IN 1847, SAM AND MARY MAVERICK WERE STILL LIVING ON
Matagorda peninsula and, like most Americans, were unaffected
by the war with Mexico. It was a happy time for Mary, after years
of hardship and anxiety on the republic's western frontier. She gave
birth to their fifth child soon after they arrived, and Sam and their
slaves built a large, three-story house for the growing family. She
enjoyed working in her garden and found the cool breezes off the
Gulf and regular ocean bathing invigorating. In Matagorda she had
the advantage of a large circle of friends, and they frequently went on
sailing excursions in the bay.[1]

But her husband was restless. The house was hardly finished
when he began to talk about moving the family back to San Antonio,
where he could better manage his land business. Since his return
from prison in Mexico, he had continued to acquire property there,
rarely selling any of it. His family would never understand Sam's
"inordinate craving for land," which up to this point had yielded decidedly mixed results. But Maverick's dogged faith in the economic
potential of the town remained undimmed. With the war in Mexico
winding down, settlers for the first time were moving into the interior in steady numbers. His years of patient investment, he told his
wife, were about to pay off.[2]

Mary seems to have had little say in the matter. In her memoirs, written many years later, she claimed to be fully in accord with her husband's decision to move back to San Antonio. The time the family had spent there she described as "a bright vision, a veritable romance," whereas the "peninsula was not home to us in the full sense of the word." Her diary suggests otherwise. "I felt really sad to leave," she wrote at the time of her Matagorda home. As for any fond recollections of San Antonio, they were surely tempered by the grisly horror of the Council House fight. Her husband must have tried to reassure her that San Antonio had changed since 1842, when the family fled just before Mexican troops seized the town. In any case, she clearly believed the decision was her husband's alone to make. If she had any misgivings, she kept them to herself.[3]

No doubt Mary was relieved to find that her husband was right. The town *had* changed. Once a dusty Hispano village of less than a thousand souls, so remote that it was only nominally part of the Texas Republic, San Antonio now thrummed with activity, with a post office, a weekly newspaper, and a stagecoach line connecting it to Houston, Austin, and the Gulf Coast. A major supply center for the War Department during the conflict with Mexico, the town was now the headquarters of the US Army's operations for the entire Southwest, home to a garrison of several hundred soldiers and their officers. The narrow streets were clogged with the wagons of Americans and German immigrants, who were looking to buy land in the rolling hills north and west of town. San Antonio's days as a distant outpost on the edge of Anglo settlement were finally over.

Sam Maverick threw himself into his land business, again leaving his family for long periods of time. In the spring he embarked on a surveying expedition that would take him 150 miles to the southwest, a wild, uninhabited expanse of scrubland on the Rio Grande. Later organized as a county that would bear his name, the area was a frequent crossing point into Mexico for Comanche raiding parties. Mary as usual worried about his safety, knowing he had cheated death in the past. But by now she knew there was nothing she could do to change his mind.

As much as he enjoyed these excursions, Sam was aware of the strain the long periods of separation placed on Mary and the children. Embarking on another expedition to West Texas the following year, he left his wife with a newborn son, Willie, so sickly that Mary feared he would not survive. His letters home, on those rare occasions when he was able to send them, were filled with solicitude, and perhaps a hint of defensiveness. "All this is nothing—not worth a moment's consideration," he insisted of his business affairs, "compared with the health of my family."[4]

Several weeks later Maverick returned, meeting an acquaintance on the outskirts of town, who gave him terrible news. Not about Willie, but his eldest daughter, seven-year-old Agatha, who had come down with a severe fever while he was gone. Mary thought the illness was due to eating unripened grapes, but the cause was probably typhoid. She had been dead two weeks. Maverick went immediately to the grave and threw himself down upon it, alone in his anguish until nightfall. The thought that he had been unable to comfort her in her final hours would torment him for the rest of his life, leaving him "a sad, changed, man," according to Mary. "Cursed land, cursed money," the grief-stricken father muttered. "I would give all, all, only to see her once more."[5]

The family had survived Indian attacks and Mexican invasion, but it was not immune to the health hazards that made life precarious for all Americans in the mid-nineteenth century. The following year, a cholera epidemic that first appeared in New Orleans—and would claim the former president, James K. Polk, as one of its early victims—ravaged San Antonio. According to one estimate, the disease killed six hundred residents of the town. In April, with most members of the Maverick household laid low by the disease, six-year-old Augusta described a dream in which she was wearing a flowing white dress, riding a carriage to a church where the congregation was also dressed in white. Two days later she was dead. "It was a prophesy

30. Mary A. Maverick and her
children, circa early 1850s. One of
the first Anglo-American women
to settle in San Antonio, Mary
Maverick would lose four of her
ten children to disease. Courtesy
of Dolph Briscoe Center for
American History, University
of Texas at Austin.

of her shroud and burial and resurrection," Mary believed, who was
inconsolable and too sick herself to attend the funeral. A son, John,
born a year later, offered some solace in her despair. He too would
be dead of cholera within a few months.[6]

The numbing grief of losing three children in the span of two
and a half years—a fourth would die in 1859—left Mary devastated.
She became introspective, overwhelmed by feelings of self-doubt,
questioning her worthiness as a Christian wife and mother. Now
more than ever she turned to her faith, consumed by the need to
better understand her place in a divine plan. Her profound sorrow
also led her to spiritualism, or "table-rapping" as the phenomenon
then sweeping the United States was sometimes called, in a poignant
quest to connect with the children she had lost. If her unending
search to find meaning in the mysteries and tragedies of life brought
her spiritual comfort, it was also accompanied by deep feelings of
melancholy. She confided to her diary: "I strive, I pray to do good,

to feel an unwavering and abiding trust in God's love & mercy & power, but I never entirely succeed in any of these." She continued to believe that "the curse of slavery" was at least partly to blame for her moral failings, a system that made her "hard & cold & evil & bitter." When a runaway slave, the family cook, was apprehended after three months of freedom, Mary noted curtly in her diary, "She is to be sold; one pest rid of, gracias!!"[7]

The end of the war with Mexico saw the return to San Antonio of another family, the Seguíns. The war years had been hard on Juan, who was now "care worn & *thread bare*" and hoping for a chance to rebuild his fortunes in his hometown. With a letter of safe passage from Sam Houston, who had always defended him, Seguín returned to the family rancho, Casa Blanca, where his father, Erasmo, still lived, and tried to resume his old life as one of San Antonio's civic leaders.[8]

It would prove to be a bittersweet homecoming for the former mayor. Remembered fondly in the Bexareño community, Seguín won election as justice of the peace, and for a time was active in the local Democratic Party. But the turbulent events of the republic years had left him suspect in the eyes of many Anglo-Texans, who could not forget his last visit to Béxar as an officer in Woll's army, or his activities as a Mexican guerilla fighter in the late war. At the same time, the political landscape had changed dramatically since his untimely departure in 1842. Anglos dominated the city council; 140 years would pass before the town elected a Mexican-American mayor again. The peace agreement ending the war only increased his feelings of alienation. By the terms of the Treaty of Guadalupe Hidalgo, Mexico formally recognized the Rio Grande as the border between Texas and Mexico, effectively severing Seguín and many Hispano Texans from kinship and business networks below the river. Never fully adjusting to his new identity as a Tejano, a term that would only now come into common use, he would spend much of his time in northern Mexico after his father's death in 1857.[9]

Seguín's experience stands in marked contrast to that of another prominent Bexareño, José Antonio Navarro, who returned to Texas

after his imprisonment in Mexico an honored hero. Of all the prominent Hispanos who had cast their lot with the Americans in the early
days of the rebellion, Navarro alone remained loyal to the cause,
giving him an unusual degree of freedom in addressing the injustices
Bexareños faced after independence. As the only Hispano delegate
to the 1845 convention, Navarro managed to have the word "white"
stricken from the clause in the state constitution that defined citizenship. He would have less success protecting the rights of Mexicans
whose land titles, issued long before independence, were deemed
"defective" by American speculators.

Navarro embraced statehood evidently because—not unlike another prominent Mexican, Lorenzo de Zavala—he believed in the
promise of American democracy. Surely, he hoped, the United States
would be better able to protect the rights of its nonwhite citizens
than the "barnyard republic." That faith would be sorely tested with
the rise of the short-lived Know-Nothing Party in the mid-1850s,
which exploited anti-Catholic sentiment among the Anglo majority
in San Antonio and called for the disenfranchisement of citizens who
were not native-born Americans. There were economic tensions,
too, which erupted in violence in 1857 when whites and Hispanos
clashed over control of the freight-hauling business between San
Antonio and the coast.[10]

Navarro remained to the end a forceful advocate for Mexican
Texans, though he could do little to remedy what he called their
"prostrated condition." Mired in wrenching poverty, most Bexareños
were despised by white residents, one local newspaper editorializ-
ing in 1852 that Mexicans were not "one whit elevated above the
Comanche, and many of them infinitely below in the scale of moral
being—repulsive objects in the eye of civilization." As a wealthy
landowner with a son at Harvard, Navarro was spared their scorn.
Tellingly, Anglos were fond of pointing out that Navarro's father had
been born in Corsica, thereby absolving him of all negative associations with the Hispano population. To many whites, Navarro was not
just a "good Mexican." He was not really a Mexican at all.[11]

As Anglos asserted their political control over the town, they sought to impose new standards of morality. The city council passed a raft of measures to prohibit Hispano cultural practices Anglos found objectionable, such as cockfighting, public nude bathing, and fandangos, while Mary Maverick joined other Protestant women to lobby for an ordinance requiring merchants to observe the Sabbath. Pushback from the Hispano community was fierce, however, and local customs generally continued in spite of Anglo disapproval. The immensely popular fandangos, which prudish whites considered to be dens of inequity that promoted drunkenness and prostitution, were the focus of a years-long campaign by moral reformers, but eventually survived, subject to municipal regulation.[12]

The new white majority would nonetheless alter forever the character of San Antonio, and it would do so with help from the federal government. Giving rise to a whole ecosystem of contractors and subcontractors that included sutlers, saddle makers, carpenters, stonemasons, and blacksmiths, the town's military base would be the key driver of the local economy well into the twentieth century. The army quickly set about making much-needed capital improvements to a town scarred by generations of war. Renting the Alamo from the Catholic Church, it converted the old mission into a quartermaster depot. Dilapidated even before the revolt against Mexico and now little more than a ruin, the structure was initially slated for demolition, then refurbished as a cost-saving measure. The original roof of the chapel having collapsed long ago, a new one was constructed to make the building suitable for storing grain and hay. For reasons that remain obscure, the architect decided to add the distinctive arched gable, or campanulate, to the facade. The renovations left one critic unimpressed, who thought the refurbished building looked like "the headboard of a bedstead."[13]

The War Department would build scores of military installations across the state, including a string of forts along a western frontier line stretching from the Rio Grande to the headwaters of the Trinity River. Thriving communities sprouted around the new army posts almost overnight; Fort Worth and El Paso's Fort Bliss would provide the seedlings for two of the state's largest metropolitan areas. Nowhere was the federal government's ability to magically transform vast swaths of open country more evident than in South Texas, the once-lawless no-man's-land that had defied the efforts of Spain, Mexico, and Texas to settle the region. During the republic years, Corpus Christi was little more than a lonely trading post for contraband at the mouth of the Nueces River, whose proprietor, Henry Kinney, bought herds of open range cattle, most of them stolen, from vagrant bands of Mexicans, Anglos, and Indians. With the onset of the war with Mexico, it became the largest population center in South Texas, home to six thousand soldiers and civilians, with its own newspaper, a theater, and even a Masonic lodge. To supply Taylor's forces in northern Mexico, the army cut a network of roads across the South Texas chaparral and chartered a fleet of steamboats to ply the waters of the lower Rio Grande. At war's end, steamboat operators Richard King and Mifflin Kenedy parlayed the fortune they had made transporting men and supplies into a ranching empire, buying up Spanish and Mexican land grants to create the King Ranch.[14]

The army would help to make Sam Maverick rich, too. He had acquired thousands of acres in some of the remotest parts of West Texas, land that would have remained undeveloped for decades but for the War Department, which signed long-term leases to build three forts on land he owned. In 1850, the family moved into a new, two-story home on Alamo Plaza; the one on Commerce Street was filled with too many painful memories. Despite their wealth the Mavericks lived modestly, Mary devoting her energies to the establishment of an Episcopal Church, her husband serving in the state legislature. Sam's relentless ambition did not diminish with age, and he was still adding to his land empire when he died after the Civil War. Mary would outlive her husband by almost three decades, dying at the dawn of a new century, in 1898.[15]

Economic growth was an unintended benefit of the US military presence, but the army could do little to keep the peace between settlers and Indians. Like the Texas Republic, the state legislature took the position that the tribes had no right to occupy land within its borders, leaving the army to deal with the violent consequences when westward-moving whites pushed into Indian hunting grounds. Comanche raids on Texas frontier settlements and Mexican border towns continued, but increasingly they were attacks borne of desperation. Overhunting had decimated the buffalo, and a prolonged period of drought kept the herds that once ranged deep into Texas up on the High Plains. Faced with starvation, the Penatekas for the first time began to steal cattle along with the usual horses, mules, and captives. For more than a decade, the southern edge of the Edwards Plateau had been a red line for the Penatekas, one they had fought to keep whites from crossing. But with the buffalo gone there was little reason to defend their old hunting grounds. In 1847, Buffalo Hump and other Comanche headmen bowed to the gloomy reality, signing a treaty with German immigrants that allowed them to settle the Hill Country west of Austin in exchange for three thousand dollars' worth of gifts.[16]

In the end, disease took the greatest toll on the Penatekas. In 1849, the cholera epidemic that had carried off young Augusta Maverick swept through the Plains tribes like a prairie wildfire, carried along overland trails by Americans on their way to northern California. Poor sanitation in Comanche rancherías made the disease, known to the Indians as the "big cramps," especially deadly, resulting in a staggering 40 percent decrease in population.[17]

In the mid-1850s, the federal government reached an arrangement with the state legislature to create two reservations on the Upper Brazos River, about seventy-five miles northwest of Fort Worth. In all, US Indian agents relocated about two thousand Indians to the Brazos Reserve, where they learned agricultural techniques, stock-raising, and attended an English-language school. The Wichitas came in willingly, grateful for the opportunity to farm plots of land under the protection of the federal government. The nomadic Comanches and the Tonkawas took considerably more coaxing. Though several groups agreed to relocate to the Brazos Reserve, they did not adapt well to the new sedentary way of life.[18]

Buffalo Hump never did come in. He occasionally appeared at the reserve trading house to ask for food and supplies, always promising Indian agents that he would return permanently after one more buffalo hunt. Still revered among his people for staying true to the old ways, he was nonetheless a relic of a bygone age, as the tribe looked to men who could negotiate more effectively with federal and state authorities. The charismatic chief who a decade earlier had swept down the Guadalupe Valley with a thousand warriors now led a few dozen destitute families who raided just to stay alive. Hounded by the US Army, Buffalo Hump and his people were eventually forced north into Kansas. The fate of the reservation Indians was hardly better. As the line of settlement bulged inexorably westward, the age-old problem of whites trespassing on Indian lands returned, and the US Army was obliged to move them again, into Indian Territory above the Red River.[19]

With news of the discovery of gold in California, a significant portion of the adventurer class, including some of the noisier, ambitious men who had come to Texas to make a name for themselves in the 1830s, quickly decamped, setting out for a new frontier and new opportunities. Thomas Jefferson Green was one of them, still consumed by his pursuit of the main chance. "He left in something of a hurry," Sam Houston would later remark snidely, "not much regretted by some, and much wanted by others."[20]

Adding "prospector" to his long list of failed occupations, Green was back in Texas by the early 1850s to promote a railroad venture. Time had not cooled the bitter feud between the two men. Houston used his considerable political clout to block the scheme, and in the summer of 1854 denounced his longtime nemesis from the floor of the US Senate in a stem-winder lasting over an hour. Green quickly fired back in a similar vein with a sixty-seven-page pamphlet, presenting a compendium of the senator's crimes, shortcomings, and "life-time of iniquity." Determined to have the last word, Houston delivered another anti-Green speech a few months later. "I would not advise any decent and respectable person to touch him with a fifteen-foot pole," Houston declared, "unless he had gloves upon his hands of double thickness, and then he should cast away the pole to avoid the influence of the contaminating shock."[21]

While some Texans headed for California, thousands of white Americans poured into the state to begin new lives as farmers and stock-raisers. Overwhelmingly, they hailed from the Southern states, and in especially large numbers from the cotton-growing regions of the Lower South. Though most would experience only marginal improvement in their economic condition, some grew rich with the sharp rise of cotton prices after the war. No longer confined to the Brazos River valley, the plantation system began to slowly extend into areas once home to Native peoples, creeping westward to the banks of the Colorado River, and northward, up the Trinity River and into East Texas. Building Greek Revival–style mansions that eclipsed in elegance the homes of the first genera-tion of planters, including even William Wharton's Eagle Island, the state's new cotton lords enjoyed enormous influence, knitting the Texas's political and economic interests tightly to those of the Lower South.

The fastest-growing population after statehood, however, was not the families who sought to cash in on the cotton boom, but the men and women needed to pick the crop. More and more, Texas slavery began to assume the character of the "peculiar institution" in the United States. For the first time, Texas farmers had access to a steady supply of enslaved labor, bringing the illegal trade of African-born people to an end. Runaways continued to find a safe haven in Mexico, much to the anger of Texas authorities, who or-ganized a slave-catching expedition that crossed the Rio Grande in 1855 and burned one of the villas del norte, Piedras Negras, causing an international incident. Nonetheless, enslaved people constituted one-third of the state's population by the Civil War, and a majority in many cotton-growing counties. Along the Lower

Brazos, where some planters began to devote some of their arable land to the cultivation of sugar, more than two-thirds of the population were enslaved.[22]

After statehood, conditions continued to deteriorate for free blacks, although, as in the republic period, considerable daylight existed between the letter of the law and its application. While the Texas Supreme Court upheld the earlier ruling that unenslaved African Americans could not reside in the state, few efforts were made to enforce the statute. Nonetheless the legislature passed a raft of new laws decreeing harsh punishments for minor offences once reserved only for slaves, including branding, whipping, and forced labor on public works. Acting on the belief that slavery was the "natural condition" for men and women of African descent, lawmakers would eventually pass a law encouraging free persons of color to reenter slavery voluntarily, allowing them to choose their own masters. It was this conviction that led O. M. Roberts, a justice on the high court, to declare that "Negroes are, in this country, *prima facie* slaves." Not surprisingly, the number of unenslaved African Americans in Texas would decline after annexation, with fewer than four hundred on the eve of the Civil War, far less than any other Southern state.[23]

As always, William Goyens proved the exception to the rule. The Cherokees were gone, and his services as an Indian negotiator and translator were no longer required. But he still enjoyed the confidence of the state's two senators, Sam Houston and Thomas Jefferson Rusk, insulating him, at least to some extent, from the resentment of his white neighbors. After statehood he kept a low profile, tending to his varied business interests from his home on Goyens Hill. As he had done throughout his successful career, he did not hesitate to use the courts for redress, expending much of his energy, as well as his income, on costly litigation. Anglo courts were rarely disposed to rule in his favor, but Goyens appears to have been motivated as much by principle as practical considerations. It still bothered him that the Land Office of the Texas Republic had rejected his claim to a forty-six-hundred-acre headright, so in 1852 he tried one more time, appealing to the state legislature. Texas lawmakers again failed to act on his petition. Goyens's wife, Mary, died in February 1856. He joined her four months later, at the age of sixty-two, leaving an estate that included more than twelve thousand acres of land.[24]

Goyens's Nacogdoches would not reap the benefits of the state's cotton boom. San Augustine and two new towns, Jefferson and Marshall, offered better access to the water routes that planters needed to transport their crop to market. American emigrants still passed through Nacogdoches along the old Camino Real, but now many came by sea, landing at Galveston and Matagorda. The town had ceased to be a frontier marketplace after the expulsion of the Cherokees and the immigrant tribes, and while a few Hispano families stayed after Vicente Córdova's rebellion, they played a negligible a role in civic life. Dismissed by the American community as "harmless vagabonds," they lived in impoverished anonymity on the outskirts of town. Now indistinguishable from the many villages carved into the Piney Woods, Nacogdoches bore little evidence of the multiracial character that once made it unique.[25]

BY THIS TIME, OF COURSE, THERE WASN'T MUCH LEFT OF THE complex system of overlapping borderland communities that existed under Mexican rule. Anglo-Texans were left to tell the story of Texas themselves, and the story they told, naturally enough, was one in which they played a starring role. Nonwhites greatly outnumbered whites during the early years of Anglo immigration. And they probably still outnumbered them, if only barely, during the struggle for independence. But in this retelling of the past, people of color appeared as obstacles to Anglo settlement or not at all. In the late nineteenth century, a cult of the pioneer emerged, with the publication of literally scores of memoirs from grizzled old-timers that recalled in vivid detail the brutalizing, hard-fought conflicts before Texas became a state. Historical preservation groups such as the Daughters of the Republic of Texas, enthralled by tales of a ragtag band of rebels locked in a desperate struggle against Santa Anna's legions at the Alamo and San Jacinto, and of frontier folk fending off merciless bands of Indians, vowed to keep the memory of the Texas pioneers alive to inspire and instruct future generations.

It was a compelling narrative, one that resonated not only with Anglo-Texans, but with a great many Americans, assuming a prominent place in the nation's historical consciousness. Compelling or not, there has always been something deeply weird about the American infatuation with the state's early modern past. For one thing, the events for which Texas became celebrated occurred well before it joined the Union; the struggle for independence was as much a Mexican story as it was an American one. The portrayal of Anglo-Texans bravely defending a homeland seemed equally disconnected from reality, since most settlers barely had time to put down roots in the area, and many had only just arrived. But all this seemed entirely beside the point to an increasingly urban, industrializing nation, which saw the region as a symbol of its frontiering past, a microcosm of the world it believed it had lost.

In fact, Texas was hardly typical of that past. Americans embraced the Texas creation myth because it seemed to offer, more than anywhere else in their push across the continent, the high drama of an embattled people engaged in a life-or-death struggle for survival. The contest between whites, Mexicans, and Indians for control of the land beyond the Sabine came to be seen as a test of the nation's core beliefs, a proving ground where white Americans defended Anglo-Saxon values against the enemies of civilization and progress. Deeply imbedded in the "epic" character of the Texas Revolution and its aftermath was an unspoken endorsement of white American cultural and racial superiority.

Only rarely did the guardians of the Texas creation myth say the quiet part out loud. But when they did, few would express the enduring appeal of the state's past more clearly than Clara Driscoll. A ranching heiress and founding member of the Daughters of the Republic of Texas, Driscoll would wage a lifelong crusade to preserve the Alamo, "the shrine of Texas liberty," and immortalize the men who died there. Speaking of the stalwart pioneers who, more than three quarters of a century earlier, defended Texas against an advancing Mexican army, she praised the "spirit of patriotism, the love of home and country" that guided them. And to these ennobling sentiments she added still another motive. They had fought to make Texas "a decent place in which a white man could live."[26]

ACKNOWLEDGMENTS

THE IDEA FOR THIS BOOK GREW OUT OF THE FORTY-EIGHTH annual Walter Prescott Webb Memorial Lecture series at the University of Texas at Arlington back in 2013. Titled "Contested Empire: Rethinking the Texas Revolution," the conference brought together a group of historians who offered new perspectives on an especially well-worn topic. I'd like to thank the scholars involved in the symposium—Will Fowler, Amy Greenberg, Miguel Soto, Eric Schlereth, and Gregg Cantrell—who made me realize that there is still a lot left to say about the founding of early modern Texas. A digital humanities project on nineteenth-century interethnic violence in the region, "Border Land: The Struggle for Texas," sponsored by UTA's Center for Greater Southwestern Studies, also helped me develop a better understanding of the role Native Americans played during this crucial period. In addition to the Summerlee Foundation, which provided seed money for the project, I'd like to acknowledge the many UTA history graduate students, too numerous to mention here, who since 2015 helped me develop the Border Land research database. The UTA Library web development team, Ramona Holmes, Andrew Leverenz, and Krystal Schenk, deserve special mention for bringing the project online.

I was indeed fortunate to receive a 2019–20 Clements Senior Fellowship for the Study of Southwestern America from the William P. Clements Center for Southwest Studies at Southern Methodist

University. Although my time at Dallas Hall was cut short, sadly, by the pandemic, I am grateful for the support and fellowship of the folks at the Clements Center, Andy Graybill, Neil Foley, and Ruth Ann Elmore, as well as Ed Countryman and graduate students Patrick Troester and Kyle Carpenter in the SMU history department. I also received financial support from my home institution, the University of Texas at Arlington, in the form of two faculty development leaves. I owe a special debt of gratitude to my administrative assistant at UTA's Center for Greater Southwestern Studies, Barbara Moore. She tracked down illustrations for the book, secured publication rights, transcribed documents, handled research travel arrangements, and, most importantly, kept me organized—no easy task.

I have benefited from the wisdom and expertise of several members of my department and the UTA College of Liberal Arts, especially Paul Conrad, Andy Milson, Gerald Saxon, David Narrett, Steve Maizlish, Chris Conway, and Ken Roemer. My editor at Basic Books, Brian Distelberg, and his assistant, Michael Kaler, offered suggestions that have made this manuscript immeasurably better. Kate Blackmer was a joy to work with on the maps; Kaitlin Carruthers-Busser was an unfailingly patient project editor. At various stages of this project I've also benefited from the input of Frank de la Teja, Ana Dekeyser, and Todd Smith, while Jimmy Bryan and Jeff Dunn gave the manuscript a careful reading and saved me from many an error. Marissa Caputo, Catherine Clinton, and Chas Haynes gave me a place to stay while doing research in Austin, San Antonio, and Houston. Finally, this is as good a time as any to give a special thanks to Chris Morris. My friend and colleague for the better part of three decades, he has been an invaluable sounding board on pretty much everything I've written during my career at UTA, and this project was certainly no exception.

Much of the work on this book was completed during the pandemic, and I am enormously grateful to the archivists who scanned materials for me when in-person visits were not possible. Fortunately, during the time many archives were closed I did have access to UTA Library's Special Collections, one of the better repositories for

Texas materials, and I am indebted to all the people who work there, especially Brenda McClurkin, Ben Huseman, and Beverly Carver. I also taxed the patience of archivists at the Dolph Briscoe Center for American History, the Nettie Lee Benson Latin American Collection, the Texas State Library and Archives Commission, the Daughters of the Republic of Texas Library Collection, the Helmerich Center for American Research at the Gilcrease Museum, the Ralph Steen Library at Stephen F. Austin University, and the Eugene P. Watson Memorial Library at Northwestern State University. I'd also like to thank Michael Daily at the Brazos County Historical Museum, James Glover and Jennifer Parsley at the Stephen F. Austin-Munson County Park, Aubrey Nielsen at the Brownsville Historical Association, Suzette Raney at the Chattanooga Public Library, and Carolyn Taylor at the Driscoll Foundation in Corpus Christi.

Finally, I'd like to thank my family for their support and interest in this project. My wife, Lisa, to whom this book is dedicated, was a source of ceaseless encouragement. She read the manuscript twice, thoroughly each time, making terrific suggestions on both style and substance every step of the way. I benefited especially from her own detective work into the lives of Lorenzo and Emily Zavala. I've never felt the need to thank a family pet before, and I doubt he'll ever read this, but my dog, Riddick, and I "sheltered in place" for a year and a half while I was writing this manuscript, and I'm not sure I could have done it without him. I should probably thank my son, Adrian, too, who says he read it, though I'm not sure he did. His only suggestion was that it needed more emojis. Who knows? He may have been right.

NOTES

ABBREVIATIONS

AHQ: *Arkansas Historical Quarterly*

AP: Eugene C. Barker, ed., *The Austin Papers* (Washington, DC: Government Printing Office, 1924).

BA: Béxar Archives

BCAH: Dolph Briscoe Center for American History, University of Texas at Austin

BLAC: Benson Latin American Collection, University of Texas at Austin

BRC: [Nacogdoches Archives] *Robert Bruce Blake Research Collection*, 75 vols., 18 suppl. vols.

ETHJ: *East Texas Historical Journal*

JAH: *Journal of American History*

JER: *Journal of the Early Republic*

JNH: *Journal for Negro History*

LHQ: *Louisiana Historical Quarterly*

QTSHA: *Quarterly of the Texas State Historical Association*

PML: Charles Adams Gulick, ed., *The Papers of Mirabeau Buonaparte Lamar*, vols. 1–6 (Austin: A. C. Baldwin, 1921).

PTR: John H. Jenkins, ed., *The Papers of the Texas Revolution, 1835–36*, vols. 1–10 (Austin: Presidial Press, 1973).

RSL: Ralph W. Steen Library, Stephen F. Austin University

SHC: Southern Historical Collection, University of North Carolina, Chapel Hill

SHQ: *Southwestern Historical Quarterly*

THQ: *Tennessee Historical Quarterly*

TSLAC: Texas State Library and Archives Commission

WHQ: *Western Historical Quarterly*

WSH: Eugene C. Barker and Amelia Williams, eds., *The Writings of Sam Houston, 1813–1863* vols. 1–8 (Austin: University of Texas Press, 1938).

INTRODUCTION

1. Eduard Ludecus, and Louis E. Brister, ed., *John Charles Beales's Rio Grande Colony: Letters by Eduard Ludecus . . .* (Austin: Texas State Historical Association, 2008), 136–139. For more on the ill-fated Beales colony, see Kyle Carpenter, "A Failed Venture in the Nueces Strip: Misconceptions and Mismanagement of the Beales Rio Grande Colony, 1832–1836," *SHQ* 123, no. 4 (2020): 421–444; and William Kennedy, *Texas: The Rise, Progress, and Prospects of the Republic of Texas . . .* London: R. Hastings, 1841), 390–420.

2. Ludecus, *Rio Grande Colony*, 118.

3. Ibid., 67, 71.

4. The Las Moras Creek area where the Beales colony was located is still uninhabited today. The closest population center is Quemado, Texas, about ten miles away, an unincorporated community with a population of less than 150 people.

5. Three decades ago, Paul Lack took scholars and popular historians of the Texas Revolution to task for perpetuating the traditional heroic narrative, arguing that the "suffocating power" of this creation story has had the effect of stifling new research in the field. See Paul D. Lack, "In the Long Shadow of Eugene C. Barker," in *Texas Through Time: Evolving Interpretations*, Walter L. Buenger and Robert A. Calvert, eds. (College Station: Texas A&M University Press, 1991), 134–164. Lack's own work remains the most thorough analysis of the revolution. See Paul D. Lack, *The Texas Revolutionary Experience: A Political and Social History, 1835–1836* (College Station: Texas A&M University Press, 1992). Despite the dearth of scholarly work on the subject, some historians have managed to break new ground by situating these events in a larger, North American context. Two works that examine the upheaval in Texas as part of the broader set of conflicts experienced by the First Mexican Republic are David J. Weber, *The Mexican Frontier, 1821–1846: The American Southwest Under Mexico* (Albuquerque: University of New Mexico Press, 1982), 158–178, 242–255; and Andrés Reséndez, *Changing National Identities at the Frontier: Texas and New Mexico, 1800–1850* (Cambridge: Cambridge University Press, 2005), 146–170. For a study that places early modern Texas in the history of the plantation economy of the American South, see Andrew J. Torget, *Seeds of Empire: Cotton, Slavery, and the Transformation of the Texas Borderlands, 1800–1850* (Chapel Hill: University of North Carolina Press, 2015). See also Sam W. Haynes and Gerald D. Saxon, eds., *Contested Empire: Rethinking the Texas Revolution*

(College Station: Texas A&M University Press, 2015). For a full-throated if less scholarly repudiation of the heroic narrative, see Jeff Long, *Duel of Eagles: the Mexican and U.S. Fight for the Alamo* (New York: Morrow, 1990); and Bryan Burrough, Chris Tomlinson, and Jason Stanford, *Forget the Alamo: The Rise and Fall of an American Myth* (New York: Penguin Press, 2021).

6. The Texas Republic era has attracted surprisingly little attention from scholars and popular writers. For two important, if traditional, studies of this period, see William Ransom Hogan, *The Texas Republic: A Social and Economic History* (Norman: University of Oklahoma Press, 1946); and Stanley Siegel, *A Political History of the Texas Republic, 1836–1845* (Austin: University of Texas Press, 1956). See also Charles Swanlund and Kenneth Wayne Howell, eds., *Single Star of the West: The Republic of Texas, 1836–1845* (Denton: University of North Texas Press, 2017).

CHAPTER ONE. WHAT MUST BE DONE WITH US POOR INDIANS?

1. John H. Reagan, *Memoirs, with Special Reference to Secession and the Civil War* (Austin: Pemberton Press, 1968), 35.

2. Often referred to as Duwali by Texas historians, Bowls frequently appears in the historical record before his emigration to the West. He signed at least three treaties with the United States, making his mark with an *X*, leaving US Indian agents to spell his name phonetically. He is listed as Too wayelloh at the 1791 Treaty of Holston, as Tulio at the second Treaty of Tellico Blockhouse in 1804, and as Toowayullau at the third Tellico treaty in 1805. See Charles J. Kappler, comp. and ed., *Indian Affairs: Laws and Treaties*, Vol. II (Treaties) (Washington, DC: Government Printing Office, 1904), 32, 74, and 84. I refer to him throughout this book as Bowls, the name by which he was known to Anglo-Texans, as well as many Western Cherokees.

3. In 1801, Indian agent Russell Meigs reported that Bowls had "five spinners in his family" who produced "ninety yards of Cotton Cloth from Cotton of his own raising." William G. McLoughlin, *Cherokee Renascence in the New Republic* (Princeton: Princeton University Press, 1986), 63. For more on Cherokee gender roles, see Theda Perdue, *Cherokee Women: Gender and Culture Change, 1700-1835* (Lincoln: University of Nebraska Press, 1998).

4. A very different story of Bowls's westward migration is told by Cephas Washburn, who incorrectly identified Bowls as the leader of an attack on a party of whites on the Tennessee River in 1794 known as the Muscle Shoals Massacre. See Cephas Washburn, *Reminiscences of the Indians* (Richmond: Presbyterian Committee of Publication, 1869), 76–78. According to Washburn's version of events, accepted uncritically by many historians, Bowls fled west after the incident to escape punishment. For a corrective to this account, see Robert A. Myers, "Cherokee Pioneers in Arkansas: The St. Francis Years, 1785–1813," *AHQ* 56, no. 2 (1997): 127–157.

5. Dianna Everett, "Ethnohistory of the Western Cherokees in Texas," PhD diss., Texas Tech University, 1985, 115–116. For more on this early Cherokee migration, see Kathleen DuVal, *The Native Ground: Indians and Colonists in the Heart of the Continent* (Philadelphia: University of Pennsylvania Press, 2006), 196–200; and McLoughlin, *Cherokee Renascence*, 146–167.

6. Jay Feldman, *When the Mississippi Ran Backwards: Empire, Intrigue, Murder, and the New Madrid Earthquakes* (New York: Free Press, 2005), 471; Myers, "Cherokee Pioneers in Arkansas," 154.

7. Willard H. Rollings, *The Osage: An Ethnohistorical Study of Hegemony on the Prairie-Plains* (Columbia: University of Missouri Press, 1992), 237; Grant Foreman, ed., "The Cherokee War Path," *Chronicles of Oklahoma* 9 (September 1931): 241 (quotation). For more on Cherokee practices of blood revenge, see Thomas Nuttal, *A Journal of Travels into the Arkansa Territory* (Ann Arbor: University Microfilms, 1966), 133–134; McLoughlin, *Cherokee Renascence*, 12–13. For more on Cherokee war rituals, see Susan Marie Abram, "Souls in the Treetops: Cherokee War, Masculinity, and Community, 1760–1820," PhD diss., Auburn University, 2009, 20–35.

8. *Niles Weekly Register* (Baltimore), September 27, 1817, 74; Rollings, *The Osage*, 239–240.

9. Grant Foreman, *Indians and Pioneers: The Story of the American Southwest Before 1830* (New Haven: Yale University Press, 1930), 58; Edwin C. Bearss, "In Quest of Peace on the Indian Border: The Establishment of Fort Smith," *AHQ* 23, no. 2 (Summer 1964), 150–152.

10. This account of Cherokee pre-battle rituals is drawn from the memoir of a warrior who took part in the attack on a Tawakoni village in Texas in May 1829. Foreman, ed., "The Cherokee War Path," 242, 253–254.

11. Rollings, *The Osage*, 239–240; Foreman, *Indians and Pioneers*, 51; Bearss, "In Quest of Peace on the Indian Border," 151.

12. Gregory D. Smithers, *The Cherokee Diaspora: An Indigenous History of Migration, Resettlement, and Identity* (New Haven: Yale University Press, 2015), 27–57.

13. C. Daniel Crews and Richard W. Starbuck, *Records of the Moravians Among the Cherokees, Volume One: Early Contact and the Establishment of the First Mission, 1752–1802* (University of Oklahoma Press, 2010), 1:244.

14. Ibid., 1:132, 1:155; Penelope Allen, "The Fields Settlement," *History of the Cherokees*, Chattanooga-Hamilton County Bicentennial Library, 514–516. For consistency, I refer to the land above the Red River as US Indian Territory, although it was known as the Arkansas Territory from 1819 until 1836.

15. Everett, "Western Cherokees," 159–166; Emmet Starr, *History of the Cherokee Indians and Their Legends and Folk Lore* (Oklahoma City: Warden Company, 1921), 187.

16. In the following pages, I have opted to use the term Hispano to refer to the Mexican inhabitants of Texas, taking the view that "Tejano," though

widely used by historians today, ascribes to them a regional identity they did not possess in the first half of the nineteenth century. The Mexicans of East Texas had little contact with those in San Antonio during this period, while many Bexareños were part of commercial and kinship networks with Mexican communities below the Rio Grande. For a description of Texas when Bowls led his band of Western Cherokees across the Red River, see Juan Antonio Padilla, and Mattie Austin Hatcher, trans., "Texas in 1820," *SHQ* 23, no. 1 (1919): 61. For more on American filibustering activity in Texas, see Gaylord Harris Warren, *The Sword Was Their Passport: A History of American Filibustering in the Mexican Revolution* (Baton Rouge: Louisiana State University Press, 1943).

17. The exodus of Native Americans from the United States into Texas in the early decades of the nineteenth century has not attracted the attention from scholars that it deserves. For a helpful overview of this migration, see F. Todd Smith, *From Dominance to Disappearance: The Indians of Texas and the Near Southwest, 1786–1859* (Lincoln: University of Nebraska Press, 2005), 67–72, 115–118.

18. For a good firsthand account of the Native peoples of Texas at this time, see Padilla, "Texas in 1820," 47–58. See also Jean Louis Berlandier, *The Indians of Texas in 1830* (Washington, DC: Smithsonian Institution Press, 1969); and José Francisco Ruíz, *Report on the Indian Tribes of Texas in 1828* (New Haven: Yale University Library, 1972). For a comprehensive overview of the many Native peoples of Texas, see William W. Newcomb, *The Indians of Texas from Prehistoric to Modern Times* (Austin: University of Texas Press, 2002).

19. Reagan, *Memoirs*, 31.

20. Manuel de Mier y Terán, Jack Jackson, ed., and John Wheat, trans., *Texas by Terán: The Diary Kept by General Manuel de Mier y Terán on His 1828 Inspection of Texas* (Austin: University of Texas Press, 2000), 80.

21. Gregg Cantrell, *Stephen F. Austin: Empresario of Texas* (Austin: Texas State Historical Association, 2016), 80–103.

22. Fields to Martinez, February 1, 1822, BA. Ernest William Winkler, "The Cherokee Indians in Texas," *QTSHA* 7, no. 2 (1903): 98–99.

23. C. A. Hutchinson, "General José Antonio Mexía and His Texas Interests," *SHQ* 82, no. 2 (1978): 118.

24. Visitors to Texas in the 1820s and 1830s wrote extensively on the region's natural environment. A good starting point is Jean Louis Berlandier, *Journey to Mexico during the years 1826 to 1834* (Austin: Texas State Historical Association, 1980), volume two. The region's buffalo and pronghorn antelope herds are described in Dilue Harris, "Reminiscences of Mrs. Dilue Harris, II," *QTSHA* 4, no. 3 (1901): 161; William B. Dewees, *Letters from an Early Settler of Texas* (Louisville: Morton and Griswold, 1852), 26.

25. On the Battle of Medina, see Bradley Folsom, *Arredondo: Last Spanish Ruler of Texas and Northeastern New Spain* (Norman: University of Oklahoma Press, 2017), 81–94; Hatcher and Padilla, "Texas in 1820," 61.

26. For recent scholarship on Comanche dominance of New Spain's far northern frontier, see Pekka Hämäläinen, *The Comanche Empire* (New Haven: Yale University Press, 2008), chs. 4–5; and Brian DeLay, *War of a Thousand Deserts: Indian Raids and the US-Mexican War* (New Haven: Yale University Press, 2008), 2–85.

27. Some confusion exists as to the name of the Comanche band that inhabited south central Texas. Brian Delay uses the term Hois, or "Timber People," arguing that the term Penateka does not come into widespread usage until the US-Mexico War in 1846. Delay, *War of a Thousand Deserts*, 351. On the Comanche horse and mule trade into the United States, see Austin to Bustamante [?], May 10, 1822, *AP*, 1:507. On Comanche captive-taking, see Joaquín Rivaya-Martínez, "A Different Look at Native American Depopulation: Comanche Raiding, Captive Taking, and Population Decline," *Ethnohistory* 61, no. 3 (2014): 391 -418.

28. Winkler, "The Cherokee Indians in Texas," 100–102.

29. Ibid., 102–103, 118. Hutchinson, "José Antonio Mexía," 118. For English translations of the Trespalacios-Fields agreement and Trespalacios's letter introducing the Indians to the governor of Coahuila, see "Agreement between the Captain of the Cherokee Nation and the Governor of Texas," November 8, 1822, and Trespalacios to Lopez, November 8, 1822, *BRC* 8(supp.): 319–321.

CHAPTER TWO. INNOCENTS ABROAD

1. Myron J. Echenberg, *Humboldt's Mexico: In the Footsteps of the Illustrious German Scientific Traveller* (Montreal: McGill-Queen's University Press, 2017), xxii. For more on living conditions for Mexico City's poorer classes, see Frederick John Shaw, Jr., "Poverty and Politics in Mexico City, 1824–1854," PhD diss., University of Florida, 1975.

2. For a discussion of the political debates in Mexico over the need to colonize Texas in the immediate aftermath of independence, see Nettie Lee Benson, "Texas as Viewed from Mexico, 1820–1834," *SHQ* 90, no. 3 (1987): 219–239; and Joseph Carl McElhannon, "Imperial Mexico and Texas, 1821–1823," *SHQ* 53, no. 2 (1949): 138–150.

3. Henry S. Foote, *Texas and the Texans; or, Advance of the Anglo-Americans to the South-West* . . . (Philadelphia: Thomas, Cowperthwait & Co., 1841), 1:215; Jordan Oliver Holt, "The Edwards Empresarial Grant and the Fredonian Rebellion," MA thesis, Stephen F. Austin State University, 1977, 213.

4. S. F. Austin to J. E. B. Austin, June 13, 1823, *AP*, 1:671 (quotation). Cantrell, *Stephen F. Austin*, 115–116.

5. Gary Clayton Anderson, *The Conquest of Texas: Ethnic Cleansing in the Promised Land, 1820–1875* (Norman: University of Oklahoma Press, 2005), 61; Winkler, "The Cherokee Indians in Texas," 102–107.

6. Hutchinson, "José Antonio Mexía," 119.

7. Information Derived from Hayden Edwards, *PML*, 3:258–259; Winkler, "The Cherokee Indians in Texas," 102–107; Allen, "The Fields Settlement," 519.

8. Hutchinson, "José Antonio Mexía," 119–120.

9. Charles A. Hale, *Mexican Liberalism in the Age of Mora, 1821–1853* (New Haven: Yale University Press, 1968), 23–27. For a useful if highly critical review of Zavala's early life and involvement in the affairs of Texas, see Alfonso Toro, *Dos Constituyentes Del Año De 1824: Biografías De Don Miguel Ramos Arizpe y Don Lorenzo Zavala* (México: Talleres Gráficos del Museo Nacional de Arqueología, Historia, y Ethnografía, 1925), 85–117. For a deep dive into Zavala's political career, see Raymond Estep, "The Life of Lorenzo de Zavala," PhD diss., University of Texas, 1942. A revised, published version of the dissertation is available in Spanish, *Lorenzo de Zavala: Profeta Del Liberalismo Mexicano* (México: Librería de M. Porrúa, 1952). The only full-length biography of Zavala in English is Margaret Swett Henson, *Lorenzo de Zavala: The Pragmatic Idealist* (Fort Worth: Texas Christian University Press, 1996).

10. J. Mecham, "The Origins of Federalism in Mexico," *Hispanic American Historical Review* 18, no. 2 (1938): 164–182.

11. Benson, "Texas as Viewed from Mexico," 219–239.

12. Winkler, "The Cherokee Indians in Texas," 131.

13. Winkler, "The Cherokee Indians in Texas," 114.

14. Everett, "Western Cherokees," 204–205.

15. On the founding of the Austin colony, see Eugene C. Barker, *The Life of Stephen F. Austin, Founder of Texas, 1793–1836: A Chapter in the Westward Movement of the Anglo-American People* (Austin: University of Texas Press, 1969), 80–118; and Cantrell, *Stephen F. Austin*, 132–170.

16. On Tonkawa and Karankawa relations with the Spanish in the late eighteenth century, see Kelly F. Himmel, *The Conquest of the Karankawas and the Tonkawas, 1821–1859* (College Station: Texas A&M University Press, 1999), 37–61.

17. "Journal of Stephen F. Austin on His First Trip to Texas, 1821," *QTSHA* 7, no. 4 (1904): 297 (first quotation), 305 (second and third quotations). For more on the Franciscans' unfavorable opinion of the coastal Indians of Texas, see Tim Seiter, "Why Are The Karankawa Indians Remembered as Savage Cannibals?" https://texoso66.com/2019/09/24/why-are-the-karankawa-indians-remembered-as-savage-cannibals/.

18. Noah Smithwick, *The Evolution of a State, or, Recollections of Old Texas Days* (Austin: University of Texas Press, 1983), 3 (quotation). Austin to Ahumada, September 19, 1825, *AP*, 1:1198. For more on the Karankawas, see Albert S. Gatschet, *The Karankawa Indians, the Coast People of Texas* (Cambridge: Peabody Museum of American Archaeology and Ethnology, 1891).

19. Austin to Bell, December 6, 1823, *AP*, 1:716 (first quotation); Austin to Wharton, April 24, 1829, *AP*, 2:212 (second quotation). On the controversy arising from the twelve and a half cent surcharge, and the colonists' ill feeling toward Austin as a result, see Barker, *Life of Stephen F. Austin*, 97–106.

20. Fields to Saucedo, March 6, 1824, BA. Emmet Starr, *Cherokees "West," 1794–1839* (Claremore, OK: 1910), 149; Everett, "Western Cherokees," 207–208; and Fields to Gegin [*sic*], August 12, 1824, *BRC*, 10:376.

21. Winkler, "The Cherokee Indians in Texas," 126–127.

22. Austin to Saucedo, September 8, 1825, *AP*, 1:1195 (quotation).

23. John Dunn Hunter, *Memoirs of a Captivity Among the Indians of North America* . . . (London: Longman, Hurst, Rees, Orme, and Brown, 1823). For more on John Dunn Hunter's reception in England, see Anna Maria Stirling and Diana Wilhelmina Pickering, *Coke of Norfolk and His Friends* (London, New York: Lane, 1912), 2:316–320 (quotation on 319). The charge that Hunter was an imposter who had never lived among the Indians stemmed from a scathing review of his book by Lewis Cass, then governor of the Michigan Territory. See Lewis Cass, "Manners and Customs of Several Indian Tribes, located West of the Mississippi, by John D. Hunter . . . ," *North American Review* 22 (January 1826): 53–119. For a contemporary defense of Hunter, see Foote, *Texas and the Texans*, 1:240–247. For more recent studies of the controversy, see John T. Fierst, "Rationalizing Removal: Anti-Indianism in Lewis Cass's *North American Review* Essays," *Michigan Historical Review* 36, no. 2 (2010): 1–35; and Richard Drinnon, *White Savage: The Case of John Dunn Hunter* (New York: Schocken Books, 1972), chs. 6–7.

24. Hunter, *Memoirs*, 460.

25. Ibid., 45–48. Why Fields did not send Hunter to Saltillo instead of the nation's capital remains a mystery, since the national colonization law made it clear that all land grant decisions would now be made by the state legislatures. Early in 1827 the military commander of Texas wrote to Fields as follows: "I am informed that in Mexico you were told to visit the State of Coahuila and Texas and select the lands that pleased you for your settlement and apply for them immediately. If you have not selected them, and not asked for them, it is not the fault of the Government." Ahumada to Fields, January 4, 1827, *AP*, 1:1561–1562.

26. H. G. Ward, *Mexico in 1827* (London: H Colburn, 1828), 1:309; Drinnon, *White Savage*, 185.

27. For Poinsett's controversial tenure as US minister to Mexico, see José Maria Herrera, "The Blueprint for Hemispheric Hegemony: Joel Roberts Poinsett and the First United States Diplomatic Mission to Mexico," PhD diss., Purdue University, 2007. For Poinsett's role in the creation of the York Rite Lodge in Mexico, see J. Fred Rippy, *Joel R. Poinsett, Versatile American* (Durham, N.C: Duke University Press, 1935), 122–123.

28. Herrera, "Blueprint for Hemispheric Hegemony," 222.

29. Winkler, "The Cherokee Indians in Texas," 131.

30. Winkler, "The Cherokee Indians in Texas," 131; Everett, "Western Cherokees," 214.

31. Fields to Commandant of Béxar, April 22, 1825, BA; Fields to the Alcalde of Nacogdoches, n.d., *BRC*, 11:193–194.

32. Alcalde of Nacogdoches to Political Chief, August 22, 1826, *BRC*, 11:193.

33. Diane Elizabeth Prince, "William Goyens: Free Negro on the Texas Frontier," MA thesis, Stephen F. Austin University, 1975, 38; Austin to Saucedo, September 8, 1825, *AP*, 2:1195; Everett, "Western Cherokees," 208.

34. Bean to Austin, December 21, 1836, *AP*, 2:1554.

CHAPTER THREE. THE RED AND WHITE REPUBLIC OF FREDONIA

1. José María Sánchez, and Carlos E. Castañeda, trans. "A Trip to Texas in 1828," *SHQ* 29, no. 4 (1926): 283. Dewees, *Letters from an Early Settler of Texas*, 20–23. "Journal of Stephen F. Austin," 289. For more on the trade between Nacogdoches and Natchitoches prior to 1821, see Matthew Babcock, "Roots of Independence: Transcultural Trade in the Texas-Louisiana Borderlands," *Ethnohistory: The Bulletin of the Ohio Valley Historic Indian Conference* 60, no. 2 (2013): 245–268. On Nacogdoches, see Sánchez, "A Trip to Texas," 283; Terán, *Texas by Terán*, 91–111.

2. Prince, "William Goyens," 35–38. Goyens is listed as William Gowings in the Cherokee regimental muster rolls. See National Park Service, "Cherokee Muster Roll from the Battle of Horseshoe Bend," March 27,1814, www.nps.gov/hobe/learn/historyculture/upload/cherokee.pdf. Goyens was a Melungeon, a term generally thought to be a corruption of the French word *mélange*. To escape the discrimination of being classified as black, Melungeons in the southeastern United States commonly claimed Portuguese ancestry. Recent genetic research has proved, however, that the group had sub-Saharan and northern European origins. Roberta J. Estes, Jack H. Goins, Penny Ferguson and Janet Lewis Crain, "Melungeons, A Multi-Ethnic Population," *Journal of Genetic Genealogy* 7 (Fall 2011). Goyens was probably a triracial isolate, of African, European, and Native American ancestry. William Goyens's father, a resident of Moore County, North Carolina, was described by Goyens's nephew as "a respectable citizen of this county, not of altogether white complection." John M. Goings Petition, July 1845, *BRC*, 50:130–131. For more on the fluid racial boundaries in colonial North Carolina, see John Spencer Bassett, *Slavery and Servitude in the Colony of North Carolina* (Baltimore: The Johns Hopkins Press, 1896), 72–74.

3. Barker, *The Life of Stephen F. Austin*, 156.

4. Commanding Officer of the Militia [Sepulveda] to Political Chief [Saucedo], March 23, 1826, *BRC*, 11:125–127.

5. Goin [Goyens] to [Court], October 25, 1826, *BRC*, 11:267; Prince, "William Goyens," 24–27. Around the same time, Austin had refused to admit English and a companion into his colony "because of the infamy of their character . . . as criminals and bad men." Austin to Political Chief, March 18, 1826, *AP*, 1:1284.

6. Holt, "Edwards Empresarial Grant," 87–88.

7. Henderson K. Yoakum, *History of Texas from its First Settlement in 1685 to its Annexation to the United States in 1846* (Austin: Steck Company, 1935), 1:249.

8. Although Edwards claimed that the rebellion was Fields's idea, Mexican authorities were already suspicious about the American's communications with the Cherokees. See Torres to Administrador de Correo, May 18, 1828, BA. For the Edwards brothers' accounts of the Fredonian Rebellion, see "Information Derived from Hayden Edwards," *PML*, 3:262–264; and B. Edwards to Gray, May 27, 1827, *The Territorial Papers of the United States* (Washington, DC: US Govt. Printing Office, 1934), 483. Henry Foote also provides a highly sympathetic account of the Edwards brothers' actions, based in part on papers given to him by Haden Edwards. Foote, *Texas and Texans*, 1:266. Holt, "Edwards Empresarial Grant," 111–112 (quotation).

9. Rick Sherrod, "The Road from Nacogdoches to Natchitoches: John Sprowl and the Failed Fredonian Rebellion," *ETHJ* 48, no. 2, article 6 (2010):23–24.

10. Torres to Ahumada, December 29, 1826, BA. The Stone House, as it was called in 1826, would be rebuilt during the 1936 Texas Centennial and renamed the Old Stone Fort. See "Old Stone Fort," Handbook of Texas, www.tshaonline.org/handbook/entries/old-stone-fort.

11. Confederation of Certain American Residents of Texas and the Cherokee and Other Tribes Against the Mexican Government, December 21, 1826, *BRC*, 11:307–309; Andy Doolen, "Claiming Indigenous Space: John Dunn Hunter and the Fredonian Rebellion," *Early American Literature* 53, no. 3 (2018): 685–712.

12. Jack Jackson, *Indian Agent: Peter Ellis Bean in Mexican Texas* (College Station: Texas A&M University Press, 2005), 67. "Edwards and Mayo to the Inhabitants of Pecan Point," December 25, 1826, *AP*, 2:1542–1545 (quotation). For more on Anglo-Texans use of the American Revolution to justify their defiance of the Mexican government during this period, see Sam W. Haynes, "Imitating the Examples of our Forefathers," in Haynes and Saxon, eds., *Contested Empire*, 32–47. On American celebrations of the nation's Jubilee year, see Andrew Burstein, *America's Jubilee: How in 1826 a Generation Remembered Fifty Years of Independence* (New York: Vintage Books, 2002).

13. Austin to Thompson, December 24, 1826, *AP*, 1:1540 (first quotation); *AP*, 1:1541 (second quotation).

14. Jackson, *Indian Agent*, 69–70.

15. Ibid., 67 (quotation); Bean to Austin, December 31, 1826, *AP*, 1554.

16. Nacogdoches Alcalde to Political Chief, January 2, 1827, *BRC*, 11:313.

17. Holt, "Edwards Empresarial Grant," 131–132.

18. "Austin to Citizens of Victoria," January 1, 1827, *AP*, 2:1558 (quotation); Foote, *Texas and Texans*, 1:266; Holt, "Edwards Empresarial Grant," 129–130.

19. Benjamin Edwards singled out the Kickapoo and their hostility toward Anglo-Americans as a major reason for the failure of the white-Indian alliance. B. Edwards to Gray, May 27, 1827, *Territorial Papers*, 483.

20. Foreman, ed., "The Cherokee War Path," 241. In this account of a Texas Cherokee war party in 1829, Bowls is mistakenly identified as "the Pan."

21. Winkler, "The Cherokee Indians in Texas," 146; Information Derived from Hayden Edwards, n.d., *PML*, 3:263.

22. Bean to Military Commander of Texas, February 7, 1827, *BRC*, 30:339.

23. Information Derived from Hayden Edwards, *PML*, 3:263; Foote, *Texas and the Texans*, 1:280 (quotation).

24. Sibley to Austin, February 18, 1827, *AP*, 1:1604–1605.

25. Jackson, *Indian Agent*, 112, 123. Military Commander of Nacogdoches to Military Commander of Texas, May 14, 1827, *BRC*, 11:378–380.

CHAPTER FOUR. AN ELYSIUM OF ROGUES

1. "Journal of J. C. Clopper, 1828," *QTSHA* 13, no. 1 (1909): 60–61.

2. Ohland Morton, "Life of General Don Manuel De Mier y Terán as it Affected Texas-Mexican Relations (Continued)," *SHQ* 47, no. 1 (1943): 33–38. Although the security of the northern frontier was undoubtedly a concern to some, including Terán's close friend Lucas Alamán, not all Mexican leaders saw the Boundary Commission as a matter of pressing importance. See Benson, "Texas as Viewed from Mexico," 253–256.

3. Ohland Morton, "Life of General Don Manuel de Mier y Terán: As It Affected Texas-Mexican Relations (Continued)," *SHQ* 46, no. 3 (1943), 239–254.

4. Terán, *Texas by Terán*, 210; Berlandier, *Journey to Mexico*, 2:306 (quotation).

5. Cantrell, *Stephen F. Austin*, 176. Terán, *Texas by Terán*, 56–59, 96 (quotation on 96); Sánchez, "A Trip to Texas," 260–261, 271; Berlandier, *Journey to Mexico*, 2:317–322.

6. Terán, *Texas by Terán*, 271–275; Sánchez, "A Trip to Texas," 271–282; Berlandier, *Journey to Mexico*, 2:322–230.

7. Terán, *Texas by Terán*, 78, 110, 129 (quotation on 129).

8. On East Texas deforestation, see Terán, *Texas by Terán*, 78–79; and Dewees, *Letters from an Early Settler of Texas*, 127. On overhunting, see Terán, *Texas by Terán*, 101.

9. Terán. *Texas by Terán*, 108–109.

10. Terán, *Texas by Terán*, 91–93, 95 (quotation on 93). In the aftermath of the Fredonian Rebellion, the commandant of the Eastern Interior Provinces, Anastasio Bustamante, seemed well-disposed to act on Bean's verbal promise, writing to the commander in Nacogdoches that he had endorsed the Cherokee land application, and believed it would be approved by the national government. However, nothing more was heard of the matter, and a land grant for the Cherokees was not contained in Terán's instructions. Bustamante to Ahumada, April 7, 1827, *BRC*, supplement, 11:106–107.

11. Terán, *Texas by Terán*, 97–101 (quotation on 100).

12. Sánchez, "A Trip to Texas," 276, 289; Terán, *Texas by Terán*, 100 (first quotation), 139 (second quotation).

13. Terán, *Texas by Terán*, 178.

14. Terán, *Texas by Terán*, 139.

15. Rippy, *Joel R. Poinsett*. For Zavala's role in the popular unrest that led to the overthrow of Pedraza, see Sylvia M. Arrom, "Popular Politics in Mexico City: The Parián Riot, 1828," *Hispanic American Historical Review* 68, no. 2 (1988): 245–268. For Zavala and the *yorkinos'* defense of their role in the riots, see Ana Romero Valderama, "Tiranía Pedracista y Derecho de Insurrección: la Justificación Periodística a la Rebelión Yorkina de la Acordada en México (1828)," *Estudios de Historia Moderna y Contemporánea de México* 55 (Enero-Junio 2018), 77–119.

16. Zavala to Santa Anna, December 24, 1828, Lorenzo de Zavala Papers, BCAH (first quotation); Santa Anna to Zavala, May 6, 1829, Ibid. (second quotation).

17. Estep, "The Life of Lorenzo de Zavala," 222, 227–231. In 1829, the Minister of the Interior was José Maria Bocanegra, who had become suspicious of Zavala's close relationship with Poinsett, blaming the two men for the factionalism among Mexico's political leadership. See José María de Bocanegra, *Memorias para la Historia de México Independiente, 1822–1846* (Mexico: Imprenta del Gobierno Federal, 1892), 16–22. Zavala clearly resented Bocanegra's interference in his colonization scheme, and in his soon-to-be-published history of the revolutionary era would describe the minister as a man of "little spirit and modest ability." Lorenzo de Zavala, *Ensayo Histórico de Las Revoluciones de México Desde 1808 Hasta 1830* (Mexico City: Fondo de Cultura Económcia, 2010), 2:115.

18. Hutchinson, "José Antonio Mexía," 125. For more on speculation in Texas lands by Mexican elites, see Miguel Soto, "Politics and Profits: Mexican Officials and Land Speculators in Texas," in Haynes and Saxon, eds., *Contested Empire*, 79–95.

19. Terán, *Texas by Terán*, 101; Sánchez, "A Trip to Texas," 283.

20. James O. Pattie, *The Personal Narrative of James O. Pattie of Kentucky* (New York: Arno Press, 1973), 366. For Robert Potter, see Edward E. Baptist,

The Half Has Never Been Told: Slavery and the Making of American Capitalism (New York: Basic Books, 2014), 196–199; and Ernest G. Fischer, *Robert Potter: Founder of the Texas Navy* (Gretna: Pelican Pub. Co., 1976). Charged with "maiming," Potter spent two years in jail and wrote a defense of his actions to the residents of his congressional district. See *Mr. Potter's Appeal to the Citizens of Nash, Franklin, Warren and Granville, 1830.* Potter's constituents were apparently willing to excuse his behavior, reelecting him to the legislature upon his release. His colleagues in the statehouse took a different view, and promptly expelled him on a trumped up charge of cheating at cards. For Richard Robinson (later Parmalee), see Patricia Cline Cohen, *The Murder of Helen Jewett: The Life and Death of a Prostitute in Nineteenth-Century New York* (New York: Alfred A. Knopf: 1998).

21. "Carta de Libertad de David Towns a Favor de sus Negroes y Mulattos," January 3, 1828, *BRC,* 1:216; Harold Schoen, "The Free Negro in the Texas Republic, 1," *SHQ* 39, no. 1 (1935): 293, 295; Benjamin Lundy, and Thomas Earle, comp., *The Life, Travels and Opinions of Benjamin Lundy* (New York: Arno Press, 1969), 116–117.

22. For more on Goyens's extensive business activities, see *BRC,* vols. 23–24; Prince, "William Goyens," 19–24.

23. Terán, *Texas by Terán,* 79 (first quotation); Sánchez, "A Trip to Texas" (second and third quotations), 271.

CHAPTER FIVE. TEXAS MUST BE A SLAVE COUNTRY

1. Erwin to Austin, September 11, 1824, *AP,* 1:894; Erwin to Austin, September 30, 1825, Ibid., 1:1213–1216; Sean Michael Kelley and Henry B. Lovejoy, "The Origins of the African-Born Population of Antebellum Texas," *SHQ* 120, no. 2 (October 2016): 220; Sean Michael Kelley, "Plantation Frontiers: Race, Ethnicity, and Family Along the Brazos River of Texas, 1821–1886," PhD diss., University of Texas at Austin, 2000, 34.

2. Rose Groce Bertleth, "Jared Ellison Groce," *SHQ* 20, no. 4 (1917): 360–361.

3. On Groce's quarrelsome personality, see, for example, Coles to Austin, November 1, 1824, *AP,* 1:931–932. Ann Raney Coleman, and Richard C. King, ed., *Victorian Lady on the Texas Frontier: The Journal of Ann Raney Coleman* (Norman: University of Oklahoma Press, 1971), 26 (quotation). On the process of girdling, see Terán, *Texas by Terán,* 144–145. William Fairfax Gray, and Paul D. Lack, ed., *The Diary of William Fairfax Gray, From Virginia to Texas, 1835–1837* (Dallas: DeGolyer Library, Southern Methodist University, 1997), 136.

4. Terán, *Texas by Terán,* 145; Kelley, "Plantation Frontiers," 38.

5. Bertleth, "Jared Ellison Groce," 367; J. H. Kuykendall, "Reminiscences of Early Texans," *QTSHA* 7, no. 1 (1903): 35.

6. Malcolm D. Mclean, *Papers Concerning Robertson's Colony in Texas* (Arlington: University of Texas at Arlington Press), 14:385; J. C. Clopper, "J. C. Clopper's Journal and Book of Memoranda for 1828," *QTSHA* 13, no. 1 (1909): 60.

7. For an extensive firsthand description of William H. Wharton, see Foote, *Texas and the Texans*, 41–48. J. H. Kuykendall, "Sketches of Early Texians," 15, Kuykendall Family Papers, BCAH (quotation).

8. Sarah Wharton Groce Berlet, *Autobiography of a Spoon, 1828–1956* (Beaumont: LaBelle Print. Co., 1971), 5–8.

9. Lorenzo de Zavala, and Woolsey Wallace, trans. *Journey to the United States of North America/Viaje a Los Estados Unidos Del Norte de America* (Houston: Arte Público Press, 2005), 20; Will Fowler, "The Texan Revolution of 1835–36 and Early Mexican Nationalism," in Haynes and Saxon, eds., *Contested Empire*, 103.

10. For the Constituent Congress deliberations, see Manuel Oropeza González and Jesús F. de la Teja, eds., *Actas del Congreso Constituyente de Coahuila y Texas de 1824 a 1827 . . .* (México: Tribunal Electoral del Poder Judicial de la Federación, 2016).

11. Austin to Durst, November 17, 1829, *AP*, 2:289 (first quotation); Austin to Martin, May 30 [1831], Ibid., 2:981 (second quotation); Austin to Saucedo, September 11, 1826, Ibid., 1:1452.

12. Lester G. Bugbee, "Slavery in Early Texas, I," *Political Science Quarterly* 13, no. 3 (1898): 403–404; Randolph B. Campbell, *An Empire for Slavery: The Peculiar Institution in Texas, 1821–1865* (Baton Rouge: Louisiana State University Press, 1989), 19.

13. Torget, *Seeds of Empire*, 135.

14. Austin to Wharton, April 24, 1829, *AP*, 2:207–212 (quotation on 210). Stephen F. Austin, et al. *Fugitive Letters, 1829–1836* (San Antonio: Trinity University Press, 1981), 17–18.

15. Houston came closest to revealing the reason for his breakup with Eliza Allen in a letter to her brother, saying, "She was cold to me, & I thought did not love me." Houston to Allen, April 9, 1829, *WSH*, 1:130. Elizabeth Crook, "Sam Houston and Eliza Allen: The Marriage and the Mystery," *SHQ* 94, no. 1 (1990): 1–36.

16. For Houston's filibustering plans, see Stanley F. Horn, "An Unpublished Photograph of Sam Houston," *THQ* 3, no. 4 (1944): 349–351; and Yoakum, *History of Texas*, 1:306–307.

17. For more on Austin's views about the future of Texas at this early period, see Euguene C. Barker, "Stephen F. Austin and the Independence of Texas," *QTSHA* 13, no. 4 (1910): 257–262.

18. William Forrest Sprague, *Vicente Guerrero: Mexican Liberator: A Study in Patriotism* (Chicago: R. R. Donnelley 1939), 105.

19. Durst to Austin, November 10, 1835, *AP*, 2:285.

20. Andrés Reséndez, "Ramón Músquiz, The Ultimate Insider," in De la Teja, ed., *Tejano Leadership in Mexican and Revolutionary Texas* (College Station: Texas A&M University Press, 2010), 134–135.

21. Berlet, *Autobiography of a Spoon*, 15.

22. William Wharton Groce, "Major General John A. Wharton," *SHQ* 19, no. 3 (1916): 272–273; Mary Austin Holley and James Perry, *The Texas Diary, 1835–1838* (Austin: University of Texas at Austin), 74; Abner J. Strobel, *The Old Plantations and their Owners of Brazoria County* (Houston: Union National Bank, 1926), 23; Holley and Perry, *Texas Diary*, 61–62.

CHAPTER SIX. THE MOST AVID NATION IN THE WORLD

1. For illegal American immigration, see, for example, "Illegal Introduction of Americans, Harrison to Commanding Officer of Nacogdoches," February 15–16, 1828, *BRC*, 12:36–37. Ohland Morton, "Life of General Don Manuel Mier y Terán," *SHQ*. Terán, *Texas by Terán*, 178.

2. Santa Anna to Zavala, October 7, 1829, Lorenzo de Zavala Papers, BCAH.

3. Ohland Morton, "Life of General Don Manuel De Mier y Terán: As It Affected Texas-Mexican Relations (Continued)," *SHQ* 48, no. 2 (1944): 198–199. Alleine Howren, "Causes and Origin of the Decree of April 6, 1830," *SHQ* 16, no. 4 (1913): 378–422.

4. Barker, *Life of Stephen F. Austin*, 267–274.

5. Herrera, "Blueprint for Hemispheric Hegemony," 305; Terán, *Texas by Terán*, 179.

6. Zavala, *Journey to the United States*, 39. For more on Zavala's conflicted nationalism, see John-Michael Rivera, "A Complete Though Bloody Victory: Lorenzo de Zavala and the Transnational Paradoxes of Sovereignty," *American Literary History* 18, no. 3 (2006): 427–445.

7. Zavala, *Journey to the United States*, 2–3, 192.

8. Zavala, *Journey to the United States*, 81 (quotation). The only Zavala biographer to devote any attention to his private life is Margaret Swett Henson. Published without footnotes, *Lorenzo de Zavala: The Pragmatic Idealist* (Fort Worth: Texas Christian University Press, 1996) makes several missteps regarding Zavala's relationship with his second wife, Miranda (later Emily) West. Describing their first meeting, Henson relies on the dubious account of Samuel A. Hammett, writing under the pseudonym Philip Paxton. Although Zavala probably met Miranda during his trip to Albany in 1830, Hammett relates in *A Stray Yankee in Texas* (New York: Redfield, 1853), 189–190, that Zavala met a "very pretty American girl . . . with two children under her charge," during his early morning walks in New York City's Battery Park.

For brief biographical information on Emily, see "Santa Anna's Wife," *New York Evening Post*, April 14, 1854; Joel Munsell, *The Annals of Albany* (Albany: J. Munsell, 1850–1859), 7:351; and George Rogers Howell and Jonathan Tenney, *History of the County of Albany, N.Y. from 1609–1886* . . . (New York: W. W. Munsell, 1886), 2:652.

9. Zavala, *Journey to the United States*, 1–2.

10. Henson, *Lorenzo de Zavala*, 53. Although Henson makes the unlikely assumption that Miranda accompanied the still-married Zavala on his eleven-month trip to Europe, she is not on the passenger list when Zavala returned to New York in November 1831. See Passenger Lists of Vessels Arriving at New York, New York, 1820–1897, Records of the US Customs Service, Record Group 36, National Archives. Henson offers no explanation for Zavala's decision to change Miranda's name on the marriage license.

11. Lorenzo de Zavala Diary, November 12, 1831, Lorenzo de Zavala Papers, BCAH.

12. Hutchinson, "José Antonio Mexía," 132–135; Morton, "Life of General Mier y Terán," *SHQ* 48 (October 1944): 212.

13. W. P. Zuber, "Thomson's Clandestine Passage Around Nacogdoches," *QTSHA* 1, no. 1 (1897): 68–70.

14. Thomas Donaldson, *The George Catlin Indian Gallery in the National Museum* (Washington, D.C.: Government Printing Office, 1886), 207. Carolyn Thomas Foreman, "Dutch," *Chronicles of Oklahoma* 27, no. 3 (1949), 252–267. For a fascinating account of the Cherokees' decision to wage war against the Wichitas, and their recruitment of tribal warriors in US Indian Territory, see Foreman, ed., "The Cherokee War Path," 233–262.

15. Smith, *From Dominance to Disappearance*, 140–141; Daniel J. Gelo, "Two Episodes in Texas Indian History Reconsidered: Getting the Facts Right about the Lafuente Attack and the Fort Parker Raid," *SHQ* 120, no. 4 (2017): 442–450.

16. Morton, "Life of General Mier y Terán," 500.

17. Terán, *Texas by Terán*, 92–93; Letona to Commandant General [Piedras], September 1, 1831, Winfrey and Day, eds., *Texas Indian Papers*, 1:1–2.

18. Jackson, *Indian Agent*, 182–184.

19. Músquiz to Letona, April 22, 1832, Winfrey and Day, eds., *Texas Indian Papers*, 1:4–5; Piedras to Músquiz, May 7, 1832, Ibid., 1:5; Jackson, *Indian Agent*, 152–153.

CHAPTER SEVEN. LONG LIVE SANTA ANNA!

1. For more on Bradburn's role in the 1832 unrest at Anahuac, see Margaret Swett Henson, *Juan Davis Bradburn: A Reappraisal of the Mexican Commander of Anahuac* (College Station: Texas A&M University Press, 1982).

The customs issue controversy is discussed on 80–81. See also Barker, *Life of Stephen F. Austin*, 327–329.

2. Peareson, "Reminiscences of Judge Edwin Waller," *QTSHA* 4, no. 1 (1900): 34–36.

3. "Stephen F. Austin—Charles G. Sayre Correspondence," *SHQ* 63 (January 1960): 456. Austin mistakenly believed the uproar over the new customs house at the mouth of the Brazos would soon blow over. See Austin to Holley, January 14, 1832, *AP*, 2:736–737. For Terán's irritated response to Austin's attempt to excuse Wharton and others for the Velasco incident, see Terán to Austin, January 27, 1832, Ibid., 2:744.

4. For a helpful overview of the extraordinarily complex set of interlocking factors that gave rise to Mexico's first civil war in 1832, see Jaime E. Rodríguez O., "The Origins of the 1832 Rebellion," in Jaime E. Rodriguez O., *Patterns of Contention in Mexican History* (Wilmington: SR Books, 1992),145–162. See also Timothy E. Anna, *Forging Mexico: 1821–1835* (Lincoln: University of Nebraska Press, 1998), 246–257. For Mexía's role, see Hutchinson, "José Antonio Mexía," 135; Estep, "Life of Lorenzo de Zavala," 266 (quotation).

5. The concern that Santa Anna was motivated less by federalist principles and more by a desire for political power was certainly the view of one of Terán's closest friends, Lucas Alamán, then serving as Minister of the Interior and Foreign Relations. See Lucas Alamán, *Historia de Mejico* (Mexico: Editorial Jus, 1968), 4:854–855.

6. Ohland Morton, "Life of General Don Manuel Mier y Terán," *SHQ* 48, no. 4 (April 1945): 524–525; Anna, *Forging Mexico*, 250–251.

7. Edna Rowe, "The Disturbances at Anahuac in 1832," *QTSHA* 6, no. 4 (1903): 265–299; "Memorial of Colonel Juan Davis Bradburn Concerning the events at Anahuac, 1831–1832," reprinted in Henson, *Juan Davis Bradburn*, 134, 143.

8. On the Stanbery episode, see Llerena B. Friend, *Sam Houston: The Great Designer* (Austin: University of Texas Press, 1954), 30–35.

9. Houston to Prentiss, June 16, 1832, *WSH*, 1:231.

10. Rowe, "The Disturbances at Anahuac in 1832," *QTSHA* 6, no. 4 (1903): 279–288.

11. For Col. Ugartechea's account of the attack on Fort Velasco, see Report of Ugartechea, July 1, 1832, *PML*, 1:132–136.

12. Morton, "Life of General Mier y Terán," 544, 546.

13. F. H. Turner, "The Mejia Expedition," *QTSHA* 7, no. 1 (1903): 12–28.

14. *Texas Gazette and Brazoria Commercial Advertiser* (Brazoria), July 23, 1832. Documents pertaining to the uprising at Velasco, as well as the reception for José Antonio Mexía when he arrived with Austin in mid-July, can be found in the pamphlet *Communication from San Felipe de Austin, Relative to Late Events in Texas*. It is reprinted in full in Mary Austin Holley, *Texas: Observations*,

Historical, Geographical And Descriptive, In a Series of Letters, Written During a Visit to Austin's Colony, With a View of a Permanent Settlement In That Country, In the Autumn of 1831 . . . (Baltimore: Armstrong & Plaskitt, 1833), 141–167.

15. Hutchinson, "José Antonio Mexía," 136.

16. Ayuntamiento of Nacogdoches to People of Ayish Bayou, July 28, 1832, *BRC*, 67:183–184.

17. H. P. N. Gammel, *Laws of Texas* (Austin: Gammel Book Co., 1898), 1:494. When the abolitionist Benjamin Lundy arrived in Nacogdoches on July 1, he found the townsfolk in a state of fevered excitement, expecting an imminent attack by the Brazoria and Anahuac rebels. Any thought of lending their support to the general uprising was temporarily abandoned, however, when "hundreds" of Indians, "armed and equipped for battle," appeared in town in support of Piedras. *Genius of Universal Emancipation*, November 1832, 4.

18. John Henry Brown, *History of Texas, from 1685 to 1892* (St. Louis: L. E. Daniell, 1892), 2:192; Gammel, *Laws of Texas*, 1:494–495.

19. Starr, *History of the Cherokee*, 197. On Filisola's land grant, see Soto, "Politics and Profits," 86.

20. Linn, *Reminiscences of Fifty Years in Texas* (Austin: State House Press, 1986), 23.

CHAPTER EIGHT. SUSPENDED OVER THE ALTAR OF SACRIFICE

1. In addition to Williams, the mob hanged in effigy Thomas Jefferson Chambers and Ira Lewis. See Austin to Williams, July 19, 1832, *AP*, 2:821. An angry Wharton said of those who condemned the insurgency, "I think I could go to San Felipe and reason some of those fellows into sense and cowhide the balance into rags." See Brown, Mitchell and Wharton to Committee at Brazoria, July 4, 1832, *PML*, 1:140. For more on those Anglo-Texans who, like Austin, favored a policy of accommodation with Mexican authorities, see Margaret Swett Henson, "Tory Sentiment in Anglo-Texan Public Opinion, 1832–1836," *SHQ* 90, no. 1 (1986): 1–34.

2. In a letter regarding the land deal, Wharton also refers vaguely to the tensions in his relationship with Austin, writing, "Our personal intercourse has always been of an undefined negative and unconfidential character." Wharton to Austin, July 14, 1831, *AP*, 2:672–673. For his part, Austin insisted that the Wharton brothers "never had any cause" for their hostile feelings toward him. Austin to McKinney, October 18, 1834, Ibid., 3:11.

3. Branch T. Archer, perhaps William Wharton's closest friend in Texas, shot James Otway Crump following a dispute involving an aggravated assault case in their home town of Powhatan, Virginia. After hearing the evidence, the jury acquitted Archer on the spot. See *New Orleans Crescent*, May 14, 1851. John A. Wharton was wounded in a duel with William T. Austin, a distant rel-

ative of Stephen F. Austin, near Brazoria in the spring of 1834. See William H. Wharton, Vertical File, BCAH. The Sandbar Fight, which occurred on a shoal in the middle of the Mississippi River in September 1827, began as a duel between Samuel Wells and Thomas Maddox, both residents of Alexandria, Louisiana. After both men missed their mark, a brawl erupted among their supporters. Though Bowie was shot several times and stabbed in the sternum during the melee, he managed to fatally stab one of Wells's seconds with his famous knife. See *Natchez Weekly Democrat*, October 19, 1827. The historiography on codes of Southern male honor is extensive. See, for example, Bertram Wyatt-Brown, *Southern Honor Ethics and Behavior in the Old South* (New York: Oxford University Press, 2007); Joanne B. Freeman, *Affairs of Honor: National Politics in the New Republic* (New Haven: Yale University Press, 2001); Amy S. Greenberg, *Manifest Manhood and the Antebellum American Empire* (New York: Cambridge University Press, 2005); and Elliott J. Gorn, "'Gouge and Bite, Pull Hair and Scratch': The Social Significance of Fighting in the Southern Backcountry," *American Historical Review* 90, no. 1 (1985).

4. Travis to Burnet, August 31, 1835, *PTR*, 1:379.

5. For Músquiz's response to the call for a convention in 1832, see Reséndez, "Ramon Músquiz," 137. Although Victoria sent two delegates to the convention, both sons-in-law of empresario Martín De León, the powerful ranching family was deeply divided about the meeting's legality. See Ana Castillo Crimm, *De León: A Tejano Family History* (Austin: University of Texas Press, 2003), 117–118.

6. Gammel, *Laws of Texas*, 1:475–504 (quotation on 489).

7. Reséndez, "Ramon Músquiz," 136–137.

8. David J. Weber and Conchita Hassell Winn, *Troubles in Texas, 1832: A Tejano Viewpoint from San Antonio* . . . (Dallas: DeGolyer Library, 1983).

9. Austin to Williams, August 21, 1833, *AP*, 2:1001 (first quotation); Austin to E. Perry, August 21, 1826, *AP*, 1:1427 (second quotation).

10. Juan Nepomuceno Almonte, Jack Jackson, ed., and John Wheat, trans., *Almonte's Texas: Juan N. Almonte's 1834 Inspection, Secret Report, and Role in the 1836 Campaign* (Austin: Texas State Historical Association, 2003), 76. Mexía to Austin, March 27, 1833, *AP*, 2:932–933 (first quotation). Zavala to Santa Anna, August 12, 1832, Lorenzo de Zavala Papers, BCAH (second quotation).

11. D. L. Kokernot, "Reminiscences of Early Days in Texas," www.sonsofdewittcolony.org/kokernotmemoirs.htm.

12. J. Villasana Haggard, "Epidemic Cholera in Texas, 1833–1834," *SHQ* 40, no. 3 (1937): 216–230.

13. Austin to Lesassier, May 6, 1833, *AP*, 2:961–962.

14. Coles to Butler, July 15, 1833, *AP*, 2:999 (first quotation); Austin to Williams, January 12, 1835, Ibid., 2:1025 (second quotation).

CHAPTER NINE. YOU HAVE TORN THE CONSTITUTION TO PIECES

1. C. A. Hutchinson, "The Asiatic Cholera Epidemic of 1833 in Mexico," *Bulletin of the History of Medicine* 32, 1958: 1–23 (quotations on 13 and 3). See also Kate Mason Rowland, "General John Thomson Mason: An Early Friend of Texas" *QTSHA* 11, no. 3 (1908): 175.

2. Austin to Ayuntamiento of Béxar, *AP*, 2:1007–1008. The town council replied soon afterward, calling his proposals "exceedingly rash." Ayuntamiento of Béxar to Austin, October 31, 1833, Ibid., 2:1012–1013. For an analysis of Austin's possible motives for advising the Béxar council to move toward statehood, see Cantrell, *Stephen F. Austin*, 272–273.

3. Hutchinson, "Jose Antonio Mexía," 136–138.

4. C. A. Hutchinson, "Mexican Federalists, New Orleans and the Texas Revolution," *LHQ* 39 (1956): 6.

5. Will Fowler, *Mexico in the Age of Proposals, 1821–1853* (Westport: Greenwood Press, 1998), 196–199; Estep, "Life of Lorenzo de Zavala," 298–300. For more on Farias' unfounded reputation for radicalism, see Fowler, "Valentin Gómez Farías: Perceptions of Radicalism in Independent Mexico," *Bulletin of Latin American Research* 15, no. 1 (January 1996): 51–53; Henson, *Lorenzo de Zavala*, 66–67.

6. *Advocate of the Peoples' Rights* (Brazoria), February 22, 1834 (quotation). Ayuntamiento of Brazoria to congress, July 1834, *AP*, 2:1069–1071; Perry to Austin, December 7, 1834, *AP*, 3:33–34.

7. *House Executive Documents*, 25th Congress, 2nd session, no. 351 (Washington, DC: Government Printing Office), 109 (quotation). For more on Butler's controversial career in Mexico, see Quinton Curtis Lamar, "A Diplomatic Disaster: The Mexican Mission of Anthony Butler," *The Americas* 45, no. 1 (July 1988): 1–17. See also Gerald D. Saxon, "Anthony Butler: A Flawed Diplomat," *ETHJ*, 24, no. 1, article 5 (1986): 3–14.

8. Published under the pseudonym O.P.Q., the two letters are reprinted in Almonte, *Almonte's Texas*, 67–74 (first quotation on 67). For Austin's response to the letters, see Austin to Williams, April 29, 1835, *AP*, 3:68; and Henry P. Beers, "Stephen F. Austin and Anthony Butler Documents," *SHQ* 62, no. 2 (1958): 235 (second quotation).

9. From a jail cell in the Accordada, Austin unburdened himself in a letter to his brother-in-law. Austin to Perry, August 26, 1834, *AP*, 2:1075–1084. For Wharton's response, see Wharton to the Public, November 9, 1834, Ibid., 3:25–26 (quotations on 25).

10. Almonte, *Almonte's Texas*, 101–102.

11. Torget, *Seeds of Empire*, 157; Almonte, *Almonte's Texas*, 273.

12. Almonte, *Almonte's Texas*, 105–106. Winfrey and Day, eds., *Texas Indian Papers*, 1:7–8; Ruiz to Alcalde, February 20, 1835, *PTR*, 1:22; Tenorio to Commander, April 9, 1835, Ibid., 1:61–62.

13. Harris, "The Reminiscences of Mrs. Dilue Harris, I," *QTSHA* 4, no. 2 (1900): 98–99; Gray, *Diary of William Fairfax Gray*, 152 (quotations). John R. Lundberg, "'Texas Must Be a Slave Country': Slaves and Masters in the Texas Low Country 1840–1860," *ETHJ* 53, no. 2, article 4 (2015): 36–37.

14. Because of the illegal nature of the trade, there are no precise figures on the number of enslaved people imported into Texas from Cuba. Early work on the importation of slaves by Eugene C. Barker estimated that between six hundred and seven hundred Africans were smuggled into Texas in the 1830s and 1840s. See Eugene C. Barker, "The African Slave Trade in Texas," *QTSHA* 6, no. 2 (1902): 156–157. More recently, however, the research of Sean M. Kelley suggests that this estimate is too low. See Sean M. Kelley, *Los Brazos de Dios: A Plantation Society in the Texas Borderlands, 1821–1865* (Baton Rouge: Louisiana State University Press, 2010), 49–50; and Sean M. Kelley, "Blackbirders and Bozales: African-Born Slaves on the Lower Brazos River of Texas in the Nineteenth Century," *Civil War History* 54, no. 4: 406–423.

15. Issued in May 1834, the Plan of Cuernavaca can be found in *The Pronunciamiento in Independent Mexico, 1821–1876*, https://arts.st-andrews.ac.uk/pronunciamientos/dates.php.

16. The Plan of Cuernavaca is generally viewed by Texas historians as a naked power grab by Santa Anna. For a more nuanced analysis of Mexico's abrupt shift toward centralism in 1835, see Michael Costeloe, "Federalism to Centralism in Mexico: The Conservative Case for Change, 1834–1835," *The Americas* 45 (October 1988), 173–185.

17. Will Fowler, *Santa Anna of Mexico* (Lincoln: University of Nebraska Press, 2007), 153–154.

18. *Philadelphia Inquirer*, October 24, 1834.

19. Joaquín Moreno, and Genaro Estrada, ed., *Diario de un Escribiente de Legación* (Mexico: Editorial Porrúa, 1970), 23, 63–64, 124 (quotation on 124).

20. For Zavala's letter of resignation as minister to France, see Zavala to Lombardo, August 30, 1834, *PML*, 1:166–167. Moreno, *Diario de un Escribiente de Legacion*, 58 (quotation).

21. Zavala's letter to Santa Anna was published in the *Mercurio de Matamoros*. See Zavala to Santa Anna, August 30, 1834, *PML*, 1:167–169 (quotation on 167).

22. Raymond Estep, "Lorenzo de Zavala and the Texas Revolution," *SHQ* 57, no. 1 (1953): 323–324.

CHAPTER TEN. THE BLOOD OF OUR ANCESTORS
FLOWS WARM IN OUR VEINS

1. Frank N. Samponaro, "Santa Anna and the Abortive Anti-Federalist Revolt of 1833 in Mexico," *The Americas* 40, no. 1 (1983): 104; George L. Hammeken, "Recollections of Stephen F. Austin," *SHQ* 20, no. 4 (1917): 374 (quotation).

2. Fowler, *Santa Anna of Mexico*,153–154; Costeloe, "Federalism to Centralism in Mexico," 173–185.

3. Barker, *Life of Stephen F. Austin*, 404–405.

4. Tenorio to Commander, April 9, 1835, *PTR*, 1:61; Unsigned to Unsigned, April 9, 1835, Ibid., 1:135; Travis to Bowie, July 30, 1835, *PTR*, 1:289 (quotation). For local resistance to the arrival of Mexican troops at Anahuac, see Eugene C. Barker, "Difficulties of a Mexican Revenue Officer," *QTSHA* 4, no. 1 (1900): 190–202.

5. Herbert Eugene Bolton, *Guide to Materials for the History of the United States in the Principal Archives of Mexico* (Washington, DC: Carnegie Institution of Washington, 1913), 345.

6. "Mexía and Farías Plan," September 4, 1835, *PTR*, 1:416. C. A. Hutchinson, "Valentín Gómez Farías and the 'Secret Pact of New Orleans,'" *Hispanic American Historical Review* 36, no. 4 (1956): 471–489.

7. For efforts of the Mexican navy to apprehend Zavala, see [Lamar], "Operations of Thompson off Texas Coast," 1835, *PML*, 3:250.

8. Sledge to Knight, July 19, 1835, *PTR*, 1:260.

9. By the fall, the news that Zavala had arrived in Texas to "encourage anarchy and provoke new convulsions" was being widely reported in the Mexican press. See *Mosquito Mexicano* (Mexico City), October 20, 1835. Raymond Estep has counted more than sixty letters written by Mexican authorities calling for Zavala's arrest during the four-month period from June to October, 1835. Estep, "Lorenzo de Zavala and the Texas Revolution," 325.

10. Alwyn Barr, *Texans in Revolt: The Battle for San Antonio, 1835* (Austin: University of Texas Press, 1990), 12–13. Smith to Chambers, September 2, 1835, *PTR*, 1:406–407 (quotation on 407). Juan Nepomuceno Seguín, and Jesús F. de la Teja, ed., *A Revolution Remembered: The Memoirs and Selected Correspondence of Juan N. Seguín* (Austin: Texas State Historical Association, 2002), 76.

11. Unsigned to Unsigned, August 18, *PTR*, 1:353; Travis to Moore, August 31, 1835, 1:382 (first quotation); "Archer to Public," September 20, 1835, *PTR*, 1:468 (second quotation).

12. "Allsbery [*sic*] to the Public," *AP*, 3:108 (first quotation); Harris, "Reminiscences, II," 157; *Texas Republican* (Brazoria), August 29, 1835. See also Alsberry to Public, August 28, 1835, *PTR*, 1:374; Columbia Meeting, September 22, 1835, Ibid., 1:479. Williamson Address, June 22, 1835, *PTR*, 1:201 (second quotation); Smith to Chambers, September 2, 1835, *PTR*, 1:406 (third quotation).

13. The alleged uprising was known as the "Murrell Excitement." For a thorough account of this episode, see Joshua D. Rothman, *Flush Times and Fever Dreams: A Story of Capitalism and Slavery in the Age of Jackson* (Athens: University of Georgia Press, 2012), chs. 3–5. On rumors of the Creeks' migration to Texas, see *Texas Republican*, July 18, 1835.

14. Cordova to Flores, July 19, 1835, *PTR*, 1:256–257; Mush and Bowls to Cherokees, September 19, 1835, *PTR*, 1:466–467.

15. As early as the third week of June, the Wharton faction was girding for battle, having learned that Mexican troops from Matamoros would soon be deployed to Texas. A concerned Henry Austin wrote to James Perry to tell him that "an attempt has been made here to involve us in an immediate Revolution." Austin to Perry, *PTR*, 1:164–165.

16. James K. Greer, "The Journal of Ammon Underwood, 1834–1838," *SHQ* 32 (October 1928): 137; "Wharton to Public," October 3, 1835, *PTR*, 2:30.

17. Jones to Bryan, September 1, 1835, *PTR*, 1:383–384; Nancy Boothe Parker, "Lamar's Texas Journal," *SHQ* 84, no. 3 (1981): 321 (quotation).

18. Columbia Meeting, August 1, 1835, *PTR*, 1:342; Nacogdoches Meeting, August 15, 1835, *PTR*, 344–345; Travis to Briscoe, August 31, 1835, *PTR*, 1:381.

19. Austin to Holley, August 21, 1835, *AP*, 3:102.

20. "Austin to the People of Texas," September 8, 1835, *AP*, 3:116–119; James A. Creighton, *A Narrative History of Brazoria County* (Angleton: Brazoria County Historical Commission, 1975), 102–103.

21. Travis to Smith, September 15, 1835, *PTR*, 1:448. Travis to Austin, September 22, 1835, *AP*, 3:133.

22. Raúl A. Ramos, *Beyond the Alamo: Forging Mexican Ethnicity in San Antonio, 1821–1861* (Chapel Hill: University of North Carolina Press, 2008), 1–2, 133–134.

23. Paula Mitchell Marks, *Turn Your Eyes Toward Texas: Pioneers Sam and Mary Maverick* (College Station: Texas A&M University Press, 1989), 3–24.

24. Ibid., 36.

25. Colonel John McIntosh was reported to have issued this reply in answer to the British army's demand that American troops surrender Fort Morris, Georgia, in November 1778. The Methodist minister was William P. Smith, who emigrated to Texas in 1835. An Old Soldier, "First Breaking Out of the Texas Revolution at Gonzales," *The Texas Almanac for 1861* (Galveston: Richardson & Co., 1861), 61.

26. During the rebellion and in the years that followed, Anglo-Texans (as well as many Americans) were determined to draw comparisons between the conflict and the American Revolution. For comparisons to Lexington, see, for example, Wm. H. Wharton, *Texas, Address of the Honorable Wm. H. Wharton, Delivered in New York, on Tuesday, April 26, 1836* . . . (New York: W. H. Colyer, 1836), 21; "Texas," *Georgia Journal* (Milledgeville), November 24, 1835. See also Foote, *Texas and the Texans*, 2:93–97. For a study of Anglo-Texans' constant allusions to the American Revolutionary era during this period, see Haynes, "Imitating the Example of Our Forefathers," in Haynes and Saxon, eds., *Contested Empire*, 43–77.

CHAPTER ELEVEN. SOLELY, PURELY, SIMPLY AMERICAN

1. Ugartechea to Austin, October 4, 1835, *PTR*, 2:39–42.

2. Wharton to Public, October 3, 1835, *PTR*, 2:30–31; Volunteers to Public, October 5, 1835, Ibid. 2:56; Wharton to Public, October 5, 1835, Ibid., 56.

3. For a colorful description of the rebel "army," see Smithwick, *Evolution of a State*, 74–75.

4. *Telegraph and Texas Register*, November 7, 1835. Vicente Filisola, and Woolsey Wallace, trans., *Memoirs for the History of the War in Texas* (Austin: Eakin Press, 1985), 2:64–65; Anderson, *Conquest of Texas*, 112; Gray, *Diary of William Fairfax Gray*, 244; Baker and Johnson to Chairman, October 23, 1835, *PTR*, 2:199–201; *PML*, 4:64.

5. Pilgrim to Austin, October 6, 1835, *PTR*, 2:61; Bell to Austin, October 6, 1835, Ibid., 2:57; White to Austin, October 17, 1835, Ibid., 2:149–150.

6. Anglo-Texans invariably drew attention to their kinship with Americans in their appeals for US aid. See, for example, Royall to Public, October 26, 1835, *PTR*, 2:224–224; Eugene C. Barker, "Journal of the Permanent Council," *QTSHA* 7, no. 4 (1904): 272–273. "To the Troops of the Department of Nacogdoches," October 8, 1835, *WSH*, 1:304.

7. New Orleans Notice, October 15, 1835, *PTR*, 2:136. For a thorough study of the role the Crescent City played in supplying financial aid and manpower to the rebellion, see Edward L. Miller, *New Orleans and the Texas Revolution* (College Station: Texas A&M University Press, 2004).

8. James Ramage to Austin, October 21, 1835, *AP*, 3:199.

9. Gammel, *Laws of Texas*, 1:489.

10. Austin to President of the Consultation, November 15, 1835, *PTR*, 2:321.

11. Noah Smithwick, *Evolution of a State*, 76; Houston to Fannin, November 13, 1835, *WSH*, 1:305–306.

12. Barr, *Texans in Revolt*, 25; Rena Maverick Green, ed. *Samuel Maverick, Texan: 1803-1870: A Collection of Letters, Journals, and Memoirs* (San Antonio: n.p. 1953), 35–36.

13. Gammel, *Laws of Texas*, 1:522–523.

14. Gammel, *Laws of Texas*, 1:533–554; "Declaration of the People of Texas," November 7, 1835, *PTR*, 2:346–347.

15. Mexía to Consultation, October 29, 1835, *PTR*, 2:262–264; Austin to President of the Consultation, November 5, 1832, *PTR*, 2:321.

16. Mexía to Smith, December 7, 1835, *PTR*, 3:106–110. See also George Fisher, *Memorials of George Fisher, Late Secretary to the Expedition of Gen. José Antonio Mexía, Against Tampico, in November, 1835* . . . (Houston: Telegraph Office, 1840); *El Mosquito Mexicano* (Mexico City), December 1, 1835. For

more on the attack on the port town, see Eugene C. Barker, "The Tampico Expedition," *QTSHA* 6, no. 3 (1903): 169–186.

17. Richard Stenberg, "Jackson, Anthony Butler, and Texas," *Southwestern Social Science Quarterly* 13, no. 3 (December 1932): 283.

18. *New Orleans Bulletin*, December 25, 1835; Mexía to Viesca, December 3, 1835, *PTR*, 3:89–90; Mexía to Smith, December 30, 1835, Ibid., 3:134–137; Farrell to Garretson, December 13, 1835, Ibid., 3:179; Robertson to Butler, December 14, 1835, Ibid., 3:191–192; Unsigned to Unsigned, December 14, 1835, Ibid., 3:195. For more on the Tornel Decree, see Richard Bruce Winders, "'This Is a Cruel Truth, But I Cannot Omit It': The Origin and Effect of Mexico's No Quarter Policy in the Texas Revolution," *SHQ* 120, no. 4 (2017): 423–424.

19. Irvine to Houston, November 7, 1835, *PTR*, 2:349.

20. Anson Jones, *Memoranda and Official Correspondence Relating to the Republic of Texas* . . . (New York: D. Appleton and Company, 1859), 12. Houston to Wharton, April 14, 1835, *WSH*, 1:294 (quotation).

21. Austin to President of the Consultation, November 8, 1835, *PTR*, 2:355; Wharton to Austin, November 8, 1835, *PTR*, 2:362.

22. Galan to Austin, November 13, 1835, *PTR*, 2:394; Pajes to Council, December 2, 1835, *PTR*, 3:80–81.

23. Dimmitt to Martin, November 15, 1835, *PTR*, 2:419–420; Filisola, *Memoirs for the History of the War in Texas*, 2:78; Smith to Council, December 9, 1835, *PTR*, 3:129.

24. Austin to Provisional Government, November 18, 1842, *PTR*, 2:450; Austin Proclamation, November 18, 1835, *PTR*, 452–454.

25. Dudley G. Wooten, *A Comprehensive History of Texas, 1685–1897* (Dallas: W. G. Scarff, 1898), 1:558–559; Austin to Perry, November 22, 1832, *PTR*, 2:487.

26. Creed Taylor and James T. DeShields, *Tall Men with Long Rifles: The Glamorous Story of the Texas Revolution* (San Antonio: Naylor, 1935), 53–56.

27. The wounded man was Thomas William Ward, who would later be elected three times as mayor of Austin. David C. Humphrey, *Peg Leg: The Improbable Life of a Texas Hero, Thomas William Ward, 1807–1872* (Denton: Texas State Historical Association, 2009).

28. Green, *Samuel Maverick, Texan*, 23. For a detailed account of the battle for San Antonio, see Hermann Ehrenberg, James E. Crisp, ed., and Louis E. Brister and James C. Kearny, trans., *Inside the Texas Revolution: The Enigmatic Memoir of Herman Ehrenberg* (Austin: Texas State Historical Association, 2021), 129–154. See also Barr, *Texans in Revolt*, 41–59.

29. Mexía to Viesca, December 3, 1835, *PTR*, 3:89–90.

30. Hutchinson, "Mexican Federalists," 35–36; Goliad Declaration, December 20, 1835, *PTR*, 3:266–267.

31. Mexía to Governor, December 23, 1835, *PTR*, 3:302.

CHAPTER TWELVE. TWO ARMIES

1. Austin was particularly upset to learn that the Wharton faction had been collecting signatures of newly arrived volunteers for a memorial demanding immediate independence, which he regarded as a flagrant attempt to undermine the Consultation's vote against secession. Austin to Royall, December 25, 1835, *AP*, 3:293 (quotation). See also Austin to Johnson, December 22, 1835, *AP*, 3:289.

2. For the capture and execution of Mexía at the Battle of Puebla, see Carlos María de Bustamante, *El Gabinete Mexicano Durante el Segundo Período de la Administración del Exmo. Señor Presidente D. Anastasio Bustamante* . . . (México: José M. Lara, 1842), 182–183; Waddy Thompson, *Recollections of Mexico* (New York, London: Wiley and Putnam, 1847), 75 (quotation). See also *Niles' National Register*, June 15, 1839.

3. S. F. Austin to H. Austin, January 7, 1836, *AP*, 3:297–298 (quotation on 297). For more on the diplomatic mission to the United States undertaken by Austin, Wharton, and Archer, see Ethel Zivley Rather, "Recognition of the Republic of Texas by the United States," *QTSHA* 13, no. 3 (1910): 167–191.

4. *New York Commercial Herald*, quoted in Carlos Castaneda et al., *The Mexican Side of the Texan Revolution* (Austin: P.L. Turner Company, 1928), 354.

5. *Georgia Telegraph* (Macon), December 7, 1835 (quotation). For more on the "Texas Fever" in the South, see Claude Elliott, "Georgia and the Texas Revolution," *Georgia Historical Quarterly* 4 (1944): 233–250; and Claude Elliott, "Alabama and the Texas Revolution," *SHQ* 50, no. 1 (1946): 315–328.

6. Andrew Forest Muir and Citizen of Ohio, *Texas in 1837: An Anonymous, Contemporary Narrative* (Austin: University of Texas Press, 1958), 135.

7. John E. Roller, "Capt. John Sowers Brooks," *QTSHA* 9, no. 3 (1906): 164, 166.

8. Ibid., 171. For more on the cult of adventurism animating young American men like Brooks, see Jimmy L. Bryan Jr., "The Patriot-Warrior Mystique: John S. Brooks, Walter P. Lane, Samuel H. Walker, and the Adventurous Quest for Renown," in *Texans and War: New Interpretations of the State's Military History* (College Station: Texas A&M University Press, 2012), 113–131.

9. Thomas Jefferson Green, and Sam W. Haynes, ed., *Journal of the Texian Expedition Against Mier* . . . (Austin: W. Thomas Taylor, 1993), vii–viii. Green's business activities in Florida are examined in James M. Denham, "The Peerless Wind Cloud: Thomas Jefferson Green and the Tallahassee Land Company," *ETHJ* 29, no. 2, article 5 (1991): 2–14.

10. For a long overdue study of Crockett's congressional career, see James R. Boylston and Allen J. Wiener, *David Crockett in Congress: The Rise and Fall of the Poor Man's Friend, with Collected Correspondence, Selected Speeches, and Circulars* (Houston: Bright Sky Press, 2009).

11. Several biographers have characterized Crockett as a naïve, unwitting dupe of the Whig Party, which enlisted him as part of its anti-Jackson campaign in the mid-1830s. See, for example, Davy Crockett and James Atkins Shackford, *A Narrative of the Life of David Crockett of the State of Tennessee* (Knoxville: University of Tennessee Press, 1973); Long, *Duel of Eagles*; and Mark Derr, *The Frontiersman: The Real Life and the Many Legends of Davy Crockett* (New York: W. Morrow, 1993). For a persuasive corrective to this view, see Thomas E. Scruggs, "Davy Crockett and the Thieves of Jericho," *JER* 19, no. 3 (Autumn 1999): 481–498.

12. Wooten, *Comprehensive History of Texas*, 1:225.

13. Houston to Soldiers, January 15, 1836, *PTR*, 4:30 (first quotation); *Telegraph and Texas Register* (San Felipe), February 27, 1836 (second quotation); Austin to Linn, May 4, 1836, *AP*, 3:35 (third quotation).

14. According to Ramón Caro, Santa Anna's private secretary, preparations for the campaign were underway by October 1835. Castaneda, *Mexican Side of the Texas Revolution*, 99.

15. Santa Anna to Sesma, December 7, 1835, *PTR*, 3:112. Pakenham to Palmerston, December 15, 1835, Foreign Office General Correspondence Mexico: Series I, 1823–1863 (London: Public Record Office, 1960), BLAC.

16. Pakenham to Palmerston, December 15, 1835, Foreign Office General Correspondence Mexico, BLAC.

17. For the difficulties of raising funds to pay for the campaign against Texas, see Castaneda, *Mexican Side of the Texas Revolution*, 9–12, 50–52, 99–101; and Fowler, *Santa Anna of Mexico*, 163–164.

18. Filisola, *Memoirs for the History of the War in Texas*; José Enrique de la Peña, *With Santa Anna in Texas* (College Station: Texas A&M University Press, 1997), 6, 19; Tina Flannery, "Mexican Military Movements in the Texas Revolution," MA thesis, University of North Texas, 1966, 53.

19. William A. De Palo, Jr., *The Mexican National Army, 1822–1852* (College Station: Texas A&M University Press, 1997), 51.

20. Castaneda, *Mexican Side of the Texas Revolution*, 100; Filisola, *Memoirs for the History of the War in Texas*, 2:144–145.

21. De la Peña, *With Santa Anna in Texas*, 24, 30. Filisola, *Memoirs for the History of the War in Texas*, 2:161.

22. Castaneda, *Mexican Side of the Texas Revolution*, 101; de la Peña, *With Santa Anna in Texas*, 26.

23. Flannery, "Mexican Military Movements in the Texas Revolution," 27.

24. Santa Anna to Tornel, February 16, 1835, *PTR*, 4:356–362 (quotation on 358). The case for Almonte's authorship is made by Jack Jackson in *Almonte's Texas*, 358–359.

25. Fowler, *Santa Anna of Mexico*, 165. For the last difficult leg of the march to San Antonio de Béxar, see de la Peña, *With Santa Anna in Texas*, 26–29. Filisola, *Memoirs for the History of the War in Texas*, 2:163.

CHAPTER THIRTEEN. MORE COMMANDERS-IN-CHIEF THAN ONE

1. Zavala, *Journey to the United States*, 195.

2. Zavala to Austin, September 17, 1835, *PTR*, 1:453–454.

3. Yoakum, *History of Texas*, 2:28.

4. Robinson Proclamation, February 12, 1836, *PTR*, 307–314. For more on the anarchy that prevailed under the General Council, see Paul D. Lack, *The Texas Revolutionary Experience: A Political and Social History, 1835–1836* (College Station: Texas A&M University Press, 1992), 53–74.

5. For more on de la Garza, see Alonzo Salazar, "Carlos de la Garza: Loyalist Leader," in de la Teja, ed., *Tejano Leadership*, 195–210; and Castillo Crimm, *De León*, 105–106. Craig H. Roell suggests that tensions between Goliad and Victoria may have played a role in the path each town and its leaders chose during the rebellion. See Craig H. Roell, "Matamoros and the Tejanos of Victoria and Goliad in the Texas Revolution: Conflicting Loyalties and 'Assiduous Collaborators,'" in Milo Kearney, et al., *Extra Studies in Rio Grande History*, 14: 24–26.

6. Fannin to Robinson, February 28, 1836, *PTR*, 4:456.

7. John C. Duval, *Early Times in Texas* (Austin: Steck Company, 1935), 31–32; Craig H. Roell, *Matamoros and the Texas Revolution* (Denton: Texas State Historical Association, 2013), 82.

8. John E. Roller, "Capt. John Sowers Brooks," *QTSHA* 9, no. 3 (1906): 177, 179, 181 (quotation on 181).

9. "Treaty between Texas and the Cherokee Indians," February 23, 1836, Winfrey and Day, eds., *Texas Indian Papers*, 1:14–17.

10. John Henry Brown, *Indian Wars and Pioneers of Texas* (Austin: L. E. Daniel, n.d.), 89.

11. John Sutherland, *The Fall of the Alamo* (San Antonio: Naylor Company, 1936), 11–12.

12. Travis to Smith, February 13, 1836, *PTR*, 4:327–328.

13. Sutherland, *Fall of the Alamo*, 13–15.

14. Sutherland, *Fall of the Alamo*, 16 (quotation); Todd Hansen, *The Alamo Reader: A Study in History* (Mechanicsburg: Stackpole Books, 2003), 332.

15. Batres to Bowie, February 23, 1836, *PTR*, 4:415 (quotation); Stephen L. Hardin, "Efficient in the Cause," in Gerald Eugene Poyo, ed., *Tejano Journey, 1770–1860* (Austin: University of Texas Press, 1996), 57–58.

16. Travis to the Public, February 24, 1836, *PTR*, 4:423.

17. Roller, "Capt. John Sowers Brooks," 183 (quotation); Fannin to Robinson, February 25, 1836, *PTR*, 4:443–444.

18. Joseph Henry Barnard, *Dr. J. H. Barnard's Journal from December, 1835 to March 27th, 1836, Giving an Account of Fannin Massacre* (Goliad: Goliad Advance, 1912), 11.

19. Roller, "Capt. John Sowers Brooks," 186 (first quotation), 187, 189 (second quotation).

20. Seguín, *A Revolution Remembered*, 80.

21. Filisola, *Memoirs for the History of the War in Texas*, 2:174–176.

22. Gray, *Diary of William Fairfax Gray*, 128–128; Filisola, *Memoirs for the History of the War in Texas*, 2:178; de la Peña, *With Santa Anna in Texas*, 49–53 (quotation on 49).

23. Gray, *Diary of William Fairfax Gray*, 129–130; Timothy M. Matovina, *The Alamo Remembered: Tejano Accounts and Perspectives* (Austin: University of Texas Press, 1995), 71–72, 88–89. Recent scholarship points to the conclusion that Joe was the younger brother of the noted abolitionist William Wells Brown. See Ron Jackson and Lee Spencer White, *Joe, the Slave Who Became an Alamo Legend* (Norman: University of Oklahoma Press, 2015), xiii–xxii.

24. De la Peña, *With Santa Anna in Texas*, 54–55.

25. General Filisola's casualty figures for the Mexican army are 60 killed and 233 wounded. Filisola, *Memoirs for the History of the War in Texas*, 2:178. Linn, *Reminiscences*, 177 (quotation). For a detailed analysis of Mexican casualties during the dawn attack on March 6, see Thomas Ricks Lindley, *Alamo Traces: New Evidence and New Conclusions* (Lanham, MD: Republic of Texas Press, 2003), 249–282.

26. Gray, *Diary of William Fairfax Gray*, 115.

27. Andrés Reséndez, *A Texas Patriot on Trial in Mexico: José Antonio Navarro and the Texan Santa Fe Expedition* (Dallas: DeGolyer Library, 2005), 54–55; David R. McDonald, *José Antonio Navarro: In Search of the American Dream in Nineteenth Century Texas* (Denton: Texas State Historical Association, 2010), 130–131.

28. Travis to Convention, March 3, 1836, *PTR*, 4:502–504 (quotation on 503).

29. For several eyewitness accounts of the battle at Refugio, see "Mission Refugio," Sons of Dewitt Colony, www.sonsofdewittcolony.org/goliadframe .htm. Salazar, "Carlos de la Garza," 200–202. See also Hobart Huson, *Refugio: A Comprehensive History of Refugio County from Aboriginal Times . . .* (Woodsboro: Rooke Foundation, 1953), 286–314.

30. Ehrenberg, *Inside the Texas Revolution*, 269–270.

31. Hermann Ehrenberg, a German adventurer and member of the New Orleans Greys, provides the most vivid account of the battle at Coleto Creek. Available in several English editions, *Texas and Its Revolution* has recently been republished with extensive annotations by James Crisp. Ehrenberg, *Inside the Texas Revolution*, 270–293.

32. Gray, *Diary of William Fairfax Gray*, 117–127; Marks, *Turn Your Eyes Toward Texas*, 58–60.

33. On March 13, only three days before the news of the fall of the Alamo reached Washington, Zavala confided to William Fairfax Gray that "Santa Anna's race is nearly run." Gray, *Diary of William Fairfax Gray*, 121.

CHAPTER FOURTEEN. TO THE LYNCHBURG FERRY

1. Houston to Royall, March 24, 1836, *WSH*, 1:384.

2. Smithwick, *Evolution of a State*, 79 (first quotation); "Uncle Jeff Parsons of Jackson Municipality," *Sons of Dewitt Colony*, www.sonsofdewittcolony.org /mustergon2.htm (second quotation).

3. John E. Roller, "Capt. John Sowers Brooks," *QTSHA* 9, no. 3 (1906): 196.

4. Yoakum, *History of Texas*, 520.

5. Linn, *Reminiscences*, 173.

6. Joseph E. Field, *Three Years in Texas: Including a View of the Texan Revolution* . . . (Boston: Abel Tompkins, 1836), 43–44 (quotation). For other eyewitness accounts of the Goliad executions, see [Joseph H. Spohn] "Colonel James W. Fannin's Execution at Goliad"; [Jack Shackelford] "Massacre at Goliad—Captain Jack Shackelford's Account"; and Andrew A. Boyle, "Reminiscences of the Texas Revolution," in *Sons of Dewitt Colony Texas*, www .sonsofdewittcolony.org/goliadframe.htm.

7. Pakenham to Palmerston, April 21, 1836, Foreign Office General Correspondence Mexico: Series I, BLAC. For the amended decree, see Tornel Decree, April 14, 1836, *PTR*, 5:475–477. For the Mexican response to the charge of war crimes committed by the Army of Operations, see Josefina Zoraida Vázquez, "The Texas Question in Mexican Politics, 1836–1845" *SHQ* 89, no. 3 (1986): 314. For an example of the public response to the execution in the United States, see *Columbus Enquirer* (Georgia), May 6, 1836.

8. John Francis Hamtramck Claiborne, *Life and Correspondence of John A. Quitman* . . . (New York: Harper & Brothers, 1860), 1:148. *Telegraph and Texas Register*, November 16, 1836 (first quotation); Linda English, "'Madam, You Ought to be the Man Such Times as These': Gendered Confrontations and the Runaway Scrape," *American Nineteenth Century History* 19, no. 2: 181 (second quotation).

9. Berlet, *Autobiography of a Spoon*, 86; Dilue Harris, "The Reminiscences of Mrs. Dilue Harris, II," *QTSHA* 4, no. 3 (1901): 164. Barker, "African Slave Trade," 153. The slave ship that landed on March 2 was the *Shenandoah*, chartered by Monroe Edwards and a business partner to bring 185 enslaved people from Havana. For more on Edwards, see Brian P. Luskey, "Chasing Capital in Hard Times: Monroe Edwards, Slavery, and Sovereignty in the Panicked Atlantic," *Early American Studies: An Interdisciplinary Journal* 14, no. 1 (2016): 89–90.

10. Harris, "Reminiscences, II," 165–166.

11. For a vivid account of the extent to which rumors of an Indian war took hold among the residents of Nacogdoches, see Friedrich W. von Wrede, *Sketches of Life in the United States of North America and Texas* (Waco: Texian Press, 1970), 21–24. Hotchkiss Report, March 21, 1836, *PTR*, 13–14; Chesher

to Committee, April 11, 1836, Ibid., 429–430; *House Executive Documents*, no. 455, 780; *House Executive Documents*, no. 351, 25th Congress, 2nd session, 22 (Washington, DC: Government Printing Office, 1837), 790; Ibid., no. 351, 777–778; *American State Papers*, 24th Congress, 6:425 (quotation).

12. Starr, *History of the Cherokee*, 209–210. Houston to Bowls, April 13, 1836, *WSH*, 1:408–410.

13. *House Executive Documents*, no. 351, 767.

14. This would come to be known as the Dade Massacre. See C. S. Monaco, *The Second Seminole War and the Limits of American Aggression* (Baltimore: Johns Hopkins University Press, 2018), 55–56, 64–67; Kenneth W. Porter, *The Black Seminoles: History of a Freedom-Seeking People* (Gainesville: University Press of Florida, 2013), 394.

15. *House Executive Documents*, no. 351, 769–770.

16. Vicente Filísola, *Evacuation of Texas: Translation of the Representation Addressed to the Supreme Government by Gen. Vicente Filisola in Defence of His Honor* . . . (Columbia: n.p., 1837), 9–10.

17. Castaneda, *Mexican Side of the Texas Revolution*, 74. In one of the many cases of Santa Anna's officers blaming the president for the Mexican defeat, second-in-command General Filisola singled out the Mexican general's decision to divide his forces at the Brazos River in an attempt to capture Zavala as a turning point in the war that "placed victory in the hands of a disheartened enemy." Filisola, *Memoirs for the History of the War in Texas*, 2:xiii.

18. Foote, *Texas and the Texans*, 2:292.

19. Rosa Kleberg, "Some of My Early Experiences in Texas," *QTSHA* 1, no. 4 (1898): 300–302; Dewees, *Letters from an Early Settler of Texas*, 207–208; Muir, *Texas in 1837*, 61; de la Peña, *With Santa Anna in Texas*, 112. S. F. Sparks, "Recollections of S. F. Sparks," *QTSHA* 12, no. 1 (1908): 63–64. Stephen L. Hardin, "A Hard Lot: Texas Women in the Runaway Scrape," *ETHJ* 29, no. 1, article 8 (1991): 37 (quotation).

20. Harris, "Reminiscences, II," 163–169 (quotation on 163).

21. Big Mush to the Committee of Safety, April 13, 1836, Andrew Jackson Houston Papers, TSLAC.

22. Marks, *Turn Your Eyes Toward Texas*, 60–61.

23. De la Peña, *With Santa Anna in Texas*, 114.

24. Information Concerning Zavala, n.d., *PML*, 1:522. Jeffrey D. Dunn, "'To the *Devil* with Your Glorious History!' Women and the Battle of San Jacinto," in Mary L. Scheer, ed., *Women and the Texas Revolution* (Denton: University of North Texas Press, 2012), 184–185.

25. Bill Walraven and Marjorie K. Walraven, "The 'Sabine Chute': The U.S. Army and the Texas Revolution," *SHQ* 107, no. 4 (2004): 577, 579. For a breakdown of the ages and origins of the men in Sam Houston's army at San Jacinto, see Paul D. Lack, *The Texas Revolutionary Experience: A Political*

and Social History, 1835–1836 (College Station: Texas A&M University Press, 1992), 126–128.

26. James Washington Winters, "An Account of the Battle of San Jacinto," *QTSHA* 6, no. 2 (1902): 141–142. For a critical account of Houston at San Jacinto, see Robert M. Coleman, and Stephen L. Hardin, ed., *Houston Displayed; or, Who Won the Battle of San Jacinto?* (Dallas: DeGolyer Library and William P. Clements Center for Southwest Studies, Southern Methodist University, 2020).

27. For Lorenzo de Zavala Jr.'s eyewitness account of the battle, see Zavala Jr. to McArdle, September 17, 1890, Lorenzo de Zavala Papers, BCAH. According to legend, a fiddler played a popular ballad, "Will You Come to the Bower," as the Texas army began its march toward the Mexican camp. In fact, the song was sung the day before the battle. See Seguín, *A Revolution Remembered*, 82. One officer in Houston's army remembered that the Texans marched across the open prairie "with the stillness of death—no fife, nor voice was heard," until the order to charge was given, which was soon followed by "the soul stirring tune" of "Yankee Doodle." *Telegraph and Texas Register* (Columbia), August 16, 1836 (quotation).

28. Pedro Delgado, *Mexican Account of the Battle of San Jacinto* (Deer Park: W. C. Day, 1919), 10.

29. Winters, "Account of the Battle of San Jacinto," 143; Holley, *Texas: Observations*, 76; Stephen L. Hardin, *Texian Iliad: A Military History of the Texas Revolution, 1835-1836* (Austin: University of Texas Press, 1994), 214; Seguín, *A Revolution Remembered*, 83; Sparks, "Recollections of S. F. Sparks," 71.

30. *El Mosquito Mexicano*, June 14, June 17, June 21, June 24, 1836; Jeffrey D. Dunn, "Mapping San Jacinto Battleground, 1836–1855" *SHQ* 114, no. 4 (2011): 390–391.

CHAPTER FIFTEEN. THE PRISONERS OF VELASCO

1. [Lorenzo de Zavala Jr. to Adina de Zavala] undated, Lorenzo de Zavala Papers, BCAH. There are several accounts of the capture of Santa Anna. See Kuykendall, "Reminiscences of Early Texans," QTSHA 6, no. 3 (1903): 244–245; Linn, *Reminiscences*, 265–268; and Sion Bostick, "Reminiscences of Sion R. Bostick," *QTSHA* 5, no. 2 (1901): 93–95.

2. Houston to General Commanding, July 26, 1836, *PTR*, 8:35. Kuykendall, "Reminiscences of Early Texans," 45.

3. De la Peña, *With Santa Anna in Texas*, 170; Raymond Estep, "Lorenzo de Zavala and the Texas Revolution," 334; Zavala to Mexía, May 26, 1836, Lorenzo de Zavala Papers, BCAH (quotation). Zavala would later have Castrillón's body interred in the cemetery at his home on Buffalo Bayou.

4. Margaret Swett Henson, "Politics and the Treatment of the Mexican Prisoners after the Battle of San Jacinto," *SHQ* 94, no. 2 (1990): 196–197.

5. "Treaty of Velasco: Public," *PTR*, 6:273–275; "Treaty of Velasco, Secret," *PTR*, 6:275–276.

6. Gray, *Diary of William Fairfax Gray*, 140.

7. Linn, *Reminiscences*, 308.

8. "To the Friends of Liberty Throughout the World!," April 5, 1836, Thomas Jefferson Green Papers, SHC. Green, *Journal of the Texian Expedition Against Mier*, viii-ix.

9. Relation of Scenes and Events Concerning Santa Anna, *PML*, 1:525–527. Estep, "Lorenzo de Zavala and the Texas Revolution," 333 (quotation); Green, *Journal of the Texian Expedition Against Mier*, ix–x.

10. Castaneda, *Mexican Side of the Texan Revolution*, 89 (first quotation); Santa Anna to Burnet, June 9, 1836, *PTR*, 7:88–89 (second quotation).

11. Castaneda, *Mexican Side of the Texas Revolution*, 138; Gabriel Nuñez Ortega, Diary of Colonel Gabriel Nuñez Ortega, Brazoria County Historical Museum; Castaneda, *Mexican Side of the Texan Revolution*, 137–147.

12. Macomb to Morgan, July 28, *PTR*, 8:58 (quotation). For more on Green's conduct with Rusk's army at Victoria, see Smithwick, *Evolution of a State*, 102–103.

13. The years 1836 and 1837 saw a major increase in Comanche raiding activity across the Southwest. See Delay, *War of a Thousand Deserts*, 61. For attacks on Laredo and San Antonio, see Robert D. Wood, *Archivos de Laredo: Documents for the History of Laredo* (San Antonio: 1999), 8; Antonio Menchaca, *Recollections of a Tejano Life: Antonio Menchaca in Texas History* (Austin: University of Texas Press, 2013), 154–156. For an account of the Mexican army's retreat, see Gregg J. Dimmick, *Sea of Mud: The Retreat of the Mexican Army after San Jacinto, an Archeological Investigation* (Austin: Texas State Historical Association, 2004), chs. 8–12. On April 4 Comanche raiders attacked the Horn party, formerly members of the ill-fated Rio Grande colony of John Charles Beales. See Brown, *Indian Wars and Pioneers of Texas*, 30–31; Sarah Ann Horn and E. House, *An Authentic and Thrilling Narrative of the Captivity of Mrs. Horn, and Her Two Children, with Mrs. Harris, by the Camanche Indians: and the Murder of Their Husbands and Traveling Companions* (Cincinnati: 1853); and Carl Coke Rister, *Comanche Bondage: Dr. John Charles Beales's Settlement of La Villa de Dolores on Las Moras Creek in Southern Texas of the 1830's, with an Annotated Reprint of Sarah Ann Horn's Narrative of Her Captivity Among the Comanches . . .* (Glendale, CA: A. H. Clark Co., 1955). The attack on Fort Parker six weeks later is perhaps the most famous Indian raid in the long history of conflict between Anglo-Texans and Native peoples. See Parker to Lamar, February 3, 1844, *PML*, 4:38; Jo Ella Powell Exley, *Frontier Blood: The Saga of the Parker Family* (College Station: Texas A&M University Press, 2001); and Dan Gelo, "Two Episodes in Texas Indian History Reconsidered," *SHQ* 120, no. 4 (2017): 450–460.

14. Barker, *Life of Stephen F. Austin*, 511 (quotation). For more on the presidential election of 1836, see Siegel, *Political History of the Texas Republic*, 45–55.

15. Lack, "The Córdova Revolt," in Poyo, ed., *Tejano Journey*, 94. Green, *Journal of the Texian Expedition Against Mier*, xi.

16. Ferris A. Bass and B. R. Brunson, eds., *Fragile Empires: The Texas Correspondence of Samuel Swartwout and James Morgan, 1836–1856* (Austin: Shoal Creek Publishers, 1978), 24.

CHAPTER SIXTEEN. THE BARNYARD REPUBLIC

1. Houston to Jackson, November 20, 1836, *AP*, 3:457–458.

2. For Wharton's diplomatic instructions, see Austin to Wharton, November 18, 1836, George P. Garrison, *Diplomatic Correspondence of the Republic of Texas* (Washington, DC: Govt. Printing Office, 1908), 2:127–140. On Wharton's assessment of the prospects for Texas annexation, see Wharton to Austin, December 11, 1836, Garrison, Ibid., 2:151–153 (quotation on 153).

3. *Telegraph and Texas Register*, July 29, 1837; Jonathan W. Jordan, *Lone Star Navy: Texas, the Fight for the Gulf of Mexico, and the Shaping of the American West* (Washington, DC: Potomac Books, 2006), 83–86. Emily Austin to James Perry, James Perry Papers, August 13, 1837, BCAH (quotation).

4. Berlet, *Autobiography of a Spoon*, 31; Jordan, *Lone Star Navy*, 87.

5. *Telegraph and Texas Register*, August 30, 1836 (quotation); Muir, *Texas in 1837*, 29; Holley, *Letters of an American Traveller*, 70.

6. On the Velasco social scene, see Holley, *Letters of an American Traveller*, 72; and Francis C. Sheridan, *Galveston Island; or, A Few Months Off the Coast of Texas: The Journal of Francis C. Sheridan, 1839–1840* (Austin: University of Texas Press, 1954), 18; "John Sharp Merchant of Velasco," Brazosport Archaeological Society, 10–16.

7. Mrs. Houstoun, *Texas and the Gulf of Mexico, or, Yachting in the New World* (Philadelphia: L. P. Smith, 1844), 91–94; Muir, *Texas in 1837*, 91–94; "John Sharp Merchant of Velasco," 1–28. Franklin, ed., "Memoirs of Mrs. Annie P. Harris," *SHQ* 40, no. 3 (1937): 246; Sheridan, *Galveston Island*, 31–47.

8. A rough estimate of the total Texas population in 1836 is 30,000 Anglos, 5,000 Hispanos (including the residents of Laredo), 20,000 Native Americans, 5,000 enslaved African Americans, and 500 free persons of color. For a more detailed analysis of the Native American population according to tribe, see Anna Muckleroy, "The Indian Policy of the Republic of Texas, I," *SHQ* 25, no. 1 (1921): 242. Richard S. Hunt and Jesse F. Randel, *Map of Texas*, 1839 (quotation); Gammel, *Laws of Texas*, 1:1193–1194.

9. Gammel, *Laws of Texas*, 1:1069–1070, 1:1073.

10. Ibid., 1:1078–1080, 1:1083–1084.

11. For Wharton's speech criticizing the planters and merchants of Texas during the rebellion, see *Telegraph and Texas Register* (Houston), November 16, 1836. The internal improvements and banking scheme was known as the Texas Railroad, Banking and Navigation Company. See Gammel, *Laws of Texas*, 1:1188–1190; *Telegraph and Texas Register*, July 29, 1837; Andrew Forest Muir, "Railroad Enterprise in the Republic of Texas, 1836–1841," *SHQ* 47, no. 4 (1944): 339–345; and Green, *Journal of the Texian Expedition Against Mier*, xii-xiii.

12. On the Homestead Exemption Law, see Gammel, *Laws of Texas*, 1:125–126; and Paul Goodman, "The Emergence of Homestead Exemption in the United States: Accommodation and Resistance to the Market Revolution, 1840–1880," *JAH* 80, no. 2 (1993): 477. On public education see *Journal of the House of Representatives of the Republic of Texas*, Third Congress (Houston: S. Whiting, 1839), 270–271.

13. Houstoun, *Texas and the Gulf of Mexico*, 171 (first quotation); Peareson, "Reminiscences of Judge Edwin Waller," 49–51. *Telegraph and Texas Register*, January 12, 1839 (second quotation). For political duels and other violent affrays during this period, see Hogan, *The Texas Republic*, 271–273.

14. A. W. Terrell, "Recollections of General Sam Houston," *SHQ* 16, no. 2 (1912): 129.

15. Notwithstanding Houston's popular appeal, British traveler Mathilda Houstoun believed the president to be "a Tory at heart." Houstoun, *Texas and the Gulf of Mexico*, 171; Stephen L. Hardin, "Sam Houston's Generalship in the Battle of San Jacinto," www.sonsofdewittcolony.org //adp/archives /feature/hardin.html (first quotation). Jackson, *Indian Agent*, 251 (second quotation). Kuykendall, "Sketches of Early Texans," 59. For Houston's sartorial eccentricities, see Mary Reid, "Fashions of the Republic," *SHQ* 45, no. 3 (1942): 247 (third quotation); and Nancy Nichols Barker, *The French Legation in Texas* (Austin: Texas State Historical Association, 1971), 66.

16. Hogan, *Texas Republic*, 281–282.

17. Jim Dan Hill, *The Texas Navy in Forgotten Battles and Shirtsleeve Diplomacy* (New York: A. S. Barnes, 1962), 84.

18. Dora Fowler Arthur, "Jottings from the Old Journal of Littleton Fowler," *QTSHA* 2, no. 1 (1898): 80 (first quotation); John A. Wharton, *Speech of the Hon. John A. Wharton, In Defence of the Hon. S. Rhoads Fisher* (Houston: Telegraph Press, 1837), 43 (second quotation).

19. Green, *Samuel Maverick, Texan*, 141; Francis Richard Lubbock, *Six Decades in Texas: The Memoirs of Francis R. Lubbock, Confederate Governor of Texas* (Austin: Pemberton Press, 1968), 43; Jones, *Memoranda and Official Correspondence*, 34 (quotation).

20. For Lamar's poetry, see Mirabeau B. Lamar, *Verse Memorials* (New York: W. P. Fetridge & Co., 1857). Bass and Brunson, eds., *Fragile Empires*, 36 (first

quotation); Herbert Pickens Gambrell, *Mirabeau Buonaparte Lamar: Troubadour and Crusader* (Dallas: Southwest Press, 1934), 165–166 (second quotation).

21. For John A. Wharton's death, see *Telegraph and Texas Register*, December 14, 1838; and Berlet, *Autobiography of a Spoon*, 34–35, 87–92. For William A. Wharton's death, see *Telegraph and Texas Register*, March 20, 1839; and Berlet, *Autobiography of a Spoon*, 38.

22. Merton L. Dillon, "Benjamin Lundy in Texas," *SHQ* 63, no. 1 (1959): 46–62.

23. Benjamin Lundy, *The War in Texas; a Review of Facts and Circumstances, Showing That This Contest Is the Result of a Long Premeditated Crusade Against the Government, Set on Foot by Slaveholders, Land Speculators, etc.*, . . . (Philadelphia: Merrihew and Gunn, 1836).

24. Siegel, *Political History of the Texas Republic*, 86; Justin H. Smith, *The Annexation of Texas* (New York: AMS Press, 1971), 64–65.

25. William Lee Miller, *Arguing About Slavery: The Great Battle in the United States Congress* (New York: Alfred A. Knopf, 1996), 284–298.

26. Sheridan, *Galveston Island*, 99. Houston to Jackson, August 11, 1838, *WSH*, 2:271 (first quotation); Gray, *Diary of William Fairfax Gray*, 212 (second quotation).

CHAPTER SEVENTEEN. HE IS UNFORTUNATELY A MAN OF COLOUR

1. *Genius of Universal Emancipation*, November 1832, 4–5. Lundy, *Life of Lundy*, 116–117.

2. David O. Watkins, "Proceed to the Prairie" [Diary of David O. Watkins], typescript, Watkins Family Papers, RWSL (first quotation); Muir, *Texas in 1837*, 47 (second quotation).

3. Harold Schoen, "The Free Negro in the Republic of Texas, 2," *SHQ* 40, no. 1 (1936): 26–34.

4. Schoen, "Free Negro in the Republic of Texas, 4," *SHQ* 40, no. 3 (January 1937): 174; Gammel, *Laws of Texas*, 1:1079 (quotation).

5. Gammel, *Laws of Texas*, 1:1079.

6. In 1850, the first year census figures are available, northeast Texas (Bowie, Red River, Cass, Lamar, Fannin, and Grayson counties) had a total population of 28,366, of whom 6,778 (24 percent) were enslaved. *Seventh Census of the United States, 1850—Texas* (Washington, DC: Robert Armstrong, Public Printer, 1853), 503–504.

7. Fred Robbins, "The Origin and Development of the African Slave Trade in Galveston," *ETHJ* 9, no. 2: 158; Creighton, *Narrative History of Brazoria County*, 171, 174; Garrison, *Diplomatic Correspondence of the Republic of Texas*, 2:148 (quotation). On the Houston administration's efforts to curb the illegal slave trade, see Kennedy, *Texas*, 759–762.

8. On runaway slaves and Native Americans, see Kenneth W. Porter, "Negroes and Indians of the Texas Frontier, 1834–1874," *SHQ* 53, no. 1 (1949): 197–204. On the "Wild Man of the Navidad," see Harris, "Reminiscences, I," 107–108. Ronnie C. Tyler and Lawrence R. Murphy, *The Slave Narratives of Texas* (Austin: State House Press, 1997), 69 (quotation).

9. On runaway slave notices, see, for example, *Civilian and Galveston Gazette*, January 11, 1843; "Runaway Taken," *National Vindicator* (Washington-on-the-Brazos), February 10, 1844. On runaway slave notices of recently smuggled Africans, see *Telegraph and Texas Register*, August 5, 1837, August 12, 1837, and April 6, 1839.

10. *Telegraph and Texas Register*, December 28, 1846, Wendell G. Addington, "Slave Insurrections in Texas," *JNH* 35, no. 4 (1950): 414; Kenneth Kesselus, *History of Bastrop County, Texas, 1846–1865* (Austin: Jenkins Pub. Co., 1987), 264; *Clarksville Northern Standard*, October 30, 1844; *Telegraph and Texas Register*, May 25, 1842 (quotation).

11. Speech on Thomas Jefferson Green, August 1, 1854, *WSH*, 6:80 (quotation). For more on Tom and Esau, see Friend, *Sam Houston*, 183. See also Frederick Law Olmsted, *A Journey Through Texas: A Saddletrip on the Southwestern Frontier* (Austin: Von Boeckmann-Jones Press, 1962), 324. According to John S. Ford, three thousand enslaved people had escaped to the villas del norte by 1855. John Salmon Ford, and Stephen B. Oates, ed., *Rip Ford's Texas* (Austin: University of Texas Press, 1963), 196. For more on what has sometimes been called the "southern underground railroad," see Alice L. Baumgartner, *South to Freedom: Runaway Slaves to Mexico and the Road to Civil War* (New York: Basic Books, 2020).

12. Campbell, *An Empire for Slavery*, 101–103; Paul D. Lack, "Slavery and Vigilantism in Austin, Texas, 1840–1860," *SHQ* 85, no. 1 (1981): 2; Madeleine B. Stern, "Stephen Pearl Andrews, Abolitionist, and the Annexation of Texas," *SHQ* 67, no. 4 (1964): 491–523.

13. *Houston Morning Star*, June 3, 1839.

14. Schoen, "Free Negro in the Republic of Texas, 6," *SHQ* 41, no. 1 (July 1937): 84–85.

15. In 1835, Goyens purchased from the Cherokees a thirty-year-old man named Jacob, who had escaped shortly after being brought to Texas from Virginia. Goyens placed a notice in a local newspaper for Jacob's owner "to come forward, prove property, pay charges, and take him away." See "Texas," *Liberator* (Boston) 6, no. 14 (April 2, 1836): 56; Prince, "William Goyens," 64 (quotation).

16. Gammel, *Laws of Texas*, I:1386, 4:1463; Schoen, "Free Negro in the Republic of Texas, 6," 93, 99.

17. Gammel, *Laws of Texas*, 1:1294–1295; Julia Lee Sinks, *Chronicles of Fayette: The Reminiscences of Julia Lee Sinks* (1975), 9; Smithwick, *Evolution of a State*, 163–166.

18. A compilation of Goyens's legal battles can be found in *BRC*, vols. 23–24. Schoen, "Free Negro in the Republic of Texas, 6," 88, 100. For more on free blacks and the court system in antebellum Texas, see Gillmer, *Slavery and Freedom in Texas: Stories from the Courtroom, 1821–1871* (Athens: The University of Georgia Press, 2017).

19. Petition of William Goyens to the Senate and House of Representatives, May 5, 1838, *Record of the Legislature, Petitions and Memorials*.

20. *Journal of the House of Representatives of the Republic of Texas, Second Congress, Adjourned Session* (Houston: Telegraph Office, 1838), 173; Prince, "William Goyens," 65–68. The following year, 1842, the Land Office did grant a headright to William Ashworth, head of a free black family in southeast Texas. Schoen, "Free Negro in the Republic of Texas, 5," *SHQ* 40, no. 4 (1937): 287, 289.

21. Adolphus Sterne, *Hurrah for Texas!: The Diary of Adolphus Sterne, 1838–1851* (Waco: Texian Press, 1969), 51, 54; *Telegraph and Texas Register*, September 1, 1841. The fate of Jake's wife, who was tried in another court, is unknown.

22. *Telegraph and Texas Register*, September 15, 1841.

23. Sterne, *Hurrah for Texas!*, 111.

24. Schoen, "Free Negro in the Republic of Texas, 6," 85.

CHAPTER EIGHTEEN. I HAVE NEVER TOLD YOU A LIE

1. Houston to Irion, January 23, 1837, *WSH*, 2:38; Houston to Snively, January 24, 1837, Ibid., 2:38.

2. Bill of Goods Furnished the Cherokee Indians by Richard Sparks and Smith, February 24, 1837, Winfrey and Day, eds., *Texas Indian Papers*, 1:19–20. Teawully [Bowls] to Houston, January 14, 1837, Andrew Jackson Houston Papers, TSLAC; Houston to Bowls, March 7, 183[7], Ibid.; Goyens to Houston, March 22, 1837, Ibid. For Goyens's full report of Bowls's trip among the prairie Indians, see *Telegraph and Texas Register*, June 13, 1837.

3. Muir, *Texas in 1837*, 47–48.

4. "Report of Standing Committee on Indian Affairs," October 12, 1837, Winfrey and Day, eds., *Texas Indian Papers*, 1:22–28 (quotation on 26); "Speech to the Texas Senate," May 21, 1838, *WSH*, 4:55–60 (quotation on 60).

5. In 1838, there were at least six attacks on Anglo surveying parties involving Wichitas, Caddos, Kickapoos, and Comanches. See *Border Land: The Struggle for Texas, 1821–1879*, https://library.uta.edu/borderland/home. Of the Comanches, Secretary of State Robert A. Irion wrote: "They have resolved to kill all the surveyors found within the territory which they consider theirs." Report from R. A. Irion to Sam Houston, March 14, 1838, Winfrey and Day, eds., *Texas Indian Papers*, 1:43. See also Forrest Deniell, "Texas Pioneer Surveyors and Indians," *SHQ* 60, no. 1 (1956): 501–506.

6. To Anna Raguet, Houston wrote after his meeting with Bowls that the Cherokee leader "has every disposition to keep peace and do all that is right and proper." Houston to Raguet, May 15, 1838, *WSH*, 2:227.

7. Everett, "Western Cherokees," 293–294.

8. Green, *Samuel Maverick, Texan*, 70.

9. Green, *Samuel Maverick, Texan*, 64, 70.

10. *US Senate Executive Documents*, no. 14, "Memorandum Book," 32 Congress, 2nd session, 15.

11. Kisner, "Tejanos and Anglos in Nacogdoches: Coexistence on Texas' Eastern Frontier Under the Mexican and Texan Republics, 1821–1846," MA thesis, University of Texas at Austin, 2017, 89–91.

12. Everett, "Western Cherokees," 294–295.

13. *US Senate Executive Documents*, no.14, "Memorandum Book," 32 Congress, 2nd session, 15.

14. For more on the violence between settlers and Shawnees and Delawares at this time, see Rowlett to Lamar, "Information from Doctr. Rowlett on the Red River," *PML*, 4:219; H. Allen Anderson, "The Delaware and Shawnee Indians and the Republic of Texas, 1820–1845," *SHQ* 94, no. 2 (1990): 231–260; Rex Wallace Strickland, "History of Fannin County, Texas, 1836–1843," *SHQ* 33, no. 4 (1930): 286–298; Rex Wallace Strickland, "History of Fannin County, 1836–1843, II," *SHQ* 34, no. 1 (1930): 38–68.

15. *Telegraph and Texas Register*, September 29, 1838. For a full translation of Córdova's manifesto, see Kisner, "Tejanos and Anglos in Nacogdoches," 94 (quotation). The Córdova rebellion has attracted surprisingly little attention from historians. Still the best work on the subject is Paul D. Lack, "The Córdova Revolt," in Poyo, ed., *Tejano Journey*, 89–109.

16. Houston to Bowls, August 11, 1838, *WSH*, 2:270; Houston to Bowls, August 14, 1838, *WSH*, 2:277.

17. Prince, "William Goyens," 50–52.

18. General Orders, August 18, 1838, *WSH*, 2:278.

19. Houston, "Speech on the Removal of the Capital from Austin," December 2–3, 1839, *WSH*, 2:319.

20. Bee to Lamar, September 6, 1838, *PML*, 2:218; Lois Foster Blount, "A Brief Study of Thomas Jefferson Rusk Based on His Letters to His Brother, David, 1835–1856, II," *SHQ* 34, no. 4 (1931): 280.

21. Fred Hugo Ford and John Lemuel Brown, *Larissa* (1930), 17–28.

22. On the so-called Surveyors' Fight, see Walter P. Lane, and Jimmy L. Bryan Jr., ed., *The Adventures and Recollections of General Walter P. Lane, A San Jacinto Veteran* . . . (Dallas: DeGolyer Library, William P. Clements Center for Southwest Studies, Southern Methodist University, 2000), 48–53; Brown, *Indian Wars*, 47–50; and Jimmy L. Bryan, Jr., "More Disastrous Than All: The Surveyors' Fight, 1838," *ETHJ* 38 (Spring 2000): 3–14.

23. McLeod to Lamar, October 22, 1838, *PML*, 2:265–266; McLeod to Lamar, October 25, 1838, Ibid., 2:270. For General Rusk's correspondence with the Houston administration and his officers during the 1838 fall campaign, see Thomas Jefferson Rusk Papers, 1824–1859, Box 2G33, BCAH.

24. This became known as the Edens-Madden Massacre. Campbell to Lamar, October 22, 1838, *PML*, 2:264; Brown, *Indian Wars*, 57.

25. On Rusk's campaign against the Caddos, see Dyer to Mayfield, October 21, 1838, *PML*, 2:256–257; McLeod to Sewell, November 21, 1838, Ibid., 2:296; McLeod to Lamar, November 21, 1838, Ibid., 2:298–299; and McLeod to Lamar, December 1, 1838, Ibid., 2:308–309. See also Anderson, *Conquest of Texas*, 16 (quotation).

26. Daniel Glenn, "Resolving the Revolution in East Texas," paper delivered at the Texas State Historical Association meeting, March 2020, 4; Lack, "Córdova Revolt," 106–109.

CHAPTER NINETEEN. WILD CANNIBALS OF THE WOODS

1. Siegel, *Political History of the Texas Republic*, 103.

2. M. B. Lamar, Inaugural Address, November 10, 1838, *PML*, 2:316–323. For more on the extremism of Lamar's states' rights views, see Anthony Gene Carey, "Parties and Politics in Antebellum Georgia," PhD diss., Emory University, 1992, 60–61.

3. Kennedy, *Texas*, 770.

4. M. B. Lamar, Message to Both Houses, December 21, 1838, *PML*, 2:352.

5. Ibid., 2:353.

6. Edward Harden, *The Life of George M. Troup* (Savannah: E.J. Purse, 1859), chs. 9–12. See also Watson W. Jennison, *Cultivating Race: The Expansion of Slavery in Georgia, 1750–1860* (Lexington: University Press of Kentucky, 2012), 19–20.

7. Houstoun, *Texas and the Gulf of Mexico*, 170 (quotation). Friend, *Sam Houston*, 93–94.

8. Madge T. Roberts, *The Personal Correspondence of Sam Houston, 1846–1848*, Vol. II (Denton: University of North Texas Press, 1998), 1:5 (first quotation); Ibid., 1:3 (second quotation); Ibid., 1:3 (third quotation). For more on the education of middle class Southern women during the antebellum era, see Anya Jabour, "Grown Girls, Highly Cultivated," *Journal of Southern History* 64, no. 1 (1998): 23–64.

9. William Seale, *Sam Houston's Wife: A Biography of Margaret Lea Houston* (Norman: University of Oklahoma Press, 1992), 10–13; Friend, *Sam Houston*, 97–98 (quotation on 98).

10. J. W. Wilbarger, *Indian Depredations in Texas* (Austin: Eakin Press, 1985), 151–157; James Wilson Nichols, *Now You Hear My Horn: The Journal of*

James Wilson Nichols, 1820–1887 (Austin: University of Texas Press, 1968), 36–38. Manuel Flores, the leader of the Mexican guerrillas, was thought to have been among the dead in the skirmish on the Guadalupe. However, Flores was undoubtedly the "Manuel Horris" Dolly Webster encountered after her escape from the Comanches a few months later. See Benjamin Dolbeare, *A Narrative of the Captivity and Suffering of Dolly Webster Among the Camanche Indians . . .* (New Haven: Yale University Library, 1986), 16–18. A. J. Sowell, *Early Settlers and Indian Fighters of Southwest Texas* (Austin: State House Press, 1986), 422.

11. *Telegraph and Texas Register*, May 29, 1839; US Congress, *Senate Executive Documents*, 32nd Congress, 2nd sess., doc. 14; Lamar to Colonel Bowls and other headmen, May 26, 1839, *PML*, 2:590–594.

12. Reagan, *Memoirs*, 29–32.

13. Ibid., 30–32.

14. Stephen L. Moore, *Savage Frontier: Rangers, Riflemen, and Indian Wars in Texas* (Plano: Republic of Texas Press, 2002), 2:240–245.

15. Reagan, *Memoirs*, 35; Brown, *Indian Wars*, 66–69.

16. Reagan, *Memoirs*, 35; *Telegraph and Texas Register*, August 7, 1839; Ibid., July 24, 1839; Ibid., August 25, 1839; Douglass to Johnston, July 16, 1839, *PML*, 3:45–47.

17. *Telegraph and Texas Register*, August 7, 1839; Moore, *Savage Frontier*, 3:8–9.

18. *Telegraph and Texas Register*, August 14, 1839.

19. Lamar took an uncharacteristically lenient position toward the Alabama-Coushattas, urging white settlers who ventured into the Lower Trinity River bottomlands to refrain from violence. "The Coushatta Indians are in themselves a weak and defenseless tribe and as such not to be dreaded." See Proclamation from Mirabeau B. Lamar to the Citizens of Liberty County, July 9, 1839, Winfrey and Day, eds., *Texas Indian Papers*, 1:73–74. For more on the tribe, see Jonathan B. Hook, *The Alabama-Coushatta Indians* (College Station: Texas A&M University Press, 1997).

20. Roberts, ed., *Personal Correspondence of Sam Houston*, 1:4–5; Friend, *Sam Houston*, 95.

21. For Houston's sharp condemnation of the Lamar administration's Indian removal policy during the Fourth Congress, see Speech Concerning the Cherokee Bill, December 22, 1838, *WSH*, 2:354–2:362 (first quotation on 355), and Speech on the Removal of the Capital from Austin, December 2–3, 1839, *WSH*, 2:315–322 (second quotation on 318), and Speech in Behalf of the Cherokee Land Bill, *WSH*, 2:323–347. Sterne, *Hurrah for Texas!*, 3:80.

22. Speech Concerning the Cherokee Land Bill, December 22, 1838, *WSH*, 2:358–359.

23. Gammel, *Laws of Texas*, 2:184–189.

24. For Burleson's account of the so-called Christmas Fight, see Burleson to Johnston, December 26, 1839, *Appendix to the Journals of the House of*

Representatives: Fifth Congress (Gazette Office), 126–128. See also Brown, *Indian Wars*, 69–70; Wilbarger, *Indian Depredations*, 173.

25. *Seventh Census of the United States, 1850—Texas* (Washington, DC: Robert Armstrong, Public Printer, 1853), 503.

CHAPTER TWENTY. AS FAR WEST AS IT IS POSSIBLE FOR AMERICANS TO GO

1. Marks, *Turn Your Eyes Toward Texas*, 61–62.
2. Ibid., 64, 67.
3. Green, *Sam Maverick, Texan*, 57–60.
4. Marks, *Turn your Eyes Toward Texas*, 77.
5. *Telegraph and Texas Register*, September 29, 1838.
6. Green, *Samuel Maverick, Texan*, 72. Although Anglo-Americans were known to exaggerate or simply invent stories of Native American violence, accounts of Tonkawa cannibalism are remarkably consistent. John Holland Jenkins related an incident in which members of the tribe, finding the body of a Waco man, "scalped him, cut off both legs at the knees, both hands at the wrists, pulled out his fingernails and toenails, [and] strung them around their necks." With some beef they boiled the severed limbs in a large pot, which they fed to the Tonkawa women, "believing that this would make them bring forth brave men who would hate their enemies and be able to endure hardness and face dangers." John Holland Jenkins, *Recollections of Early Texas: The Memoirs of John Holland Jenkins* (Austin: University of Texas Press, 1987), 77–78. For a similar account, in which all members of the tribe feasted on a stew of corn, potatoes, and the flesh of a Comanche warrior, see Smithwick, *Evolution of a State*, 179. Jean Louis Berlandier also noted that the Tonkawas "have been seen carrying the bleeding severed limbs of the [Tawakonis] they have slain as trophies of victory." Berlandier, *The Indians of Texas in 1830*, 147.
7. Green, *Samuel Maverick, Texan*, 72–73.
8. Ibid., 65.
9. Ibid., 85–86.
10. Ibid., 87, 125–126.
11. Smithwick, *Evolution of a State*, 136.
12. Ferdinand Roemer, *Texas: With Particular Reference to German Immigration and the Physical Appearance of the Country* (Austin: Eakin Press, 1995), 269.
13. *Telegraph and Texas Register*, March 17, 1838. Smithwick, *Evolution of a State*, 138 (quotation).
14. Green, *Samuel Maverick, Texan*, 125; Marks, *Turn Your Eyes Toward Texas*, 88.
15. Brown, *Indian Wars*, 51.
16. Brown, *Indian Wars*, 51; Wilbarger, *Indian Depredations*, 1–2.
17. Brown, *Indian Wars*, 61–62.

18. Alex W. Terrell, "The City of Austin from 1839 to 1865," *QTSHA* 14, no. 2 (1910): 114. For a history of the founding of Austin, see Jeffrey Stuart Kerr, *Seat of Empire: The Embattled Birth of Austin, Texas* (Lubbock: Texas Tech University Press, 2013).

19. Dolbeare, *Dolly Webster*, 3.

20. Dolbeare, Ibid., 4–7.

21. Dolbeare, Ibid., 11, 23.

22. Dolbeare, Ibid., 12, 24–25.

23. Dolbeare, Ibid., 21.

24. Dolbeare, Ibid., 9, 12–13.

25. Dolbeare, Ibid., 18–19.

26. Karnes to Johnston, January 10, 1840, Winfrey and Day, eds., *Texas Indian Papers*, 1:101–102.

27. Dolbeare, *Dolly Webster*, 24.

28. Green, *Samuel Maverick, Texan*, 118–119. The practice of disfiguring captive women was also observed by Jean Louis Berlandier, a botanist who accompanied General Mier y Terán to Texas in 1828. See *The Indians of Texas in 1830*, 118.

29. Johnston to Fisher, January 30, 1840, Winfrey and Day, eds., *Texas Indian Papers*, 1:105–106 (quotation on 105).

30. Republic of Texas, *Journal of the House of Representatives, Fifth Congress, Appendix* (Austin: Gazette Office, 1841), 1136–1139.

31. James Wilson Nichols, *Now You Hear My Horn: The Journal of James Wilson Nichols, 1820–1887* (Austin: University of Texas Press, 1968), 39–40. Green, *Samuel Maverick, Texan*, 107–109.

32. For an official account of the Council House episode, see McLeod to Lamar, *Appendix to the Journals of the House of Representatives: Fifth Congress*, 136–139.

33. Green, *Samuel Maverick, Texan*, 107–109.

34. Green, *Samuel Maverick, Texan*, 119.

35. In 1828, members of the Texas Boundary Commission led by General Mier y Terán had the opportunity to observe Comanche prewar rituals. See Sánchez, "A Trip to Texas in 1828," 264–265; and Berlandier, *Indians of Texas*, 73–74, 115.

36. *Telegraph and Texas Register*, September 2, 1840; Brown, *Indian Wars*, 79. For an eyewitness account of the sack of Victoria, see Linn, *Reminiscences*, 338–344. For an overview of the raid, as well as its causes and consequences, see Donaly E. Brice, *The Great Comanche Raid: Boldest Indian Attack of the Texas Republic* (Austin: Eakin Press, 1987).

37. Brown, *Indian Wars*, 81–82.

38. Nichols, *Now You Hear My Horn*, 63, 65–66; A. J. Sowell, *Early Settlers and Indian Fighters of Southwest Texas* (Austin: B.C. Jones & Co., Printers, 1900), 314; Peareson, "Reminiscences of Judge Edwin Waller," 52.

CHAPTER TWENTY-ONE. A FOREIGNER IN MY NATIVE LAND

1. *Telegraph and Texas Register*, March 28, 1837.

2. Seguín, *A Revolution Remembered*, 89 (quotation). Roell, "Matamoros and the Tejanos," in Kearney, et al., *Extra Studies in Rio Grande History*, 14: 35. Castillo Crimm, *De León*, 165–166.

3. Houston to Karnes, March 31, 1837, *WSH*, 2:77.

4. Green, *Samuel Maverick, Texan*, 136, 142.

5. Linn, *Reminiscences*, 345–346.

6. Information Derived from Anson G. Neal, May 30, 1847, *PML*, 6:101–102. Anglo historians have generally assumed that the so-called Republic of the Rio Grande was a legitimate separatist movement. See, for example, David M. Vigness, "A Texas Expedition into Mexico, 1840," *SHQ* 62, no. 1 (1958): 18–28. Recent research by Hispano scholars using Mexican archival sources dispute this view, arguing that Canales only claimed to be fighting a war for northern Mexico's independence to gain Anglo-Texan financial and military support. See Josefina Zoraida Vázquez, "La Supuesta República del Río Grande," *Historia Mexicana* 36, no. 1 (1986): 49–80; Juan José Gallegos, "'Last Drop of My Blood:' Col. Antonio Zapata: A Life and Times on Mexico's Río Grande Frontier, 1797–1840," MA thesis, University of Houston, 2005, 168–180; and Miguel González Quiroga, *War and Peace on the Rio Grande Frontier, 1830–1880* (Norman: University of Oklahoma Press, 2020), 385.

7. *Telegraph and Texas Register*, June 9, 1841; Brown to A. S. Johnston, September 13, 1838, *PML*, 3:106–107; Linn, *Reminiscences*, 323 (quotation); Sowell, *Early Settlers and Indian Fighters*, 151–157.

8. McDonald, *José Antonio Navarro*, 167.

9. Green, *Samuel Maverick, Texan*, 141.

10. Reséndez, *A Texas Patriot on Trial in Mexico*, 32.

11. For more on the ill-fated expedition's trek to New Mexico, see George Wilkins Kendall, Gerald D. Saxon, and William B. Taylor, eds., *Narrative of the Texan Santa Fé Expedition: Comprising a Description of a Tour through Texas, and Across the Great Southwestern Prairies . . .* (Dallas: William B. Clements Center for Southwest Studies, Southern Methodist University, 2004), Vol. 1 (quotation on 121).

12. For more on Navarro's trial, see McDonald, *José Antonio Navarro*, 180–199; and Reséndez, *A Texas Patriot on Trial in Mexico*.

13. Siegel, *Political History of the Texas Republic*, 182.

14. Seguín, *A Revolution Remembered*, 43–44; Green, *Samuel Maverick, Texan*, 152–153.

15. Green, *Samuel Maverick, Texan*, 155–156.

16. Green, *Samuel Maverick, Texan*, 159; Joseph Milton Nance, *After San Jacinto: The Texas-Mexican Frontier, 1836-1841* (Austin: University of Texas Press, 1963), 100.

17. Marks, *Turn Your Eyes Toward Texas*, 103.

18. Mary Maverick Diary, June 17, 1852, Maverick Family Papers, BCAH; Ibid., January 17, 1856; Ibid., February 16, 1856; Ibid., March 17–19, 1856.

19. Green, *Samuel Maverick, Texan*, 164–165.

20. Green, *Samuel Maverick, Texan*, 167; Houston Wade, *The Dawson Men of Fayette County* (Houston, 1932), 8–15.

21. Huson, *Refugio County*, 475–476; and Nichols, *Now You Hear My Horn*, 101–102.

22. Mary Ann Maverick, *Memoirs of Mary A. Maverick* (San Antonio: Alamo Printing Co., 1921), 74; *Telegraph and Texas Register*, November 16, 1842.

23. Linn, *Reminiscences*, 322–324; *Telegraph and Texas Register*, December 21, 1842.

24. Seguín, *A Revolution Remembered*, 49; Houston to E. Seguín, July 6, 1842, *WSH*, 4:125; Maverick, *Memoirs*, 59.

25. Seguín, *A Revolution Remembered*, 103.

CHAPTER TWENTY-TWO. STRIDING WITH GIANT STEPS TOWARD DISSOLUTION

1. Green, *Samuel Maverick, Texan*, 196 (first quotation), 199 (second quotation).

2. Sam W. Haynes, *Soldiers of Misfortune: The Somervell and Mier Expeditions* (University of Texas Press, 1990), 24–27, 89–90.

3. Bass and Brunson, eds., *Fragile Empires*, 185 (quotation), 203. For the economic motives of Texas militiamen and ranger companies in the campaigns against Indian villages during this period, see Anderson, *Conquest of Texas*, chs. 9–11.

4. Samuel H. Walker, *Florida and Seminole Wars: Brief Observations on the Conduct of the Officers, and on the Discipline of the Army of the United States*, 1–5, Samuel Hamilton Walker Papers, TSLAC.

5. S. H. Walker to Mrs. A. M. Walker, January 22, 1842, Samuel Hamilton Walker Papers, TSLAC. See also Bryan Jr., "The Patriot-Warrior Mystique," 113–131.

6. Although unpopular with the men he was about to lead into Mexico, Somervell would become a neighbor and close friend of Sam and Mary Maverick when the couple moved to Matagorda Peninsula in 1844. Mary would write that his "famous fits of laughter" could be heard "all over the point." Maverick, *Memoirs*, 69. Harvey Alexander Adams, "Diary of Harvey Alexander Adams, in Two Parts: Rhode Island to Texas and Expedition against the Southwest in 1842 and 1843," 64, Harvey Alexander Adams Papers, BCAH (quotation).

7. Adams, "Diary," 26, BCAH.

8. On the sack of Laredo, see William Preston Stapp, *The Prisoners of Perote: Containing a Journal Kept by the Author . . .* (Austin: University of Texas

Press, 1977), 18 (quotation); Sterling Brown Hendricks, "The Somervell Expedition to the Rio Grande, 1842," *SHQ* 23, no. 1 (1919): 128; Adams, "Diary," 55; and Joseph D. McCutchan, and Joseph M. Nance, ed., *Mier Expedition Diary: A Texan Prisoner's Account* (Austin: University of Texas Press, 1978), 25.

9. Siegel, *Political History of the Texas Republic*, 211–212.

10. Seale, *Sam Houston's Wife*, 75–78; John Washington Lockhart, and Jonnie Wallis and Laurance Landreth Hill, eds., *Sixty Years on the Brazos; the Life and Letters of Dr. John Washington Lockhart, 1824–1900* (Waco: Texian Press, 1967), 96.

11. *New Orleans Commercial Bulletin*, January 12, 1843.

12. Houston to Elliot, January 24, 1843, *WSH*, 3:299–302. Green would go to great lengths to show that Houston had callously abandoned the Mier prisoners, reprinting all the correspondence he could find on the controversy in an appendix of his memoir, *Journal of the Texian Expedition Against Mier*, 221–229.

13. Bass and Brunson, *Fragile Empires*, 199–200.

14. Lockhart, *Sixty Years on the Brazos*, 119.

15. Green, *Samuel Maverick, Texan*, 212–222 (quotations on 216, 217).

16. Green, *Samuel Maverick, Texan*, 239–242; Marks, *Turn Your Eyes Toward Texas*, 116.

17. For more on the Texans' escape at the Hacienda el Salado and their eventual recapture, see Samuel Hamilton Walker, and Marilyn McAdams Sibley, ed., *Samuel H. Walker's Account of the Mier Expedition* (Austin: Texas State Historical Association, 1978), 44. Stapp, *Prisoners of Perote*, 68–87; McCutchan, *Mier Expedition Diary*, 83–85; Haynes, *Soldiers of Misfortune*, 104–115.

18. *Niles' National Register*, May 13, 1843 (quotation); *Boston Cultivator*, May 27, 1843, 165.

19. *Telegraph and Texas Register*, July 16, 1843; Llerena B. Friend, "Sidelights and Supplements on the Perote Prisoners," *SHQ* 68, no. 4 (1965): 490; Haynes, *Soldiers of Misfortune*, 144 (first and second quotations).

20. Green would later claim that he left in the care of William Fisher a wry note addressed to the Mexican president. Since the climate at Perote was "not suiting my health," he wrote, "I should, for the present, retire to one in Texas more congenial to my feelings." Green, *Journal of the Texian Expedition Against Mier*, 148–149. For more on Green's escape and return to Texas, see Ibid., 149–176.

21. Creighton, *A Narrative History of Brazoria County*, 181. Haynes, *Soldiers of Misfortune*, 131–132.

22. Haynes, *Soldiers of Misfortune*, 145–147.

23. Ibid., 145 (first quotation), 179 (second quotation).

24. When Houston took the oath of office in December 1841, the 320 Texans captured on the Santa Fe Expedition were being marched to Mexico City. Thirty Texans were already in prison in northeastern Mexico, having been captured by Mexican troops on the Nueces River in July. The 67 men

captured by General Woll in San Antonio in September 1842, and 248 men who laid down their arms at Mier three months later would bring the total to 665. Joseph Eve, "A Letter Book of Joseph Eve, United States Chargé d'Affaires to Texas, Part III," *SHQ* 43, no. 4 (1940): 493–494 (quotation on 494).

CHAPTER TWENTY-THREE. WE ARE NOT ASHAMED TO CONFESS THAT WE WANT REPOSE

1. William W. Bollaert, and W. Eugene Hollon, ed., *William Bollaert's Texas* (Norman: University of Oklahoma Press, 1956), 185–186, 198.

2. For more on the decline of pro-war public opinion in Texas in the aftermath of the Mier Expedition, see Haynes, *Soldiers of Misfortune*, 157.

3. *Clarksville Northern Standard*, October 14, 1843.

4. Houston to Neill and Williams, May 1, 1844, *WSH*, 4:314.

5. Anderson, *Conquest of Texas*, 203.

6. Mopechucope to Houston, March 21, 1844, Winfrey and Day, eds., *Texas Indian Papers*, 2:6–9.

7. For more on Houston's relationship with Elliot, see Haynes, *Soldiers of Misfortune*, 36–37, 89–90, 96–96, 150–151.

8. Elliot to Aberdeen, February 5, 1842, Ephraim Douglass Adams, ed., *British Diplomatic Correspondence Concerning the Republic of Texas, 1838–1846* (Austin: Texas State Historical Association), 162 (first quotation); Elliot to Addington, November 15, 1842, Ibid., 126 (second quotation).

9. Friend, *Sam Houston*, 131 (first quotation). For more on Elliot's career as a diplomatic troubleshooter for Her Majesty's government, see Clagette Blake, *Charles Elliot, R. N., 1801–1875: A Servant of Britain Overseas* (London: Cleaver-Hume Press, 1960). Jackson to Houston, March 15, 1844, *WSH*, 4:266 (second quotation).

10. The Lone Star Republic's tortured road to annexation—and the efforts of European powers and Mexico to prevent it—is covered in exhaustive detail in David M. Pletcher, *The Diplomacy of Annexation: Texas, Oregon, and the Mexican War* (Columbia: University of Missouri Press, 1973), chs. 5–7.

11. For more on the annexation treaty negotiations and their impact on the 1844 campaign, see Joel H. Silbey, *Storm over Texas: The Annexation Controversy and the Road to Civil War* (New York: Oxford University Press, 2005), 52–72; and Sam W. Haynes, *Unfinished Revolution: The Early American Republic in a British World* (Charlottesville: University of Virginia Press, 2010), 238–248.

12. Western to Houston, June 16, 1844, Winfrey and Day, eds., *Texas Indian Papers*, 2:72–73. See also *Telegraph and Texas Register*, July 3, 1844; and *New York Herald*, November 26, 1847.

13. Council Ground, Tehuacana Creek, July 22, 1844, Winfrey and Day, eds., *Texas Indian Papers*, 2:81; Conner and Shaw to Houston, October 2, 1844, Ibid., 2:102–103.

14. Western to Torrey, September 23, 1844, Winfrey and Day, eds., *Texas Indian Papers*, 2:98. The Tonkawas did not attend the Tehuacana Springs conference. By 1843 the Karankawas, though not extinct, had been assimilated into other tribal groups or enslaved to labor on the plantations of the Gulf Coast. Himmel, *Conquest of the Karankawas and the Tonkawas*, 77–82.

15. No account of Indian dancing at the Tehuacana Springs meeting survives. However, Cherokee leader and newspaper editor Elijah Hicks provides a vivid description of these performances during an intertribal council held on the same site in May 1846. Elijah Hicks, "The Journal of Elijah Hicks," *Chronicles of Oklahoma* 13, no. 1, 96–97.

16. Lockhart, *Sixty Years on the Brazos*, 98; Reagan, *Memoirs*, 48.

17. Winn, "Minutes of Council at the Falls of the Brazos," October 7, 1844, Winfrey and Day, eds., *Texas Indian Papers*, 2:104–106.

18. Ibid., 2:109.

19. Ibid., 2:109–111 (first quotation, 109); Ibid., 110 (second quotation); Ibid., 111 (third quotation).

20. The Mier prisoners were released at the personal request of Wilson Shannon, who replaced Waddy Thompson as the US minister to Mexico. Haynes, *Soldiers of Misfortune*, 198–204. For more on the imprisonment and escape of José Antonio Navarro, see McDonald, *José Antonio Navarro*, 196–202.

21. Valedictory to the Texas Congress, December 9, 1844, *WSH*, 4:403 (quotation); Haynes, *Unfinished Revolution*, 253–254.

22. For more on the congressional debates that ultimately led to the so-called joint resolution offering to annex Texas to the United States, see Pletcher, *Diplomacy of Annexation*, 172–185; and Sam W. Haynes, "Anglophobia and the Quest for National Security," in Sam W. Haynes and Christopher Morris, eds., *Manifest Destiny and Empire: American Antebellum Expansionism* (College Station: Texas A&M University Press, 1997), 115–145.

23. Aware that his movements were being closely watched by proannexation Texans, Elliot traveled to Mexico in disguise. The plan backfired when Americans in the port city of Veracruz reported that a mysterious Englishman wearing a white hat had arrived on his way to the capital on important official business with Mexican leaders. Elliot's identity was soon discovered, and the scandal surrounding the "Man in the White Hat" caused an uproar in Texas and the United States, further solidifying support for the annexation proposal. For more on Elliot's secret mission to Mexico, see Sam W. Haynes, "'But What Will England Say?': Great Britain, the United States, and the War with Mexico," in Richard V. Francaviglia and Douglas W. Richmond, eds., *Dueling Eagles: Reinterpreting the U.S.-Mexican War, 1846–1848* (Fort Worth: Texas Christian University Press, 2000), 19–39; and Haynes, *Unfinished Revolution*, 253–261. For Houston's speech declaring his full support for annexation, see "A Review of the San Jacinto Campaign . . .," *WSH*, 6:12–13 (first quotation). Jackson to Polk, May 26, 1845, James Knox Polk, and Herbert Weaver,

ed., *Correspondence of James K. Polk* (Knoxville: University of Tennessee Press, 1996), 9:410 (second quotation).

24. M. L. Houston to S. Houston, October 6, 1843, Roberts, ed., *Personal Correspondence of Sam Houston*, 1:295 (first and second quotations); M. L. Houston to S. Houston, September 20, 1844, Ibid., 1:319.

25. S. Houston to M. L. Houston, January 27, 1845, Roberts, ed., *Personal Correspondence of Sam Houston*, 1: 324 (first quotation); Friend, *Sam Houston*, 157; Sam Houston, and F. N. Boney, ed.,"The Raven Tamed: An 1845 Sam Houston Letter," *SHQ* 68, no. 1 (1964): 90–92 (second quotation).

26. Maverick, *Memoirs*, 89.

CHAPTER TWENTY-FOUR. TO CONQUER A PEACE

1. Darren L. Ivey, *The Ranger Ideal, Texas Rangers in the Hall of Fame, 1823–1861* (Denton: University of North Texas Press, 2018) 1:239–240.

2. Douglas A. Murphy, *Two Armies on the Rio Grande: The First Campaign of the US-Mexican War* (College Station, Texas: Texas A&M University Press, 2015), 48–73.

3. James K. Polk, and Milo Milton Quaife, ed., *The Diary of James K. Polk During His Presidency, 1845 to 1849* (Chicago: A.C. McClurg, 1910), 1:386.

4. Murphy, *Two Armies on the Rio Grande*, 170–171.

5. Foreman, "The Texas Comanche Treaty of 1846," *SHQ* 51, no. 4 (1948): 313–332; Treaty with the Comanches and Other Tribes, May 15, 1845, Winfrey and Day, eds., *Texas Indian Papers*, 3:43–51.

6. Polk, *Diary of James K. Polk*, 2:2–5; Delay, *War of a Thousand Deserts*, 260.

7. *New York Evening Post*, July 22, 1846; *Washington Union*, July 23, 1846; Polk, *Diary of James K. Polk*, 2:29, 46.

8. Treaty with the Comanches and Other Tribes, May 15, 1845, Winfrey and Day, eds., *Texas Indian Papers*, 3:52; "Report of Robert Simpson Neighbors," *Executive Documents*, 30th Congress, first sess., no. 8, no. 22, 893. *Tri-Weekly Times* (Austin), February 11, 1854 (quotation).

9. George Wilkins Kendall and James Freaner covered the war for the New Orleans *Daily Picayune* and the New Orleans *Delta*, respectively. See George Wilkins Kendall, and Lawrence Delbert Cress, ed., *Dispatches from the Mexican War* (Norman: University of Oklahoma Press, 1999); and Alan D. Gaff and Donald H. Gaff, eds., *From the Halls of the Montezumas: Mexican War Dispatches from James L. Freaner, Writing Under the Pen Name "Mustang"* (Denton: University of North Texas Press, 2019). For more on American press coverage of the Texas Rangers in the US-Mexico War, see Jimmy L. Bryan Jr., "Agents of Destiny," in Jimmy L. Bryan Jr., ed., *The Martial Imagination: Cultural Aspects of American Warfare* (College Station: Texas A&M University Press, 2013), 53–70.

10. *Niles' National Register*, May 23, 1843; Ivey, *Ranger Ideal*, 245.

11. For more on Walker's press coverage, see "Capt. Samuel H. Walker," *Spirit of the Times* (New York City), May 30, 1846, 165. *New York Daily Tribune*, June 1, 1846. *Niles' National Register*, May 30, 1847; *New York Herald*, November 27, 1847. See also Robert Walter Johannsen, *To the Halls of the Montezumas: The Mexican War in the American Imagination* (New York: Oxford University Press, 1985), 135–136.

12. *Niles' National Register*, August 1, 1846 (quotation). Miguel A. González Quiroga, *War and Peace on the Rio Grande Frontier, 1830–1880* (Norman: University of Oklahoma Press, 2020); George Gordon Meade, *The Life and Letters of George Gordon Meade* (New York: Charles Scribner's Sons, 1913), 1:122; Justin Harvey Smith, *The War with Mexico* (New York: The Macmillan Company, 1919), 1:213.

13. Samuel C. Reid, *The Scouting Expeditions of McCulloch's Texas Rangers; or, The Summer and Fall Campaign of the Army of the United States in Mexico, 1846* (Philadelphia: G. G. Evans, 1859), 51–52. For a thorough examination of atrocities committed by US volunteers during the war, see Paul Foos, *A Short, Off-hand, Killing Affair: Soldiers and Social Conflict During the Mexican-American War* (Chapel Hill: University of North Carolina Press, 2002), 113–132; and Peter Guardino, *The Dead March: A History of the Mexican-American War* (Cambridge: Harvard University Press, 2018), 124–132. Both Foos and Guardino single out the Texas rangers for special censure, while Guardino notes that American troops had generally behaved themselves until the Texas volunteer units arrived.

14. Meade, *Life and Letters*, 1:111 (quotation). One Texan volunteer, whose brother had died on the Mier Expedition, received a reprimand from Zachary Taylor for scalping his victims. See Haynes, *Soldiers of Misfortune*, 210. Lane, *Adventures of Walter P. Lane*, 69.

15. Compton Smith, *Chile Con Carne; or, The Camp and the Field* (New York: Miller & Curtis, 1857), 297–298.

16. For more on Walker's return to the United States, see *New York Herald*, December 5, 1846; Ibid., February 10, 1847; Ibid., February 19, 1847. See also *Democratic Telegraph and Texas Register* (Houston), February 15, 1847.

17. For more on guerrilla activity against US troops in central Mexico, see Irving W. Levinson, *Wars Within War: Mexican Guerrillas, Domestic Elites, and the United States of America, 1846–1848* (Fort Worth: TCU Press), 2005.

18. J. Jacob Oswandel, *Notes of the Mexican War 1846-47-48, Comprising Incidents, Adventures and Everyday Proceedings and Letters While with the United States Army in the Mexican War . . .* (Philadelphia, 1885), 198 (quotation). See also *New York Herald*, July 24, 1847; Ibid., September 18, 1847; Ivey, *Ranger Ideal*, 1:258.

19. Thomas Claiborne, "Reminiscences," Thomas Claiborne Papers, 1845–1935, SHC, 31–33.

20. Oswandel, *Notes of the Mexican War*, 348–351; Claiborne, "Reminiscences," 36–40. For newspaper accounts of Walker's death, see *New York Herald*, November 13, 1847; Ibid., November 15, 1847.

21. George Winston Smith and Charles Burnet Judah, eds., *Chronicles of the Gringos: The U.S. Army in the Mexican War, 1846–1848; Accounts of Eyewitnesses & Combatants* (Albuquerque: University of New Mexico Press, 1968), 271.

22. See, for example, Mayne Reid, *The Rifle Rangers: or, Adventures of an Officer in Southern Mexico* (London: Shoberl, 1850); *The Scalp Hunters, or, Romantic Adventures in Northern Mexico* (London: Charles J. Skeet, 1851); Charles W. Webber, *Tales of the Southern Border* (Philadelphia: Lippincott, Grambo, 1853); *The Shot in the Eye, and Adventures with the Texas Rifle Rangers* (London: H. Vizetelly, 1853); and Jeremiah Clemens, *Mustang Gray: A Romance* (Philadelphia: J.B. Lippincott & Co, 1858).

CHAPTER TWENTY-FIVE. A DECENT PLACE IN WHICH A WHITE MAN COULD LIVE

1. Maverick, *Memoirs*, 67–75.

2. Marks, *Turn Your Eyes Toward Texas*, 162.

3. Maverick, *Memoirs*, 76; Marks, *Turn Your Eyes Toward Texas*, 145.

4. Marks, *Turn Your Eyes Toward Texas*, 147.

5. Maverick, *Memoirs*, 78–79.

6. Maverick, *Memoirs*, 83.

7. Marks, *Turn Your Eyes Toward Texas*, 205 (first quotation); Mary Maverick Diary, January 17, February 16, March 17–18, 1856 [single entry], Maverick Family Papers, BCAH (second and third quotations); Ibid., April 19, 1856 (fourth quotation).

8. Veatch to Lamar, February 23, 1848, *PML*, 4:193–194.

9. For more on Seguín's life after the US-Mexico War, see Seguín, *A Revolution Remembered*, 50–56.

10. Larry Knight, "The Cart War: Defining American in San Antonio in the 1850s." *SHQ* 109, no. 3 (2006): 319–336.

11. Lawrence Knight, "Becoming a City and Becoming American: San Antonio Texas, 1848–1861," PhD diss., Texas A&M University, 1997, 32 (quotation); James Crisp, "José Antonio Navarro: The Problem of Tejano Powerlessness," in *Tejano Leadership*, 156; McDonald, *José Antonio Navarro*, chs. 7–8.

12. Knight, "Becoming a City," 31; *Frank Leslie's Illustrated Newspaper*, January 15, 1859.

13. Thomas "Ty" Smith, "The US Army and the Alamo, 1846–1877," *SHQ* 118, no. 3 (2015): 262–285. Joel Kitchens, "San Antonio's Spanish Missions and the Persistence of Memory, 1718–2016" PhD diss., Texas A&M University, 2016, 135.

14. For the War Department's impact on the state's economic development, see Thomas T. Smith, *The US Army and the Texas Frontier Economy, 1845–1900* (College Station: Texas A&M University Press, 1999). For Corpus Christi, see Robert Wooster and Ariel Kelley, "'Nothing but Rascally White People': George B. McClellan Returns to Texas, 1852–1853," *SHQ* 117, no. 1 (2013): 26–46.

15. Marks, *Turn Your Eyes Toward Texas*, 178.

16. DeLay, *War of a Thousand Deserts*, 306. For the Comanche treaty with the Germans, see Roemer, *Texas*; and Daniel J. Gelo and Christopher J. Wickham, *Comanches and Germans on the Texas Frontier: The Ethnology of Heinrich Berghaus* (College Station: Texas A&M University Press, 2018).

17. James H. Leiker and Ramon Powers, "Cholera among the Plains Indians," *WHQ* 29, no. 3 (1998): 317–340.

18. Anderson, *Conquest of Texas*, 289; Smith, *From Dominance to Disappearance*, chs. 7–8.

19. Anderson, *Conquest of Texas*, 289; Jodye Lynn Dickson Schilz and Thomas F. Schilz, *Buffalo Hump and the Penateka Comanches* (El Paso: Texas Western Press, 1989), 40.

20. Always a lightning rod for controversy, Green continued to draw attention to himself in California. He arrived on the Yuba River with a dozen Anglo-Texan prospectors and fifteen enslaved men in July 1849, flouting local mining bylaws barring the use of slave labor. Free-Soilers ran off Green's party, prompting delegates at the state constitutional convention to include a provision prohibiting slavery. California entered the Union as a free state the following year. His prospecting career at an end, Green served two terms in the California Senate, the fourth state in which he would hold elected office. See Green, *Journal*, xxi–xxii; and Stacy L. Smith, *Freedom's Frontier: California and the Struggle over Unfree Labor, Emancipation, and Reconstruction* (Chapel Hill: University of North Carolina Press, 2013), 47–50. *US Congressional Globe*, 31st Congress, 1st sess., Appendix, 1244 (quotation).

21. Speech on Thomas Jefferson Green, August 1, 1854, *WSH*, 74–93. Upon publication of his anti-Houston pamphlet, Green had copies placed on every senator's desk in the capitol chamber. See Thomas Jefferson Green, *Reply of Gen. Thomas J. Green, to the Speech of General Sam Houston, in the Senate of the United States, August 1, 1854* (Washington, DC: 1855). For Houston's rebuttal, see "Remarks Concerning the Pamphlet of Thomas Jefferson Green," February 15, 1855, *WSH*, 6:165–166 (quotation on 166).

22. The exact motives of the so-called Callahan Expedition into northern Mexico in 1855 are a matter of some dispute. Taking the view that it was principally a slave-catching enterprise are Ronnie C. Tyler, "The Callahan Expedition of 1855: Indians or Negroes?" *SHQ* 70, no. 4 (1967): 574–585; and Alice L. Baumgartner, *South to Freedom: Runaway Slaves to Mexico and the Road*

to the Civil War (New York: Basic Books, 2020), 212–213. This thesis has been challenged by Thomas O. McDonald, who argues that the expedition was intended to punish Lipan Apache and Seminole Indians for their depredations in South Texas. See Thomas O. McDonald, *Texas Rangers, Ranchers, and Realtors: James Hughes Callahan and the Day Family in the Guadalupe River Basin* (Norman: University of Oklahoma Press, 2021), chs. 12–17. Creighton, *A Narrative History of Brazoria County*, 210–230.

23. Campbell, *An Empire for Slavery*, 112.

24. Prince, "William Goyens," 69–70, 56.

25. Olmsted, *A Journey Through Texas*, 78–79.

26. Clara Driscoll to the Texas Club of New York City, January 27, 1914, Clara Driscoll Papers, Clara Driscoll Foundation.

INDEX

SAM W. HAYNES is a professor in the department of history and the director of the Center for Greater Southwestern Studies at the University of Texas at Arlington. He lives in Dallas, Texas.